Eugene Schuyler

Turkistan

Vol. I.: Notes of a Journey in Russian Turkistan, Khokand, Bukhara, and Kuldja

Eugene Schuyler

Turkistan

Vol. I.: Notes of a Journey in Russian Turkistan, Khokand, Bukhara, and Kuldja

ISBN/EAN: 9783744798655

Printed in Europe, USA, Canada, Australia, Japan

Cover: Foto ©Andreas Hilbeck / pixelio.de

More available books at **www.hansebooks.com**

TURKISTAN

VOL. I.

JEWS OF SAMARKAND.   [*Frontispiece of Vol. I.*

TURKISTAN

NOTES OF A JOURNEY IN RUSSIAN TURKISTAN,

KHOKAND, BUKHARA, AND KULDJA

BY

EUGENE SCHUYLER, Phil. Dr.

MEMBER OF THE AMERICAN GEOGRAPHICAL SOCIETY AND OF THE IMPERIAL
RUSSIAN GEOGRAPHICAL SOCIETY, ETC.

WITH THREE MAPS AND NUMEROUS ILLUSTRATIONS

IN TWO VOLUMES
VOL. I.

NEW YORK:
SCRIBNER, ARMSTRONG & CO.
1877.

John F. Trow & Son,
Printers and Bookbinders,
205-213 East 12th St.,
New York.

PREFACE.

My readers must not expect either stories of personal adventure or accounts of geographical exploration. The care which the Russians, Bukhariots, and Khokandians took that I should incur no personal danger, and should penetrate into no regions previously unexplored, prevented both one and the other. The chief aim of my journey in Central Asia was to study the political and social condition of the regions which had been recently annexed by Russia, as well as to compare the state of the inhabitants under Russian rule with that of those still living under the despotism of the Khans. In this I was in a measure successful.

I have attempted in this book to give my impression of what I myself saw, and of what I learned from my intercourse both with Russians and natives. In endeavouring to give a true picture of the condition of affairs, I have sometimes felt obliged to speak at length of subjects upon which it has given me little pleasure to dwell. I think, however, that my friends in Russia will not mistake my object in speaking. I have lived too long in Russia, and have made too many friends there, to have other than kind feelings for the country and the people. I hope, then, that my readers will believe that the criticisms made upon certain acts of the Russian administration in Central Asia are not made in a spirit of fault-finding. It is evidently for the interest of Russia that the mistakes and faults of the Russian policy should be known, and should be remedied as soon as possible.

I have felt the more free to mention some of these things in this book, because the substance of the later chapters was embodied in an official document which was subsequently made public and excited considerable discussion.

Besides my own observations, and the information which I have received from persons of very different grades and stations in life, both Russians and natives, from official documents, and from private letters, I have made use of whatever materials, either printed or written, were accessible, some of which are little known to any except Russian specialists. I have, however, I trust, followed no authority blindly; I have never accepted a statement without enquiry and comparison with the accounts of others; and if I sometimes state things which seem opposed to all that has been written or printed before, upon any particular subject, it has not been without good reason.

It is of course impossible, and would be unwise, in every instance to name the authorities for my statements; I can only say that I have endeavoured in all cases to obtain exact and accurate information.

It is impossible for me to thank by name the many friends who assisted me in my enquiries and with my work; but I desire to express my special gratitude to the Russian authorities, both in St. Petersburg and in Central Asia, particularly in Samarkand and Semiretch, where I was rendered so much kind assistance about my journey. My thanks are also due to Professor Grigorief, Professor Zakharof, and Mr. Lerch, of the University of St. Petersburg, for all their patience and kindness in opening to me their stores of Oriental information. I desire also to express my obligations to General Milutin, the Russian Minister of War, for his polite attention in allowing the Topographical Department of the Staff at St. Petersburg to prepare the two special maps of Central Asia and of the Kuldja region which are annexed to this book.

CONSTANTINOPLE: *September* 1876.

CONTENTS

OF

THE FIRST VOLUME.

CHAPTER I.

THE STEPPE.

PAGE

The start—Prince Tchinghiz—The German Colonies on the Volga—Bashkirs—Uralsk—The Cossacks—Their great merits—Orenburg, the threshold of Central Asia—Old acquaintances—Our final preparations—Crossing the mountains—Orsk—The road through the steppe—Camels—Imaginary dangers—The steppe—Karabutak—Irghiz—The Aral Sea—Desert of Kara-Kum—Arrival at Kazala—The Kirghiz—Their history and present condition—Their character and peculiarities—Their life—Amusements—Horse races—Marriages 1

CHAPTER II.

THE SYR DARYA.

Kazala—Fort No. 1—Commercial importance—Cordial reception—Talk of the Khivan expedition—Prospects of joining it—Suspicious—Frustrated hopes—We explain—Arrival of Russian captives from Khiva—The Syr Darya—Obstacles to navigation, and efforts to improve it—The Aral flotilla—A strange birthplace—Fort No. 2—A Kirghiz cemetery—A Mussulman saint—Fort Perovsky—MacGahan starts for Khiva—The Kyzyl Kum desert—Hazreti-Turkistan—Mausoleum of Akhmed Yasavi—Inscriptions—Ikan—Its brave defence—Tchimkent 44

CHAPTER III.

TASHKENT.

First impressions—Similarity to American towns—Rapid growth—Houses —Garden of Governor-General—The Church—Earthquakes—Hotels and fare—The Club—Ming Uruk—Society—The Governor-General's State —Rigid etiquette at his balls—Bad tone—Cliques—Ignorance of the country displayed by officials—The 'Central Asiatic Society'—Jura Bek —Baba Bek—A nephew of the Amir of Bukhara—Alim Hadji Yunusof —A Court doctor—Murder of Malla Khan—A political execution in Bukhara—The mercantile community—Said Azim—The native town— Mills—Walls—Population—Sarts—Tadjiks—Uzbeks—Their characteristics—Arabs—History of Tashkent—Its capture by General Tchernaief —His first proclamation. 76

CHAPTER IV.

MUSSULMAN LIFE IN TASHKENT.

A merchant's house—Its furniture—Mussulman devotions—Dress—Food— Drinks—Narcotics—Native games—Sporting—Falcons—Horses—Vehicles—Singing—Musical instruments—Dances of boys—A dance of women —The festival of Zang-ata—Veneration for old trees—Circumcision— Marriage—Wedding feasts—Divorce—Maladies of the Sarts—Cholera— Parasites—Medicines—Funerals—Mourning—Asiatic influence on Russia —Islam—Different sects of Mohammedans—Mosques and worship there —Religious orders—Visit to performances of Jahria—Education—Primary schools—Colleges—Their arrangements and studies—The Kazis —Native courts among the nomad and settled population—Mussulman law—Christianity and Islam. 118

CHAPTER V.

THE BAZAARS AND TRADE.

The Tashkent bazaar—Sunday bazaar—Silversmiths—Brassworkers— Cutlery and arms—Iron-foundries—Teahouses—Barbers—Apothecaries —Cosmetics—Oils—Dyes—Shoes and Leather—The Kirghiz bazaar— Caravanserais—Hindoos—Money-lending and its subterfuges—Pottery— Embroidery—Cotton goods—Silk and silk culture—Legendary history of silk—Weights and measures—Money—Duties and Taxes—The Fair and its results—Statistics of Central Asiatic trade—Transportation—Trade routes—Proposed railway. 173

CHAPTER VI.

SAMARKAND.

The Mullah—Tchinaz—The Famished Steppe—Assafœtida—Murza Rabat—Jizakh—Gates of Tamerlane—Rock inscriptions—Tchupan-Ata—First view of Samarkand—Hafistas—Early history—The Græco-Bactrian dynasty—Chinese travellers - Clavijo—Baber's description—The Russian conquest—Siege of the citadel by the natives, and its heroic defence by the Russians—Mosque of Shah Zindeh—Bibi Khanym—Shir-dar—Tomb of Timur—The *Kok-tash*—Hodja Akhrar—Koran of Othman—Bazaars—Dervishes—The Jews—Abdur Rahman Khan of Afghanistan—Russian adventurers—Russian soldiers—Russian administration . 225

CHAPTER VII.

THE ZARAFSHAN VALLEY.

Urgut—Our idyl—A second visit—The mountain ranges—The glacier—The Upper Zarafshan—Kohistan—The petty Beks—Iskender Kul Expedition—Annexation—Small extent of arable land in Central Asia—Irrigating canals—Regulation of irrigation—Water supply of Bukhara—Methods of irrigation—Systems of husbandry— Rotation of crops—Cereals—Famines—Lack of statistics—Cotton—Gardens—Price of land—Land tenure—Proposed land settlement—Land taxes. . . . 268

CHAPTER VIII.

HODJENT AND KURAMA.

encontre at Jizakh—Zamin—Ura-tepé—Peak of Altyn-bishik—Nau—Hodjent—Its situation—Defence against the Khokandians—Coal mines—Lead—Gold—Naphtha—Exaggerated accounts of mineral wealth—Bridge over Syr Darya—Prefect's residence—Population of Kurama—Stock-raising—Climate of Central Asia—Earthquakes—The calendars—Agricultural solar year—Zodiacal months—Their Chaldæan origin—The Kirghiz calendar derived from the Mongol—The twelve-year cycle. 308

APPENDICES.

PAG

I. A Sketch of the History of Khokand in Recent Times . . 337

II. Review of Vámbéry's 'History of Bukhara,' by Professor Grigorief 360

III. Mediæval Travellers in Central Asia . . . 390

ILLUSTRATIONS

IN

THE FIRST VOLUME.

JEWS OF SAMARKAND (*by Verestchagin*) . . *Frontispiece*

A VIEW OF THE SYR DARYA (*by Verestchagin*) . . . *To face p.* 50

THE MOSQUE HAZRET AT TURKISTAN (*by Verestchagin*) . „ 70

TURKISTAN (*by Verestchagin*) . . . . „ 73

STREET IN TASHKENT, WITH MOSQUE (*from a photograph*) . „ 101

VIEW IN TASHKENT, LOOKING OVER THE ROOFS OF THE BAZAAR TO THE MEDRESSÉ OF BEKLAR-BEK (*from a photograph*) . „ 104

THE CITADEL AT TCHIMKENT (*by Verestchagin*) . . „ 112

MEDRESSÉ OF HODJA AKHRAR, SAMARKAND (*from a photograph*) „ 238

MEDRESSÉ SHIR-DAR AT SAMARKAND (*from a photograph*) . „ 254

WOMEN OF SAMARKAND (*from a photograph*) . . . „ 266

A TARTAR LADY OF ORENBURG (*from a photograph*) . . 13

KIRGHIZ CHANGING CAMP (*by Verestchagin*) 29

KIRGHIZ WOMEN (*from a photograph*) 36

KIRGHIZ HORSEMEN (*by Verestchagin*) 40

ILLUSTRATIONS IN THE FIRST VOLUME.

	PAGE
A Kirghiz (*by Verestchagin*)	42
A Kirghiz Tomb (*by Verestchagin*)	63
Bara Bek and Jura Bek (*from a photograph*)	87
An Uzbek (*by Verestchagin*)	107
A Tadjik (*by Verestchagin*)	110
A Boy of Tashkent (*by Verestchagin*)	142
A Bazaar-Cook (*from a photograph*)	179
A Hindoo (*by Verestchagin*)	185
The Tomb of Timur (*by Verestchagin*)	253
A Youth of Urgut (*by Verestchagin*)	273
A Hodjent Merchant (*by Verestchagin*)	315

TURKISTAN.

CHAPTER I.

THE STEPPE.

The start—Prince Tchinghiz—The German Colonies on the Volga—Bashkirs—Uralsk—The Cossacks—Their great merits—Orenburg, the threshold of Central Asia—Old acquaintances—Our final preparations—Crossing the mountains—Orsk—The road through the steppe—Camels—Imaginary dangers—The steppe—Karabutak—Irghiz—The Aral Sea—Desert of Kara-Kum—Arrival at Kazala—The Kirghiz—Their history and present condition—Their character and peculiarities—Their life—Amusements—Horse races—Marriages.

I HAD long been desirous of visiting Central Asia, but various circumstances had prevented my doing so.

Finally the opportunity presented itself unexpectedly to me; and leaving St. Petersburg on the 23rd of March, 1873, pausing for a day at Moscow, I arrived in Saratof, some 940 miles, on the morning of the 26th, by rail. I was accompanied by Mr. J. A. MacGahan, the Correspondent of the 'New York Herald,' whose desert ride, on his way to Khiva, was a few months later the subject of general wonder and admiration.

I could not help thinking it a good augury for our journey that almost our only fellow-passenger in the carriage was Prince Tchinghiz, a lineal descendant of the famous Tchinghiz Khan, and son of the last Khan of the Bukeief Horde of Kirghiz. Strange, that on the threshold of Asia I should meet the descendant of its greatest conqueror! After the death of his father, he, the eldest son, was given the Russian title of Prince, in memory of his ancient lineage, and of the services of his father.

The Prince, who is a good Mussulman, had just returned from

Mecca, where he had been on a pilgrimage, and was going to spend the summer on his estates in the Government of Samara. He seemed a cultivated gentleman, and was most of the time deep in a French novel.

From Saratof we were obliged to travel in sledges, as the country was still covered with snow, though the violent thaw which had set in at Saratof made us fearful that the roads would be very bad. The remainder of the day we spent at Saratof in purchasing various articles of outfit that we had previously neglected, and in making arrangements for our journey, having to get a *podorozhnaya* or road-pass for post horses, as well as to lay in a stock of provisions.

We finally got off at ten o'clock the next morning in two small, low sledges of country make, discovering just at starting that we should not have to go up the Volga to Samara by the usual route, but that we could take a cross-cut to Uralsk, and so to Orenburg, the snow-roads still being good. We accordingly struck across the Volga, where the ice showed no signs of weakness, and soon made our twenty-four miles to Krasny Yar, one of the German Colonies. The left bank of the Volga in the neighbourhood of Saratof is for a long distance covered with German Colonies, some of them sectarians and Catholics, but the most of them Lutherans, who were induced to come here about 1769 by the Empress Catherine II. They had certain privileges conferred upon them, one of which was exemption from military service, and are in a most flourishing state. It is very curious, however, to see that they have had no effect whatever upon the civilisation of the Russian peasants who surround them, nor have they themselves at all changed by their contact with Russians. The Colonists remain as German now as were their ancestors a hundred years ago, though many of them know some words and phrases of Russian, which they speak with a most vile accent. In the German towns, which are close to each other, there are comfortable well-built houses, with neat roofs and fences, large and capacious barns and granaries, fine churches, and every evidence of prosperity. The Russian villages near by are no better than those seen in any of the interior provinces.

The Germans look with dislike and contempt upon the Russians, a feeling which is returned by the latter with interest.

Intermarriages are very rare, and there is little intercourse, except for business. Some of the Germans themselves told me that both priests and pastors were equally to blame for this state of things, the Russian priests inveighing against the Germans as heretics, and the Lutheran preachers condemning the Russians as idolaters. Other influences, too, have been at work to make the differences between these two classes. The Germans were exempt from military service, were never serfs, and were burdened in proportion with far less taxation. Their position was thus exceptional.

The post stations here were always comfortable, and we were sure of finding good bread and butter, and always a cup of coffee, while at the Russian post villages it was impossible to procure anything more than black bread and an occasional egg. It was only at Nikolaiefsk, the single large town on our road, that we were able to get a meal, wretched, it is true, but hot, and therefore lingering in our memories for days, when in our benumbed state we gnawed at our wholly frozen provender, while bargaining at the stations for horses, and vainly trying to instil into lazy peasants a sense of the value of time. Not knowing whether we were to find snow or mud, we had purchased no vehicles, and were therefore obliged at every station to change our sledges as well as our horses, to our great discomfort. At last, on the third day we reached Kuzebai, a Bashkir village, where we had our first glimpse of Oriental life. The houses were rudely built of clay, half under-ground, and with flat clay roofs, on which the dogs of the household were constantly promenading and barking at us. At the other end of the village rose the wooden cone-capped minaret of the mosque.

The Bashkirs are a people said to be of Finnish origin, though they speak a language of Tartar or Turkish stock. They live chiefly in the Government of Orenburg, on both sides of the Ural mountains, but there is a large number of them in the Government of Samara. In all the race amounts to perhaps 500,000 souls. Formerly devoting themselves to rapine and a nomadic life, they were first made useful as a frontier army similar to the Cossacks, have gradually taken up agriculture, and have become quiet peaceable citizens. Their chief town is Ufa, which is now the centre of the Government of the same name.

The road we were following not being a direct post-road, we had at every station great difficulty in obtaining horses, but nowhere so much as here. Driving into a dirty court, full of slush and melted snow, we descended two or three steps, and, bending our heads, went through a small door into the single room which constituted the habitation of the Bashkir horse-owner. The inside of the house was scrupulously clean, with an immense stove on one side, half of the room being divided off by print curtains. Along the wall was a broad divan, covered for our benefit with a gay felt rug, and in the corner next the door were a calf and a young colt, which had been brought in for protection against the extreme cold outside. A young woman and a number of small children clustered about the low stove built of rude bricks, and on one end of the divan lay a worn-out-looking woman, with a diminutive infant, apparently born only some hours before. The proprietor of the house, a very neat-looking Bashkir, wearing a long caftan, and with a small black skull-cap on his shaven head, was amiable enough, and evidently disposed to further our journey. He explained that the regular *yamstchiks* or drivers had all gone away with their horses, and sent out into the village to see whether others could not be had. Soon a large number of men appeared, old men with grizzly beards, and awkward thick-lipped youths; one of them especially was, in his way, quite a dandy. The broad collar of his shirt was whiter and finer than the rest, and his dark blue cloth caftan was girt with an ornamented silver belt. He felt his position, and was indisposed to let us have horses for anything except a most extortionate price, and the rest followed his example; so that we found it impossible to make any bargain, and consequently sent them all away. Others then came in, and after a prolonged discussion, our host, whose features were always lighted with a grave smile, kindly interpreting for us, we were at last obliged to take two pairs of bad horses for seven rubles, to go a distance of sixteen miles. The regular postal charge is one and a half kopeks a verst for each horse, which would be only about one and a half or two rubles for the same distance. When we agreed to take the horses one of the old men glibly recited the first chapter of the Koran, all stroked their beards, and the bargain was made. But we were obliged even then to pay down part of the money before we could start, and had a long delay in getting the horses to. We whiled away the time by observing the housekeeping of the Bashkir women, who were mending the fire, and boiling some compound in a huge pot, and at intervals sweeping the floor to clear off any particles of snow or dirt. The children gradually grew less shy and showed us what proficiency they had made in reading a Tartar book.

At the next station, Kutchambai, also a Bashkir village, we had the same trouble, it being impossible of course to get the horses for any less than we had paid at the previous station, each driver telling the next what we had already given, so that we found the prices rising as we went on. Miles and miles we went on over low hills all white with snow, and nothing visible but the track before and behind us, when it suddenly became intensely cold, and there was every sign of a violent storm. At the Russian station of Tobaeva, which we reached late in the evening, we were able to obtain horses, and desired to go on at once, but we were urged to wait, so as not to be caught in the *buran*, or whirlwind of snow, which is very common on this waste plain. Many stories were told us of persons who had been lost, and especially of one young man from the nearest village, who had set out in a snow-storm the week before, and had not since been heard of.

The chief room at the station was occupied by a justice of the peace, who was engaged during the whole evening in settling disputes between various peasants who came in—chiefly cases about boundaries or rents. We at last decided to stay the night, spread our sheepskin coats on the floor, and went to sleep; but at one o'clock we were awakened with the news that it was now fine weather, and that the moon and stars were out, and with the advice to go on, as another sledge was coming, and if we did not take the horses at once we would not be able to get them later. We therefore quickly drank a glass of hot tea, and started off at two o'clock, crossing the last ridge that separated us from the valley of the Ural, and making the twenty-six miles to the next station by half-past six o'clock in the morning. Here we were delighted to come upon a neat house in a Cossack village, where a couple of fine old Cossacks immediately bestirred themselves to get us our horses and to give us some breakfast. They were venerable-looking old fellows, dressed in long wadded

Bukharan dressing-gowns, which they tucked into a most enormously wide pair of leather trowsers before starting off in the snow. When our tea was ready we found some excellent white bread and fresh cream, a luxury we had not known for a long time. The horses turned out to be good, and we were quickly in sight of the green domes which mark the city of Uralsk. We had no desire to delay here, but we wished at least to get a good dinner, and to procure the road-paper to Orenburg. It was, however, Sunday, which made difficulties. The wretched rooms at which we stopped were kept by a man, who did not conceive it possible to give us any meat during the Lenten fast, and we had great difficulty in getting anything to eat, as nothing seemed to be in the house. Of course the public offices were not open, and everybody told me it would be impossible to get farther before the next night. But after writing a note to the Governor and telling him of our haste, we succeeded in getting an order to the head police-master to give us a certificate, with which I went to the Treasurer of the district, and, luckily finding him at home, by great persuasion induced him to sign a road-paper, which procured us the desired horses; this, however, took from noon until nine o'clock at night.

I was much disappointed at the appearance of Uralsk, which I had imagined to be a neat and thriving town ; neat, because it is inhabited by Cossacks, and thriving, because it is their capital. It may be that in ordinary times these epithets would be applicable, but a spring thaw is apt to make any country town look utterly wretched. Here the snow was nearly gone, and on this warm sunny day the mud in the streets was so deep that it was even dangerous to walk across them in goloshes, which might have been left behind. So far as we were able to move about it seemed as though there was hardly a respectable-looking building in the town; all were dirty and dilapidated. There was a little boulevard, which perhaps in early summer would be very pretty, with a pavilion at one end, and a statue or monument erected to the memory of the late Cesarevitch, but so completely veiled with a large black cloth, that it was impossible to tell what it was. The streets were full of Kirghiz, most of them mounted on camels, which at once gave the town an Oriental aspect, and altogether it seemed far more Kirghiz than Cossack. The cause of this is to be found in the new regulations for the government of the Kirghiz Steppe, issued in 1869, which placed it under the same Government as the Ural Cossacks, with the head-quarters at Uralsk; before that a Kirghiz was rarely seen on the Russian side of the river. About five o'clock, as I was returning from the Treasury, I saw about the 'White' Church a large crowd of young Cossacks, and great animation in the streets and on the neighbouring bazaar. This turned out to be a sort of labour market. The men serving at the different frontier stations come to hire volunteers for the various expeditions to take place during the summer; while others who have nothing to do, or who have lost their all in some unlucky fishing venture, come to seek employment. Two or three, who had somehow learned that I was going to Tashkent, were anxious to enter my service. One had been in Central Asia before, and the others had been led by the stories they had been told of the easy life and the profit which was to be gained there. All such offers I refused, as I expected to take servants at Orenburg who knew the language, and could interpret; but afterwards I regretted that I had not taken one of these men, who would, I think, from what I learned of Cossack character, have been far more faithful and adroit. I could not help noticing, on the whole road from Saratof to Uralsk, the interest which was felt in Central Asia by everyone. Many had relatives or townsmen there, and all were influenced by the idea that Tashkent was a place where fortunes were to be made, and where life was adventurous and pleasant.

It is strange what an erroneous notion prevails in the West with regard to the Cossacks. They are thought to be an uncivilised, savage race, given to nothing but plunder and acts of barbarity. These opinions, arising from old legends, were probably strengthened during the partisan war of 1812, when the Cossacks played such an important part as light cavalry in the West, and when the skirmishers of the Russian army excited everywhere an irrational terror, and passed into tradition as bugbears and scarecrows, occupying much the same position as the Prussian Uhlan will for some time hold in France. In reality the Cossacks are mild, amiable, and hospitable. They are the pioneers of Russian civilisation. If anything has to be done, and brave manly fellows are required to do it, the Cossacks are employed. When a country is to be colonised the Cossacks guard it, and themselves take part in the work of settlement. Though given perhaps to occasional raids, when next to some Kirghiz or uncivilized tribe, they are in the main peaceful and orderly citizens, brave, industrious, and enduring. The women are hard workers and good housekeepers, and during my whole journey in Asia I was only too delighted when I came to a post-station kept by a married Cossack, for there I was sure to find everything clean and neat, with eggs and milk at least, and possibly something more substantial to eat.

The name 'Cossack,' or 'Kazak,' as the Russians spell it, is Eastern, and is not properly the name of a people, but a word originally belonging to the Tartar-Turkish language, meaning a vagabond, and then a partisan or guerilla. The people living under the shadow of the Caucasus first came into history with the name of Kazaks, and subsequently the bands who settled on the river Don, forming an outlying frontier colony of the Russians, took the same name, constantly using Tcherkess, the real name for the inhabitants of Circassia, as synonymous with it. Though the name is Tartar, the Cossacks themselves are chiefly a Russian race. Deserters, outlaws, peasants flying from the tyranny of their masters, brave and adventurous spirits of every sort, who could not find room for themselves in Russia, joined the tribes living on the Don, and made up the community which soon became known as the 'Cossacks of the Don.'

With the Church troubles, many who held to the old faith, and opposed the new reforms introduced by the patriarch Nicon, and all who sought for independence of action or of thought, joined them. Offshoots of them settled also on the Dnieper. Though always calling themselves Russians, the Cossacks insisted on maintaining their independence; virtually being a state within a state. They often made war and pillaging excursions on their own account, and refused to deliver up their prisoners without ransom. Such proceedings forced the Russian Tsars to send expeditions to punish them; and in the latter part of the sixteenth century, the boldest of them finding things too hot for them at home, moved Eastward in search of greater freedom for adventure. The first results of this were the capture and colonisation of Siberia by the band of Yermak, and the expulsion of the Tartars from the banks of the Yaik—now the Ural

—followed by the formation of the Yaik or Ural Cossacks. Here, on the Ural, they were so far removed from the Moscow Government that it was long before any settled regulations could be made for their administration and entire subjection. Among their other expeditions some predatory attacks on the Persian territory led to complaints, and the Tsar Alexis, by promise of pardon, prevailed on the Ataman to come with some of his companions to Moscow, and they were sent in 1655 against Poland and Riga. This was the first service of the Cossacks in the Russian army. In 1735 Orenburg was founded, the lines of the Ilek and Yaik established, and Russian posts and authorities introduced there. The Cossacks, feeling that these acts were in some way an invasion of their privileges, complained against the exactions of the Russian Governors, and were constantly in commotion.

The discontent finally culminated, just one hundred years ago, in the rebellion of Pugatcheff, who gave himself out as the Emperor Peter III., dead shortly before. The rebellion soon took tremendous proportions; all the country of the Volga was pillaged, and Moscow even was threatened, when finally, in 1775, the rebels were beaten, and Pugatcheff was executed. The name of the river and province was changed from Yaik to Ural (a thoroughly Asiatic punishment), and since that time the Cossacks have been peaceful and willing subjects, when no attack has been made on their privileges, except that it has been found almost impossible to restrain them from making pillaging forays into the dominions of the Kirghiz on the other side of the river.

The male Cossacks from eighteen to twenty are in the military service within the district; then, after a year of rest, they are liable to service outside the boundaries of their district for nominally fifteen years, though they are always sent home again long before the expiration of that period. Every Cossack is supposed to be in the army, though exceptions are made in favour of a father who has three sons in the service, or in case of one out of four brothers. In time of war all can be called upon. The actual number of the Ural Cossacks in service is estimated at over 10,000, though really not more than 3,000 actually serve at one time. It has long been the practice of the richer Cossacks to hire the poorer to take their places in the ranks, three hundred rubles being paid for two years' service in Turkistan.

The abolition of this custom by the new military law was the cause of the disorders in September, 1874.

The Cossacks form an almost ideal community. The land belongs to the whole army collectively, and each member has the right to till the ground, to cut hay, or to pasture his cattle where he pleases, provided, of course, he does not infringe on the rights of others, as settled by custom. Even the fishery in the Ural and in the sea is common property. The days of fishing are regulated; and though all are ready, none dare to cast a net or throw a harpoon before the cannon signal has been given by the Ataman, under penalty of confiscation of all his fishing implements. The 'golden bottom' of the Ural was once the main source of wealth to the Cossacks; but owing to the rapid and careless extermination of the forests above Orenburg, the river is drying up, and filling with shoals, and the fish seem seeking some other locality. Yet even now the produce of caviare, isinglass, salted sturgeons, and *beluga* is very great. By this commercial system the spread of wealth is much more even and regular than elsewhere, and there are no rich and no poor, or at least only in a comparative sense, for a poor man here is one who has nothing more than what is indispensable, *i.e.* his house, horse, and cattle. This system, however, in a country so limited in its capacities as the Ural region, will, with all its merits, be found inadequate to a rapidly growing population.

The Cossacks are almost entirely dissenters, chiefly 'old believers,' though apparently without the bigotry and religious hatred which characterize Russian dissent in general. In 1862, out of a population of over 70,000, there were only sixty-two who belonged to the orthodox Russian Church, chiefly Russian officials in the towns; and it is worthy of note that in 1859, the last year for which statistics have been published, thirty-eight out of eighty crimes were committed by orthodox, and only ten by dissenters, the remainder being by Jews, Mohammedans &c. The whole orthodox population at this time was eighty-nine.[1]

We had some difficulty in getting started in the evening, as when the horses finally arrived the drivers were ill-natured, and pretended that the loaded sledges were far too heavy for the

---

[1] 'The Army of the Ural Cossacks.' Collection of statistics published by the Staff. St. Petersburg, 1866. P. 305-333.

horses. All along the road we had great trouble in procuring horses, as it had been understood that the Governor-General of Orenburg was coming that way. Fortunately I had heard at the station that his journey had been postponed for two or three days, and sometimes persuaded the station-masters that this was actually the case. They wished to reserve all the horses for him, and we had on some occasions to take private horses belonging to the Cossacks, paying, of course, double price for them. That night and the next were intensely cold, and with the cold and the bright sun of the day our faces grew red and swollen, and the skin began to peel off in blotches. The reflection from the snow was so blinding that we were obliged to put on the dark spectacles set in wire-gauze which we had brought as a protection against the dust of the desert. The road followed the bank of the Ural, though, as the river was frozen and covered with snow, it was often not specially noticeable, and our travelling was without variety, except an occasional overturn of our sledge on account of the inequalities of the road, for where there was a little side-hill or hollow the sledge would invariably slide down into it and pull up with a jerk, which would throw us both out. As we approached Orenburg the river-bottom began to be covered with thin woods. At the last station we were heartily glad to find that, owing to the snow being still deep, we were able to cut off a distance of some twenty miles and proceed along the river bank through what in early summer must be a lovely country; and at last, on Tuesday morning about noon, we reached a broad plateau, on the farther side of which we saw the spires and buildings of Orenburg.

We brought up at the Hôtel d'Orenburg, commonly known as 'Antons,' situated in the chief street, where we were able to procure two decent rooms, and had at last baths and comfortable beds. Our appearance on arrival was anything rather than calculated to inspire the host with confidence in us. It had been, I think, the coldest weather in which I was ever out, and we suffered much, although we were very warmly dressed. I had a long sheepskin coat, such as is worn by the peasants, and my ordinary fur-lined paletôt, with a fur collar, thrown over my shoulders besides, for the sheepskin coat was without a collar, and the wind came down my neck. Besides this there was a red tippet about my throat, and a brown bashlyk of soldier's cloth tied over my head, with its tall peak sticking up. With beards of a week's growth, and red and scaly faces, we were certainly not attractive objects.

Orenburg contains just that mixture of European and Oriental that one might expect to find at the threshold of Central Asia. The wide streets crossing one another at right angles, the well-built wooden and plastered houses, the shops, the churches, the boulevard and public square, the immense Government buildings used for barracks, storehouses, and schools, give the place a thoroughly Russian air; while, on the other hand, the caravanserai, with its beautiful mosque and minaret of white stucco; the Tartar mosque, the camels, in caravans, single, or harnessed to wagons; the crowds of Tartars, the Kirghiz on horseback, in their dirty rags, with rude caps; the bazaar, with the Bukharan, Khivan, and Tashkent merchants, in long robes striped with many colours, and with turbans on their heads, showed that the inhabitants of the place were thoroughly Asiatic. In reality only about 5,000 of 35,000 inhabitants are Tartars and Asiatics; but they are enough to give an Eastern tone to the place. There is a very pleasant society among the officials, and nearly all the Russians are either officials or merchants. I found more than a dozen persons who spoke English very well, as well as French and German; and there is a theatre and musical society. The merchants in general live very meanly, but there are some of them worth several millions, and on the occasion of a grand dinner or fête they show much luxury.

Orenburg seemed to me much improved in the five years that had elapsed since my last visit: very many new and large buildings had been constructed, such as the military gymnasium (high school), the pro-gymnasium, and the city gymnasium, with one or two hotels, and there seemed much more life and movement in the city. As the centre of the Administration of the large province of Orenburg, of the Orenburg Cossacks, and of the Kirghiz of the Turgai district, as well as the military headquarters, it brings together no inconsiderable number of officials. Orenburg is one of the chief entrepôts of the trade carried on between Tashkent and Central Asia in general and Russia, though much passes through Troitsk, another city of the same province, coming chiefly by way of Southern Siberia, though the main trade of both places is with the Kirghiz Steppe. On the completion of the railway which is now being constructed between Samara and Orenburg the business of Orenburg will undoubtedly increase. It needs but greater facilities for transport to permit the introduction of more capital and the better working of the numerous mines which the Ural mountains contain. The Central Asiatic caravans arrive and depart from what is called the Myenovoi Dvor, or Exchange Court, situated on the other side of the river.

A TARTAR LADY OF ORENBURG.

We were detained in Orenburg from Tuesday until Saturday, as there were many little things to be done preparatory to a journey over the Steppe, where provisions could not be had. I renewed my acquaintance with my former friends, and received the greatest politeness and most substantial assistance from all of them. All treated me with the greatest kindness, and did everything possible to further my plans. The shops in Orenburg are much better than I had expected, and I was enabled to purchase many little things which I had forgotten or neglected. We had to lay in not only provisions of all kinds—taking of course about three times as much as was really necessary for us, owing to the stories of detention and utter nakedness of the land—but had besides to procure a tarantass—a large covered travelling carriage, without springs, but balanced on long poles which serve the purpose. There are no seats, but when we had spread mattresses and pillows we could lie comfortably at night and travel with great ease. It is the only possible vehicle that is adapted to stand Russian roads, and is certainly very comfortable and convenient. We found, however, that this was too small to carry some of the heavy luggage we had brought with us, for we were provided with a considerable amount of ammunition and some few firearms, in case of any little expedition we might wish to make in a hostile country or of the possibility of an attack on the road. We therefore procured a small cheap country sledge, which we resolved to take as far as we could, and then trust to luck. The roads at this time were covered with snow, though it was thawing in Orenburg, and we were told that we could with difficulty get as far as Orsk, where we should probably change to wheels. We had had the wheels taken off the tarantass and the vehicle lashed on a sledge.

It was necessary also to make arrangements about money, for we were warned to take as little as possible, as we should in all probability be robbed on the road by bands of Kirghiz, or possibly of Turkomans; and consequently, after procuring a large quantity of small silver and several bags full of copper pieces to pay away at the post-stations, and taking enough notes to last us for the road, we deposited the rest in one of the banks at Orenburg. This was a great piece of folly on our part, as, there being no bank at Tashkent, I found it rather difficult to obtain money, and only did so through the kindness of a merchant who had a house at Orenburg.

The first thing we did here was to look about for servants, and with the kind assistance of my friend Professor Bektchurin, a Tartar gentleman, who is professor of Arabic and the Eastern languages in the military gymnasium, we got two Tartars, one an old fellow named Ak-Mametef, who had been twice in Tashkent and Central Asia, and spoke Persian as well as Turki and Kirghiz, and the other a young fellow named Akhmet, who spoke Kirghiz perfectly, having been much in the Steppe. Unfortunately, Ak-Mametef turned out to be an utter rascal, and MacGahan especially had great difficulty with him. Akhmet would have been a good enough fellow, as he was perfectly docile and amenable, had it not been for his utter stupidity, and I was subsequently obliged to discharge him.

In Orenburg the talk was chiefly about the Khivan expedition, the Orenburg detachment having started some weeks before. News had been received that it had safely arrived at the fort on the Emba. The men had been well clad in sheepskin coats, and at every station *kibitkas* had been erected, and plenty of tea and *vodka* provided to protect them against the cold.

The army had been conveyed by horses which had been stationed there by the Kirghiz, at the command of the authorities, in sledges, and though the weather had been very cold there had been no suffering and no illness. The provision-train, however, met with a heavy storm before reaching the Emba fort, and had greatly suffered; so that apprehensions were felt lest all might not be ready for the forward advance of the detachment. My friends regretted that I had not come a month sooner, in order that I might have accompanied the expedition, evidently knowing nothing of the restrictions which had been placed at St. Petersburg on free travelling in that direction; and it was suggested to us that when we reached Kazala we might still have an opportunity to go, either by catching up with the detachment or by taking a passage on one of the steamers now plying on the Aral Sea.

We were two whole days going the 177 miles to Orsk, on account of the unsettled state of the roads and the bad condition of the horses. The stations were nearly all large villages, *Stanitzi* of Orenburg Cossacks, and at them we had little difficulty. At one, however, which we reached at seven in the evening, we were told that it would be impossible to travel at night in the soft state of the ground, and were besought to wait till morning. But about midnight we became impatient, and insisted on being off, taking some extra horses to get better over the difficult road. To the tarantass we had eight horses, but they were hardly better than four, as they all pulled different ways. Add to this our driver took a short cut through a wooded valley, where we got stuck several times among the stumps; so that it took us six hours and a half to make the stage of seventeen miles.

The Orenburg Cossacks are much farther from the ideal than those of the Ural. They have never had the free life and the natural development of their neighbours, but have been colonized there to order, and their ranks filled with retired soldiers and peasants. They have never had the same trouble to defend their frontier against raids, and lack the old military traditions. The conditions of their life, too, are in many respects very different, though far superior to those of the ordinary Russian peasant.

There are no fisheries here, and agriculture and cattle-raising are the main occupations. At every station we were offered the beautiful Orenburg shawls, both white and grey, knit by the Cossack women of the long fleece of a peculiar breed of goat kept here. Some of the more delicate ones require months and even years for their completion.

As we neared Orsk we crossed with some difficulty, on account of the melted snow, the Guberlinsky mountains, the southern portion of the Ural chain. They are very low, mere hills in fact, but they have all the characteristics of mountains, bare of trees, rocky and stony, with snowy patches, leaving the dark brown ridges bare. They are chiefly composed of gravel, but a curious strata of rock crops out at a high angle, and is visible in long straight lines for a great distance. When we reached the very summit of the hills, near the station which marks the boundary between Europe and Asia, we had a most wonderful view—on every hand a sea of dark brown peaks and ridges, with snow lying in the hollows and valleys, and showing better their contours. We looked far to the south beyond the Ural, and everywhere there were hills, which gradually grew smaller and smaller until they creep up again into the Mugojar mountains, on the northern coast of the Aral Sea.

During the last stage we were very wretched, for experience had made us wary of following the advice of station-masters, who usually knew nothing of the road, and we had retained our sledges instead of changing them for wheels, though we were obliged to submit to having fifteen animals, four of them camels, harnessed to our two sledges. We stuck in the mud, and bumped and scraped over bare ground for hours, till at last, about six o'clock, we came on a plain, and saw in the distance the fort and group of houses which showed us what we had looked forward to as the last stage of civilisation—it being the last telegraph station. We could endure no longer the slow motion of the vehicle, and got out to walk. But near as Orsk seemed, our sledges always appeared to be making a large circuit to the left, and it was a very long time before we crossed the frozen Ural and arrived at the station-house.

With the experience of the last stage we were quite ready to be convinced, when the station-master assured us that beyond this there was no snow at all, and that we had better take to wheels. As we had no intention of delaying longer than was necessary we at once gave the order, and the sledge was taken off, and the wheels properly greased and put on. For our luggage we had to look about for a wagon; and finally, after many vain attempts, found one belonging to a merchant, who had the post contract for the route beyond Kazala, which he was desirous of sending on, and which he offered to us free of charge as far as we wished, if we would only leave it at one of the stations. Some little thing, however, was necessary to be done, which would take about half-an-hour, but it was impossible to get it into the head of anyone that it could be done at once. They would not promise it to us earlier than the next morning. There was nothing then to do but to wait. We took a little walk through the town, which, though an old frontier town—the original site of Orenburg in 1735—is very wretched; a church or two, and one or two shops where everything is sold. The bazaar was utterly insignificant, which much surprised us, for Orsk is one of the chief centres of trade with the Kirghiz Steppe, and the amount of business transacted is very great. We went to the little dirty *traktir* bearing the name of *Hôtel de Berlin* and ordered our dinner—such as could be obtained—to be sent to the post-house, despatched our last telegrams, and wrote our last letters.

In the morning we discovered, when it was already too late, that we had been far too hasty the night before. The weather had changed, and it had turned most fearfully cold, so that we were obliged to wrap up warmly. More than this, we found afterwards that there was a perfectly good snow-road as far as

Irghiz, two-thirds of the distance to Kazala; but luckily for us it was so cold, and the road so hard-frozen, that we travelled for the most part as if over a macadamised road, so that wheels were equally serviceable with runners. Our vehicles were neither of them heavy; but it is of no use to state the number of horses you want, or to have your luggage weighed, even should there be a possibility of doing so. The post-master will insist that more horses are required to draw such heavy loads, and there is no help but to submit. We took, therefore, the ten horses that were given us, and started off in the face of a fearful wind. We had, however, but reached the edge of the town, when we discovered that in the hurry of departure one of the axles had been put on wrongly, and that the forward movement was gradually unscrewing both of the front wheels. We fortunately saw this in time, and, with the assistance of the people living near by, unharnessed the horses, raised the tarantass, and changed the axle. With this began our experience of the real difficulties of Asiatic travelling. At this time the post-track to Terekli was kept by Kirghiz contractors. They were careless and improvident, and laid in little or no forage for the horses during the winter, which had to live on what they could grub up under the snow or starve; consequently they were nothing but skin and bone, and were often scarcely able to move. The stations along the road were wretched. Sometimes there was nothing but a Kirghiz kibitka, the felt walls of which were incapable of keeping out the cold, in spite of the fire of roots in the centre, or, as we found in one instance, of a red-hot iron stove, which a Kirghiz girl was constantly busily feeding with dried camel's dung—the usual fuel on the Steppe. Very often they were underground huts, down to which we stumbled through a long dark passage, which were at least cozy and warm, however dark and filthy. At present the road is rather better, for soon afterwards a new contract was made with some Russians, and when I reached Orsk on my return from Tashkent, I heard that neat wooden stations had been put up along the line, and saw numbers of good sledges and tarantasses that were being sent out there. It was stated that the stations were all well furnished, and that it was even possible to obtain a meal there. How long this will continue it is of course impossible to say.

Frequently we had great difficulty in getting horses. This happened even at the first station, Tokan. Now, Tokan is marked on the map, and we therefore supposed that there would be a village of some sort there. There was, however, nothing but the station, though about a mile off there was a little Kirghiz, winter *aul*, a little group of earthen hovels, surrounded by manure-heaps, the population of which changes from year to year. After waiting for more than an hour, we were told by the Cossack in charge that the Kirghiz station-master had refused to give us horses, although all were in, and had sent off the driver with blows. The Cossack said that if he went there the old Kirghiz would certainly beat him, and suggested to us that it would be much better that we should go and beat him instead, offering to lead the way. There was nothing else to be done, and after a long walk through the snow we found the station-master, on whom our solicitations made not the slightest impression. Words being spent in vain, our Tartar servant began to belabor him with a rusty sword, quite against all rules and regulations, it is true, but we were too angry and too hurried to protest. The Kirghiz at once gave in, knelt down, and began to embrace our knees and beg for mercy, saying he would give us the horses immediately. He had, however, only furnished two, when he leaped on the third and rushed off over the plain. We immediately sent in pursuit of him, and brought him back, when he said he was going to another village to fetch other horses. We refused to take this excuse, and insisted upon at once having them all, and after considerable delay they were furnished. It was, however, three hours from the time we reached the station before we were ready to start. Even then the horses were so bad that we were almost sorry we had any.

Frequently there were no horses, and we had to have camels harnassed to our tarantass, which was very annoying, as they went so slowly, seldom more than two and a half miles an hour. Still they would take one through anything, mud, snow, sand, or water. It is no doubt very fine to speak of camels as 'ships of the desert,' and use other poetical expressions for them, but practically they are the most disagreeable, unpleasant animals that I have ever seen; ungainly, unamiable, and disgusting in odour, they seem to be a sort of a cross between a cow and a cassowary. Seen in the distance they make one think of a big over-grown ostrich, with their claw-feet and long necks, which they turn about so as always to observe everything which comes by, and stare at you with their big vacant eyes until you have passed fully out of sight. They seem to stand cold very well, although they will take cold and die if allowed to lie down in the snow. Hence during the winter on the Steppe their bodies are wrapped up in felt, which, when taken off in spring, carries most of the hair with it, and they then look entirely naked. If they get an idea into their heads that the road is long, or the weight too heavy, or that some part of the harness is wrong, they commence to howl. It is not exactly a groan nor a cry, but a very human, shrill and disagreeable sound; and this they never cease—they keep it up from the time they start until they reach their destination, varying their performances by occasionally kneeling down and refusing to advance; or if they do go on, holding back in such a manner as to make progress all the slower. In this case there is nothing to do but to unfasten the animal, turn him loose, and tie his legs together, when he will begin to browse about, poking the snow away with his nose, and his driver will find him when he comes back. Camels are much too stupid to go home, as any other animal would, but they will continue to walk on in the same direction their faces are turned without ever thinking of master or stable or anything else. They are very revengeful, and in the spring season the male camels are very often dangerous. Many instances are known where they have bitten persons to death, and they then have to be carefully muzzled. There was one comfort to be got out of them notwithstanding—their walk was so quiet and sauntering, that in the morning, when it was not too cold, we could read with ease in the carriage, as there was not motion enough to jolt the book. In this way we got through 'Middlemarch,' some books on Central Asia, and the whole of the Koran, to say nothing of spelling through Tartar exercises, and trying each other as we went along in pronunciation and phrases. It was not only the camels that gave us trouble—the harness was always in disorder; a rope would perhaps be too long, or then too short, and occasionally some strap or string would break, so that half an hour rarely elapsed without the driver being obliged to dismount and arrange something. If nothing else happened he would drop his whip. The drivers were for the most part Kirghiz, stupid and stolid enough, but still good-natured, and cheerily singing to themselves as they went on, though usually, if the camels went very slowly, they were apt to go to sleep, and by this means our night journeys were rendered very tedious.

Both in St. Petersburg and at Orenburg our friends had prophesied to us many imaginary dangers. I was even advised by Government officials in St. Petersburg to go by way of Siberia, as my safety could not be guaranteed if I went over the Steppe. At Orenburg we were urged to keep a sharp look-out, as we might at any time be attacked by bands of hostile Kirghiz, or possibly Turkomans, coming from Khiva, but we found the road perfectly safe, and speedily laid aside all thoughts of precaution, though we took care to have a pistol near us; but our large revolvers were stowed away at the bottom of the tarantass, where they remained undisturbed until we reached Kazala. The road was so safe, in fact, that ladies were travelling on it alone, with only a servant; even the war-time seemed to make no difference; and as it turned out afterwards my companion went as far as Khalata, where he joined the Russian forces, without meeting the slightest danger of any kind except from fatigue and want of water.

As far as Kazala our greatest hardship was cold. It being winter, water was plentiful, and we always had enough to eat. We had brought some hams and preserved meats and plenty of eggs, so that our usual diet consisted of fried slices of ham, which we prepared ourselves over a spirit-lamp, boiled or fried eggs, with sausages, jams, and potted meat. The bread we had found at Orsk was good, but it usually took some time to warm it to a temperature at which it could be either cut or eaten. We had plenty of good butter, and really lived very well. When we felt that the miseries of the day made us deserve a more luxurious feast, we had a stew of some tinned American oysters, if we could find any milk. Our servants looked rather askance at the ham and bacon, and apparently lived on nothing but bread and eggs, though I think Ak-Mametef had conquered his Mussulman prejudice sufficiently to have frequent swigs at the whisky-bottle. Of course the cooking took some little time, and the washing of the dishes and packing up much more; so that we tried to get along with as few meals as possible, and at last satisfied ourselves with a good supper, provided we had tea and bread-and-butter two or three times a day; but we found from long experience that in order even then to be kept from waiting we must command our horses as soon as we arrived at the station. It was fortunate that we had brought our own provisions, for we should have found nothing; indeed, we had to help others with a little sugar or even bread. I well remember one underground hut, where a Cossack and his young wife asked us to spare them a loaf, as they had not tasted bread for a week, living only on porridge.

Our eleven days' journey over the Steppe from Orsk to Kazala was not, of course, without its varieties and its little incidents. Of the Steppe, as far as Irghiz at least, we saw very little, for being covered with snow, it presented but one white plain, rising and falling gently in places, but never-ending. Still there were the lights and shadows, the dazzling glare of the sun, and the wan light of the night, the tracks of animals by the roadside, the caravan trails, which made us think we could never lose our way, if thrown alone by accident, and the occasional bivouacs of Russian carters, with the picturesque groups around the camp-fires, to lend interest to the monotony. In general the whole of this Steppe has a declivity towards the Aral Sea, but there are at times slight elevations of ground—it would be wrong to call them hills—and there are the almost imperceptible valleys in which are torrents or river courses. On our right we could see at times low ranges of hills, which sometimes, when near at hand, were white, and sometimes in the distance, without the snow, were of a tender blue. These were the continuation of the chain of the Ural, which finally towards the Sea of Aral becomes what is called the Mugojar mountains. Between these, and the Guberlinsky, on the north side of the Ural river, there is no specific name for the chain. At times we crossed or followed little streams, which as a general rule were still covered with ice and snow, and were therefore invisible. One of them, the little river Or, which flows into the Ural near Orsk, we had some difficulty in crossing. This was at the station of Istemes. We arrived at the river about one o'clock A.M. at a place where the ice, owing to the recent thaws, had become so thin that it was incapable of bearing us, and the drivers refused to go on; although it was evident that some one not long before had crossed the stream; neither were they willing to risk their lives—as they said—by endeavouring to cross the ice on foot to the scattered huts on the other side, in order to ask where a better crossing for our vehicles could be found. My companion and myself vainly wandered up and down the banks, misled in the bright starry night by faint tracks, hoping to find some place where the ice was more solid, but it always began to give way as soon as we put our feet on it. Finally, we persuaded one man to risk the crossing; and though he assured us the water was up to his neck, if not higher, he managed somehow to get safely across—the ice breaking through only once—and was told at the huts that our best way was to go straight on; so at last we started, having taken the leaders from one tarantass and added them to the other, sending all the horses back again for the wagon we had left behind. To our surprise we found not only the ice so thin as not to incommode the horses, but the water only about a foot and a half deep.

The largest river that we passed was the Irghiz, which flows into Lake Tchalkar without continuing so far as the Aral Sea. These rivers of the Steppe are all much alike. In the spring there is a great deal of water, which overflows a considerable extent of country. In the summer there is often no water at all, or only a succession of small pools and lakes at distances of many miles. In spite of the wintry weather the Steppe, even from Orsk, abounded in birds of all kinds, especially in crows, blackbirds, and eagles. When our horses and camels went very slowly, and the day was not too cold, we often amused ourselves by trying to get a shot at either the birds or the small fur-bearing animals which live on the Steppe. These latter from their dark colours, especially with the aid of the sharp eyes of our Kirghiz drivers, could be seen a long distance off; but even with the best of long-range rifles they always succeeded in getting to their holes before we came up. Near Irghiz there were some small reedy ponds, which were covered with thousands of wild duck; but unless we went gradually towards them in our vehicles, to which they paid no attention, it was impossible to get a shot at them, and even then it did us no good, as they always fell too far out in the water for us to reach them. One day we were unusually lucky, for MacGahan shot a couple of bustards, large and very graceful white and grey birds, with long necks, which are frequent in that part of the Steppe. We cooked them when we arrived at the station, and found them excellent eating.

There were two breaks in the monotonous journey—the forts of Karabutak and Irghiz, situated respectively at 140 and 262 miles from Orsk. They were welcome reliefs to us; and had it not been for the kindness of Colonel Strashny-Senukovitch, the Commandant of Karabutak, I know not how we should have got on. At the previous station we could only get two worn-out wretched horses and a small sledge, in which with great exertions we made the thirteen miles to the fort in five hours. We found the station to be a very small earth hut, quite cold, and apparently with no means of making a fire, and with no persons about. We therefore drove directly to the house of the Commandant of the fort, to whom I had a letter from General Kryzhanofsky, of Orenburg. It was quite dark at his little house, and we were afraid at first that he had gone to sleep; but there was no help for it, and we had to run the risk of awakening him. At last he appeared, and received us both very kindly, had tea immediately prepared for us, and gave us some cold supper, which we were glad enough to get, as we had had nothing to eat since the morning. He at once sent a soldier with his own horses to the last station to bring on our vehicles and luggage, and kindly insisted on our passing the night with him, for which purpose he had his divans made up into beds, and we slept luxuriously until late the next morning. It was not until the afternoon that our servants appeared and told us that we could now go on, as six horses were also provided for us by the commandant.

This fort, which is a very small one, was built in 1848, to assist in keeping up the communication with the fort of Uralskoe, which had been raised in the Steppe some three years before. It is situated on a little eminence, at the foot of which runs a small stream of saltish water, which cannot be used for drinking purposes. There is no verdure or vegetation about the fort, and the Commandant has even found it impossible to make a garden The garrison numbered less than a hundred, which is quite sufficient, as now the Steppe is so peaceful there is really nothing to do except to show the Kirghiz that force can be used in case anything goes wrong. About the fort a few small clay houses have been built, but there are no merchants, and the doctor and one or two officers are the only company for the Commandant. I went through the fortification and into the barracks, where I found everything in excellent order. They had been baking bread that day—black bread, such as is so loved by the Russian peasantry and soldiers—and it really was excellent. I tasted the dinner, also excellent, which had just been brought on the table, consisting of boiled beef and cabbage-soup. There was no view from the heights except the wide snowy plain, but as it was too cold to enjoy even that we quickly returned to the house again. After an excellent breakfast, or really a dinner, the Commandant allowed us to depart, though he urged us much to stay another day. As we were leaving he gave the driver strict injunctions to take us on as quickly as possible.

Irghiz, which before it was made into a district city was called Uralskoe, is somewhat larger perhaps than Karabutak. The fort is a wretched earthen construction, situated on the steep high bank of the little river Irghiz. The place is as dull as can be, and utterly unpicturesque, with rows of flat-roofed, one storied, mud houses, in which live the hangers-on of the fort and the traders with the Kirghiz. A few shops containing iron kettles, felt, cloths, and prints, and other articles for Kirghiz trade, and a broad muddy street, comprise the whole of the town. The Commandant, Colonel Ryedkin, received us very kindly, and gave us a paper addressed to all the stationmasters, to facilitate our getting horses.

We were lodged here in a dirty damp room, in what purported to be a cook's shop, where we spent the most of the day in resting, renewing our ammunition, and getting some fresh provisions. When we started, late in the afternoon, it was warm and sunny, and the snow was fast disappearing, so that the Steppe took for us a new appearance, though there was yet nothing green. The ground was in some places so soft that at last we were unlucky enough to get into a mud-hole and stick there, near some Kirghiz *kibitkas*. Both men and women assisted to pull us out, but for a long time their efforts were useless, as the horses would not pull together, and it was very difficult to make the Kirghiz driver understand that he must turn the vehicle in order to wrench the wheel out of the rut. The thaw had begun in earnest, and the approach to the desert began to be filled up with deep sand, so that our progress became more difficult. In places there were small ravines filled with melted snow and water—*aksai*—which were very hard to pass. The Steppe became more and more desolate until we reached the station of Terekly, on the edge of the great desert of Kara-Kum, (black sand), where begins the province of Turkistan. This was formerly the great bugbear of the route; but owing to the energy of the district prefect of Kazala and the efforts of the post-contractors, it has now become one of the easiest portions of the road. The stations themselves are all well-constructed buildings of unburnt bricks, neatly covered with white plaster, and have a large warm room, with a divan, so that if a traveller wishes to pass the night there he can sleep with comfort. The road was at that time very bad, being over deep snow, but the short distances between the stations and the better horses and camels made us travel much more quickly. One station, I remember, of eleven miles we made in an hour and a quarter. The Kara-Kum did not, however, conform to my preconceived notions of the desert, being by no means a desolate expanse of sand, as it was covered in every direction with small bushes and shrubs, and the ground frequently rose in little hillocks. There were no shifting sands, and the grey sand seemed hardly black enough to warrant the name. Some indeed believe that this desert is gradually disappearing. The young grass and the wild tulips were just venturing to come up, so that the waste had at times a greenish tinge, and the shrubs, though they had no leaves upon them, all had a certain colouring—grey, red, blue, and purple—in dull shades, so that where a hillock was thickly covered with them there was at a little distance quite a landscape effect.

One day, near the station of Ak-julpas, for about three hours before sunset our road lay along the smooth beach of a bay of the Aral Sea. Far out to the west we looked over an expanse of shallow water rippled by the wind, and forming pools on the flat sandy beach. In the distance was a low dark blue promontory, and faint blue coast-lines, and to the east and south the desert rising and falling in low hillocks, covered with low leafless shrubs, the coloured stems of which gave an aspect of purple, rose, and yellow, mingling with the yellow-brown of the sand. But the charm lay in the sky, light blue with fleecy clouds, and a sun which lighted up the clear, very clear, shallow pools of water and shore and sea with silver and pearly hues. White gulls soared and dipped into the bay, hovering even over our heads ; while farther away the water was covered with flocks of ducks and other water-fowl, but they were too wary to allow us to approach them. It was the same here as elsewhere on the road : as long as we remained in the tarantass the birds would be quite indifferent to us, and sit still as we passed them, but the moment they saw a person on foot they were astonished at the novelty of the sight, and immediately made off.

The water looked so clear and pure that I scooped up a cup of it and drank it. In taste it was slightly brackish, but not strongly saline.[1] The troops of the Orenburg detachment on their way to Khiva used it for two days, without disagreeable results, though with rapidly increasing disgust.

The appearance of this shallow bay of Sary-Tchaganak is an example of the whole of this vast inland sea, a veritable waste of

---

[1] The first analysis of the water of the Aral Sea was made by Mr. Teich, director of the Tashkent laboratory, on water collected at Ak-Julpas, on August 1, 1871. A second analysis was made by Professor Schmidt, of Dorpat, on water collected by Dr. Grimm in 1873. The results, as given in the 'Bulletin of the Imperial Russian Geographical Society,' 1873, No. 3, p. 95, and the 'Russische Revue,' No. 5, 1874, p. 468, are, in 1,000 parts of water, as follows:—

	Professor Schmidt, 1873.	Mr. Teich, 1871.
Chloride of rubidium, Rb Cl.	0·0030	?
Chloride of potassium, KCl	0·1115	?
Chloride of sodium, NaCl	6·2356	6·7087
Chloride of magnesium, $MgCl_2$	0·0003	0·4510
Bromide of magnesium, MgB_2	0·0033	?
Sulphate of lime, $CaSo_4$	1·5562	1·9330
Phosphate of lime, CaP_2O_4	0·0016	?
Sulphate of magnesia, $MgSo_4$	2·7973	3·1830
Bicarbonate of magnesia, MgC_2O_3	0·1942	?
	10·9089	12·2757
Specific weight at 17° 5 C =	1·00914	= 1·0106

Two later analyses by Pratz give the percentage of foreign substances in 1,000 parts of water as 12·359 and 12·567 respectively (' Bull. Imp. Russ. Geog. Soc.,' 1874, No. 5, p. 194). This shows that the water of the Aral Sea is less salt than that of the Caspian or of the ocean.

waters, 270 miles long by 160 broad. The surroundings are utterly desolate and uninhabited—everywhere sandy hills and stretches of desert. Except birds there are very few signs of life. The fauna of the sea is poor in forms, the fish being all of the species found in the rivers emptying into it, while the mollusks are in part fresh-water forms, and in part a remnant of the inhabitants of the old Aral-Caspian basin. The sea itself is shallow, it being in no place deeper than 245 feet, and that only on the western rocky shore, while in the middle its depth is only about 100 feet. On the east and south one can walk for miles through the shallow water, and during the time of strong winds the bed is for a long distance almost dry. Owing to the absence of good harbours, and the difficulties of getting into and out of the mouths of the Syr-Darya and Oxus, the sea is almost unnavigable. If we may judge from tradition and the reports of previous travellers, it seems to be gradually drying up. There are evidences on nearly all sides that it once occupied a far greater extent, and the Khivan expedition found that the Aibugir Lake, which was formerly connected with its southern end, is now become a dry bed. The level of the Aral sea, according to the measurements of the exploring expedition of 1874 under Colonel Thilo, is about 165 feet above the level of the ocean, and 250 feet above that of the Caspian Sea.[1]

At last the Kara-Kum was passed, and we arrived at the station of Yuniisk, some sixteen miles from Kazala, where we were obliged to pass the night, as it was too dark to go on, the road being in parts much flooded, and there being nothing but camels to take us. Starting early in the morning with horses, we went on, and soon came in sight of the town and the tall masts of vessels, which showed that at least we had reached the river. Many of these *masts* as we had supposed them to be on our nearer approach turned out to be well-sweeps. We had to go by a very round-about road through the Steppe, which was completely cut up with small canals, as the Kirghiz sometimes irrigate and cultivate this part of the country; and when we had nearly reached the town we found in our way a large and deep canal, which had much overflowed, and looked somewhat dan-

---

[1] The observations of Zagoskin, Anjou, and Duhamel in 1826 gave the level of the Aral Sea as 117·6 feet above the Caspian, while those of Struve in 1358 fixed it at 132 feet.

gerous to cross, as the water was rushing swiftly by. Having got safely almost to the deepest part, we stuck there, and for nearly an hour our efforts to move were entirely useless, the wheels sinking deeper into the mud every moment. We piled our pistols, guns, and hand-bags in the back of the carriage, as the water nearly reached up to the floor, and began to think that we should have to leave them there for the present and ride in on the horses. At last, after great exertion, we had other horses brought to us from the station, and succeeded in dragging the vehicles out one after the other, after which we drove at once to the Hôtel d'Europe, where we had two or three bare but tolerably clean rooms, a luxury we had not calculated upon.

KIRGHIZ CHANGING CAMP.

All through the Kara-Kum we met numbers of Kirghiz families, who were going from their winter to their summer quarters, seeking pasturage for their cattle and flocks in the Steppe south of Orenburg—long caravans of horses and camels laden with piles of felt, tent-frames, and household utensils, on top of which sat a woman, perhaps with an infant in a cradle before her. Sometimes we caught them as they were setting up their kibitkas or arranging the fences of reed-mats to protect their flocks from the prowling wolves. Some of them spend the winter in the Kara-Kum itself, but the most of them pass south of the Syr Darya, near the bounds of Khiva.

These nomads who inhabit the western Steppe are not the same people as the true Kirghiz or Buruts who live about the lake Issyk-Kul and in the mountain ranges of Khokand, and are called by the Russians Kara-Kirghiz (Black Kirghiz), and also *Dikokamenny*, or wild mountain Kirghiz. They do not call themselves Kirghiz, which is a name given them by the Russians, but are known only as *Kazak*, the same as the Russian Cossack. In order to distinguish this from the Russian word the Russians are in the habit of calling the race *Kirghiz Kaisak*, an entirely erroneous and meaningless name. The name *Kazak*, as used in Central Asia, means simply a vagabond or wanderer, and its application is evident. It is convenient, however, to follow usage and continue to speak of them as Kirghiz.

The Kirghiz speak a language which is one of the purest dialects of Tartar,[1] though as a race they contain many foreign elements. They originated from several Turkish tribes and families, which in the second half of the fifteenth century followed Sultans Girei and Jani Bek in their flight from the tyranny of their rulers to the neighbourhood of Lake Balkash. They were soon joined by others, and rapidly became a flourishing community, known by their neighbours as *Kazaks*. The kernel of the race is evidently Turkish, and many of the tribes and families have the same names as Uzbek tribes in Khokand and Bukhara. Gaining more and more strength and importance, they soon numbered a million of men, with over 300,000 warriors, and in 1598 their Khan, Tevvekel, conquered the cities and provinces of Tashkent and Turkistan, which were the seat of the Kirghiz dynasty till 1723. It was in this flourishing period of their sway that the Kirghiz became divided into three parts, the provinces of Tashkent and Turkistan forming the Middle Horde, the Great Horde going to the east, and the Lesser Horde to the west and north.[2]

---

[1] The Kirghiz language differs from Tartar in the interchange of certain letters, *j* for *y*, *b* for *p*, *zh* for *j*, *sh* for *tch*, *t* for *d*, *p* for *f*, *d* for *l*, &c. Few Persian or Arabic words are used, and there are many words peculiar to this dialect only, as it has not passed the growing stage.

[2] The word Horde, Russian *orda*, comes from the Turki *ordu*, a camp, seen now in *urda*, citadel, which is the accepted term in Tashkent, Khokand, and the neighbouring places. *Orda* is now commonly used by the Russian soldiers and

In the beginning of the eighteenth century the Kirghiz, through intestine disputes, found themselves in a very bad position—attacked on the south-west by the Kalmuks, on the north by the Siberian Cossacks, and on the east by the ruler of Jungaria; and, under the leadership of Abul-Khair Khan, they asked Peter the Great to receive them under Russian protection. This request was at that time refused, on account of the want of unanimity among the tribes.

In 1723 the Khan of Jungaria took the city of Turkistan, when, rather than submit to him, the Middle and Lesser Hordes made a despairing movement westwards, drove out the Bashkirs, and occupied all the Steppe between the Aral Sea, the Caspian, and the river Ural, and thus became the immediate neighbours of the Russians. It is with this, the Lesser Horde, that the Russians have had the chief trouble. Abul-Khair, the Khan of the Lesser Horde at this time, was a remarkable man—enthusiastic and able, but cunning and false, and therefore unable to maintain long his influence or carry out his plans. Besides being Khan of the Lesser Horde he was also chosen Khan of the Greater Horde, but was subsequently deposed. He was also for a short time Khan in Turkistan, and reigned in Khiva until the report of the approach of Nadir Shah drove him away. In one of his moments of difficulty, hard-pressed by his rivals, he, with a small number of his followers, offered to become Russian vassals. This was in 1730, but his proposition to the Russians was repudiated by the most of the Kirghiz, and it was only after much difficulty that they were brought to recognise him again as Khan, and that finally in 1734 an agreement was made by which Abul-Khair bound himself to keep the Russian boundaries intact and to protect the Russian trading caravans; and the Russians in return agreed to affirm the dignity of Khan to his descendants. This agreement, combined with the ignorance of the Russians of the real feelings and wishes of the Kirghiz, was probably the cause of all the troubles of the Steppe. By it the principle of the free election of the Khans was overthrown; and the descendants of Abul-Khair, being neither personally popular among their countrymen, nor being of the

Cossacks in a very amusing manner as a contemptuous term for an Asiatic. The Great, Middle, and Lesser Hordes are called in Kirghiz *Ulu-juz*, *Urta-juz*, and *Kitchi-juz*.

oldest tribe or family, would never have been voluntarily chosen. But the Russian generals were blind, and continued for nearly a hundred years the mistaken policy of maintaining titular Khans, who often possessed not a shadow of influence or authority among their people, and lived chiefly in the Russian forts. Though the Kirghiz were now accounted Russian subjects, the Steppe was even more unquiet and dangerous than before, and frequently the Russian authorities were compelled to maintain their *protégés* and put down their unruly subjects by force of arms, while the trade with the settled countries of Central Asia was greatly obstructed. In 1824 the Khanate was abolished, and the whole country was divided into three districts, which were governed by three Sultans Regent. These divisions were, however, carelessly made, tribal distinctions and rights of land not having been recognised, and the difficulties of the situation were not removed. The Kirghiz had great respect for their aristocracy, and the common people, or 'black bone,' were led by the 'white bone' (the Kirghiz for *blue blood*), or the descendants of the old Khans and ruling families. These men stood up for their tribes and families in defence of the honour and safety of their members. Reverencing at the same time bravery, dash, and boldness, and loving their freedom, they were always ready to follow the standard of any '*batyr*' or hero, such as Syrym, Arunbazi, or Kenisar, who might appear in the Steppe. The Sultans Regent were either mere Russian creatures, entirely destitute of influence, or they were themselves inclined to revolt at times, and neither they nor the annual military expeditions from Orenburg could succeed in maintaining order in the Steppe.

The establishment of Russian forts and garrisons in commanding positions in the Steppe by the Governor-General Obrutchef, in 1845, and the subsequent advances on the Syr Darya, brought about a better state of things; but it was not until the final overthrow of the bandit Iset Kutebarof, and the death of the celebrated *batyr* Jan Hodja, that the Steppe became quiet and safe, and the Russians really gained the position of *protectors* of the Kirghiz. Even then all the causes of danger were not removed.

Some years ago an effort was made to abolish, as far as possible, the tribal distinctions of the Kirghiz aristocracy, and for the purposes of a better government the so-called reform was introduced into the Orenburg Steppe in the year 1869. By this all the Lesser Horde of the Steppe was divided into two large districts—the district of Uralsk, and the district of Turgai—and each district was placed under the command of a Russian military governor, district prefects, and the *volost* or *aul* elders. The district prefects were of course appointed by the Government, while the rulers of the *volosts* or *auls* were elected by the inhabitants. It was perhaps carrying the system of elective government very far to introduce it into the Steppe among people who were accustomed to nothing else than hereditary and arbitrary rule, for the Khans, when they were still elective, were chosen by the aristocracy only, and the result was very great discontent, which broke out into open insurrection.

It is said by the Russians that the distrust and dislike of the common people for the Sultans and native aristocracy was shown by the fact that very few of the officers who were elected belonged to the aristocracy, and that persons who enjoyed the confidence of the community were refused election merely on the ground that they were Sultans; and it is alleged that the disturbances were chiefly stirred up by the Mullahs, who saw that their livelihood would be cut off if they were deprived of the position they had held as scribes to the Sultans. There is, however, no doubt that the great cause of the disturbances was the belief, in great measure founded on fact, that the new regulations would give the Kirghiz entirely up to the rule of the Cossacks, with whom they had always been at variance. In the Turgai district the military governor was entirely independent of Orenburg, although he has thus far always resided in that city; but the Uralsk district was amalgamated with the Ural Cossacks, as the military governor of the Uralsk Kirghiz is also the Ataman of the Ural Cossacks. The disturbances were also to some extent fomented by the Khan of Khiva, and the result was that during the whole of the years 1869 and 1870 the Steppe was in great commotion. The postal route was blockaded, stations were destroyed, and even travellers were captured, some being killed and others sold into slavery by the Khan, while the small garrisons in the Russian fortresses in the Steppe were in a very dangerous position. Order was ultimately restored, and the Steppe is now in a most tranquil state. The Kirghiz have rapidly become accustomed to the new order of things, and it is even said that the clannish feeling for the members of the same family and tribe is being transferred to the members of the same volost and district. The Middle Horde followed the Lesser Horde in demanding Russian protection, but it was only in 1781, on the death of the bold Sultan Ablai, who by skilful coquetry with both Russia and China had managed to retain a real independence, that the Russian sway became fixed. The Greater Horde became subject to Russia only in 1847.

It is very difficult to calculate the numbers of the Kirghiz, but so near as can be ascertained by the return of taxes, which amount to three roubles on each *kibitka*, there are in all about a million and a half. In the Greater Horde, in the district of Alatau, there are about 100,000 of both sexes; in the Middle Horde, occupying the whole of Southern Siberia and country north of Tashkent, there are 406,000; and in the Lesser Horde, between Fort Perovsky, the Ural, and the Caspian, there are 800,000. There is still another horde, the Bukeief, or Inner Horde, living in Europe, between the Ural and the Volga, numbering perhaps 150,000. This horde was formed in the early years of the present century by about 7,000 of the Lesser Horde, led by Bukeief, a grandson of Abul-Khair, who crossed the Ural to occupy the land left vacant by the Kalmuks. In 1812 Bukeief was confirmed Khan. This is the ancestor of Prince Tchinghiz, mentioned in the opening of the chapter.

The flocks and herds of the Kirghiz form their only wealth, and are without doubt a source of income to the empire, though it is not easy to calculate the amount. According to the statistics of 1869 there were sold by the Kirghiz at the exchange bazaars of Orenburg and Troitsk: camels, 1,150 head; horses, 1,001 head; herding cattle, 16,031; sheep, 273,823, amounting in all to 1,500,000 roubles, or 200,000*l*. At Petropavlovsk, on the Siberian border, the sales of cattle from 1856 to 1865 amounted to over two and a half millions of roubles yearly (340,000*l*.), and the sale of leather and hides to 400,000 roubles (55,000*l*.) yearly.

In spite of its Turkish origin the Kirghiz race has almost as much of a Mongol as of a Turkish type. This is especially noticeable in the aristocratic class, above all in their women; and one reason is said to be that the Kirghiz, until recent times, preferred, whenever possible, to marry Kalmuk women, carrying them off from the confines of China or the Astrakhan steppe. It would be very difficult to describe any one face as showing the typical Kirghiz traits, for, ranging through slight gradations, there are at last strong contrasts to be observed. Still the Kirghiz type readily impresses itself on the memory, and seen a few times is not soon forgotten. The Kirghiz are in general short of stature, with round swarthy faces, insignificant noses, and small sharp black eyes, with the tightly-drawn eyelid which is seen in all the Mongol tribes.

In winter the Kirghiz sometimes live in underground huts, entered by crooked passages, where children, calves, and colts all sleep and play together; but usually their habitation, both in winter and summer, is a *kibitka*, a circular tent made of felt spread over a light wooden frame. This frame is easily taken apart and put together, and is so light as to form a load for a single camel only. The broad pieces of felt are easily stretched over it, so that the whole can be put up in about ten minutes. On one side is a door covered by a flap of felt, and the fire is built in the middle, the smoke escaping through an opening in the roof. The interior of the tent is decorated with pieces of ribbon of various kinds, used to fasten down the felt, and around the sides the Kirghiz place and hang all their valuable goods, consisting of carpets, silk mattresses, and clothes, and sometimes, in cases of the richer men, of even silver articles, with the trappings of horses and household utensils. The *kibitka* forms a most comfortable abode, being cool in summer and warm in winter.

Being Mussulmans, the men all shave their heads and allow their beards to grow, although usually their beards are very insignificant—a straggly tuft of hair scarcely covering the chin. They wear immense baggy leather breeches, and a coarse shirt with wide flapping collars. Their outer garment is a dressing-gown, and they usually wear two or three, according to the weather. The rich and distinguished have magnificent velvet robes, richly embroidered with gold and silver. A red velvet robe is given by the Government as a mark of distinction, and there is nothing the Kirghiz are more proud of, unless it be a medal or a cross. They wear on their heads embroidered skull-caps, and over those oddly-shaped hoods of sheepskin, with the wool inside, or conical felt hats cut with two slits for convenience of turning up the brims, and not, as has been said, that it might not be like a Christian hat, of which they know nothing. On grand occasions the wealthy don tall steeple-crowned hats, with the brim turning up in two immense horns, made of felt or usually of velvet, embroidered often with gold. But their greatest adornments are their belts, saddles, and bridles, which are often so covered with silver, gold, and precious stones as to be almost solid. The women are dressed the same as the men, but have their heads and necks swathed in loose folds of white cotton cloth, so as to make a sort of bib and turban at the same time.

KIRGHIZ WOMEN.

They spin, embroider—very well too—cook, and do most of the work, as the men are too lazy to do more than look after the horses. The boys are either naked or in a shirt and baggy breeches, with capless shaven heads. The girls dress like their mothers, with their hair shorn behind, and hanging in front in a score of very long fine braids.

The Kirghiz are in general breeders of cattle and sheep, and the search for fresh pastures is the main cause of their migrations over the Steppe. They do not, however, wander indiscriminately over the vast expanse, but have their settled winter and summer quarters, each *volost*—as they are now divided by the Russians—keeping its own limits.

Along the Syr-Darya the Kirghiz have to some extent begun to cultivate the ground, but in general a person who engages in agricultural pursuits is looked down upon by the rest. Still, love of gain has been sufficient to counterbalance this contempt among the Kirghiz in the vicinity of Aulié-Ata and the northern slope of the Alexandrofsky range. There it has been found such a lucrative occupation to raise wheat, that the Kirghiz Sultans, and after them the lower classes of the community, have with eagerness engaged in agriculture. It is perhaps one characteristic of nomad life to be utterly improvident, and the Kirghiz are particularly so. They are able to go without drink for a whole day, and food for several days, and will then gorge themselves to repletion. Their food consists principally of mutton, although sometimes, especially at great feasts, they will indulge in horse-flesh. They, of course, have no bread, but they make a sort of porridge of millet or other easily cultivated grain, although many of them never use this from one year's end to the other. As a drink tea is now greatly used in the Steppe, the Kirghiz buying the cheapest kind of what is called 'brick tea'—tea which is hard-pressed into moulds, so that it resembles bricks—otherwise they always have *kumys*—a liquor made of fermented mare's milk. *Kumys* is sourish to the taste, but not unpleasant, and possesses agreeable exhilarating although not intoxicating qualities. It is rapidly coming into use in Russia, especially in the neighbourhood of Samara, as a cure for many diseases. One of their favourite drinks, especially in Central Asia, is *buza*, a kind of beer made of grain, the effect of which is immediately to stupefy and deaden the senses rather than to inebriate.

In religion the Kirghiz are regarded as Mohammedans, although few have any fixed religious principles, as they have no settled priests, and but few can read or write. The rite of circumcision is performed by Tartar Mullahs, who wander through the Steppe, some kept as secretaries to rich Sultans, and others endeavouring to gain a livelihood by the profession of a pious life or the profession of medicine. They rarely pray, and their faith is mingled with many superstitious notions derived from paganism and Shamanism. It is only externally that they are Mussulmans. On being asked what religion they have, unaccustomed to such a form of the question, they will say they do not know, but at the same time they would repel with vigour any insinuation that they were not good Mussulmans.

It is a curious fact that the Kirghiz were converted to Mohammedanism by the mistaken efforts of the Russian Government. At first but a few of their sultans and chiefs had any idea of the doctrines of Islam, and there was not a mosque nor a mullah in the Steppe, but the Russians (just as they insisted on using the Tartar language in intercourse with them) insisted on treating them as though they were Mohammedans, built mosques and sent mullahs, until the whole people became outwardly Mussulman, although the farther from the Russian lines, and the nearer to the settled populations of Central Asia, the weaker was the faith. In the same way the Buriats during the present century were made Buddhists by the Russian officials, when they were nothing but Shamanists. It would have been easier, had the Government known it, to convert both races to Christianity at the outset. In the reign of Alexander I., when mysticism and religious enthusiasm were in vogue, and the Russian Bible Society flourished, English and Scotch missionaries had colonies in Irkutsk, Astrakhan, and Orenburg. Mirza Kasem-Beg, the well-known professor of St. Petersburg, was the most prominent convert of the Presbyterian mission under John Mitchell at Astrakhan. At Orenburg the colony headed by Fraser left an excellent name after their forced departure, and the house they built, just beyond the town, is still known as 'the English house.'

The Kirghiz, owing to the simplicity of their life, are far more children of nature than most other Asiatics, and have all the faults and virtues of children. Probably the first acquaintance with them will be found disagreeable, and certainly the side a traveller sees is their worst, but on knowing them more intimately one cannot help liking and even respecting them, and it is the verdict of everyone who has lived in Central Asia that the Kirghiz are superior to all the other races.

The men devote themselves almost entirely to the care of their horses, leaving all the work to be done by the women, and leading in general a lazy shiftless life, although when it comes to riding they are indefatigable, and will go hundreds of miles without seeming to be in the slightest degree tired. They are hospitable, often to a fault, to one of their own race or to a fellow Mussulman, nor do I believe that a Christian would fare worse among them. I certainly, whenever I happened to meet them on the Steppe, was well received, and everything which the family possessed was offered to me. They are sociable, and always eager for fresh news; even the telling or repeating it has a great charm for them; and as soon as a man arrives among them with a piece of news one of the family will immediately start off on a fresh horse and convey the intelligence to some distant acquaintance. In this way news travels through the Steppe almost as if by telegraph. Contrary to most other Asiatics, the Kirghiz are unsuspicious, and with child-like innocence believe all that is told them; they are, however, themselves far from truthful, though rather from laziness than wilful intent to deceive. Their promises are little to be depended upon, and in making a bargain with them, if they once obtain what they want, it is difficult to secure the performance of their part of the contract. They are light-minded and fickle, and easily influenced by the persons with whom they are for the moment associated. One of their best traits is their respect for age and the authority of their superiors. In war they are in general cowardly, though they are found to make excellent scouts, partly from their untiringness, and partly from their acquaintance with nature and capacity for observation. They can see or somehow divine a way in the darkest night, and it seems hardly possible for them to get lost in the desert or steppe. They measure space by the distance which the voice will reach or the eye can observe. They are not cruel by nature, and their wars or expeditions, when they undertake them, are rather for purposes of plunder than revenge. Plundering expeditions are frequent among those Kirghiz who are under Russian rule, though such *barantas* are severely punished if the perpetrators are discovered. The loss of horses or sheep is a sufficient reason for a *baranta*, or plundering expedition on a large scale, against one's neighbours, to indemnify oneself—really a sort of lynch-law. In disposition they are merry and good-natured, and devoted to music, constantly singing to themselves. They have many songs not devoid of much simple poetry, and as musical instruments have, besides the jewsharp, a sort of guitar and a drum.

Being Mohammedans, they use to the full extent the privilege of having many wives, though the first wife is always the mistress of the *kibitka*, and takes rank over the others. The seclusion of the harem is impossible in a tent on the Steppe, and the women are therefore unveiled, nor is any effort made to keep them from the observation of the men. One curious thing, however, in connection with their life is that, as a mark of respect to their husbands and male relatives, they are not allowed to mention their real names in the presence of others, but must either call them by some term adopted for the purpose or use a circumlocution. An incident is related of

KIRGHIZ HORSEMEN.

a Kirghiz woman who wanted to say that a wolf had stolen a sheep and taken it to the reedy shore of the lake. Unfortunately the men of the family bore names corresponding to most of these words, and she was obliged to gasp out that 'in the rustling beyond the wet a growler gnaws one of our woollies.'

A circumcision, a marriage, or a funeral feast among the Kirghiz is the signal for a large festival, accompanied by games and horse-races. To these men will sometimes ride one or two hundred miles for the mere chance of regaling themselves for two or three days at another's expense and take their share of gorging on whole-roasted sheep and horses. If the horses—for racing—are good, the races are the main feature of the feast, and large crowds remain seated with the utmost attention to look for the winner. The races being long, often twelve, fifteen, or twenty miles, the horses are usually started at a distance, as the race is generally in a straight line, and not round a circular course. Sometimes very high prizes are offered. I was invited to a *toi*, or feast, near Aulié-ata, where it was said would be some celebrated racers from Khokand, and the highest prize was as much as 500 roubles, which to a Kirghiz is a very great sum. Usually horses are given as prizes. The Kirghiz horses are wiry and enduring, and when really of good stock will show qualities in these long races which are truly wonderful. I saw one race of this kind some years ago, near Orenburg, where about a hundred horses were entered, ridden by boys and girls of various ages, all dressed in much the same way, and all sitting their horses alike, without either saddle or stirrups. This being a race got up for the Grand Duke Vladimir, who was then there, it was four times round a course marked out on the Steppe, making in all 20 versts, or over 13 miles, and was won in 29 minutes and 30 seconds. At first the horses ran pretty well together, but by the time they had made the course once they were widely scattered, and some passed on the second round the horses which had not yet completed the first. I saw at the same time a camel-race, for which three camels and a dromedary were entered. The poor animals were much frightened and confused by the crowd, and had to be dragged along and whipped on by horsemen, both when they started and as they came in. They started off with a shuffling uneasy trot; but on the other side of the course, where they were free, they went along very well. The dromedary—which was ridden by a dark-looking fellow, who seemed as if he were being thrown high into the air from the animal's single hump at every step— led the race in; but the horseman who had seized the bridle to guide him let go too soon, and away he went blindly among the crowd. A camel ridden by a young girl of about eighteen actually came in first, and took the prize.

Besides the racing there is usually wrestling, and especially the national sport of *baiga*, where one man holds a kid thrown over his saddle, and everyone else tries to tear it from him.

There is one race, called the 'Love Chase,' which may be considered a part of the form of marriage among the Kirghiz. In this the bride, armed with a formidable whip, mounts a fleet horse, and is pursued by all the young men who make any pretensions to her hand. She will be given as a prize to the one

A KIRGHIZ.

who catches her, but she has the right, besides urging on her horse to the utmost, to use her whip, often with no mean force, to keep off those lovers who are unwelcome to her, and she will probably favour the one whom she has already chosen in her heart. As, however, by Kirghiz custom, a suitor to the hand of a maiden is obliged to give a certain *kalym*, or purchase-money, and an agreement must be made with the father for the amount of dowry which he gives his daughter, the 'Love Chase' is a mere matter of form. The kalym often consists, with rich individuals, of as many as forty-seven horses, and perhaps a medium would be thirty-seven cattle and a few horses. In the dowry given by the father must always be included a kibitka for the use of the bride. As mullahs are very rare in the Steppe, a religious ceremony of any kind at a marriage is unusual, but one thing must be strictly performed: after the women have sung the virtues of the bride, and the men have chanted those of the husband, telling of his great exploits, how many cattle he has stolen, and in how many marauding expeditions he has engaged, the young man must enter the kibitka where the bride is seated and take her out, although both entrance and exit are forcibly opposed by all her friends. This is probably a remnant of the old primitive custom when marriage was an act of capture.

CHAPTER II.

THE SYR DARYA.

<small>Kazala—Fort No. 1—Commercial importance—Cordial reception—Talk of the Khivan expedition—Prospects of joining it—Suspicions—Frustrated hopes—We explain—Arrival of Russian captives from Khiva—The Syr Darya—Obstacles to navigation, and efforts to improve it—The Aral flotilla—A strange birthplace—Fort No. 2—A Kirghiz cemetery—A Mussulman saint—Fort Perovsky—MacGahan starts for Khiva—The Kyzyl Kum desert—Hazreti-Turkistan—Mausoleum of Akhmed Yasavi—Inscriptions—Ikan—Its brave defence—Tchimkent.</small>

Our first care on arriving at our hotel at Kazala and taking possession of our three rooms, with their dusty tiled floors, was to order a hot bath in the little Russian bath-house, and a good dinner; and while these were preparing we set out to see the river, for that, after so much desert, was the main attraction to us. We had not far to go through the wide streets, with their low mud houses, before we found ourselves under the regular slopes of the fortress, on the ramparts of which were standing some new rifled cannon, and just beyond it the Syr Darya rushed along in a wide turbid yellow flood. Workmen were busy putting together a small iron barge; and farther down, close under the guns of the fort, lay anchored the steamers of the Aral flotilla.

In 1847 the Russians built a little fortification at the very mouth of the Syr Darya, which they called Fort Raim—the first step in that course of Asiatic conquest which is not even yet terminated. This post was, however, very unhealthy, and subject to frequent overflows, and in 1855 the fort was transferred to the present position, where the little branch Kazala parts from the main river, and where two years before a small fort, called No. 1, had been erected. Since that time it has been called indiscriminately either Kazala, Kazalinsk, or Fort No. 1. Even here in the spring the inundations are so great that Kazala is then nothing but a small island in a waste of waters. The fort is so close to the bank of the river that it is expected that with the constant changes and wearings of the current the walls will be undermined and gradually washed away. It is a regular fortification, with thick walls of mud-bricks, glacis, and ditches, and would be capable of good defence even against civilised enemies; of course against Khivans or Turkomans it is absolutely impregnable. Inside are the barracks, the shops, and the houses of the different officers. The usual garrison consists of a battery of artillery, and two *sotnias* of Cossacks.[1] Round the fortress has grown up a little town, now containing at least 3,000 or 4,000 inhabitants, and in the bazaar a lively trade is kept up with the Kirghiz. Kazala lies at the junction of all the trade-routes in Central Asia, as the road from Orenburg meets here with the Khivan, Bukharan, and Tashkent roads. Here, too, is the chief post on the river Syr Darya. Should the Asiatic trade be developed, Kazala is likely to become a considerable commercial centre, and even now the trade is large. The advantages of Kazala would, however, be much increased by the erection of proper storehouses for goods, and by the establishment of a branch of some bank. At present goods arriving from Orenburg or other places frequently come here at the times when, owing to the state of the roads, it is impossible to carry them farther, and they must therefore be stored here for some weeks, or possibly months. In addition to there being no good store-houses, the owners of the goods are sometimes small capitalists unable to afford the delay, and are therefore forced to sell the goods at a low price to the local traders of Kazala, who take advantage of their necessities. With the extension of railways the great fair at Nizhni-Novgorod, where the products of the East and West have for centuries been exchanged— will probably be moved eastward, and in that case Kazala will reap great advantages.

Orenburg seems the natural centre of the Bukharan and Khivan trade; many of the merchants of those cities have personally been to Orenburg, and have several commercial connections there, and would always prefer to continue their trade

---

[1] A *sotnia* contains usually 120 men.

through that city, even should the possible advance of railways in a different direction—through Southern Siberia, for instance—effect a slight economy of freight on sending their wares to a different market. This relation of the two Khanates to Orenburg will always make Kazala a trade-centre, as being the only place of importance on the road. It is, however, a most dull and uncomfortable place of residence, as the sun streams down with great force here during the whole of the summer, and hot winds prevail.

It has not yet been found possible to raise any trees, or at most their number can be counted on one's fingers. Even at this time we found the heat great, as, when rested and refreshed, we strolled about the bazaar, inspecting and pricing the horses and camels, with a view to eventualities; peering into the little shops kept by Bukharans, and even Khivans, in their long striped robes; wondering at the ringleted Jews, living so far from the rest of their race, and yet so very Hebrew-like. We inspected the piles of felt, the heaps of kibitka frames, and the rows of iron caldrons, and watched the broad-shouldered hard-faced Kirghiz chaffering and bargaining. Passing beyond the bazaar, we entered one good shop, where wines, potted meats, *pâtés de foie gras*, English ale, and tinned American lobsters are in store for famished travellers, and were accosted by a kindly old Colonel, who asked if we were not the Americans who had just left him a letter of introduction from General Kryzhanovsky. He proved to be Colonel Kosaref, the Commandant, and gave us at once a most cordial invitation to take tea with him. The simplicity and kindliness of our reception made us at once feel at home, and we passed a pleasant evening in chatting with our host about the Steppe, which he knew so well, the Kirghiz, and the lonely life which he had led here at Kazala; before that at Fort No. 2, and still earlier for sixteen years at Fort Alexandrovsk, on the Caspian Sea, where there was at times communication with Russia but once or twice a year. Two or three officers entered, with whom we made acquaintance; and one, Captain Verestchagin, acting for the nonce as district prefect, observed us so narrowly and curiously that it was evident his suspicions were aroused about our purposes. Though the town was small, the Commandant insisted on having his droshky brought up for us, lest we might lose our way in the dark, and we were safely convoyed past all the sentries.

The next day was the Russian Easter day, and we took advantage of the Russian custom to call on all our acquaintances of the previous day, as well as to make new ones. It seemed strange to us, after our tiresome journey, when we felt that we were so far from Europe and civilisation, to hear persons talking of going home on leave of absence, and of visiting the Vienna Exposition, or of spending the summer in Switzerland, as though the journey were nothing at all. I made acquaintance with one lady, for instance, who had come alone all the way from the borders of Poland in order to marry a man whom she had never seen, the marriage having been arranged by common friends. As the Russian customs do not allow a marriage in Lent, the lady, who had arrived a fortnight before, was still in a state of single blessedness, although the marriage was expected to come off during the week, and the happy husband was to leave immediately for the Khivan expedition.

At Kazala all the talk was about Khiva. The Kazala division had left some time before, and was now supposed to be at Irkibai, where a fort was to be erected. Couriers were arriving from it once or twice a week, and occasionally there was one from the Orenburg division, beyond the Emba. A good part of the garrison had joined the expedition, and the rest were therefore much interested in it. We were urged to go on to Khiva, and it was even suggested that a passage might be given to us on the steamer 'Samarkand,' which was to start in a few days, and was expected to join the expedition in the neighbourhood of Kungrad, if it should succeed in getting so far. Circumstances looked so promising that I had nearly made up my mind to accompany my companion to Khiva, if it were possible to secure a passage on the steamer, as thus the journey would be comparatively easy, even should we be obliged to stay a week or so on the shallow waters of the Aral Sea.

We were both doomed to disappointment. One morning Captain Verestchagin—the same who had looked at us so curiously the first night at the Commandant's—called on us. He now stated that he had strict orders to allow no one whatever to go on to Khiva, and he had thought it perhaps his duty to send us back to Orenburg, but that, as I had brought an official letter to the Commandant, and he was willing to vouch for us, we would be allowed to go on to Tashkent. In support of his statement he wished me to read two papers. One of these was an order from the Governor-General, signed by the Governor of the province, stating that should Europeans desire to enter the province of Turkistan for purposes of trade they were not to be allowed to do so without a special written permission from the Governor-General, and in default of this were to be sent back to the place from which they had come. I laughingly said to Captain Verestchagin that I was much obliged to him for showing me this document, but that I could not see how it affected me, as I was not an European, nor had I come there for purposes of trade. The other paper was an exceptional order, stating that on the recommendation of Admiral Bock two Swiss gentlemen of good family, M. Picquet, of Lausanne, and M. Rivas, of Neufchatel, who were travelling for scientific purposes, and without political aims, and who intended to go from India through Central Asia, would be allowed to proceed, and that facilities were to be offered them. It would, indeed, have been rather absurd had these poor travellers arrived at the Russian frontier, after passing through the dangers of Afghanistan and Bukhara, only to be ' sent back to the place from which they had come.' I have never been able to hear more of these two travellers, except that many months afterwards I received information from Balkh that two persons, whom I fear to be the same, one disguised as a Jew and the other as a Tartar, supposed to be Russian spies, as they had papers on them written in Russian, had been murdered by order of the Amir of Balkh.

The communication of this zealous official convinced my companion that there was no possibility of reaching Khiva from Kazala, and he resolved to start at once for Tashkent, hoping to have better luck either there or on the road to that place. It was probably very fortunate for us that we did not sail in the 'Samarkand.' The steamer was detained a long while at the mouth of the river by the obstructions in the channel, and the party which left it to join the army of General Verevkin at Kungrad were all murdered by the Turkomans. As we were about starting the next day the Commandant came to us and of his own accord gave us an explanation of the action of Captain

Verestchagin, saying that as he was a young official left for a short time with brief authority he was fearful of taking upon himself any responsibility, and desired to recommend himself to the Government by the strictness and zeal with which he performed his duties.

A short time before we were at Kazala the Khivan Embassy arrived, bringing the Russian prisoners who had been enslaved there, and for whose delivery the war was nominally begun. They did not meet with the expedition, as they had taken a route close along the eastern shore of the Aral Sea. It being winter they were able to obtain water by melting the snow. As the letters brought by the ambassadors were addressed to General Kaufmann no one at Kazala was willing to take the responsibility of opening them, and accordingly information was sent to him by courier, and after some time word came back that the ambassadors as well as the prisoners were to be forwarded to him at the head-quarters of the expedition. There were twenty-one of these prisoners, and during my stay at Kazala they could be seen about the town in the striped cotton gowns which had been presented to them by the Khan on their departure. They all said they had had a hard time of it, but apparently had not suffered very much, although they were heartily glad at their release, and most of them were celebrating their freedom by getting drunk. The majority of them were Cossacks, and common soldiers, although there were three or four clerks and merchants among them. Three of these men were brought to see me—a Cossack soldier, who had been captured at Fort Irghiz in 1869, and two clerks, who together with a companion were taken also in the same year. One of these clerks was aged thirty-two, and the other about twenty-four. They were engaged in supplying the military stations with salt meat, and were also engaged in trading with the Kirghiz, when suddenly, near a station on the Aral Sea, they were captured by a band of hostile Kirghiz, tied to their saddles, and taken by long marches, day and night, to Khiva, where they were sold. This was during the disturbances in the Kirghiz Steppe consequent on the new regulations. As soon as they reached Khiva they were bought by the Khan, with most of the other prisoners, for his private use, and lived for the greater part of the time in one of his gardens outside of the city, where most of them were obliged to act as gardeners, though those who knew any special trade were made to work by preference at that. As to fare they were treated in the same way as the Persian slaves, of whom there were very large numbers, and lived chiefly on fruit, rice, and an occasional bit of mutton or tallow. They were at first treated with great severity, and efforts were made to compel them to become Mussulmans, force even being threatened; but the Khan on finding this out at last gave orders that no one should be made to change his religion unless he wished. They described the Khan as being personally good-natured, and frequently saying a word or two to them as he passed through the garden, and laid on the Divan-Beghi, or Vizier, the whole blame of the hostile relations of the Khanate to Russia.

While at Kazala I had an opportunity of visiting and inspecting the steamers and barges of the Aral flotilla which were then moored there; but before speaking of this flotilla and of its utility I must say a few words about the river Syr Darya itself.

The Syr Darya or River Syr, (*darya* meaning river or watercourse) was known to the Greeks as Iaxartes, and was said by Strabo and others to empty into the Caspian Sea. The Arab geographers of the Middle Ages called it the *Sihun*, just as they called the Amu-Darya, or Oxus, *Jihun* or *Gihon*, but speak of it as flowing into the Sea of Aral. No European traveller in Central Asia mentions the river before the Englishman Anthony Jenkinson, and in his map, made in 1558, he marks it as falling into the Aral Sea, which he calls the 'Chinese lake.' But even in spite of this on the maps of the sixteenth and seventeenth centuries it is marked as flowing into the Caspian. The Russians, however, through their intercourse with the Asiatic tribes, knew more about the river, and in the ' Book of the Great Survey,' written in 1627 to explain previous maps, it is said that the river Syr Darya flows into the Blue Sea (Aral Sea) from the east.

The river takes its rise amid the high plateaus and ranges of the Tian Shan, to the south of the lake Issyk-Kul, at an elevation of from 11,500 to 12,000 feet, being formed chiefly from the Petrof Glacier. At an elevation of 11,000 feet the small streams already make a considerable river, which is soon known by the name of Taragai, and after its junction with the

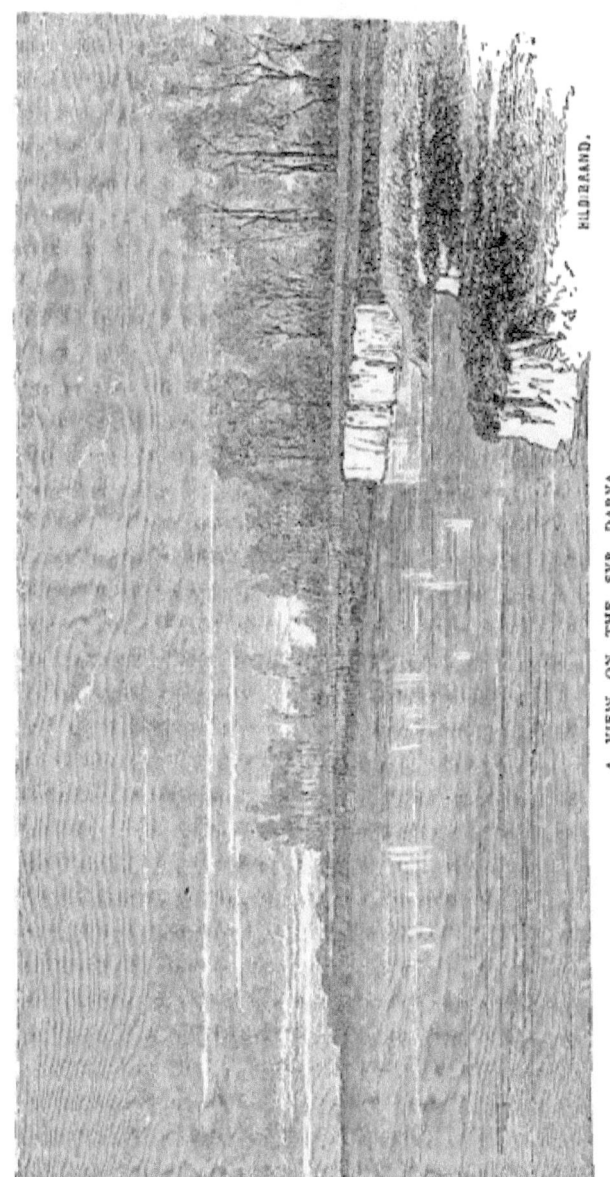

A VIEW ON THE SYR DARYA.

Karasai and the Kurmenta, a distance of about 100 miles from its source, it receives the name of Naryn. The Naryn flows through mountain defiles, always with a swift current, over a bed full of rocks, with a rapid fall, until near Balyktchi, in Khokand, it unites with the river Kara Kuldja. This latter river is chiefly called by the natives Syr Darya, and is held by them to be the real river, the Naryn being considered only a branch. The Kara-Kuldja takes its rise in the Alai mountains, near the pass of Terek-Davan, which leads to Kashgar. The character of this stream, the course of which has not yet been thoroughly explored, is far different from that of the Naryn, as it flows along quietly and peacefully, is not deep, and is in many places fordable. Its valley is wide and fertile, and was formerly known as the vale of Fergana. But the valley of the Naryn, on the contrary, is at times merely a narrow defile, although widening out in places to a breadth of from three to five miles. The junction of the two rivers is about 470 miles from the source of the Naryn. From the junction, the river, now called by all the Syr Darya, becoming broad and turbulent, and partaking in a great measure of the characteristics of the Naryn, both as to the swiftness of its current and the muddy colour of its waters, flows on in a south-westerly direction, somewhat past the town of Hodjent, when it turns to the north and north-west. In the neighbourhood of Hodjent the river receives some small tributaries from the mountains of the south, but after that the only water which it receives comes from the small streams rising in the Kara-tau mountains, especially the Tchirtchik and Agengeran, in the neighbourhood of Tashkent, and the Arys and Bugun, between Tchimkent and Turkistan.

As long as the Syr Darya receives the mountain streams there is plenty of water in the river, the depth being from twenty to forty feet, and the width in places more than a third of a mile. The current is very swift at times, even as much as eight feet in a second, although this is of course during the high water. The rapidity of the stream changes several times during the day, being greatest at ten or eleven o'clock in the morning, then gradually diminishing till two in the afternoon, and then increasing again. The amount of water in the river changes several times in the year, but this is especially noticeable at three seasons: about the end of March, on the breaking up of the ice, when the high water lasts for about ten days; in May, on the melting of the snow on the lower hills; and in June and July, on the melting of the snow on the mountain-tops, when the increase of water is greatest.[1] From the station of Tiumen-aryk the Syr Darya, still with plenty of water, runs on in a broad stream through a tortuous channel between tolerably high banks as far as Fort Perovsky. Here begins the third phase of the river, for it runs over level ground, with scarcely any fall, to the Aral Sea. The banks are covered with reeds and swamps; and the river, instead of taking in tributaries, sends off numerous branches, which become lost in the sand, and the lack of water and the numerous shoals greatly impede navigation. The chief of these branches is called Jany Darya, or Yany-Darya—the y of Turki becoming j in the Kirghiz dialect—and leaves the main river nearly opposite to Fort Perovsky, running in a south-westerly direction towards the mouth of the Amu Darya. The name means 'new river,' and there is a Kirghiz tradition that it was formed in part artificially towards the end of the last century, but this is evidently an old channel of the river which perhaps had become closed up, and in which at that time the water began again to flow. The water rarely flows for more than about 150 miles in this river, when it is lost in the sand. The marshes below Fort Perovsky are very great. Of the two arms into which the main river is here divided, the right, Kara-Uziak, is at first a broad stream of five or six hundred feet, and flows with a rapid current for about twenty-five miles, when it is entirely lost in the marshes, and forms lakes and islands, including many floating islands, covered with jungles of reeds. After some forty miles of such swamps this branch again flows out as a large river for about fifty miles, till it joins the main river at Karamaktchi, or Fort No. 2. The left branch, the Jaman-Darya, or 'bad river,' must therefore be considered the main stream. It is nearly 150 miles long, and has received its name on account of its shoals and the narrowness and tortuousness of its channel. In some parts it is not more than 200 feet wide. Below Fort No. 2 are some small arms which branch from the river, but from this point to the sea it is more easily navigable.

[1] The periodical floods of the Syr Darya have a most important influence on the cultivation of the land along its banks.

THE FORMER COURSE OF THE OXUS. 53

It is now, I believe, a well-settled fact that the Amu Darya, or Oxus, formerly flowed into the Caspian Sea. The explorations which have been conducted with regard to what is called the 'ancient bed' show that it really was the channel of a deep and broad river. There is good reason to believe also that the ancient geographers were right in saying that the Syr Darya also discharged its waters into the Caspian, although in a somewhat different manner from what has generally been imagined.[1]

The following theory was suggested to me by my friend Colonel Tchaikofsky, at Samarkand, who had lived a long time in Central Asia and was familiar with the country; and subsequent study and personal investigation have satisfied me of its great plausibility.

It would seem strange that such a powerful river as the Amu Darya, after flowing in a general north-westerly direction, should suddenly turn almost at right angles in its course and run south-westerly to the Caspian. Rivers do not do this unless there is some natural obstacle to prevent their keeping on in a straight course, and in this case it is evident there is no such obstacle, from the fact that the river now flows in the same general north-westerly direction to the Aral Sea.

Some have supposed that this change of bed was owing to a gradual change of inclination and level in the surface of the Steppe towards the NE., and it may be that such a change has really taken place, but it will be noticed on looking at the map that the Jany Darya, which leaves the Syr Darya at Fort Perovsky, running in a south-westerly direction, is nearly in a line with the 'ancient bed' of the Oxus; and as far as investigations have been made there seem to be traces of an 'ancient

---

[1] A map of the Russian dominions was made in the reign of the Tsar Fedor (1584-1598). In 1627 this map had become very old and worn, and it was renewed and corrected, and accompanied by an exact written description, to which the title was given of 'Book of the Great Survey.' The map has unfortunately disappeared, but the book is full of precious materials for geography, and contains some curious indications for that of Central Asia. Among them is the following, Ed. Yazykof, 1838, p. 72: 'From the Khvalym (Caspian) Sea to the Blue Sea (Aral) toward the place of sunrise in summer, in a straight line is 250 versts. Along the Blue Sea to the mouth of the river Syr is 280 versts. Across the Blue Sea is 60 versts; and in the Blue Sea the water is salt. The river Arzaz, or Argaz, flows out of the Blue Sea and into the Sea of Khvalym. Into the river Arzaz from the east flows the river Amu Darya. To the source of the Amu Darya is 300 versts, and to the source of the Arzaz is 1,060 versts.'

bed' in the same line from the Amu Darya, in a north-westerly direction, as if to meet the Jany Darya.[1] There are also traces of an old river-bed in an easterly and north-westerly direction, from Fort Perovsky, on the other side of the Syr Darya. It would seem that the waters of the Tchu and Sary-su, which are now lost in the Saumal Kul, Tele Kul, and other lakes and swamps, were formerly conveyed into the Syr Darya near Perovsky.

The Tchu is now barely navigable in the upper course to below Tokmak, and is then so lost in the sands that even a small boat cannot proceed on it.

The Tchu takes its rise in the Tian Shan, to the south of the Alexandrovsky range, and to the south-west of Issyk Kul. At the head of the Buam Pass the river is about four miles distant from the Issyk Kul. There is now a small channel connecting the lake with the river, and in spring floods the river is as apt to flow into the lake as the lake is to flow into the river. Lake Issyk Kul, which is a large body of water, 120 miles long by thirty-three wide, has at present no outlet. Its shores, however, afford indubitable evidence of numerous elevations and depressions. At one time the water evidently reached the bases of the surrounding mountains, at a height of some hundred feet above the present river.

From the Buam Pass, and along the valley of the Tchu, far below Tokmak, there is every evidence of the river having been formerly much greater and higher than at present. It is probable, therefore, that at some previous time in the world's history Lake Issyk Kul—itself fed by small streams and the snows of the surrounding mountains—discharged its waters into the Tchu. The Tchu, running north-westerly, with a broad and rapid stream, received perhaps also the water of the great lake of Balkash, with its large tributaries the Ili and the

---

[1] Since writing the above I have been informed by Colonel Sobolef, of the Amu Darya Exploring Expedition of 1874, that he found a wide and well-marked river-bed extending from the Amu Darya at Shurakhana to the north-east, in the direction of the Jany Darya. This he explored for some forty miles. Major Wood, who accompanied the expedition, believes that the course of the Amu Darya may have been changed through the irrigation canals near Khiva, which took off so much water during the summer floods that the remainder was unequal to the task of washing away the silt deposited in the river-bed during the low water of winter.

Karatal; then turned westerly and received other rivers, such as the Sary-su, to the neighbourhood of Fort Perovsky, and then probably ran in a south-westerly direction through the bed of what is now the Jani Darya and the 'ancient bed' of the Amu Darya, until it emptied into the Caspian Sea. The Syr Darya and Amu Darya were, therefore, probably only large branches of the river Tchu. When a depression of the basin of lake Issyk Kul took place the waters of the lake were prevented from emptying into the Tchu. The volume of water in this river was therefore much lessened, and owing to the spongy nature of the soil, it formed large marshes and small lakes, and became entirely lost before it reached the meridian of Fort Perovsky. The rapid current of the Syr Darya, no longer turned by a powerful river coming from the east, impinged violently upon the opposite bank, creating large swamps and morasses, and finally found its way through them along the almost level Steppe until it emptied by various channels into the northern end of the Aral Sea, as at present.

In the same way the Amu Darya continued its course in a north-westerly direction, forming marshes about the places where it formerly turned at right angles into the 'ancient bed,' and found a new outlet in the southern end of the Aral Sea. This would be quite sufficient to account for the legends which exist with regard to the sudden change of the waters of the Amu Darya, and for the fact of its having been found impossible to restore the river to its ancient bed, although dykes and dams were erected by its inhabitants to prevent it from overflowing the country and creating marshes.

The stretch between Fort No. 2 and Fort Perovsky is the great obstacle to the successful navigation of the Syr Darya. All attempts to better it seem to have been unsuccessful. The ill success of the first attempt, in 1853, at the navigation of this portion of the river was attributed to the breaking of the dyke at Kara Bugut, near the separation of the Jani Darya, which was said to have lowered the water in the Jaman Darya. In the autumn and winter this dyke was rebuilt, but in the next year it was again broken. In 1856 Lieutenant Butakof attempted to widen a small stream connecting the Kara-uziak with the Jaman Darya, in hopes of avoiding the navigation of the very narrowest part of the river, and letting water into it from the Kara-uziak, and at the same time of cutting off some of the capes and of straightening the channel. These works were continued with vigour during 1856 and 1857, but had to be given up, as the water did not rise sufficiently high to wash away the barriers in the manner proposed. In 1860 it was proposed to clean out the channel of the Kara-uziak for a distance of nearly four miles, which it was calculated would occupy sixty-five men for 180 days. The work was undertaken against the stream, in order that the water might immediately carry away the obstructions. Operations were carried on for twenty days only during the year. The next year little was done, as the troops were occupied with constructing the fortress of Julek, and besides this convictions began to be entertained of the uselessness of the proceeding. Again in 1862 an attempt was made to increase the water in the Jaman Darya, but failure once more resulted. Led by the idea that the two new steamers which had been constructed for the flotilla would be sufficient to overcome all the difficulties of navigation, nothing was done during the next year, but in 1864 there was a small expedition sent out by Captain Schott to explore the Kara-uziak, and it was reported that it would not take long to clean it, and that navigation was always possible on it for seven or eight months of the year. In the autumn, however, the expedition reported that this was impossible. Two years were then spent in projects; and in 1866, it being resolved that the cleaning of the channel of the Karauziak would be dear and difficult, it was decided to dig a canal from the Syr Darya to the Jaman Darya, above its commencement. The work continued for seventeen days, employing 400 men a day, and the cost of the canal amounted to 2,471 roubles. On June 21 the canal was opened, and it was hoped that the high water of the following spring would widen it and render it navigable for ships. On the contrary, the canal was filled up with sand, and the navigation was made worse. Since that time nothing has been done.

With such obstructions to navigation it is not to be wondered at that the Aral flotilla has been of little service, though there are also other reasons for its inutility. The formation of the fleet was contemporary with the establishment of the fortress of Raim, and in the year 1847 there were constructed in Orenburg two two-masted schooners, the 'Nikolai and 'Mikhail.' The first was intended for surveying purposes, and the second for starting a fishery; but as the ships did not dare go far out to sea little was done in 1847 besides surveying the Kos Aral and the other islands which lie near the eastern coast. Meanwhile another schooner was constructed in Orenburg, the 'Konstantin,' somewhat larger than the others, and in this vessel Lieutenant Butakof, in 1848 and 1849, completely surveyed the Aral Sea.

In 1850, upon the proposition of General Obrutchef, an order was given to the Mutal factory, in Sweden, for the construction of two vessels, a forty-horse-power steamboat called 'Perovsky,' and a twelve horse-power iron barque, with a screw, the 'Obrutchef.' These vessels cost in Sweden 37,445 roubles, and with their transport and the payment for the mechanicians brought out from Sweden cost at Kazala 49,347 roubles. The steamer 'Perovsky' was launched on the Syr Darya in 1853, but owing to the non-arrival of its wooden parts the 'Obrutchef' could not be used before 1855. The 'Perovsky' was armed with three nine-pounders, and the 'Obrutchef' was fitted to receive two similar guns in case of necessity. The 'Perovsky,' however, was found to be too large for the successful navigation of the difficult parts of the river, and was continually getting aground. During the season available for navigation the 'Perovsky' could make only three round trips from Fort No. 1 to Fort Perovsky, towing two barges. The up trip occupied from ten to twelve days, and the down trip seven or eight days. After the order for these two steamers it became necessary to provide fuel. During the whole of 1851 the two schooners 'Konstantin' and 'Mikhail' were engaged in conveying *saksaul* and other roots from the banks of the Aral Sea to the island of Kos Aral, but General Perovsky wrote that it would be impossible to supply the steamers with this fuel alone, as it was very difficult to obtain and to use it. *Saksaul* (*Haloxylon ammodendron*, Bunge,) is of a very close fibre, full of knots, and most difficult to be sawn or split, and breaks into very crooked and unmanageable pieces. Accordingly a contract was made for bringing anthracite coal from the Don, and in 1852 one hundred and eighty tons were brought to the fort, at a cost of six rubles per ton. When anthracite was used for fuel each round trip of the 'Perovsky' to Fort Perovsky and back cost about 2,500 rubles (344*l.*). When the furnaces were heated with *saksaul* it was necessary to use four times as much fuel, though, owing to the much smaller price, six kopeks a *pud* (thirty-six pounds), the trip cost only 520 rubles. Consequently, by calculating the carrying capacity of the 'Perovsky' and of her barges, it was found that the transport of every *pud* of cargo between Fort No. 1 and Perovsky cost the Government thirty kopeks, which was but slight economy, as by land carriage it cost only forty or fifty kopeks. But by heating with *saksaul* the cost of transport was not more than three kopeks a *pud*, which was consequently a saving to Government of forty-seven kopeks. The resolution was therefore adopted to transport as far as possible, all provisions, materials, &c. by water from Fort No. 1 to Perovsky and Julek.

In 1860 two new steamers were ordered in Liverpool, at the Hamilton Works, to be built of corrugated iron, according to the Francis system, flat-bottomed, and stern-wheelers. At the same time there were ordered at Liverpool a floating pontoon dock and six shallops, and at the Kama-Votka Works three barges. The steamers were brought in pieces from Orenburg, on the backs of camels, and being put together at Kazala, were launched in the autumn of 1862. They were both armed with 9-pounders, and were called respectively the 'Syr Darya' and the 'Aral.' The first was of twenty-horse-power, costing when delivered 16,000 roubles, and the second, of forty-horse-power, costing 30,080 roubles; but the navigation returns for 1863 showed that the new steamers, instead of being better, were worse than the old ones. The 'Aral,' which ought to carry at least 540 tons weight, could not take more than 216 tons. The iron turned out very fragile, and the vessel was not sufficiently strong. The machinery also was badly built. The boilers were placed so far from the engines that the steam lost 10 per cent. of its force, and necessitated a very great expenditure of fuel, seventy-two *puds* of *saksaul* an hour for every horse-power, so that it used in one month what should have lasted for six. Besides, the construction of the engines rendered the working of the steamer very difficult, subjecting it to the danger of being blown up. The vessel was very deep in the water, and unfitted for river navigation. The stern being too low down, the steamer got aground very deeply; and being of thin iron was very difficult to get off the shoals. The 'Syr Darya' had the same defects as the 'Aral,' although it was in parts better constructed; but instead of carrying at least 216 tons of freight at a speed of four versts an hour, it could not move at that speed more than 172 tons. These defects were, however, in some measure overcome by reconstructing the engines. The floating pontoon dock, which cost about 30,000 roubles, was also constructed of corrugated iron, in two parts, each 42 feet by 30 feet, united by diagonal bridges passing over it for 20 feet. The current of the river, however, was so strong, being more than two miles an hour, that had the dock been put in the water it would have been lost in the spring, if not in the autumn, and it was found better to repair the vessels on the shore itself rather than place them in the dock. For these reasons it has never been used. The barge, which was to carry 36 tons of freight, was found to be useless, because it would not obey the rudder, but turned its side to the current, and therefore the commanders of the steamers have never dared to use it. The barges built in Russia were more successful; they were 99 feet long by 18 broad, with two masts and sails, and could carry 63 tons, but with this load they drew $3\frac{1}{2}$ feet of water, and therefore were not fully suitable for river navigation. The great increase of traffic rendered it necessary in 1865 to increase the flotilla, and three large barges, to carry 162 tons each, were bought in Russia, and another ferry-boat in addition to the two already existing; and in 1866 the steamer called 'Samarkand' was built at Cockerill's works, in Belgium, at a cost of 78,700 roubles. It was of 70 horse-power, 150 feet long, and 22 broad, of 154 tons, with three furnaces, and carried two guns. In addition to this another steamer, the 'Tashkent,' was added in 1870, built in Russia, costing 35,000 roubles, of 35 horse-power, 104 feet long by 16 broad, and with single furnaces. Of all these steamers the 'Samarkand' is the only one which seems to be capable of doing good service, although in this, as I was informed, the iron-plates are in places as thin as paper, and it was considered to be a great risk to send her to the mouths of the Amu Darya to join the Khivan expedition. When I was in Kazala she was still undergoing repairs, having been injured in coming down shortly before from Fort Perovsky to Kazala, where she had got on a shoal, and it had become necessary for over one hundred men to dig a canal through the shoal to get her off, a proceeding occupying over a week. Besides the *saksaul*, which is becoming somewhat difficult to obtain, coal was used in a great measure for fuel on the steamers, being brought from the mines near Tashkent, but always at considerable expense, although much cheaper than if brought overland from the Don. The working of these mines has, however, now ceased.[1]

So far as we have statistics of the traffic of the flotilla there were carried in

	Government freight.	Private freight.	Passengers.
1865	1,491 tons	218 tons	1,208
1866	1,416 „	318 „	1,767
1867	2,633 „	404 „	2,328
1868	2,081 „	56 „	3,558
1869	2,920 „	24 „	3,025

We thus see that while the use of the steamers for Government has greatly increased, in consequence of the larger amount of Government stores and troops, for the passengers are chiefly soldiers, which have to be transported to the upper portions of the river, the private traffic has much fallen off. This is chiefly owing to the difficulties of navigation, and especially to the peculiarities of the transport business between Orenburg and the river. The freight is very apt to accumulate at Kazala in quantities too great to be transported in one season, and for that reason private business is chiefly carried on by the old mode of camel transportation.

It was on Tuesday, April 22, that we finally got off from Kazala. The day was extremely warm, although there was a fresh breeze on the Steppe, where the coming spring had begun to spread a slight yellowish green tint over the whole surface of the country, and the first flowers were appearing, especially the small yellowish fragrant tulips. The first two stations, which were small Kirghiz kibitkas, where two or three

[1] The account of the navigation of the Syr Darya and the Aral flotilla is chiefly based on an article in the Military Review' ('*Voennoi Sbornik*') for April 1872.

families seemed to be living, we made in good time, but it soon began to rain violently, and we lost our road and got into very rough ground, neither of our drivers having the least idea where we were. At last we saw a light in the distance, which we hoped was the station, but on coming to it we found it to proceed from a kibitka of some poor Kirghiz, who professed utter ignorance of any station, saying that they were strangers. We went in and made tea with very muddy water, and a supper of sardines and cold goose, to the delight and admiration of our host, his wives and numerous dependents, who sat around the fire. For us was reserved the post of honour, and we reclined on the best cotton quilt, propped up against our pillows, carrying on a lively conversation through Ak-Mametef. There was no light but the fire in the middle of the floor, the smoke going out by a hole in the roof, which let in the rain at the same time, except a bit of candle we had part of the time, for which we extemporised a candlestick by rolling a handkerchief round it. It was a scene for Rembrandt, or rather for Gherardo della Notte. Great wonder was manifested at our clothes, at the articles of our provision-basket, and especially at our knives and forks; and we could not resist delighting the jolly looking Kirghiz by giving him a knife and fork from our small store. But we at last got warmed through; and becoming tired of inquiries about Kirghiz family and domestic life, went to sleep in our carriage in spite of the rain, waking up in the morning to find that we were only about a mile from the station, although far off from the road.

Owing to this misadventure and to difficulties in getting horses and camels, we did not get to Fort No. 2, only 120 miles, until Thursday noon; but the way was not without its amusement. At the station of Ak-jar we were obliged to wait for several hours, where we really enjoyed ourselves, as it was a splendid day. There was a lovely view of a bend in the river; and the station itself, which was kept by a Cossack and his newly married wife, was beautifully clean. We passed our time in shooting at a mark—practising against possible Turkomans—and when tired of that were treated to some fresh bread, hot from the oven, to say nothing of an omelette and a cold pheasant.

At one station we found the room occupied, much to our regret, as we were desirous of stretching ourselves, but when we heard the cause we could not help laughing, and were willing to have a felt spread for us in the sun out of doors. It seems that the wife of an officer, who was accompanying him from Tashkent to St. Petersburg, had just presented him with an heir, in spite of the uncomfortableness and difficulties of the situation. We endeavoured to be as friendly as travellers should be to one another, and the officer was glad to accept a bottle of red wine for his wife and some cans of condensed milk for his child. Everything seemed to be going on well, and he hoped to be able to start the next day.

Fort No. 2, or Karamaktchi, is almost as bad and uncomfortable a place as Karabutak. It has but a small garrison, and is situated directly on the bank of the river, which seems, indeed, to be eating away its walls. A few huts along the river-bank make up the town. There was no ferry and no bazaar, so that it was useless to attempt crossing the river here, and MacGahan saw himself forced to wait till Perovsky at least, though chafing at the delay, which might prevent him from seeing the fall of Khiva.

Not far from the station there was a large Kirghiz burying-ground, which was not without interest, as it contained very many tombs, some small mounds of earth, others temples and pavilions of different kinds and descriptions, some even looking like small castles, in which were placed the actual tombs, There appeared nowhere to be any inscriptions. Such cemeteries are not infrequent in this part of the Steppe, especially along the river-banks, and at a distance look like the ruins of some antique city. At Khorkhut, the last station before Fort No. 2, there is a similar cemetery, but there most of the tombs are built of burned bricks, and there are many stone slabs with Arabic inscriptions. In the neighbourhood are many mounds and heaps, and in all probability this was the site of the ancient Jend. One of the largest of these tombs, now half-ruined, is pointed out as that of the famous saint Khorkhut, concerning whom is a curious local tradition. This Khorkhut, who was fourteen feet tall, was once living on the extreme edge of the world, when he dreamed one night that some men were digging a grave there. 'For whom do you dig it?' said the saint. 'For Khorkhut,' was the reply. The anxious Khorkhut, wishing to avoid the death which threatened him,

went the next day to live on the other edge of the world.
There he had the same dream. Again at dawn he set out, and
in this way, followed by his vision, he went over all the corners
of the earth. In despair, not knowing where to go, he resolved
to remove to the centre of the world, which proved to be the
bank of the Syr, on this spot. No sooner thought than done.
But his dream still pursued him. The holy man then thought
to cheat fate. Concluding that there was no safety for him on
land, he made up his mind to live on the water, so spread his

A KIRGHIZ TOMB.

mantle on the Syr and sat down on it. Here he sat for a
hundred years, always playing on the lute, till at last he died.
The pious Mussulmans took his body and buried it here.

From Fort No. 2 to Perovsky we could no longer follow the
river, on account of the swamps, but were obliged to make a
long *détour* to the north. Formerly the road lay on the other
side of the river, it being necessary to cross it at Fort No. 2,
and again at Fort Perovsky. The new route has hardly yet
been put into good order. All of the stations are as yet underground huts. The road, however, was good, and the horses were

much better than usual, so that we reached Perovsky late the next night.

These marshes are said to be infested with tigers and wild boars, and tiger-shooting is a favourite sport of some of the officers of the garrison. Along the road we heard many frightful stories of the depredations of the tigers, when, in cases of extreme hunger they came to the stations and carried off cattle, and even children and men, and we were recommended to be constantly on our guard, and have our revolvers ready, in case of attack—advice which of course was intended well, but which proved utterly useless, for we saw no tigers.

It was nearly midnight when we reached Fort Perovsky, and to our disgust we found the post-station—where we preferred to stop, thinking it would be better to avoid observation—already occupied by other travellers. We were therefore obliged to pass the night in a filthy little room at what was called an hotel, although the next day by good luck we found excellent quarters in the house of a Finnish lady, whose husband was engineer of the steamer 'Samarkand.'

Fort Perovsky was originally a fort and town belonging to Khokand, called Ak-Masjid (white mosque), which was captured by the Russians under General Perovsky in 1853, after a very stubborn defence conducted in part by Yakub Khan, the present ruler of Kashgar. During the twenty-five days' siege the Russian artillery had such an effect upon the mud-walls of the fort that the Khokandians were quite ready to give up the place, and sent a letter to General Perovsky to that effect. It is said that notwithstanding this the Russian general was determined to win a little glory at any expense, and, throwing the letter into the fire, replied to the messenger, 'We shall take the fort by assault,' which he did on the following morning. The fort has of course been completely rebuilt by the Russians, although some portions of the ancient constructions are still standing. The town has thriven since its occupation by the Russians, and now covers considerable space. While it is full of Kirghiz, like Kazala, it differs from that town in having a very large population of Sarts and Khivans as well as Bukharans, and has in consequence a thoroughly Oriental aspect. In my wanderings about the town I was particularly struck with the *makhtab*, or primary school.

It was in a little room that opened directly on the street; and although the boys manifested some little curiosity as we passed and looked up, the teacher dropped his eyes at once, and made them go on with their tasks, each repeating the lesson in the loudest tone of voice, and seesawing his body backwards and forwards, kneeling as he was, in order better to impress upon his memory the Arabic task, of the meaning of which, being taught by rote, he had no idea. There was a large public garden, full of trees, and beyond this a grove, extending for a considerable distance. Further on still is the monument erected to the memory of the Russian soldiers who fell in the siege.

The weather had now changed from winter to midsummer, and the days were oppressively warm. The grass was beginning to spring up, and the peach trees had begun to blossom. It was even at times uncomfortably hot to walk across the broad place which separated the fortress from the surrounding houses. At sunset, however, it was very pleasant, and even at night it was sufficiently warm to stay out of doors in the moonlight.

I remained at Fort Perovsky five days, as MacGahan had decided to start from here at all hazards, to try and make his way across the desert to the head-quarters of the expedition, and I was desirous of seeing him safely off, and doing what I could to facilitate his departure. Our days were taken up in vain searchings for camels, horses, and guides. Many times were we deceived, and it was only when we, as a last resort, had recourse to Captain Rodionof, the acting district prefect, that all obstacles were as by magic removed.

Up to this time, remembering our experience at Fort No. 1, we had avoided the officers and the official world. MacGahan was the happiest of men, as he felt that, official consent having been secured, nothing but the desert and the Turkomans stood in the way of his joining General Kaufmann. Horses were at once forthcoming, and were soon packed and saddled, and with light hearts the little caravan started over the ferry, while I regretfully stood on the bank and saw them safely across the river. I heard but once from MacGahan during the whole summer, as in some singular way all our letters which were not sent by private hands failed to reach us. I frequently, however, heard of him, his ride across the desert being spoken of everywhere in Central Asia as by far the most wonderful thing that had ever been done there, as he went far through a country which was supposed to be hostile, knowing nothing of the roads or of the language. Even the officer whose scouts had failed to catch MacGahan, from whom long afterwards, on coming from Khokand, I first heard of my companion's safe arrival at Khiva, was delighted at his pluck, and used the significant Russian expression, '*Molodetz*'—'a brave young fellow'—the greatest possible praise under such circumstances. At Tashkent, however, there was great alarm over possible English spies, and I feared for a moment that it would fare hardly with Captain Rodionof; but in the end General Kaufmann's good sense triumphed over the foolish fears of his officials.

Having seen MacGahan safely across the river, I started off myself about 7 o'clock for Tashkent. It was a lovely evening, and I was fully disposed to enjoy the scenery, which, in spite of its flatness, is really pretty in the neighbourhood of Fort Perovsky. There are large numbers of shrubs, especially saksaul and calligonum, and many were thickly covered with white and pink blossoms. Others, again, were clothed in pale green, and the pleasant evening light added a peculiar charm. At every step magnificent golden pheasants started up. They are not wild, and suffer one to approach very near, and are therefore very easily killed; but unfortunately MacGahan had taken with him all the fowling-pieces, so that I had nothing to shoot with. All along the Syr Darya the shooting is very good; not only pheasants, geese, ducks, grouse, and partridges, but even much larger game can be met with.

The horses which they had given me were really excellent, and for the only time, I think, in my whole trip we did not stop once to arrange or repair the harness, and consequently made the sixteen miles in an hour and three-quarters.

Travelling all night, I reached Julek, a Russian fort on the banks of the river, distant some seventy miles from Perovsky, at 9 o'clock. In order to make myself fresh for the day's travel I was just on the point of stripping to take a bath, when to my great regret two carriages came up with some ladies and children, so that I was obliged to content myself with a basin of water behind the house. We had tea and breakfast together, soon made acquaintance, and had a very pleasant time. We were then seized upon by one of the officers of the fort, who insisted that we should come and breakfast with him, which of course detained us all for an hour or two longer.

This *rencontre* turned out very well for me, for one of the ladies whom I met was the wife of an officer in Tashkent, and sent letters to him by me. She asked me where I intended to stop there; and as I had no place in view, almost insisted that I should go to her husband, who had a large house; and as I willingly complied with her request, I was made comfortable during the whole of my stay in Tashkent.

The fort, which was constructed in 1856, on the site of a Khokandian fortress captured and destroyed in 1853, during the siege of Ak Masjid, was, until the campaign of 1863, the farthest Russian outpost in Asia. It is especially noticeable for having the prettiest Russian church of any fortress in these parts. There was at that time no resident priest there, and one from Perovsky had just come on to officiate for two or three days.

Not long after leaving Julek I began to see a faint blue line to the north-east, which soon grew larger and more distinct, and proved to be the beautiful mountain range of Kara-tau, which with its branches extends beyond Tashkent. The summits were still covered with snow, and after so much barren and arid steppe this was a most beautiful feature of the landscape.

The Steppe was now covered with flowers of all kinds, especially scarlet poppies, wild tulips, geraniums, and many cruciferous and leguminous plants. It frequently became necessary to cross the beds of small streams which came down from the mountains, and in many of these there was considerable water. The whole of this region shows traces of ancient cultivation, and it is evident that a very large population at one time existed here. In various parts there are mounds, now covered with growths of saksaul and other shrubs, which are evidently the ruins of former cities. There is an old legend that the whole valley of the Syr Darya was at one time so thickly settled that a nightingale could fly from branch to branch of the fruit-trees, and a cat walk from wall to wall and housetop to housetop, from Kashgar to the Sea of Aral. From the traces of former culture one can in part believe this. We know, indeed, from history that the banks of this part of the river had numerous large and flourishing towns, noticeable among which were Otrar, Sauran, Jend, and Jany-Kend. The ruins of Jany-Kend (Yany-Kend, or 'New Town,') are placed by Lerch and other investigators some sixteen miles below Kazala. Several of the mounds which compose these ruins have been opened, and various articles of pottery and household ware have been found there, but nothing which could enable the age of the ruins to be ascertained.

I came to the ruins of Sauran the next morning, passing several large forts and ruined towns which, like Saganak, had apparently been abandoned in recent times. The ruins of Sauran itself lie at some distance from the post-station, so that I was unable to visit them. They were noted a few years ago for containing two tall brick towers or minarets of very graceful construction, having spiral staircases within. One of these fell some years ago; and as the other was greatly injured by the Kirghiz, it is now probably also in ruins.

On the opposite side of the Syr Darya stretches the great waste called the Kyzyl-Kum, or 'Red Sands.' One great arm of this desert extends from Fort No. 1 southward along the Sea of Aral to the Bukan mountains, even touching the Amu-Darya in several places opposite to Khiva. Along the Jany-Darya there are places where the desert gradually dies out into an ordinary waste steppe, and along the left bank of the Syr Darya from Tchardara to Julek there is also a clayey steppe, in places even cultivable, and filled with the ruins of ancient cities.

On the south the desert is bounded by the Famished Steppe between Tchinaz and Jizakh, and by the low ranges of hills, where are the wells Aristan-bel-kuduk, Tamdy, &c., nearly to the Bukan-tau. Through an opening in the mountains an arm of the desert called Jaman Kyzyl, or Bad Red Sand—for it is the very worst part of the desert—reaches the Amu Darya, and extends along it from Montchakli to the south of Bukhara even. This desert is constantly extending itself to the southward under the influence of the north and north-east winds, which blow almost without cessation. During the three months' stay of the Russian Expedition in the desert in 1872 there were but three days when the wind was not from the north-east.

The Kyzyl-Kum does not, however, consist entirely of

bare and shifting sand, but is full of small hillocks covered with vegetation of various kinds, especially saksaul and other similar shrubs which can be used as fuel, and among the herbs there are very many of the ferulaceous order, especially the three from which are obtained the gums asafœtida, ammoniac, and galbanum. Among the rocks contained in the mountains are limestone, marble of a bad quality, flint, and slate; and there are numerous traces of iron, which even tinges the hillocks of sand with an orange-red colour, and has without doubt given the name to the desert. The Kyzyl Kum is intersected with caravan-roads, the most of which, running north and south, were formerly—and are now to some extent—the main ways of communication between Northern Asia, and Khiva and Bukhara. Along the roads there are numerous wells; in fact, without these it would be impossible for human beings to live there. In winter especially the Kyzyl-Kum is inhabited by numerous Kirghiz, who wander there from the steppes on the right side of the Syr Darya, crossing on the ice in autumn, and returning in the spring before the ice breaks up, or afterwards on rafts or bridges of reeds. Water is obtained from very small basins produced by the melting snows, which last only for a few weeks, from natural springs which form large basins, either open or underground, and from artificial wells. These last are from six to a hundred feet deep, much larger at the bottom than at the top, and often built up for a half or a quarter of their depth with limestone or sandstone or the hard wood of the saksaul. The Kirghiz who has dug a well—and he knows where to dig it, from the abundance of the plant called *adrasban* or *hazorasband* (*Peganum Harmala*)—considers it as his special property, and is careful to prevent other wandering Kirghiz from settling near by. In some cases the water is excellent, but in most of the wells it is salt, sometimes slightly so, at others thoroughly impregnated with Glauber's or other mineral salts. It frequently happens that the well when first dug will contain pure water, but in the course of a few days, or even a few hours, this will become bitter and undrinkable, from dissolving out the salts which are contained in the earthy sides.

At the station before Sauran I left the banks of the Syr Darya, and from here to Tashkent the road lies at some dis-

tance from the river. It was with great delight that on
Friday afternoon I saw what at first seemed a black spot, but
soon turned out to be thick groves of dark green trees, looking
darker and richer by contrast with the Steppe around them.
These were the groves and orchards which surround the city of
Turkistan, and it was not long before I forded the river, and
passed along narrow lanes between high clay walls, over which
I saw branches of apricot trees, and occasionally the faces of
little boys and girls looking with curiosity at the equipage, till,
making a circuit of the town and fort, above which rose the
immense vault of a splendid mosque, I came to the post-
station. A short walk through the deep ditch or ravine which
surrounds the ruined walls of the citadel, where soldiers and
natives were making clay bricks, brought me to the famous
mosque over the tomb of Hazret Hodja Akhmed Yasavi. The
construction of this mosque was begun by Timur in 1397, who
went on a pilgrimage to Turkistan, or Yassy, as it was then
called, while waiting for his new bride, Tukel-Khanym.
Sheikh Akhmed Yasavi, who was the founder of the sect Jahria,
and died about 1120, is one of the most celebrated saints of
Central Asia, and is the especial patron of the Kirghiz. The
mausoleum is an immense building, crowned by a huge dome,
and having annexed to the rear another small mosque, with
a melon-shaped dome. The front consists of an immense
arched portal, at least a hundred feet high, flanked by two
round windowless towers with crenelated tops, which reminded
me in some indefinite way of the front of Peterborough Cathedral.
In the archway there is a large double door of finely carved
wood, and over this a small oriel window, dating from the last
reconstruction by Abdullah Khan. The walls are of large
square-pressed bricks, well burnt, and carefully laid together.
Only the rear and side still bear the mosaic facings of enamelled
tiles, though in a very injured condition. The blue tiles
which covered the dome have nearly all fallen off, and of the
inscriptions in large Cufic letters which surround it only the
end can now be deciphered. It reads thus: 'The work of
Hodja Hussein, a native of the City Shiraz.' Similar inscriptions—gigantic ornamental texts from the Koran, in blue on a
white ground—run round the frieze, and the building, which is
still grand in its decay, was evidently once wondrously beau-

THE MOSQUE HAZRET AT TURKISTAN.

tiful Earthquakes and despoilers have ruined it, leaving large cracks, now filled up in many places with coarse plaster. The front was apparently never completed, for the old beams, which once served as a scaffolding, remain standing in the walls, occupied now by immense storks' nests. These birds, which seem to be regarded with reverence, are frequently seen perched on one leg upon the top of Mussulman mosques. In the middle of the mosque is an enormous hall, under the lofty dome which rises to a height of over a hundred feet, and is richly ornamented within with alabaster work in the style common in Moorish buildings, and especially seen in the Alhambra. On the right and left are rooms filled with tombs of various Kirghiz Sultans of the Middle and Lesser Hordes, among them the celebrated Ablai Khan. One room answers for a mosque, where the Friday prayers alone are said, while under the small dome at the back of the building are the tombs of Akhmed Yasavi and his family; and opening out of a long corridor full of tombs is a large room with a sacred well. Next to the tomb of the saint the most interesting monuments are those erected to a great-granddaughter of Timur, Rabiga-Sultan-Begim, daughter of the famous Ulug-Bek. She was married to Abul Kheir-Khan, and died in 1485. One of her sons lies next to her.

The walls of the first room are covered with numbers of inscriptions, chiefly short prayers, or verses from the Koran, one of which is said to have been written by Mohammed Ali Khan of Khokand, who was killed by the Amir of Bokhara, in 1842; and in the middle, standing on a pedestal, there is a large brass vessel like a kettle, which would contain at least fifty gallons of water, for the use of the persons who live in the mosque and the pilgrims and students who come there. It is said to have been cast at Tchurnak, now in ruins, about fifty miles from Turkistan. Around this vessel there are several lines of Arabic inscriptions, in different characters; the first and longest reads: 'The highest and Almighty God said, "Do ye place those bearing water to pilgrims and visiting the sacred temple."'[1] He (*i.e.* the Prophet) said, "May peace be on him!

---

[1] The beginning of this inscription is part of the nineteenth verse of the ninth Sura of the Koran, speaking of unbelievers, and should be followed by inserting after the word 'temple,' 'on the same level with him who believeth in God and

Whoso sets a vessel of water for the sake of God, the Highest, him will God the Highest reward doubly in Paradise. By command of the great Amir, the ruler of nations chosen by the care of the most merciful God, the Amir Timur Gurgan. May God prolong his reign!" This water-vessel was made for the tomb of the Sheikh-ul-Islam, chief of all Sheikhs in the world, the Sheikh Akhmed of Yassy. May God give repose to his worthy soul! The twelfth of Shavval, in the year 801 (1399).' The other inscription is: 'The work of the servant, striving Godward, the Abul-aziz, son of the master Sheref-uddin, native of Tabriz.'

There are besides in the mosque four large candlesticks, but the inscriptions are so defaced that one can only read the name of Timur, and that of the maker, a Persian from Ispahan, with the date 799 (1397). The Sheikh-ul-Islam has several documents from various rulers of Central Asia in whose possession Turkistan has been, conferring privileges on the shrine, one of them of the year 1591, signed by Abdullah-Khan.

This mosque is considered the holiest in all Central Asia, and had very great religious importance, as previous to the capture of the city by the Russians pilgrims of all ranks, even khans and amirs, assembled there from all quarters.

Being in the citadel, it served as a point of defence, and its bastions and minarets were mounted with guns. In order to hasten the fall of the city the Russian artillery was ordered to destroy it, and did considerable damage, the balls leaving their marks in many places. It is probable that this ancient monument would have been entirely ruined had it not been that the Sheikh-ul-Islam mounted the minaret and showed the white flag, which was the precursor of the surrender.

The mosque is entirely supported by property which has been given to it by various worshippers, including the revenues from several caravanserais and shops in the city, and very large amounts from land. Before the capture of the city the Khan of Khokand used to send 500 tillas a year, and even now pilgrims are in the habit of offering sheep every Friday, the meat of which is distributed to the poor of the city.

In the little enclosure in front of the portal are numerous

the last day, and fighteth on the way of God? They shall not be held equal by God: and God guideth not the unrighteous.'

TURKISTAN.

tombs bearing inscriptions, and in a corner of the large courtyard is a small and very elegant mosque, with a melon-shaped cupola, covered with blue tiles. The local legend runs that this was the temporary resting-place of the body of Rabiga-Begim, whose early death caused Timur such grief that he built the great mosque. Unfortunately history shows that she died some eighty years after him, and it was very doubtful if he ever saw her.

The termination of the great mosque called Hazret was almost contemporaneous with Timur's death. The word *Hazret*, an Arabic word, meaning literally 'presence,' is used in the sense of 'majesty' for rulers, and with the meaning 'sanctity' is frequently applied to saints, especially to those most reverenced, and in this case the celebrity of the saint has even given a name to the town, which is often called ' Hazreti-Turkistan,' or even simply ' Hazret.'

Besides the mosque there is little in Turkistan to interest one. The city has much fallen off, and now barely numbers 6,000 souls. Everything looks dilapidated and desolate, though I found the straggling bazaar very curious, as it was the first really genuine Oriental bazaar which I had seen, that at Perovsky being half-Russian.

I wandered for a long time, in spite of the heat, past the little rows of shops, looking at the silversmiths plying their trades, and seeing the general idleness and listlessness of the shopkeepers, for there seemed almost no business going on. The central point of interest was a raised platform, where stood a man with a little mountain of snow, which he was dealing out to the little boys in small portions, with a sauce of sugary syrup. The eyes of the boys were big and greedy, yet their timidity or their hatred of a Kaffir was such that I had some difficulty in inducing them to allow me to treat them.

Leaving Turkistan at seven o'clock in the evening, with good horses and good roads, I arrived at Ikan, a town of considerable size, though much ruined, which, on December 16, 17, and 18, 1864, was the scene of a most heroic contest on the part of a small body of Russian soldiers. After the capture of Tchimkent, Alim Kul and the Khokandians raised a large body of troops and resolved to attempt the recapture of Turkistan the Holy. There were numerous messengers announcing the approach of this army, and especially one asking for aid sent by the inhabitants of Ikan, who had preferred to remain under Russian protection, and Captain Serof with a *sotnia* of Cossacks and one gun was sent out to Ikan. When near that place he became entirely surrounded by large masses of the enemy, and found it impossible either to advance or retire; and from the evening of the 16th until that of the 18th, without tasting food, these brave Cossacks defended themselves against the overwhelming forces of the enemy; and then, having spiked their gun, the little remnant made a sortie, and bleeding and breathless joined the Russian forces, which were standing three miles from Turkistan. The Russians lost in all fifty-seven killed and forty-three wounded.

A small force had just been sent out from Turkistan, but on seeing the enemy they immediately retreated; and though the firing was continually audible at Turkistan, no other effort was made to relieve the detachment, the time being passed in councils of war and debate. In consequence of this affair the commander of Turkistan was subsequently compelled to leave the army.

The Khokandians lost many in this desperate fight, and were astonished at the bravery and perseverance of the Russians, not only at their refusing to surrender, but at their refusing to accept the terms they offered, which were an honourable and safe retreat to the main detachment at Turkistan. This was told me by the man who was sent by Alim Kul to carry on negotiations with Serof.

From Turkistan to Tchimkent, 100 miles or more, the road goes through a very pretty country, the Steppe being rich in verdure and flowers, and constantly rising and falling, owing to the nearness of the mountains. A number of torrents had to be traversed, and two of these, the Bugun and Arys, were especially difficult. At the latter it became necessary to unload entirely the tarantas, and place all the luggage on a large native cart, as the current was very swift and the water far above the floor of the carriage. In crossing one of these mountain ravines the driver locked the wheel of the tarantas in such a careless manner that two spokes were at once taken out, and I began to fear that I would find it difficult to reach Tashkent or even Tchimkent, but after thoroughly lacing up the wheel with rope, the tarantas was still strong enough to stand.

The town of Tchimkent,[1] which I reached on the next evening after leaving Turkistan, presents nothing remarkable except the picturesque citadel, which is built on what seems an almost inaccessible height. The new bazaar, with its ponds and well-built shops, which has been constructed by the Russians, shows that the town is still flourishing. The occupation both of Turkistan and of Tchimkent was, as is well known, in pursuance of a plan made as long ago as 1854 for the formation of a fortified line which would connect the line of Orenburg with that of Siberia, and thus completely protect the Kirghiz. The first intention was to have this line run to the north of the Kara-tau range, but on the representations of the local commanders the plan was modified. During and just after the Crimean war it was impossible to take active measures in the Steppe, and it was not until 1864 that Colonel (now Major-General)—Tchernaief, with 2,500 men from Siberia, and Colonel (now Lieutenant-General) Verevkin, with 1,200 men from Orenburg, were sent to carry out this plan. Turkistan was taken in June, about the same time as Aulié-ata, while it was not until October that Tchimkent was stormed. I am told that the successful assault was owing to a ludicrous mistake. In the first outset one of the soldiers was slightly wounded and cried out for the surgeon— 'Dok-tu-ra!' His comrades heard only 'u-ra!'—the Russian 'Hurrah,' rushed forward, pressing the enemy before them, and within an hour had full possession of the citadel, with only five men killed. It is said that the bazaar was sacked and many of the inhabitants massacred; if so, this was an exceptional case, for the Russian movements in Central Asia have been marked by great discipline and humanity.

[1] The name Tchimkent is derived by the natives from the Turki *tchim*, turf, and the Persian *kent*, town, like many other local names taken from the two languages. Lerch considers it a corruption of *Tcheshmkent*, fountain-town, and identifies it with the ancient Isbyjab. I may remark here that the terminations *kent* and *kand* are the same, *kent* being used when the vowels of the first part of the word are *i* or *e*, and *kand* when they are *a*, *o*, or *u*, as in Khokand, Yarkand, Samarkand. Tashkent as thus written is improper, but as it is sanctioned by usage, and the town is now Russian, I keep to it. The natives say 'Tashkand.'

CHAPTER III.

TASHKENT.

First Impressions—Similarity to American towns—Rapid growth—Houses —Garden of Governor-General—The Church—Earthquakes—Hotels and fare—The Club—Ming Uruk—Society—The Governor-General's State— Rigid etiquette at his balls—Bad tone—Cliques—Ignorance of the country displayed by officials—The 'Central Asiatic Society'—Jura Bek —Baba Bek—A nephew of the Amir of Bukhara—Alim Hadji Yunusof— A Court doctor—Murder of Malla Khan—A political execution in Bukhara—The mercantile community—Said Azim—The native town—Mills —Walls—Population—Sarts—Tadjiks—Uzbeks—Their characteristics— Arabs—History of Tashkent—Its capture by General Tchernaief—His first proclamation.

As I sat in the porch in the bright moonlight, the first night of my arrival at Tashkent, I could scarcely believe that I was in Central Asia, but seemed rather to be in one of the quiet little towns of Central New York. The broad dusty streets, shaded by double rows of trees; the sound of rippling water in every direction; the small white houses, set a little back from the streets, with trees and a palisade in front; the large square, full of turf and flowers, with a little church in the middle—all combined to give me this familiar impression. By daylight, however, Tashkent seems more like one of the Western American towns—Denver, for instance, though lacking in the busy air which pervades that place, and with Sarts, in turbans and gowns, in place of Indians and miners. The conditions of the town are, indeed, much the same; it is built on the Steppe, and owes its green and fresh appearance to the canals, which bring streams of fresh water through every street. The sides of the streets are planted with poplars and willows, which in this country grow quickly and luxuriantly; a small stake driven into the ground soon becomes a fine tree; gardens spring up almost like magic; and I saw in the garden of a laboratory a peach tree bearing peaches the third year from the seed.

There are about 600 houses in Tashkent—I speak of the Russian town—and a population of 3,000, exclusive of the garrison of about 6,000. New houses and streets are everywhere springing up, and the growth of the city in the nine years of its existence seems something really wonderful. Still when one comes to examine into the matter there is something artificial in all this; the real, permanent population of the city is small, for trade is not great, manufactories do not exist, and, with the exception of the merchants, no one lives here who is not obliged to do so on account of his official duties. No one comes to Tashkent to remain, which distinguishes it from similar American towns, and most of these pretty houses have been built on money loaned by the Government, of which, by the way, but little is ever repaid.

The houses are in general built of sun-dried clay bricks, covered with plaster, and washed with some light colour, and are seldom more than one story high. Owing to the scarcity of wood and the dearness of iron, the roofs are very peculiar; between the rafters which compose the ceilings pieces of small willow-branches are closely fitted together, the whole is then thatched with reeds, and on this is placed a layer of clay and sods, it being necessary to put on a new layer of clay every year to render the roof in any degree waterproof. During the summer, when it does not rain, these roofs are excellent, and very pretty, as they are often covered with wild poppies, capers, and other flowers. When the rainy autumn season commences one must be very careful : it may be that too many layers of clay have been placed on the roof, and the timbers have become worn, so that the whole thing falls through; or perhaps not enough clay has been put on, and one violent rainstorm is sufficient to wash a large hole in it.

Furniture and household goods of all kinds have to be brought from Russia or Siberia, for there are no cabinet-makers or upholsterers in Central Asia, and simplicity is therefore the rule. Still the houses are comfortable in spite of their fragility, and the great wide divans, the profusion of Turkoman carpets, the embroidered cushions, and the display of Eastern weapons, armour, and utensils give them an air of elegance and luxury.

During the summer all who can afford it leave their town

houses and remove to one of the numerous gardens in the suburbs, where they either have a small house of a similar kind or live in Kirghiz *kibitkas*. Nothing can be more delightful than this. The heat does not penetrate through the thick elms and poplars; a freshness constantly exhales from the square pond and from the canals which water the garden, mixed with the perfume of roses and syringas. The *kibitka* is spacious and comfortable; and if to this is added a Bukharan pavilion-tent, with its embroidered and variegated walls, for a *salon*, the abode is charming. When at night the paper lanterns stand out against the dark green of the pomegranates, while the nightingale sings as the light shimmers over the still surface of the water, it is a scene taken bodily from the 'Arabian Nights.'

The palace of the Governor-General is by far the best building in Tashkent, being very large, and covered with an iron roof. It is situated in an immense garden, which has been very prettily laid out with hills, trees, flowers, ponds, canals, and even cascades, and here, three evenings in a week, the military band plays, and the gardens are thrown open to the public. They are then the rendezvous of all the Russians, and much of the native population of the place, for the Sarts are attracted by the band, which occasionally plays native airs. Near by the palace of the Governor-General is a large new fort, not yet entirely finished, intended for the protection of the city. This fort is mounted with heavy cannon, and has a large garrison, though many of the troops are quartered in different barracks, and during the summer are in the camp near the town.

There are, of course, the usual number of public buildings for Government offices, without which no Russian town can possibly exist; and there is the little church, in addition to which the foundations of a large stone cathedral have been laid. This seems almost a waste of money in a place where are so few Russians, and where missionaries are forbidden. The church is quite large enough for present wants, and is somewhat out of repair, a negligence which astonishes the pious Mussulmans, who are also shocked that so few Russians attend church regularly. As their own religion is not attacked, the natives treat the church with reverence, though they call it *bud-khaneh*, idol (Buddha) house, and the more liberal and curious spirits sometimes are attracted by the services. The building of this cathedral is looked on as a dangerous experiment, on account of the earthquakes, though they are not frequent, and it is several years since there was a severe one. I looked for one with some curiosity, being anxious to experience a new sensation; but alas! when it came I slept soundly, and did not hear of it until breakfast-time. There were three shocks, about five o'clock in the morning, severe enough to make the walls tremble and the pictures swing outwards, and even small objects were thrown down.

There is not in Tashkent what can be called an hotel, though there are one or two places, such as Gromof's, where there are furnished rooms and some provision for meals, but they are dirty and uncomfortable. There is a fair restaurant, kept by a Pole, Gizhitzky, which has one or two rooms to be let out to sojourners. I was not, however, entirely dependent on it, for owing to my fortunate *rencontre* at Julek I received quarters in a private house, where I was treated with all kindness and hospitality. Fare in Tashkent is much the same as in any other Russian town, and if there exists there any local delicacy or any new undeveloped possibility the Russians have not yet discovered it. Beef was scarce and bad, but mutton was plentiful, cheap, and delicious. At first the colonists complained of a scarcity of potatoes, but where Russian soldiers live their cabbages soon grow, and there is now plenty of all the usual vegetables. Game is abundant, but fish is very rare; for the Syr Darya, where sturgeon abound, is still unfished. Excellent fruit and melons of all kinds are to be had almost for the asking, but I heard complaints of the difficulty of raising rye, and the consequent scarcity of black bread. Wine is of course to be had at about four times St. Petersburg prices, and one can even get English ale and porter—the latter is a special favourite—at about ten shillings a bottle. A very bad beer is brewed there, and several kinds of native wines are made, but all strong and sour. With time and experience good wine will doubtless be made in such a climate, and with such profusion of good grapes.

Of course there is a club, as stupid and unclublike as all Russian clubs. A bad dinner can be had there every day, and men occasionally drop in to read the newspapers when the mail arrives or to play at billiards; but as a general rule people reserve themselves for the social evenings during the winter, when the large ball-room is open and there is a dance or concert. There is now attached to the rooms of the club an excellent library, which was originally collected for the Chancellery of the Governor-General, and has since that time been enlarged by gifts from other persons. It contains now about 4,000 volumes, including the standard works of Russian, French, and German literature, and an exceedingly good collection of books and articles relating to Central Asia.

Among the other institutions of the place I should mention the Chemical Laboratory, which is mounted on a far better and more costly scale than seems warranted by the necessities of the country; and the 'Turkistan Gazette.' This is a small weekly journal, containing besides official matter articles on the history, ethnology, and statistics of the country, which are often very interesting and valuable. Of news from the rest of the world there is nothing whatever, and even the current events of Central Asia are rarely mentioned, except in extracts from the newspapers of St. Petersburg and Moscow. It has only about 300 subscribers, and costs the Government some 22,000 rubles a year, or 37 kopeks a copy. While thankful for many of the articles contained in the 'Gazette,' I sometimes wonder at its existence. A supplement in Turki is published for the spread of literature among the natives, but when I was in Tashkent its contents were chiefly drawn from the tales of the 'Arabian Nights.' Just outside of the town, on the east, in the direction of the fair, is a large garden, known by the name of Ming-uruk (or the thousand apricot trees), which was formerly the evening promenade of the place. As its name implies, it is a large orchard of apricot trees, most of them very large and extremely old, surrounded by a high clay wall. The very day I arrived a festival was held there, with the usual accompaniment of lottery *allegri*, and the green sward and the wide paths were covered with loungers and promenaders. A temporary restaurant was also put up, and in various tents and pavilions the ladies of Tashkent distributed the little lottery-tickets at twenty kopeks apiece, perhaps one in 2,000 drawing some slight prize. The natives take very kindly to this form of gambling, and it has been noticed of late that the chief revenue of such little charitable lotteries is derived from the Sart population, who are eager to have this chance of possibly winning something without more exertion than drawing the little rolls of paper from the glass urn, slipping off the wire ring, and unrolling them. The word *allegri* on the ticket always marks a blank, while a number indicates a prize. Now that the Governor-General's garden is open so often the Ming-uruk has somewhat fallen into disrepute, and the good roads and introduction of droshkies and carriages have to a certain degree stopped horseback exercise; but three years ago vehicles were scarce and the mud was deep, so that all men and women were constantly on horseback. Now few but officers and natives ride, and even natives are sometimes to be seen in droshkies—struck with the charm of civilisation.

During my stay in Central Asia I considered Tashkent my head-quarters, and was there for more or less time at four different periods. Fortunately perhaps for me, the magnates of the Russian official world were all on the Khivan expedition, and I was thus cut off from the higher official society. Among those who remained I found some very pleasant acquaintances, though I was received at first with perhaps a shade of suspicion. I had sent on my letters of introduction to General Kaufmann, at the head-quarters of the expedition, and arrived in Tashkent with no recommendations to the officials there. Still, even before the approval of my visit by General Kaufmann arrived, the idea that I might be an English spy in disguise had, I think, worn off, and my relations with the authorities were most pleasant. After the arrival of General Kolpakofsky from Vierny, as the acting Governor-General, I was treated with still greater politeness, and was enabled to carry out all my plans. Still, out of mere curiosity, perhaps, I regret not having seen the life of the little court—for it is really nothing else—that ordinarily goes on at Tashkent. The Governor-General or Yarim Padshah (the half-king), as he is called, imitates in the state he keeps the Eastern monarchs by whom he is surrounded. He never rides out, so I am told, without a select guard of Cossacks, and even his wife and children had their escorts. These I believe were abolished after the unfortunate remark of some newly-arrived officer, who innocently enquired what lady that was under arrest. The Governor-General rarely goes out in society, but does his part by giving two or three balls during the course of the winter, to which the leading natives as well as the Russians are invited. These must be very amusing affairs. The guests are obliged to arrive punctually at the moment, as at the Winter Palace at St. Petersburg, and they are kept waiting for perhaps an hour until the Governor-General, his wife, and suite enter the room, and are received by deep bows and curtseys. Before this it is impossible for dancing to begin, and even then etiquette is so much stricter than at St. Petersburg, that no gentleman is allowed to sit down in the presence of the Governor-General. The poor unfortunate who should do so would at once receive from an aide-de-camp a strong hint to rise. Should the Governor-General be seen shaking a person warmly by the hand or conversing with him for five or ten minutes, the man so honoured immediately becomes a figure in society, and is considered necessarily a rising man and one of great influence. Such is the effect of court favour.

When the Governor-General returns to Tashkent triumphal arches are erected, all the officials go several miles out of the city to meet him, and he is received with salutes of cannon. When a branch of the Control Department was founded at Tashkent it was found that there was no law authorizing these salutes, and a request was made that the money expended for the powder fired should be returned to the Treasury. The money was paid, but the salutes continue, though not at Government cost. The triumphal arches and the receptions are supposed to be the outspoken expression of popular feeling, but these demonstrations are hardly spontaneous. When Khiva was taken a meeting was called to devise a means of commemorating the victory. Some proposed a permanent triumphal arch, others a scholarship of the Oriental languages—to be named after the Governor-General—in some university. It was finally decided to do both. The money was to be raised by voluntary subscriptions, but all the officers and officials, even in other parts of Turkistan, received an official paper from their superiors asking for their contributions, which few dared refuse.

Besides the Governor-General there are the military governor and the vice-governor, and a staff of generals and other grand officials, for this being a little capital there must be in every department a central administration mounted on a large scale. The wives and families of these chiefs of the official hierarchy consider themselves as the *sommités* of society, and vastly superior to the other ladies of the place, for it must not be thought that Tashkent is destitute of ladies, most of the officers having brought their wives and families with them. Society is therefore divided into cliques and coteries, for though, with the exception of the highest officials, nearly everyone who is there has either come there to avoid his creditors or been sent away to keep out of some scrape, or has come on account of increased pay or the shorter time of service necessary before receiving a pension, or in the hope of making a rapid fortune, yet they all bring with them their St. Petersburg ideas. There is the same etiquette with regard to morning calls, full dress, and other customs of society that prevails in the larger Russian towns. People meet, it is true, at the soirées or private theatricals, which are occasionally given at the club, or at the Governor-General's palace, but each coterie keeps apart from the others, and there is nothing like real general social life. These absurd divisions in such a small society, and the fact that Tashkent is looked upon as a temporary place of exile, are very bad for the younger officers and officials. There being few amusements, society being dull and broken up, and their scientific and literary pursuits discouraged or at least not encouraged, the officers have little resource but gambling and drinking, and in many instances young men have utterly ruined themselves, some even having to be sent out of the country—and a man *must* be bad to be exiled from Tashkent—and others having died or committed suicide. A Russian writer of growing repute, Mr. Karazin, formerly an officer in Central Asia, has given a good picture of Tashkent in his novel 'In the Distant Confines.' I know that this book is looked upon as a libel in Tashkent, but nearly every character is recognizable, and the tone of society as depicted there is, as nearly as I could gather the truth, exactly such as really existed there two or three years ago. There is now a little improvement. There is not so much of open debauchery and dissipation as then, but the same general tone prevails. Home is far away, public opinion is lenient or silent, and many allow themselves liberties of conduct which elsewhere they would not imagine possible.

I could not but be struck in the Russian society of Tashkent, not only with the want of knowledge of the country, but with the lack of interest in it which was manifested, and it seemed to many difficult to understand how I could be interested in a country, and come so far to see it, which for them was the epitome of everything disagreeable. Of course there were exceptions to this, but I speak of the general impression. The number of Russians who know either Persian or Turki, or who care at all for the history, antiquities, or natural productions of the country, or who interest themselves in any way in the life of the people about them, is wonderfully small. A branch of the 'Society of Natural History and Anthropology' was once started in Tashkent, and held its meetings at the house of the Governor-General; but whether it was the incubus of official presence or the lack of real interest in the thing, it soon died out.[1]

The Tashkent branch of the 'Society for the Encouragement of Russian Trade' also leads a very lingering existence.

A 'Central Asiatic Society' was formed, but was forbidden by the authorities.

The man in all Tashkent who interested himself the most about the natives was Mr. P——, the agent of the Ministry of Finance. He had learned Turki perfectly, and spoke it with accuracy and elegance, and his house was the head-quarters of prominent natives. His wife also took great interest in the

---

[1] I was told that when the Central Asiatic Society was started General Kaufmann expressed a wish to become a member. It was then considered necessary to elect him the honorary president, and at his urgent request the meetings were held at his house. On one of these occasions Colonel R——, one of the most active members of the society, appeared in the usual white linen undress uniform worn at Tashkent. When the meeting was over the Governor-General sent word to him through the police that it was not proper to come to the house of the Governor-General otherwise than in full uniform. At the next meeting of the society a letter was read from Colonel R——, in which he informed the society—through its president—that he had been reprimanded by the Governor-General for not appearing in full uniform at one of its meetings, because it was at the house of the Governor-General. He stated that undress uniform was permitted at meetings of learned societies, and referred especially to the Imperial Russian Geographical Society, at St. Petersburg, of which the Grand Duke Constantine is President, where members dress as they please, and smoke even in his presence, and stated that under the circumstances he felt compelled to offer his resignation as a member of the society.

native population, and constantly visited them, and received visits from them. Apart from the friendship and kindness which I received from Mr. P—— and his agreeable family, I delighted to visit his house as often as possible, because I was sure at any hour of the day of meeting two or three natives whose stories or conversation were of great interest and value.

Prominent among the *habitués* of this hospitable house were the various deposed Beks, and chiefly Jura Bek and Baba Bek, of Shahrisabs, a little province just south of Samarkand. The fathers of both of them had been prominent there before the country had been finally annexed to Bukhara by the bloodthirsty Nasrullah. After the death of his father Kalentar Bek, Jura was taken into the service of the Amir as one of the youths in waiting, where he remained until the death of the Amir in 1860, when he escaped to Shahrisabs. Six months after the death of Nasrullah the new Amir, his son, Mozaffar-eddin, went from Samarkand to Shahrisabs. The presence of Mozaffar could awake no sympathy in such a purely Uzbek place. Unsociable by nature, fat and lazy, already known and detested as a dissolute man, the Amir rode in, a strong contrast to his father, amidst the laughter of the population, who were accustomed to a certain degree of freedom. On that very night he demanded the sister of Baba Bek, who had once before been forced in a similar way to serve the passions of his father. This could not remain concealed, and on the next day there were crowds of people in the streets loudly crying out against the Amir. Being afraid of still greater publicity, and perhaps rebellion, Mozaffar immediately returned to Bukhara, but he did not forget Shahrisabs. Many important personages were seized and imprisoned, but they were released by the populace, now fully aroused, and Jura Bek, then about twenty years old, was elected the Bek of Kitab, one of the twin cities. He succeeded in expelling the officials of the Bukharan Amir, and in connection with Baba Bek, who succeeded his father, maintained the independence of his little valley until August 1870, when Shahrisabs was taken by the Russians and delivered up to the Amir. He and Baba Bek then escaped to Khokand, but were treacherously delivered up by Khudayar Khan, who bore an old grudge against Jura Bek for laughing at him and calling him an old woman when he was once complaining to the Amir Nasrullah of his troubles and his exile. Brought as prisoners to Tashkent, they lived there for some time under surveillance; but finally obtaining pensions of about 2,000 rubles a year from the Bukharan Government, through the agency of the Russians, they now reside there unmolested, although, owing to the irregularity of the payments, they are sometimes reduced to great straits, as they both have large families. Jura Bek has become thoroughly convinced that the Russians are and are to be the masters of Central Asia, and sees that any chance for him in the future must come from them. His allegiance to them therefore is unwavering; and though cognizant of plots in the neighbouring countries— for he is occasionally appealed to by emissaries, as being of good judgment and experience—he does not fail to inform the Russians of anything which may be hostile to their interests, and has refused to take part in anything against them, no matter how brilliant the inducements were.[1] He is one of few natives I have met—if not the only one—whose word I would implicitly trust on any subject. It is rare to find a Mussulman and an Asiatic of such delicacy of mind and feeling, such an appreciation of what is due to himself and others, and of such an aristocratic bearing in every look and movement. Jura Bek is a tall handsome Uzbek, with a thin dark beard, pleasant gray eyes, and a serious face. His dress is always very simple, but exquisitely neat, and there is something about the sadness of his expression and the suave grace of his gestures which never fails to attract and to interest. He is indeed a perfect gentleman. He is a strict Mussulman, but he has now been sufficiently with the Russians to have lost all fanaticism, and to be willing to conform to many of their usages. He will associate with them, eat with them, and even, if he chooses, drink wine, having sufficient dignity to act as he pleases, never, as many others do, wearing one face to the Russians and another to his fellow-believers. Jura Bek is besides a good judge of character, has the politeness of Central Asia at his finger-ends, and is certainly not without ambition; and therefore, as he is an honest and straightforward man, he might, if properly treated, be of the greatest service to Russia. Should it become necessary to overturn the Amir of Bukhara or the Khan of Khokand,

---

[1] The son of the Khan of Khokand, on his visit to Tashkent, tried in vain to bribe him; and he first gave information of the attack on the station of Kara-sa.

and place a vassal on the throne, no better person could be found in the interest either of the natives or of the Russians than Jura Bek, and his birth—for he comes from the noble family of Keninghez, one of the four whose hereditary duty it is to raise the Amir on his throne—would cause him to be accepted without a murmur by the population.

Baba Bek, his companion in exile, is a man of much weaker stamp, a stout man of thirty-six, though looking twenty years

BABA BEK AND JURA BEK.

older, so much have his troubles told on him, and is without either the ability or the courage of his companion. He passes his life quietly, and is so amiable that one cannot help pitying his downfall; but he is not the kind of man that one would ever think of setting up again.

As occasional visitors we had other deposed Beks, the petty rulers of the small districts of Kshtut and Farab, high up in the mountains near Samarkand, Shadi Bek and Seid Bek,[1] who are

---

[1] Hussein Bek, the Bek of Magian, was, when caught, arbitrarily exiled to Siberia, because, when still an independent ruler, he did not come to Samarkand

now dependent on Russian charity, and Abul-Gaffar Bek, the former Governor of Ura-tepé. Abul-Gaffar comes of a family that has held many high stations in the Bukharan service, and was for a long time the Bek of Ura-tepé, where he was very unpopular, as he was both unjust and severe. He was at continual war with the mountain districts, and had the reputation of being a great coward, in spite of which he made a strong defence against the Russians of the fortress he commanded. He afterwards had part of his property returned to him, and received in addition a small pension, on which he lives at Ura-tepé and Tashkent. He is an educated man, a Mullah, fond of talking and repeating verses, and evidently of a sociable disposition, as he has had twenty wives, and has ten grown sons, one of whom was formerly Bek of Zamin. One of his brothers was the brave Omar Bek, who fought against the Russians at Jizakh, and was killed in 1872 by the Amir; and another is Ibodullah Bek, whom I sometimes saw, the former ruler of Hissar, an educated man, and well acquainted with the regions of the Upper Oxus.

Seid Khan is a young man of about thirty-five, the son of a sister of the Amir Mozaffar-eddin, who escaped from Bukhara after the accession of that monarch, when his father, mother, and the whole of his family were put to death. He claims that his right to the throne is superior to that of the present Amir; and were he as able as he is ambitious, he might easily overturn the Amir and set himself in his place, provided, of course, that the Russians consented to such an arrangement. He is nominally in the Russian service, and receives a pension of 2,400 rubles a year, but dreams his time away, and wastes his money on dancing-boys and riotous living, so that he is always in debt. His long residence in Tashkent and his intercourse with Russians of all kinds have taught him how to speak and write Russian. Being of royal blood, he has his party in Bukhara, with whom he is in correspondence; and in spite of his many defects he would perhaps make as good a figure-head as anyone else, although he has no head for plots; and the letters of importance which he receives from persons even near to the Amir are often left for weeks unheeded. He has a way of

to pay his respects to the Governor-General. Escaping from there, he was caught and sent back. His cousin, Mussa Bek, is now a leading official in Kashgar, and very hostile to the Russians.

changing his residence every few weeks, which renders it somewhat difficult to visit him; and the last time that I saw him he greatly amused me by his belief that emissaries of his uncle were in Tashkent with designs upon his life. He sat on the floor, surrounded by weapons, and changed the position of his bed every night. His head was full of grand projects as to what he would do when he became Amir, of the certainty of which he seemed to have no doubt. He frequently used to come with a mysterious air and talk in a dark way about highly important letters he had received, about which he wanted advice, but which he had always forgotten to bring with him. Usually his visit terminated with a request for a slight loan. When I at last saw some of these letters, in whose existence I had begun to disbelieve, I found them really very interesting. One from the astrologist of the Amir began with Persian verses and stilted compliments, and at last said, 'You know that the real owner of the estate where we live resides in Tashkent. Tell him that the steward who is here is very bad, and excites great discontent among the tenants. He must remove this steward; if he does not we shall do it ourselves, and ask you to come or choose another. He need not punish him, for it will be enough if he orders him to go live in Tashkent; or should he come himself, the steward will be frightened and at once run away.' When we are told that the estate is Bukhara, the real owner General Kaufmann, and the steward the Amir, we can at once understand the parable, which was cleverly carried out to great length. Unfortunately for both tenants and owners, the same steward still remains.

An amusing type of the native was the tall thin Mussa Mahomet Bii, who at the capture of Tashkent was acting as governor, and as such surrendered the place to the Russians. He told me that his excitement and fear were so great that he galloped through the streets weeping violently and crying to all he met, 'Bid farewell to your wives and children, for the Russians have come.'

The morning after the capture of Tashkent a deputation from the city came to wait upon General Tchernayef. He immediately sent for his interpreter, but to his astonishment the venerable leader of the deputation began to talk to him in pure Russian, about science, philosophy, and the benefits of civilisation. He turned out to be a certain Alim Hadji Yunusof, a Tartar, from Penza, in South Russia, who had received his education at Moscow, and had been as a pilgrim to Mecca and through India. I saw a great deal of him in Tashkent, and he was certainly one of the most striking characters I met. He was, I think, much more of a philosopher than a Mussulman, and was continually in search of new ideas of some kind. During the twenty years that he had lived in Tashkent under native rule he had lived quietly, attending to his gardens and cotton and silk-raising, and marrying one wife after another. He had tried nearly all the races procurable there, and shortly before my visit had married a young Persian. He was civilised enough to be willing to discuss family matters, and on one or two occasions I got a glimpse of some of his wives. Even here his idiosyncrasy showed out, and he told me in an apologetical tone of voice that his favourite wife had received her education among the Kirghiz, which was merely a polite way of saying she was a Kirghiz girl. Since the Russian occupation he has tried his hand at civilisation, has built houses, planted American cotton, established a soap factory, tried to introduce machines for spinning silk, and gins for cleaning cotton, but I fear that all these attempts were failures. His large house in the Russian town is still unfinished, and his soap factory had already come to an untimely end before the silver medal he gained at the Moscow exhibition reached him. Still he kept on with his experiments. I well remember one visit I paid him in his garden just out of town. Persistent knocking at the little door brought the Hadji himself to let us in. He was attending to his plantations, and appeared in a long loose pink calico shirt, open at the throat and showing his bronzed muscular neck. Stroking his long grizzly beard, pulling down his sleeves, and tying a handkerchief about his waist, he led us through the vines and pomegranate trees to where a mat was spread in the shade, where he regaled us with the choicest peaches and grapes, while he discoursed on the diseases of mulberry trees, and the consequent epidemic among the silkworms, with many shrewd observations on botany and gardening. The Hadji reads a great deal; his interests are world-wide, and his dabblings in science have brought him to be a member of several learned societies in Moscow and St. Petersburg.

With all this he is a man of good heart and excellent sense, and a few more such would do much good in Tashkent. Unfortunately he is there no longer, as I shall tell farther on.

Asudullah Bek was one of the well-known doctors of Tashkent. I do not know at what medical institution he had taken his degree, for he was a Persian, born in the Caucasus, who had come to Central Asia early in life, and had always had a large practice. He had been the intimate friend of Alim Kul and Yakub Khan, and doctor to various Khans of Khokand. He was not really a Bek, though he bore this appellation, which is sometimes given as a pet name, sometimes as a nickname. He spoke Russian tolerably well, and was always glad to have a chat or take a hand in a game at cards, in which he was an adept. He had passed a very adventurous life; and as he was a Persian and a heretic Shiite, he was not much loved by the orthodox Sunnites who surrounded him. I was always glad to see him, for he needed very little provocation to tell some of the episodes in Central Asiatic history with which he had been connected. When questioned as to why he ran away from the Caucasus, Asudullah Bek was very uncommunicative, though ready enough to talk about his later life. 'I came,' he said, 'to the city of Turkistan in 1856, and lived there a year. At this time the Russians had come to Julek, and our army went there, and Batyr Bek was wounded. They asked for a doctor, and collected all the Bukharans and other men, but none pleased them. They then said, "There is a man from Roum; you ought to call him." I had a shop at that time. They brought me to Batyr Bek, and I pleased him, for I was then very handsome, and without a beard. Khanayat Shah, the general of the army, said to me, "You must cure him in twelve days, or have your head cut off. Now the Khan is in Tashkent; if you cure him we will take you there and present you to the Khan." Then I washed myself and prayed to God, for I was very fearful, as the people had treated me badly, because they had taken me for a spy of the Russians; but I was given ten tillas, and was ordered to buy everything that was necessary. The wound of Batyr Bek was really very bad. The ball had gone into his mouth and out at his ear and knocked his teeth out. He could not eat, drink, or speak. I immediately washed him with hot water, and then put on a plaster of oil and roots, and fed him through a tube. After four days his tongue was better, and he opened his lips, moved his tongue, and began to talk. On the eighth day he was so much better that they gave me twelve tillas, and told me to wait in Tashkent while Khanayat Shah and Yakub Bek (the present ruler of Kashgar) went on ahead. After a week they sent for me. "Give him a man and a horse, and make him many compliments—the Khan has sent him a letter of invitation." In Tashkent I became acquainted with Alim Kul and Shah Murad Bek, the nephew of the Khan, for the Khan himself had gone to take Ura-tepé. When I was taken to Shah Murad Bek, I did as I had been taught, and took him by the hand and rubbed it over the whole of my face. He was pleased with me, for I was then handsome, and told me to live with Yakub Bek, where I stayed for two weeks. After that we went to Khokand, where I began to practise medicine, and was made the doctor of the Khan, and received one tilla (about eight shillings) a day.' From being the physician Asudullah Bek became the intimate friend of Malla Khan, and was present at his murder. He had already suspicions that something was up, but was unable to fix upon anything, so as to warn the Khan. During the night he occupied the next room to the Khan, who was sleeping soundly, having taken during the day many love-potions. During the night he heard his door bolted from without and a voice which said, 'The Khan is here.' A crowd then rushed into the room of the Khan and beat him and stabbed him with their knives. He defended himself bravely, but was finally cut almost to bits. Asudullah Bek then heard the conspirators propose to murder him also, as being one of the nearest friends of the Khan, but one of them spoke in his favour, saying that he was a foreigner and a physician, living there only temporarily, and had done no harm, and these pleadings obtained his release. Poor Asudullah was more dead than alive during the colloquy which interested him so much. The conspirators then found Shah Murad, who was living in Khokand at that time, tossed him in the air on a large white felt, and saluted him as Khan.

In the morning a proclamation was made through the streets that Malla Khan was dead and that Shah Murad was Khan, and all the officials and great personages of Khokand went up to make *salaam* at the palace. Asudullah was of course among them. When the Khan saw him, he smiled and said, ' Do not be afraid; I will not hurt you, but you shall be my court doctor also.' He thereupon gave him a complete suit of clothes, a turban, and a purse of gold pieces. The money he took home and divided with Yakub Bek, who was then living with him.

When the first attack was made upon Tashkent, Asudullah Bek was there, and was by the side of Alim Kul when he was wounded. The wound and death of Alim Kul caused great consternation among his followers; and as his clothes were taken off one by one the doctor gave them to the bystanders to hold, and tried to give some fresh air to the dying man. These articles of dress were immediately carried off by the persons who had received them, so that by the time Alim Kul died he was stark naked, and the doctor was obliged to use his own *khalat* to cover him. After the capture of Tashkent the doctor, as he spoke Russian, was of considerable service to the Russians, and remained there some time; finally, however, he obtained permission from General Tchernayef to go to Khokand in order to settle his affairs and bring back his wife, whom he had left there. When he arrived at Khokand the Amir of Bukhara was in occupation of the city, and the doctor was at once denounced as a Russian spy. He was brought before the Amir, and was about to be sentenced to immediate execution, when he fell at his feet and besought him for mercy, saying how well he had fought at Tashkent for Khokand, and how he had stayed with Alim Kul until the last; that he had now fairly succeeded in getting away from the Russian clutches, and desired to settle in Khokand in peace for the rest of his days. This tale produced a good effect upon the Amir, who took the gold-embroidered skull-cap from his head and tossed it to him, saying he would not only spare his life but would make him his court doctor, and take him to Bukhara with him. He immediately ordered a full suit of clothing to be given to him and a purse of money. The doctor was pleased with the turn affairs had taken, but still was not anxious to accept the kind offer of the Amir, as it seemed to him that Bukhara would be even a more dangerous place than Khokand. He, however, waited until the day of the Amir's departure before taking any steps. When the Amir's people sent him four carts on which to load his househood goods he consulted with his wife, and resolved to escape if possible. He sent the soldiers who drove the carts all off on various errands, and fled with his wife, taking only what little money they had about them. Getting outside of Khokand, they concealed themselves in a field, lying down in a drain; but thinking that this would be dangerous, as the Amir would probably send men on their traces, the doctor's wife went to a small house near by and procured for him a female dress, which he put on, and was just coming into the house when the soldiers sent by the Amir passed and asked him if he had seen the doctor, Asudullah Bek, and his wife, who had run away from the Amir. He replied that no such persons had been in the vicinity, and the soldiers went on. He was concealed in this house for some days, and then in another, until the Amir, finding himself unsuccessful, had left for Bukhara. He then thought it best, as he was almost without money, to return to Khokand, where he concealed himself; but his wife being in the bazaar was recognised by one of the police officers; and a chief of police, who had formerly been a friend of his, came to him at once, but told him he need not fear anything, because the Amir had gone, and the Khan was certainly well-disposed towards him. He was then summoned to the palace of Khudayar Khan, who told him he would not allow him to go to the Amir, and would protect him. A few days after this the Amir sent a letter to the Khan, urging him to pursue to the utmost this traitor and send him on to Bukhara, where he would punish him. This of course made Asudullah Bek more anxious, but he resolved for the present to wait, taking his chance of escaping if anything should happen, for he felt that the time might come when the Khan could not feel it possible to resist the Amir's demands. Soon after one of his friends, the secretary of the Amir, gave him a letter from the Amir to the Khan again demanding his instant surrender. Asudullah Bek took the letter, though he did not deliver it to the Khan, but still has it in his possession, and showed it to me. He resolved to leave Khokand at once, first saying to his wife, 'I cannot take you with me this time, for it is too dangerous, but I will give you a divorce.' This is a fair specimen of Eastern conjugal fidelity. The wife accepted the divorce, as there was nothing else to do, and is now living in Khokand, married to somebody else. Asudullah Bek went alone through the mountains, and after some privations and danger reached Tashkent, where a new danger awaited him, for General Tchernayef having been removed, he was unknown to General Romanofsky and his officers, and was thought by them to be a spy from Khokand, but he was fortunate enough at last to find a friend to guarantee him, and has remained in Tashkent ever since, though frequently invited to Khokand by Khudayar, as well as to Bukhara by the Amir, who professes to have entirely pardoned him, and only desires the presence of such an agreeable companion. He lately received a message from his old friend Yakub Khan, through his ambassador, urging him to go to Kashgar, but he thinks that 'a bird in the hand is worth two in the bush.' On his return to Tashkent he married the widow of Alim Kul, the sister of the Khan of Khokand, but she is now dead, and he at present has a pretty Tartar wife and some very lovely children. Not everyone lives up to the letter of the law, and when I called on him one day and found his wife and daughters unveiled there was no screaming or objurgation, but I was welcomed as one of the family.

In this connection perhaps I may be allowed to insert the account of a political execution in Bukhara, as told by Mirza Kashbar, and taken down in his words:—

'At that time I was aid of the police-master of Bukhara, who was a relative of mine, Mirza Abdullah Babai; you have probably heard about him—he lived a long time in Orenburg and traded there. Batyr Khan (the Amir Nasrullah) was very fond of him. He called him to him and made him police-master. He took me as one of his aids, and I served him in this duty a long time, almost to the time when Mozaffar became Amir. Mozaffar killed all whom Batyr Khan liked, and killed my relative. Every day people made *salaam* to the Amir, as many as 1,000 men, all great people, Datkhas, Biis, and all the officials. We were there every time if there were no council; then we made *salaam* and went away. Iskender and his brother, Tchumtchu Khan, came once to the salaam, bowed, and went away. As soon as they had gone the Amir called me and ordered me to call them back and make them sit in a little court in a separate room. I went after them and brought them back, as they had not yet got as far as their houses. They were put into the separate room. They asked what was the matter, and said, "It cannot be that they have called us to the council. This is something bad. Our affairs are wretched." I said to them, "I know nothing about it. They probably call you for some council."

'That same day Mirza Abdullah, who lived in the fortress, received an order from the Amir not to leave his house. We were very much frightened, since we thought that something bad would happen to Abdullah, because in Bukhara nobody knows what is going to be done: to-day you are alive, to-morrow they behead you. We were for a long time unquiet, then said our midday prayer, and sat still and waited.

'Suddenly another message came from the Amir, "from above," to let all our people go home for the night, and to have only three trustworthy men stay, and after sunset prayers to be in the fortress at the drum-beat, and to send for the executioner and a woman to wash the dead and to prepare two shirts.

'We began to guess that they were going to punish Iskender, but could not understand what woman was to be punished with him, because we knew nothing about it before.

'After this a *badatcha* came from the Amir ordering us to execute Iskender and the woman he would send to us.

'A *badatcha* is a small seal like an almond, which the Amir uses when he orders some one to be executed. For other matters the Amir has a large seal.

'As soon as we received the order we immediately sent for Iskender and brought him to the place of execution. In the Amir's fortress there is a place like a well, deep, and covered with boards. As soon as they execute them they throw the body there. There are many corpses there.

'The executioner was already waiting for us. He immediately seized Iskender, threw him on the ground, and as Iskender had no beard he put his fingers in his nostrils, and, taking hold of his head, cut his throat. After this they brought a woman from the Amir. As soon as she saw the dead body of Iskender she immediately began to weep and to abuse the Amir. We then saw that the woman was the sister of

Iskender, the wife of the Amir. She was of the family of Keninghez, and all called her "My moon of Keninghez." The executioner tied her hands, and shot her with a pistol in the back of the head.

'With us they do not cut the throats of women, but shoot them.

'He did not kill her at once. She fell and struggled for some time. The executioner kicked her twelve times on her breasts and back till she died.

'They say that she was punished because she, according to the order of her brother, poured mercury into the ear of the Amir when he was asleep.

'For a long time they did not know what disease he had. He went to Hissar and Karshi, but did not get better. At last they guessed why he was ill. Yes, it is written in our books how diseases are caused. Yes, I saw a great deal in Bukhara, and some time will tell you about it.'

In Central Asia nearly everyone is a merchant as well as agriculturist, and our little circle of natives was not without its mercantile representatives. One of these was Doda Mohammed, a stout, jolly merchant, whose business was in great part to act as a sort of court furnisher and agent, if not spy, to the Khan of Khokand, whom he provided amongst other things with champagne, under the name of lemonade. The Amir of Bukhara buys it under the name of *kan-su* (sugar-water), of course to prevent scandal in passing the custom-house. Doda Mohammed has even sold boys from Tashkent as slaves in Khokand. Then there were one or two old merchants from Bukhara, and I several times met a man from Peshawur who had come all the way from India by Kabul and Balkh, that road which was so easy to him and is so difficult for us, to collect some money which was owing to him.

There are in Tashkent two merchants who have much influence both with Russians and natives; one of these is Sheraffei, a Tartar by birth, and a runaway Russian soldier, who has been in this country about forty-years, and by his adroitness and commercial capacity succeeded in making himself a large fortune, and in enjoying a high reputation as a merchant before the Russian times. He lent much money to the Khan and people about the court, and much of this is still due to him.

Of late he has interested himself a good deal in army contracts, and has officially ruined himself. I say 'officially,' because it is one of the rules in the Russian commissariat department that if a contractor be unable to fulfil his contract he may give notice of his inability, and on paying down twenty per cent. of the contract is released. Sheraffei has on one or two occasions done this, but the person who took the contract after him bought the grain of Sheraffei at about three times its previous value, so that Sheraffei easily made up the twenty per cent., together with a nice additional profit.

The other, Said Azim, a very sharp and intriguing man, is a native of Tashkent, who learned Russian by being frequently at Orenburg and Troitsk for trading purposes. He was absent at Troitsk when Tashkent was taken, and when, on his return, he found out what high honour and repute certain Sarts and Tartars enjoyed among the Russians as interpreters and mediators between them and the population of the town, he immediately attached himself to the Russian officials, and since then, by universal politeness and flattery, and by presents even, has succeeded in keeping on the very best possible terms with them. Though a man of no great property he lives in very fine style, is always dressed well, and rides a magnificent horse. He has also engaged in the business of army contracts, and has fulfilled them with great accuracy, though to do so he has been obliged to borrow much money of Hindoos and others, to whom he is still largely indebted. If rumour speaks correctly he uses his influence among the natives very badly, and takes bribes right and left. The position of Said Azim is in some respects very peculiar. The Russian officials believe that he has vast influence with the native inhabitants, and honour him accordingly, and make him their representative in matters which concern the natives, who on their part, seeing that he is on the best of terms with the Russians, and that he is much favoured by them, all treat him with respect and use him as their mediator with the officials. In reality the Sarts hate him, and I more than once heard people say that should the Russians ever leave Tashkent the first thing that would be done would be to kill Said Azim. He meddles in every matter, and is said, in carrying or his numerous lawsuits, to hire witnesses and buy up the Kazis, and there are few affairs of importance among the natives in which he does not somehow manage to have a ruling voice. Here is a slight instance. On one occasion a feast was given to me by a young merchant, Azim Bai, at which there were to be a large number of guests, and where it was proposed to have dancing and other amusements. Said Azim heard of this, and felt hurt to think that he, as the most important Sart, had not been requested to get up this festivity. He had previously had a quarrel with Azim Bai on account of an inheritance which he had managed to get hold of by breaking into his house at night. He therefore went to his intimate friend, the Vice-Governor, and represented to him that any such performance as was proposed to be given for me would be contrary to the feelings of the people, and would be looked upon in the light of an insult to their religion and customs, as all the better class of the population were desirous of putting down such performances, which were not allowed by the strict letter of their religion. It would seem that a private party of this sort, to which two Russians only were invited, was hardly worth the interference of the Government, but still a hint was given, and it was accordingly found necessary to confine the festivity to a dinner and some quiet singing. The people apparently did not entirely sympathise with the representations of Said Azim, judging from the fact that more than a thousand loiterers were gathered about the garden of Azim Bai, waiting for the performance to begin, when they hoped to obtain entrance. The sincerity of Said Azim in this matter is shown by the fact that after the return of the Russians from the Khivan expedition he himself gave a large feast, at which he had all the amusements and dancing which had so offended his religion and morality on the previous occasion.

Since then he has been engaged in a very scandalous affair, which, however, does not seem to have at all compromised him with the authorities. Said Azim, it seems, took a fancy to marry the daughter of Ishan Hodja, a native of Tashkent and nephew-in-law of Yakub Khan of Kashgar, but her father opposed this, partly because she was yet a child of nine years old, and partly because Said Azim was not of sufficiently good family, as Hodjas can only marry with Hodjas. Said Azim, finding himself opposed, devised a plan to carry the girl off, when her father and friends asked for the interference of the Kazi.

Said Azim on his part obtained the influence of some friends in the Government, and the result was that an order was made forbidding Ishan Hodja to allow his daughter to be married until she had reached the full age, and then only on condition that she was first to be proposed to Said Azim, if he should then wish to marry her. This was a very strange decision in itself, but the matter went even farther. Among the persons who acted on behalf of the girl were a son of Yakub Khan and Alim Hadji Yunusof, of whom I have already spoken. They refused to sign this decision, and protested against it, on the ground of its being illegal. Alim Hadji Yunusof was then arrested on the charge of being a disturber of the public peace and of speaking slightingly of the Russian authorities; and in spite of his having the diploma of 'hereditary honourable citizen,'—which indeed he was the first in Tashkent to obtain, Said Azim being the second,—was conveyed to the common prison and stripped and searched. Subsequently, in the face of all complaints and protests, he was exiled without any trial to Lepsa, on the confines of Siberia. The son of Yakub Khan was so frightened that he ran away to Kashgar.[1]

On walking up the chief street of Russian Tashkent to the north one imperceptibly comes into the native town. The square stuccoed buildings cease, low clay walls and little native shops begin, and almost before one knows it the place has entirely changed its aspect. No town in Central Asia presents such a variety as the real native Tashkent. The streets are rarely straight, and in rambling about the town we go up and down hill, turning to this side and that, sometimes between high walls, sometimes beneath the wooden portico of a mosque which mounts high in the air, now along the edge of some deep ravine, and now crossing some rushing stream on a low wooden bridge. Everywhere trees are leaning over the walls, for everywhere there are gardens, and we can leave the street and take a by-path up the edge of some stream where an old wooden millwheel is busily turning, and feel ourselves almost in a country

---

[1] An order was also given to exile Ishan Hodja, if anything could be found against him, but it was not carried out. When Mahmud Yakub Khan, the Envoy of Kashgar, visited St. Petersburg in 1875, his main object was to settle this question and to obtain possession of the girl, who had, he said, been betrothed to the son of his master.

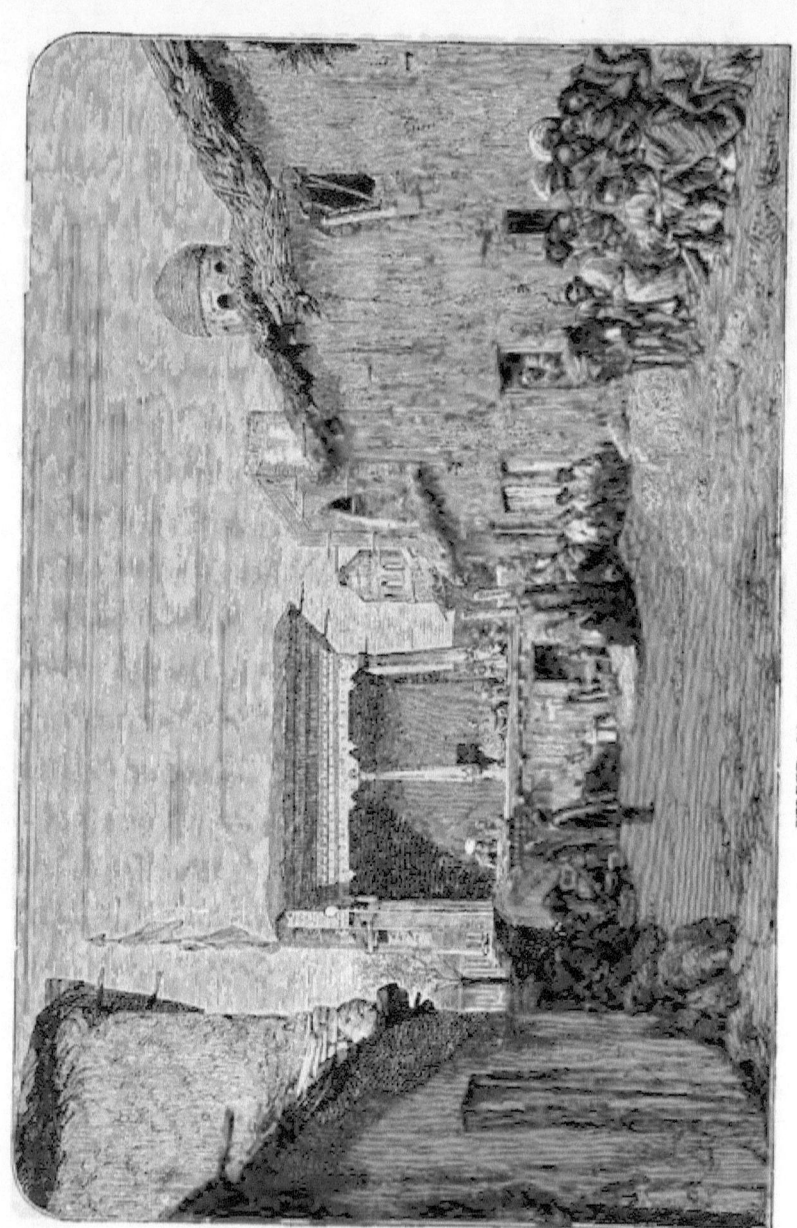

STREET IN TASHKENT, WITH MOSQUE.

nook. An Asiatic mill is a curious affair. The water turns a rude wheel, from the axle of which project large wooden teeth, if so they may be called; on these teeth lie huge beams, and as the wheel goes round these beams slide one by one over the ends of the teeth, causing the other end, made like the head of a hammer, to come down with a crash into a mortar, pulverizing the wheat which is lying ready there.

Sometimes we pass into the large garden of some *medressé* or college, where are shady walks, and where the turf about the edge of a square pond is covered with idlers from the town, for the pupils are mostly in their little rooms reading or reciting their lessons. In some of these retired quarters of the town old Sarts quietly live who never even think of going into the Russian city, and it is said that many of them have never even seen one of the 'infidels.' There are few old buildings, and most of the mosques are small and dilapidated. The only ones worthy of mention are the old ruined mosque of Hodja Akhrar, with its broken mosaics, and the modern *medressé* of Beklar-Bek, with its brick turrets and galleries, which occupies a commanding position over the bazaar. The chief streets are in places, especially on the hills, paved with large stones, intended as aids to vehicles, but which serve rather as obstacles. It is quite possible that in the mud of the winter and autumn these stones may be useful as a safe foundation for the feet of passengers, but during the summer they are deeply buried in the abundant and suffocating dust.

The walls of Tashkent are said to be sixteen miles in length, and had formerly twelve gates, the three adjoining the Russian town having been lately taken down. The wall is in places twelve or fifteen feet high, built of hard blocks of clay, and then plastered over; much thicker at the base than the top, which is crenelated, and has embrasures for cannon. There are places on the inside about half-way up where there is a narrow path and platform, on which it was possible for soldiers to stand and cannon to be placed. A narrow street separates the wall from the houses. Outside of the walls—and the town is about six miles across—the gardens extend for several miles. These gardens, which are thickly planted with trees, and at a a distance entirely conceal the town, are still very beautiful, though they have greatly suffered since the Russian occupation. On one side they were destroyed to make room for the fair, and to afford parade, drill, and practice-grounds to the troops. In addition to this there has been great destruction of trees for the purposes of fuel. At present coal, which is brought from beyond Hodjent, is very dear, and it is found cheaper and pleasanter to cut down the native orchards and burn the wood of peach, apricot, and cherry trees, the supply of which must soon run short. The revolutions of centuries destroyed most of the forests and plantations in Central Asia, and unfortunately Russian colonists, accustomed as they are at home to consider forests as enemies, and to be extravagant in the use of wood, have now almost exhausted what had hitherto been spared. Beyond the gardens we find the open Steppe, which stretches from the Syr Darya, here some forty miles distant, to the mountains. Villages, with their trees and gardens, are seen on all sides, for the population of this district of Kurama is almost as thick as in the valley of the Zarafshan. One of these—Kuiluk, on the Tchirtchik—is the residence of the Russian prefect, and is full of Russian houses; another, Nogai Kurgan, is inhabited solely by Tartars, who had fled here in former times from Russia, or who have come for trade. At Kaplan-Bek is a horse-breeding establishment, the chief use of which is to afford a fat place for a Russian official. While nominally a private enterprise started for the improvement of the race of horses in Turkistan, it was endowed by the Government with some 5,000 acres of land taken from the Kirghiz and 20,000 rubles in money, and has since then received 15,000 rubles more from the fund established for savings banks in the district. The mountains here, called Tchatkal, which are about thirty miles from Tashkent, and which form a beautiful feature in the landscape, contain some interesting villages, inhabited by Tadjiks, especially up the valley of the Tchatkal, where is the picturesque little town of Hodjakent, with its frail bridges resting on huge rocks in the bed of the stream.

The prosperity of Tashkent is entirely dependent on its water-supply, which is the most abundant in Turkistan. All the water is brought from the river Tchirtchik, running down from the neighbouring mountains by a large canal called Bos-su, which leaves the river at Niazbek, some sixteen miles above the city. This canal divides into four others, and these with their ramifications are brought through every part of the town. For the needs of the Russian town it was resolved to construct a new canal, and the work was entrusted to a Russian engineer, who evidently had not studied under the natives the art of irrigation, in which they are so skilful. A huge embankment was erected and a ditch was dug at great cost, but not a drop of water has ever flowed into it, and the work has been abandoned.

The town is divided into four parts or quarters—Shaikantaur, the north-eastern corner of the town; Bish-agatch, the southern part, next the Russian town; Koktchi, the western quarter; and Sibzar, the north-western. The old tradition is that these quarters were formerly separate villages, sometimes at enmity with each other, and that gradually with the increase of trade they became consolidated into one huge town. Each of these quarters has its special *aksakuls* (literally greybeards) or elders, and its chief of police, the whole town being under the government of a Russian commandant or prefect, who lives in a large house on the side nearest the Russian part of the city. The present commandant, Colonel Medynsky, has been in Central Asia since the time of General Tchernaief, and has a thorough knowledge of the people with whom he has to deal, and understands the Turki language sufficiently well to prevent his being imposed upon by incapable interpreters. With the exception of the prefect and his immediate assistants all of the officers of the town and of the police are natives, and the order and good government are very remarkable. Crimes are very rare, theft being the most common; and it is possible to walk or ride through any part of Tashkent at any hour of the night without incurring the slightest danger, or even meeting persons who molest or insult you. I could not but be struck with this evidence of the order kept by the native police, and of the good feeling which existed between the natives and the Russians. The expenses of the town, which are rapidly increasing, are paid out of the taxes, of which there are four kinds; the land, the weight, the *zemsky*, and the communal tax. The land tax, which replaces the old *heradj* and *tanap*, is assessed on the numerous gardens and grain fields within the city limits, and brings in about 22,000 rubles, which go to the government. The weight tax, which is nominally for the preservation of order in the bazaars, amounts to about 7,000 rubles. The *zemsky* tax, which is affected to the repairs of roads, bridges, &c., is a fixed tax of 75 kopeks on each house or kibitka, and brings in nearly 11,000 rubles, the number of houses being estimated at 14,222 with 300 kibitkas. The communal tax is properly for the town expenses, and one quarter of the amount to be raised is assessed *en bloc* on each of the four quarters of the town, it being left to the native officials properly to distribute it on the inhabitants. This tax in 1874 amounted to over 86,000 rubles, making with the other taxes 3·04 rubles per head. In 1868 it was only 16,000 rubles, but has been yearly increasing. As no receipts for taxes are given, a wide door is left open to fraud and extortion.

It is difficult to ascertain exactly the number of inhabitants in Tashkent, as no careful and accurate census has yet been taken. The number of mosques is stated to be 300; and according to the usual estimate of a parish of from thirty to fifty houses to every mosque, and of five inhabitants to each house, the population would be about 60,000. This estimate appears to me to be much too low. There must be very few houses in Tashkent that do not have more than five inhabitants, and persons who know the city well consider the population to be about 120,000, which seems tolerably correct. For the purposes of taxation, the population is estimated at 41,799, or less than three to a house, and taxes are *officially* reported for only that number.

The inhabitants of Tashkent are chiefly Uzbeks, though there are some Tadjiks, and a number of Tartars, Kirghiz, Hindoos, and others. The natives here, as well as in many other places of Turkistan, are known by the name of Sarts, but this name has no ethnological significance, as Mr. Shaw was one of the first to show. According to the natives the whole population of the country is divided into two classes—settled and nomad; the nomads are called *Kazak*, vagabond, or wanderer, as I have previously remarked; and the settled population go by the name of Sarts. If the theory of Mr. Lerch be correct, Sart means merely a city inhabitant.[1] It is remark-

---

[1] Mr. Lerch, in No. 1 of the 'Russische Revue,' traces the words *Iaxartes* and *Iaxartai* to a root *Xartai*, which is the representative of an old Iranic root, *khsatra*,

VIEW IN TASHKENT, LOOKING OVER THE ROOFS OF THE BAZAAR TO THE MEDRESSÉ OF BEKLAR-BEK.

able that in the older writers the word Sart was used at first almost exclusively for the inhabitants of the valley of the Syr, and was not known in Bukhara or Samarkand, though it passed over into Kashgar, Khokand, and Khiva. Abul Ghazi speaks of the Sarts as the settled dwellers in his own country, Khiva, as distinguished from the Uzbeks; whereas in the country conquered by him, as Bukhara, he uses the word Tadjik. At present the name Sart is also known in Bukhara. As used by the nomad tribes, the word 'Sart' is almost a word of abuse, and synonymous with a cowardly and effeminate person.

So far as race is concerned the inhabitants of Turkistan may be broadly divided into those which are of Iranic or Persian origin and those of Turkish descent. To the former belong the Tadjiks, who were the original inhabitants not only of the country between the Syr and the Amu, the ancient Maverannahr, but also of the right bank of the Syr, Khokand and Kashgar. It was Firdusi in the *Shah-nameh* who first made the Amu the boundary between Iran and Turan, but Professor Grigorief has clearly shown that these terms were used in a purely geographical and not in an ethnological sense, and that the contest between Iran and Turan was not a contest between two different races, but a rivalry between two tribes of the same origin.[1] In later times Turan has been confounded with Turk, and it has been used not only as a general term for all races of Turkish descent, but even still more broadly and improperly to express everything which is neither Semitic nor Aryan, and in fact everything of which ethnologists and philologists knew little or nothing. A part of the country was undoubtedly inhabited by the Sacae or Scythians, a people of Aryan race, the distant ancestors of the Germans and Slavonians. The Turkish races were comparatively late immigrants into this region. When they did come they dispossessed in a great measure the Persian or Iranic tribes of the land, confining them either to the cities or compelling them to take refuge in the moun-

as seen in the later Persian *shehr*, city. *Iaxartai* would thus mean the dwellers in cities, and *Iaxartes* the river of cities; and the word *Sart*, the corruption of *Iaxartai*, was passed over from the Iranic nomads to the Turkish nomads as a designation for the settled inhabitants of the lower valley of the Syr, which was then thickly populated and full of flourishing cities.

[1] 'Trudi Vostochnago Otdieleniya Imp. Russ. Archæologitcheskago Obstchestva,' vol. xvi. p. 286. 'The Scythian people Sacae.'

tains, and accordingly we find that not only in the Ak-tau mountains, near Tashkent, are there small scattered villages inhabited exclusively by Tadjiks, but that the mountain ranges about the head-quarters of the Zarafshan are thickly settled with them. With each new wave of Turks the Tadjiks were driven farther back into the mountains. These Tadjik mountaineers are usually called Galtchas. In Bukhara, Samarkand, and Hodjent, Tadjiks form the main element of the city population, but on the right bank of the Syr the proportion is much smaller, the population being nearly all of Turkish origin. The Turkomans call the Tadjiks *Tad*, but this latter name is especially used for the inhabitants of Merv, who were forcibly colonised in the neighbourhood of Samarkand after the capture of that city by the Amir of Bukhara, Shah Murad.

The Uzbeks are the descendants of the Turkish tribes who at various times migrated to this part of Asia, both before and since the time of Tchinghiz Khan. The population of Central Asia has never become fixed, and even now movements among tribes and races continue. Their name means 'independent' or 'free,' from *Uz*, self, and *bek*, a bek, and their origin must be sought in one of those free confederacies which, like that of the Kirghiz-Kazaks, was founded in the fifteenth century. In this way the names of former great nations, such as the Naimans, are preserved to us as appellations of Uzbek clans. According to opinions current in Tashkent and Bukhara the Uzbeks are divided into ninety-two clans or families, but hardly two lists of these clans will agree. In each clan there are several divisions and subdivisions, but many of these have in the course of time even come to be considered as original families. In some cases new clans have arisen, as Yus-ming-kyrk, from the coalescence of parts of three different tribes. Though many of the Uzbeks are settled in the cities north of the Syr, the greater part of them still pursue their nomad life under certain restrictions, and they do not by any means keep to the same places, so that localities which twenty or thirty years ago were inhabited by one clan are now possessed by another. Some of the leading clans are the Ming, to which the present Khan of Khokand belongs, who inhabit Urgut and the mountains to the south-east of Samarkand; the Manghit, of which the Amir of Bukhara is a member, who dwell in the neighbourhood of Karshi, but also have some settlements near Samarkand; the Keneghez, who live in Shahrisabs; the Yus, Kyrk, Kiptchak, Kitai, Kungrad, &c. The Kirghiz, as I have already explained, are of the same stock as the

AN UZBEK.

Uzbeks; and the Karakalpaks, the most of whom occupy the delta of the Amu, near Khiva, though a number of them live near Samarkand, are considered to be only a clan of Uzbeks. The Turkomans, the Guz of old times, are thought by some to be Uzbeks who have become somewhat more separated from the rest; at all events they were a similar confederacy of the same race. The Tartars are known everywhere in Central Asia as Nogai, which is also the name of an Uzbek clan.[1]

The Tadjiks and Uzbeks are readily distinguished from each other, not only in appearance but also in character. The Tadjik is larger and fuller in person, with an ample black beard, and with an air of shrewdness and cunning. He is fickle, untruthful, lazy, cowardly, and boastful, and in every way morally corrupted. The Uzbek is taller and thinner, with a scanty beard, and a longer and more strongly marked face. He is simple in his manners and dress, while the Tadjik is devoted to his personal appearance, and fond of adorning himself. The Uzbeks look upon the Tadjiks with contempt, but at the same time they are dependent upon them. The Tadjiks treat the Uzbeks as fools and children of nature, and smilingly say that they have them entirely in their power. Intermarriages, however, are not uncommon. The Tadjik has none of the pride of race which the Uzbek possesses, and will rarely call himself by the name Tadjik. If asked who he is he will say, 'I am a man of Tashkent;' 'I am from Hodjent;' 'I am a Samarkandi,' as the case may be; while the Uzbek will say, 'I am an Uzbek of the clan of Jalayr or Kalagar,' and will even in many cases particularise the division and subdivision of the clan to which he belongs, though these distinctions have greatly dropped out of use in Turkistan.

The popular story of Shirin and Ferhat well shows the difference between the Uzbek and Tadjik natures. There was once a queen, Shirin Hatun, of great beauty, who lived on the farther side of the Syr Darya. She had two wooers, one a Tadjik and the other an Uzbek named Ferhat. Both were persistent, and as she was at a loss which to choose, an old woman counselled her to give them some difficult work, and to marry the one who succeeded. She therefore commanded them to dig a canal through the Famished Steppe. Ferhat, a strong stalwart fellow, with a simple and straightforward nature, took his spade and dug away all day, trying to turn the

---

[1] Full lists and accounts of the Uzbek clans, which are of some historical and geographical interest, will be found in Khanikoff's 'Description of the Bukhara Khanate,' and in 'Russian Turkistan,' part II., Moscow, 1872; 'Materials for the Statistics of Turkistan,' part III., St. Petersburg, 1874; both in Russian.

channel of the river, and thus formed the cataracts at Bigavat. The Tadjik, crafty, and full of expedients, plaited a wicker of reeds and laid it on the ground across the steppe. Early in the morning the sun's rays reflected from the shining reeds made them appear like a stream of water, and Shirin Hatun thereupon called for the Tadjik and married him. When the Uzbek learned of the deception that had been practised upon him, he was in despair, and threw his spade high up in the air so that as it came down it cut off his head with a single stroke.

The Tadjiks speak a dialect of Persian, which has been greatly influenced by the Turkish dialects of the neighbourhood, and has taken in many Turkish words. It retains, however, many Aryan words that are not used in modern Persian, which is an evidence of the long continuance of the race in these regions.[1] While few Uzbeks speak Tadjik most of the Tadjiks speak the Turki, which is the language of the Uzbeks. The dialect of Turki spoken here is that known to some European scholars by the name of Jagatai, though few in Central Asia now know the name. On being asked what language he speaks a native will either say, 'I speak Turki,' or 'the Uzbek language.' The name Jagatai was, I believe, given to this dialect by the Persians, as the Uzbek tribes of this part of Asia were known to the Persian historians as 'the men of Jagatai,' from the son of Tchinghiz Khan, to whom this region was allotted. As most of the Tadjiks, except in the districts inhabited exclusively by them, speak Turki, it is possible with that language to go anywhere in Central Asia. At the same time the Tadjik is the language of politeness and culture, in which most letters and all state and official documents are written.

The whole population of the Russian province of Turkistan is estimated at about 1,600,000, of whom fully 1,000,000 are nomads. Besides the Tadjiks and Uzbeks there are fragments of other races. For instance, there are many Persians, some who have been originally brought from Persia as slaves, and their descendants, and others who have been forcibly colonised there during some of the wars, as, for example, the inhabitants of Merv, who were settled in the neighbourhood of Samarkand. There are also a few Arabs living in the neighbourhood of

---

[1] A critical study of the Tadjik dialect, by Prof. Grigorief, will be found in his edition of the 'Memoirs of Mirza Shems.' Kazan, 1861.

Katta-kurgan, near Karshi, and at Kukertli, on the Amu Darya. Those near Katta-kurgan speak Tadjik and Turki; the rest speak a debased and corrupted Arabic. With regard to them there are two traditions—one that they are the descendants of the Arabs who forcibly introduced Moham-

A TADJIK.

medanism into the country, which they themselves believe; and another that they were settled here by Timur after he had conquered the Western powers. They weave woollen and cotton stuffs and make excellent carpets. The number of Arabs in the district of Zarafshan is estimated at 2,000 families.

In every city, and even in many of the smaller towns of Central Asia, there are numbers of Hebrews and Hindoos, the former having been in the country for centuries, the latter coming temporarily from the neighbourhood of Shikarpur for the purposes of trade. There are to be seen at times in the towns people called Liuli, who are apparently the same as our gypsies. The women tell fortunes, cure the sick, and carry on a small traffic. The men trade in horses, and have almost a monopoly of leeches, which they collect from the ponds and streams. Connected with these are two other races apparently much the same—the Jiutchi, who are probably Kafirs from Kafiristan; and the Mazang, who are settled in some small villages, and are agriculturists, though their women traverse the whole country as pedlars with small wares. The Liuli, on the contrary, are nomads, as gypsies are everywhere. Externally they are all Mussulmans, but it is doubtful whether they would be able to repeat a single prayer, and as a general rule they neglect all the ordinances of religion. I should also mention here another small, mysterious people, called Andi, who inhabit Mashad, the second post station between Tchimkent and Aulié-ata and three other villages in the immediate neighbourhood. They speak a dialect of Turki, allow the women to be unveiled, intermarry among themselves, and seem to be ashamed of their origin, as they are unwilling to admit that they are Andi.

The history of Tashkent is surrounded with much obscurity, as the historical documents relating to the troublous times in Central Asia are but few; and though it is said that a chronicle of Tashkent exists, European eyes have not yet seen it. A city existed on this spot, or more probably some twenty-five miles to the south-west, at a place now called Old Tashkent, which was known by the name of Tchatch or Jadj, and is mentioned in the Shah-nameh, and even earlier by the Chinese traveller of the seventh century, Hiouen-Thsang. The Arabic writers found difficulty in pronouncing and spelling the name, and it then became altered to Shash. The present name Tashkent probably originated with the Turkish nomad tribes when they came into the country, Shash, which meant nothing for them, being changed to *Tash*, a stone. *Kent* is a Persian word meaning town. Lying on the borders of Maverannahr,

Tchatch, or Tashkent, which must even then have been a large and rich town, belonged sometimes to the sovereigns of Bukhara and Samarkand, and sometimes to the Turkish tribes, who lived farther to the north-east — and whose capital for a long time was Bala-Sagun. When this kingdom was overthrown by Tchingbiz Khan, Tashkent passed into his possession, and was ruled over in connection with the neighbouring countries by his son Jagatai and his successors. After the reign of Timur it remained in the possession of his successors until they were conquered by the great Sheibani Khan. In 1598 it was taken by the Kirghiz, who were just then at the height of their power, from Abdullah Khan, the last great sovereign of Samarkand and Bukhara. The Kirghiz retained possession of the place and the adjacent province until 1723, when it was taken by Galdan-Tsyran, the ruler of Jungaria, who was then greatly extending his dominions. This dynasty was overthrown in 1769, and it is probable that from that time the bekship of Tashkent enjoyed a semi-independent position, paying allegiance at times to the ruler of Bukhara, until about the beginning of the present century, when it was captured by Alim Khan of Khokand. With the exception of the short period when Khokand was subjugated by Bukhara, Tashkent remained in the possession of Khokand until it was captured by the Russians, although always a great rival to Khokand, and ready on the slightest provocation to rebel. At times, indeed, it was the seat of the government.

The capture of Tashkent by General Tchernaief, considering the small force he had at his disposal, is one of the most remarkable things in the history of the Russian conquests in Central Asia. Immediately after the capture of Tchimkent, in October 1864, General Tchernaief thought that as the Kushbegi of Tashkent had died at Tchimkent, and many of the garrison had been drawn from Tashkent, it might be possible to take that city by a *coup de main*. He accordingly advanced to it, and on October 15 placed a battery in position, and after making a breach in the walls gave the assault. He found, however, that the city was much more strongly defended than he had expected, and was repulsed with a loss of sixteen killed and sixty-two wounded, and returned to Tchimkent. A large body

THE CITADEL AT TCHIMKENT.

of Khokand troops soon after marched towards the city Turkistan, but after the severe fight at Ikan were obliged to retire. It was found that the Amir of Bukhara, being alarmed at the progress of the Russians, was massing troops near Uratepé with the design of taking possession of Tashkent, to prevent it falling into Russian hands. As the disposition of the inhabitants of Tashkent was not very favourable towards the rulers of Khokand, and they were suffering under the despotism of the Regent Alim Kul, General Tchernaief feared lest they might be enticed over to the Bukharan side, and therefore considered it necessary to take some measures to prevent this. He accordingly attacked and took the small fortress of Niazbek, situated more than sixteen miles to the north-east of Tashkent, on the river Tchirtchik, which commanded the water supply of Tashkent, and thus placed the city to a certain extent at his mercy. As the peaceful party in Tashkent were favourably inclined towards the Russians, but was not yet able to declare itself openly in their favour, General Tchernaief moved down to a new position some six miles from the city, and made a reconnaissance of its north-eastern side, during which it had been agreed that the Russian partisans should attack the garrison and open the gates of the city, but on the same day the Regent of Khokand, Mullah Alim Kul, with an army of 6,000 men and forty guns, arrived and entered the city. On the next day, May 21, Alim Kul and 7,000 men made an attack upon the Russian camp, but after a severe fight were driven to the very walls of the town, where they took refuge, though it was thought unadvisable by the Russians to make an assault at that time. In this affair the Russians had some twenty wounded and bruised, and the enemy lost more than 300 killed, among whom was, as was soon learned, Alim Kul himself. The death of Alim Kul made a great impression not only in Tashkent but in all Khokand, but the tide of affairs was rather to the profit of the Bukharan partisans, and an embassy—among whom was Ata Bek, the present Atalyk of Khokand—was sent to the Amir of Bukhara with a request for aid and the expression of a desire to be received as Bukharan subjects. In order to prevent any possibility of aid being sent by the Amir, and to show the inhabitants that any resistance was useless, General Tchernaief moved his forces in the direction of the fortress of Tchinaz, which covered the ferry across the Syr Darya; but when he was still some twelve miles from the place the aksakal came to inform him that the garrison had fled across the river and that the ferry was destroyed. Only a small force was then sent to occupy Tchinaz, and General Tchernaief returned to take up his position on the Bukhara road, some three miles from the walls of Tashkent. The inhabitants of the city were in great distress from want of water, there being but one spring in the town, and were even short of provisions. They were in the habit of sending parties out into the surrounding gardens and fields to cut the then ripe corn and to pasture the cattle. This was often prevented by the Russian attacks, and the cattle were seized. They rested their only hope of deliverance upon the Amir, who had not refused assistance, but had demanded that the young Khan, Seid Sultan, should be sent to him as a hostage. On receipt of this intelligence the Khan, with 200 of his immediate followers, fled on the night of June 21, and at the same time a small party of Bukharans led by Ishan Bek entered Tashkent and took command of the city. The forces of the Amir also began to show themselves at various points along the Syr Darya. It was impossible formally to besiege the city, the walls of which were sixteen miles round, and enclosed a population of considerably over 100,000. It would also have been as disastrous to the Russian policy to retreat from the city and allow it to be taken possession of by the Bukharans as it was dangerous to risk a drawn battle with the strong army of the Amir, when the forces of General Tchernaief amounted at the most to only 2,000 men and twelve guns. It was finally resolved to attempt an assault, which was fixed for the early morning of June 27, on the Kamelan gate, which, leading into the highest part of the city, would, when taken, render it possible to command the town. At three o'clock the storming party, under command of Captain (now Major-General) Abramof, made a successful assault on the walls, surprised the watch party and opened the gates, after silencing the artillery fire which was opened on them from various barbettes, and Abramof went along the city wall some six miles to the Kara-Sarai gates, leading to that part of the city where the Russian partisans were supposed to live. Major De La Croix at the same time entered by the Khokand gate and took possession of that part of the citadel. During the whole of that day the troops were occupied in making progress through the various streets of the bazaar, finding at every step barricades, and the strongest resistance from soldiers and others stationed in the gardens and houses. At night everything seemed to be quiet, but on the next morning, the 28th, when a force was sent to collect the enemy's guns and to blow up the citadel, the affray was renewed, and it was found that barricades, hastily formed of carts and trees, had been everywhere erected. It was necessary first to clear these away, and to stop the fire of the enemy, and the whole day was spent in the contest. At last in the evening messengers came asking for quarter, and promising to formally surrender the city on the following morning. At the appointed hour a deputation from the city, consisting of the aksakals and magistrates and the most respected inhabitants, arrived and surrendered the city unconditionally, and measures were immediately taken for the restoration of order. Complete tranquillity prevailed, and not another shot was fired. The whole number of the defenders amounted to some 30,000, of whom more than 5,000 cavalry escaped, and were pursued by 39 Cossacks as far as the river Tchirtchik, into which they threw themselves in great confusion. Among the trophies were 16 large standards, 63 cannon, and 72,000 lbs. of powder. The Russian loss was 25 killed and 117 wounded. The moderate party in the town explained to General Tchernaief, that they were very anxious to keep order, and a few days after the surrender requested his signature to a proclamation, in which they gave the strongest injunctions for discipline, and for the resumption by the people of their usual employments, and, what was strange for Mussulmans, spoke in the highest terms of the Russian Emperor.[1] The conduct of

---

[1] This proclamation, which was written in Turki by the Mussulman authorities of Tashkent of their own motion, is so curious that I quote its beginning and end:

'By order of the great white Tsar, and by command of his lieutenant, the Governor Iskender Tchernaief (this is a compliment referring to Alexander the Great, his name being Michael), we hereby declare to the inhabitants of the city of Tashkent that they must in everything act according to the commands of Almighty God and the teaching of the orthodox religion of Mohammed, on whom and on whose descendants be the blessing of God, and to the laws established by him, not departing from them one iota. Let all, so far as they can, act for the advantage and profit of the country. Let them say everywhere their prayers five times a

General Tchernaief made a most favourable impression upon the natives, and from that time on there was not the slightest trouble of any kind on the part of the native population. Innumerable stories are told of the courage and simplicity of General Tchernaief, and among them that, on the evening of the surrender of the town, he rode through the streets, which were hardly then clear of the dead, attended by only two or three Cossacks, and took a native bath. Immediately afterwards one of the crowd that followed him offered him a bowl of tea, which he drank without the slightest hesitation. Such things excited the greatest admiration for him, and when he was removed from command his departure was witnessed with regret, and the natives long for his return. There is even a legend that on the anniversary of the capture of Tashkent people go to the Kamelan gate, where the storming took place, and pray for his soul. The people of Central Asia are in the habit of

day, not passing by the appointed time an hour or even a minute. Let the Mullahs constantly go to their schools and teach the laws of the Mohammedan faith, and not waste the time of their pupils by an hour or by a minute. Let children not for one hour miss their lessons, and let the teachers try to collect the children in school, and not give them hours of idleness, and in case of need use strong measures, even beating, to make them learn, and if the parents show carelessness in this, let them in accordance with the Mohammedan *Shariat* be brought to the Reis, the head of the city, or Kazi Kilian, and be well punished. Let the inhabitants of the country occupy themselves with their work. Let the people of the bazaar carry on their trade and not pass their time idly. Let every man carry on his own work. Let nothing be thrown into the streets, and let them be kept clean. Your Mohammedan religion forbids you to drink *buza* and whisky, to play at games of chance, or to be licentious, therefore beware and keep back from every innovation which is contrary to the laws of religion.' [Here follow various minute regulations about weights, measures, trade, &c.] 'All the inhabitants of Tashkent, rich and poor, must exactly fulfil all that has been said above. Houses, gardens, fields, lands, and water-mills, of which you have possession, will remain your property. The soldiers will take nothing from you. You will not be made Russian Cossacks. There will be no quartering of soldiers on you. No one in service will come into your courtyards, or if he come let us know at once, and he will be punished. Great kindness is shown to you, and therefore you should pray for the health of the white Tsar. If any one kill anybody, or rob a merchant, he will be judged by Russian laws. If any one kill himself, his property goes to his heir according to the *Shariat*; we will take none of his property. The tenth part which is taken from the products of Government land, I, the Governor Iskender Tchernaief, remit to you for the present year, but afterwards it will be in accordance with the will of our great white Tsar to show you according to his own disposition still greater kindness. 1282, 6th day of the month Safar (July 2, 1865).'

giving nicknames to their rulers; calling, for instance, Nasrullah Khan, the late Amir of Bukhara, 'the Butcher,' and the Khan of Khokand 'the dog.' The name of Tchernaief they metamorphosed into Shir-Naib, 'the Lion Viceroy.' Some apparently mistook the name for a title, for the Bek of Jizakh in writing, in 1866, to General Romanofsky began, 'To the newly-arrived Tchernaief from the White Tsar.'

CHAPTER IV.

MUSSULMAN LIFE IN TASHKENT.

A merchant's house—Its furniture—Mussulman devotions—Dress—Food—Drinks—Narcotics—Native games—Sporting—Falcons—Horses—Vehicles—Singing—Musical instruments—Dances of boys—A dance of women—The festival of Zang-ata—Veneration for old trees—Circumcision—Marriage—Wedding feasts—Divorce—Maladies of the Sarts—Cholera—Parasites—Medicines—Funerals—Mourning—Asiatic influence on Russia—Islam—Different sects of Mohammedans—Mosques and worship there—Religious orders—Visit to performances of Jahria—Education—Primary schools—Colleges—Their arrangements and studies—The Kazis—Native courts among the nomad and settled population—Mussulman law—Christianity and Islam.

FROM my numerous acquaintances I soon had an opportunity of obtaining an insight into Mussulman life at Tashkent, for I was taken to make visits, and was very frequently asked to little entertainments, or to go in the evening and take tea and *pilaf*. These entertainments are all very much alike, but let us take as an example an evening with Doda Mohammed.

Going down through the bazaar we turn up hill into a street so narrow, and so full of large sharp stones, that it was evidently not made for wheels, and after some time come to another narrow lane, with its long reach of blank clay wall, for here no windows ever look into the street. Eventually, after two or three mistakes, we arrive at a small door which is half-open; on calling out, three handsome lads in long loose shirts, girt with handkerchiefs round the waist, and close-fitting skull-caps, appear with smiling faces, greet us with the customary 'Aman,' and take our horses. We enter, and find a large court-yard nearly surrounded with sheds filled with horses—the only kind of stable which is used here. We are taken through another door into still another courtyard, on two sides of which are the balconies of the house. This is the *tish-kari* or man's court, and beyond, through a door and a narrow passage, is the *itch-kari*, or woman's court. Doda Mahammed, being rich, has as many as three courtyards, but no one who pretends to have a house at all has less than two; for the women must have some place where they can be at their ease, and where men do not enter. This man's court has a smooth hard clay floor, with little strips of turf, and on one side a platform raised a foot or eighteen inches above the ground, and near by a square pond, shaded by trees, which is fed by a little ditch from one of the main canals, and which provides the water for drinking as well as for purification.

We are shown into the guest-room, where we sit on Turkoman rugs, which cover the floor; meanwhile, the air being pleasanter outside, other rugs are taken out and placed on the platform; thin striped silken mattresses are laid along the edge, and pillows are given us to put our elbows on in case we find sitting too fatiguing. The natives sit at times cross-legged, but it is considered much more polite and respectful to kneel down and sit upon the feet. Tiresome as it is at first, one gradually becomes accustomed to it, though much depends upon the dress, and with the loose native trousers one finds it perfectly easy to do without chairs. The houses are all much alike; there is one large room opening on the portico, the guest-chamber, and opposite one or two smaller ones opening out of it. The living-rooms in the woman's court are in every respect similar to these. In each room there are two or three doors, with double leaves, opening inwardly, hung on a sort of pivot, let into the lintel and threshold instead of hinges, usually carved with delicate arabesques, in which work the natives have great proficiency. There are no windows, except oblong openings over the doors, sometimes filled in with a little lattice-work, and usually covered with white paper. The walls are plastered, and sometimes decorated with a pretty cornice in alabaster work, and usually have a large number of niches with arched tops, which serve as shelves for the few books, the clothes, jars of sweetmeats, ewers, and teapots. The walls are frequently painted with representations of fruit, bouquets or pots of wonderful flowers, and sometimes with small arabesques; in rare cases there is the representation of some animal, but this is avoided, as being in contradiction to the injunctions of the

Koran. The ceiling is made of small round willow-branches fitted between the rafters, and is usually painted a bright ultramarine blue, picked out with red and yellow, and even occasionally with a little gold, so that when nicely done it is really very beautiful.

Besides the rugs and mattresses there is no furniture, except perhaps a small round table, a few inches in height, on which sweets and fruits are placed for the guests, or a carved or painted wooden cupboard. I should not omit one peculiarity: in the corner of the room there is very frequently a little basin, sunk a little below the floor, for the purpose of ablution before prayers, beside which a small ewer of water is placed. The floors themselves are of clay, though in all good houses well covered with rugs and carpets. In the outer court are kept all the things necessary for the horses, saddles, bridles, blankets, and so forth, and those objects which are specially used by men. In the inner, or woman's court, are the cooking utensils, and the special articles of female use, besides bundles of cotton, silk, cloth, and all the articles which women gather about them. The women have no more furniture than is found on the men's side, except possibly a broad bed made of a wooden frame, raised but a few inches from the floor, over which a net work of rope is stretched. Most people, however, sleep on a rug, or a thin quilt or mattress laid on the floor. After trying a quantity of such beds on various occasions I began to understand how the prince in the Arabian tale could feel a pea under seven mattresses. Indeed, he would have been well hardened if he had not felt it. Externally the houses have no ornament, except possibly the carved pillars of the portico, and they often rest upon no foundation except the earth, being built immediately up from it, of sunburnt clay bricks. The roof is flat, made of reeds or thatch, and then thickly plastered over with clay, furnishing abode to innumerable scorpions, which are constant guests in the native houses, and occasionally to tarantulas and other venomous spiders. The houses are generally but of one story, though sometimes there is a small upper room, called *balakhana* (Persian *bala*, or *baliand*, upper, and *khana*, room), whence we get our word *balcony*.

When we get well seated on the platform a piece of striped coloured calico or silk is laid down, and trays of sweets are brought in to us. This is called a *dostar-khan* (literally table-cloth), and is a necessary accompaniment to hospitality in Central Asia. The dishes consist of almonds and pistachio nuts, either alone or in sugar coverings, pastes and candies of various flavours, and known by the name of *halvah*, little cakes, and always the thin wafer-like bread which is eaten here. If fruit is to be had it is also introduced, and there are occasionally some rare sweet dishes, such as almonds in sugar-syrup, or rose-leaves preserved in honey, or one dish which is much liked here, carrots chopped fine in honey. While we tempt our appetite with these various delicacies we talk on various subjects, from common acquaintance and the news of the day to points of religion or of local history. One native, a tall good-natured man of forty, amuses me immensely, for he has learned Russian, and has taken a great fancy to Russian society, knowing almost every lady in Tashkent by her Christian name; he has even picked up a few words of French, with which he interlards his conversation. It is now, however, towards sunset, and our entertainers, without any excuse, one by one retire to the pond to perform their ablutions, for everyone has carefully to wash his face and hands and his arms up to the elbows. It is amusing to see what dexterity is acquired by a little practice; the hand is raised, there is one twirl of the wrist, and the water runs evenly from the hand to the elbow. In drinking too, the Asiatic applies his mouth to the hollow at the wrist, and not a drop is wasted. Each arm must be washed three times, and then there is a triple ablution of the face, 'including all the seven orifices,' eyes, ears, nose, and mouth, and as far back as to the nape of the neck. After this it is the turn of the feet, but this is an amusing example of formality and practice. The men, as a general rule, object to taking off their boots, and merely draw their wet fingers over the toes, as a symbol that their feet have been washed. They then put on their turbans, pull the dangling end well down over the left side, and standing on a carpet or a clean robe spread on the ground, with their faces towards Mecca, they repeat their prayers. On this occasion, the prayer is a short one, the *Namaz Digar*, said immediately before sunset. There is not the slightest hesitation or feeling of shamefacedness because foreigners are present, but the religious duty is gone through as a matter of course. They then return to our company, but so soon as the sun has set it becomes necessary to repeat the second evening prayer, or *Namaz Sham*, though additional ablution is not in this case practised, the effects of the former one lasting at least ten minutes. There are five prayers during the day, which every Mussulman is bound to observe: the *Namaz Bomdat*, immediately before sunrise: the *Namaz Pishim*, about noon, though an hour or two later makes no difference; the *Namaz Digar*, of which I spoke, just before sunset; the *Namaz Sham*, immediately after; and about nine o'clock in the evening the *Namaz Hoftan*, which is the signal for sleep. This last prayer is the longest, but none of them are long. These names of the prayers are those used in Central Asia, though not those sanctioned by Mussulman law. Popular usage has given to each a rhyme, specifying some daily duty which is coincident in time, as for instance: *namaz digar kari digar*, put the kettle on; *hoftan-horaftan*, go to bed; *sham*, light the candles.

Prayers being over, Doda Mohammed and his friends find it more comfortable in this hot weather to take off their turbans, and sit merely in their little embroidered skull-caps, even taking these off to cool their shaven skulls. The dress of the Central Asiatic is very simple. He wears loose baggy trousers, usually made of coarse white cotton stuff, fastened tightly round the waist with a cord and tassel; this is a necessary article of dress, and is never or rarely taken off, at all events not in the presence of another. Frequently when men are at work this is the only garment, and in that case it is gradually turned up under the cord or rolled up on the legs, so that the person is almost naked. Over this is worn a long shirt, either white or of some light-coloured print, reaching almost to the feet, and with a very narrow aperture for the neck, which renders it somewhat difficult to put the head through. The sleeves are long and loose. Beyond this there is nothing more but what is called the *tchapan*, varying in number according to the weather or the whim of the person. The *tchapan* is a loose gown cut very sloping in the neck, with strings to tie it together in front, and inordinately large sleeves, made with an immense gore, and about twice as long as is necessary, exceedingly inconvenient, but useful to conceal the hands, as Asiatic politeness dictates. In summer these are usually made of

Russian prints, or of the native *alatcha*, a striped cotton material, or of silk, either striped or with most gorgeous Eastern patterns in bright colours, especially red, yellow, and green. I have sometimes seen men with as many as four or five of these gowns even in summer; they say that it keeps out the heat. In winter one gown will frequently be made of cloth, and lined with fine lambskin or fur. The usual girdle is a large handkerchief or a small shawl; at times a long scarf wound several times tightly round the waist. The Jews in places under native rule are allowed no girdle but a bit of rope or cord, as a mark of ignominy. From the girdle hang the accessory knives and several small bags and pouches, often prettily embroidered, for combs, money, &c. On the head, there is a skullcap; these in Tashkent are always embroidered with silk; in Bukhara they are usually worked with silk or worsted in cross-stitch, in gay patterns. The turban, called *tchil-petch* or 'forty turns,' is very long; and if the wearer has any pretence to elegance it should be of fine thin material, which is chiefly imported from England. It requires considerable experience to wind one properly round the head so that the folds will be well made, and the appearance fashionable. One extremity is left to fall over the left shoulder, but is usually, except at prayer-time, tucked in over the top. Should this end be on the right shoulder it is said to be in the Afghan style. I have said that the majority of turbans are white, and this is true in Tashkent, though white is especially the colour of the Mullahs and religious people, whose learning is judged by the size of their turbans. In general merchants prefer blue, striped, or chequered material. At home the men usually go barefooted, but on going out wear either a sort of slippers with pointed toes and very small high heels, or long soft boots, the sole and upper being made of the same material. In the street one must in addition put on either a slipper or galosh, or wear riding-boots, made of bright green horse-hide, with turned-up pointed toes and very small high heels.

The dress of the women in shape and fashion differs but little from that of the men, as they wear similar trousers and shirts, though in addition they have long gowns, usually of bright-coloured silk, which extends from the neck to the ground. They wear an innumerable quantity of necklaces and little amulets, pendents in their hair, and earrings, and occasionally even a nose-ring. This is by no means so ugly as is supposed: a pretty girl with a turquoise ring in one nostril is not at all unsightly; on the contrary, there is something piquant in it. Usually when outside of the houses all respectable women wear a heavy black veil, reaching to their waists, made of woven horsehair, and over that is thrown a dark blue or green khalat, the sleeves of which, tied together at the ends, dangle behind. The theory of this dull dress is, that the women desire to escape observation, and certainly for that purpose they have devised the most ugly and unseemly costume that could be imagined. They are, however, very inquisitive, and occasionally in by-streets one is able to get a good glance at them before they pull down their veils. The look of an infidel, or Kaffir, is not supposed to be so injurious to them as that of a Mussulman.

In the towns under native rule the morals of the people are thoroughly looked after by the officials, but in Tashkent and other Russian towns there are increasing numbers of women of loose character and morals, for many native women take up this life rather than live with husbands whom they do not love, and even to get a divorce they will pretend to be ill and go to the Russian hospital to be examined by the doctors, a proceeding which of course disgusts their husbands, and renders a separation possible and easy. These women are always unveiled, and are seen constantly walking in the streets, or riding on carts to pic-nics or places of pleasure, and from them one soon gets some idea of the female type. It is perhaps unfortunate that the unveiling of the women has begun with that class, because now no respectable woman dares to go unveiled, and even the Jewish and Tartar women wear veils to preserve themselves from disagreeable remarks as they pass through the streets. It is believed that if General Tchernaief at the capture of Tashkent had ordered the women to go without their veils, the command would have been readily acquiesced in, but now it is somewhat difficult to bring about such a reform by external pressure, and it is not easy to know when the Mussulmans themselves will become sufficiently enlightened to allow their wives to show themselves in public.

But while my friends have been discussing the last scandal

—a woman who unsuccessfully demands a divorce from her husband, who refuses to live with her, but has just married an unveiled woman, and questions are raised as to who is the proper person to bring it before the Kazi, for the woman herself is kept prisoner in the house—and while I have been examining their dress and thinking about their wives, supper has been brought in. It consists of *pilaf* or *palau*, a dish composed of rice and mutton. Its preparation is very simple: a quantity of mutton tallow or fat is melted in a pot, and the mutton, after being cut into pieces, is stewed in this; when the meat is cooked it is taken out, and the rice, which has been properly washed and cleaned, is put in and stewed until done; with this are mixed usually small thin slicings of carrot, and the whole is turned out on a large platter, the pieces of meat and bones being placed artistically on the top. One of the company then takes his knife from his girdle and cuts the meat into smaller pieces, distributing it at different sides of the rice; so as to be convenient for the guests. Everyone eats with the right hand (as the left is destined for more menial services), taking up the rice with his fingers, pressing it into a ball in the palm of his hand, and skilfully thrusting it into his mouth. If it be a grand feast the *pilaf* is occasionally improved by having a chicken cooked with it, in place of the mutton, and raisins and pistachio nuts are added. An occasional dish of *pilaf*, with plenty of salt and pepper, is pleasant, but it is too greasy and insipid to be long agreeable to an European palate. Other native dishes are *kavardak*, composed of scraps of mutton stewed in grease, together with pieces of bread, and *kavap* (a name which is naturalised with us as cabobs), small bits of meat roasted on a spit, and a hash of mutton and carrots, which is not bad. I have frequently eaten also *tchushvara*, *pilmen* and *nanty*, mutton mixed with onions and thickly sprinkled with pepper, enclosed in paste, and boiled or stewed. Mutton is almost the only meat. Horse-flesh—on which, as all storybooks inform us, Tartars exclusively feed—I never saw used, and when I spoke of it everyone denied having eaten it, but said that it was very common in some other place. I once, in passing through a small village, saw a horse being cut up, apparently for food, by Kirghiz, and I was told that the horse-sausages and roast young colt of Khokand were celebrated, but

I never could get a taste. The bread, which is usually of wheat, is made very small and round like a bun, and is cooked by being plastered on to the side of a round oven. Sometimes it is very large and very thin, like a tremendous wafer, and when fresh is very good.

For drink there is nothing but water and green tea. It is always considered necessary to drink water after eating *pilaf*, for the natives say the rice has to be planted in water: it grows in water, it is boiled in water, and consequently one must drink water with it. Green tea—for black tea was not known here till the Russians came—is drunk at all times of the day, and is sometimes very good; it is certainly a great restorative on a warm day, as it cools rather than heats one, and though I drank it often I found that I experienced no bad effects from it. A favourite drink, especially in the early morning, is *shirin-tchai*, green tea thick with cream or melted tallow. The Koran prohibits the use of wines or other liquors, and none are to be had here, though now the natives, except of the strictest principles, rarely refuse a glass of liquor when offered by a Russian, and the Jews have long been known to make a coarse red wine. It is strange, however, that with all the different fruits which abound in this country the natives have not invented some cooling fruity drink which would not have intoxicating powers. There is a liquor something like beer made from grain, called *buza*, which is very intoxicating, having a stupefying effect, and is much used by the Kirghiz. If I may judge of *buza* from one trial, the taste is not unpleasant. The effects of this drink have been found so great on the Russian soldiers that an attempt has been made to stop its sale in Tashkent. Twice I wandered through the Kirghiz quarter vainly asking for *buza*, but no one knew where it was made or could be had, though several whom we asked were evidently tipsy from it. At last a boy, after a great display of ignorance as to the drink, admitted having some in a jug he was carrying, and permitted us to taste it. Sometimes on hot days sour milk is drunk mixed with water, and in Tashkent one can get the *kumys*, or liquor made of mare's milk, which is so much drunk by the Kirghiz on the Steppe. At intervals the *tchilim*, or Bukharan water-pipe, is passed round, for Doda Mohammed is not a puritan and smokes. This pipe, which is in principle the same as the *nargileh*, is usually made of a gourd prettily mounted in brass, with a long tube coming up through the water, which holds at the top a small earthern or brass receptacle for the coals and tobacco, and on the side a similar tube for the mouth-piece. The mouth-pipe is often wanting, and the smoker must apply his lips directly to the hole in the gourd, but he needs much practice before he can draw up the smoke, and then place his finger on the opposite orifice and get a good whiff. Tobacco is chiefly used by the natives in the form of a fine dark green powder, varying in colour according to the quality, of which a small quantity is placed on the tongue and sucked or chewed. This tobacco, if the user can afford it, is carried in a small bottle of Chinese jade or nephrite, but more usually in a very small gourd fitted with a stopper. Snuff, as such, I rarely saw used. Opium is smoked by some, but it is rather rare in Tashkent, and only persons very far gone in dissipation would indulge in this taste. The narcotic which is usually smoked is *bang*, which is prepared from the Indian hemp. Another substance frequently used for its narcotic effects is *kukhnar*, a liquor made by soaking in water the bruised capsules of the poppy after the seeds have been taken out; this is a dark brownish liquor with an intensely bitter taste, and when taken habitually it produces very bad effects. Temporary exhilaration is soon succeeded by stupefaction, and that by nervous prostration. The *kukhnar* drinker is soon forced to take large quanties several times a day, and to use the greatest caution in his diet; above all he must abstain from very hot and from very sour drinks.

At last the time came for us in the forms of Tashkent politeness to ask permission of our host to retire. Hands were pressed on each side, and the whole company, with candles and small iron lamps, in form like those from Pompeii, saw us to our horses.

As we were riding homeward through the moonlit streets I asked my friend the Mullah Hair-ullah what were the amusements of Mussulmans. His answer was that he himself read or sometimes made translations, or said his prayers, but that in Central Asia people had no amusements. The men occupy themselves with their horses or sometimes shoot, but otherwise, he said, with the exception of festivals, where a large number of persons were collected together, and where dancing sometimes took place, there were no amusements of any kind, and people passed their days in sleeping or in conversation. 'But the children?' I said. 'Our religion, you know,' he replied, 'forbids children to have any toys. Their studies must be directed towards religion and towards war, and for that reason they may be allowed to ride, and may use the bow and the gun, but nothing else.' This method of education, which reminds one of how Xenophon said that the Persian boys were taught to ride, to use the bow, and to speak the truth, is, however, not thoroughly carried out in practice, for I have often seen the boys in Tashkent and Samarkand playing games similar to those played in Europe, and especially a game with knucklebones, which is quite as common in Central Asia as it is in Russia, and another game where bones are placed at intervals on the ground, and the players, standing off at some distance, toss another bone at them, pocketing as many as they are able to knock down and displace. Girls have dolls roughly made of rags, and commonly play ball. Chess is frequently played, and in Samarkand there is a great deal of gambling and betting, with cards, dice, and especially at odds and evens, for which last game some even have a real passion, constantly tossing little stones from one hand to another and rapidly counting them. Cards were first brought from Russia, although long before the Russian occupation, and most of the games played are those which are favourites with the Russian peasantry and merchants. A very common gambling game is, for a group of men to sit in a circle, each placing before him a copper coin, and bets are then made as to whose coin will first have a fly on it. At the Yak bazaar at Tashkent, for a fortnight during the early spring, there are wrestling matches.

The chase is rarely practised by city dwellers, though all who live in the country indulge in it, especially with falcons, which are here trained in large quantities for this purpose, as well as other birds of prey of all kinds, and even large eagles. A matchlock, which is the most common firearm, is an uncomfortable article of sporting equipment, because it is large and heavy, the barrel being very long and solid, and takes a long time to reload. The match is so placed that on pulling the trigger it drops down into the priming-pan. The matchlock is usually provided with two supports, so that it can be rested on the ground, and in this case, as the supports are short, it is necessary for the marksman to lie at full length. I have seen men who were very good shots, and on one of my visits to him I remember that Jura Bek stood on the portico, and leaning the matchlock against a column, took the head off a sparrow at the top of a large tree. Jura Bek too shot very well with the blow-gun, a weapon which I was surprised to see, as I was not aware that it was used in Asia, though he told me that in Shahrisabs it was very common. It is a long tube, usually of reed, in which a small bullet is put in at one end and expelled by the breath, and its use is much less difficult than one might suppose, requiring no great expenditure of wind.

All Uzbeks are extremely fond of horses, and they certainly have some remarkably good ones, the two chief breeds here being the Kirghiz and the Argamak. The Kirghiz horse is a small hardy animal, capable of enduring the extremes of cold and heat, and of going long distances without fatigue; it is much the same as the little Cossack horses which are used on the Ural, and which are frequently seen in St. Petersburg. The Argamak is probably a mixed breed, the best being found in Bukhara. The animal is rather large, but slightly built, and for short distances is very fast; but it is fitter for show than for use. A good Argamak will command a very large price, but the horses in common use, which seem to be of a mixed breed, are by no means dear, thirty rubles being an average price. Another breed, *Kara-bair*, made by crossing an Argamak with a Kirghiz mare, is highly esteemed. The Turkoman horses, which are not seen at all in Tashkent, are still different from the Argamaks, being of purer breed and more like the Arabian horses, and are capable of undergoing any amount of fatigue and hardship. A thoroughly good Turkoman horse it would be almost impossible to buy, as only great necessity would make its owner part with it. The bridles in use are of the ordinary description, with a rough, jointed bit; the saddle is very small, made of wood, brightly painted red or green, and with a sharp peak flattened at the top, which is made of bone or ivory, with which substance the edges of the saddle also are inlaid. Quantities of elk-horns are brought from beyond Lake Issyk-kul to Tashkent, to be used in the manufacture of saddles. The natives always use a saddle-cloth, which is frequently of velvet, richly embroidered with gold and silver. A horse would not be permitted to go from the stable unless it wore round its neck one or two carved wooden balls called *dulaneh*, from the wood-thorn (*Cratægus*) of which they are made, which are considered an amulet against all evil influences. Asses are in Tashkent nearly as common as horses, and in Bukhara, seem to be still more used, while in Khokand one rarely meets any. They are small, usually white or grey, and capable of bearing very heavy burdens. Of course one sees everywhere in the streets numbers of camels.

The only vehicle used by the natives is a large wide cart on two immense wheels, called an *arba*. The wheels are very roughly constructed with wide felloes and heavy spokes, usually made of elm-wood, and without tires. The shafts are prolongations of the main body, which rest on a wide strap over the back of the horse, where the driver sits on a small saddle, with his feet on the shafts instead of taking his place in the cart. Sometimes these *arbas* are covered with matting, and although the vehicle is rude yet it is comfortable, because on account of the great size of the wheels the inequalities of the road are not much noticed.

Dogs occupy a very anomalous position in the Sart household. While there is at least one in every family they are not petted, but rather ill-treated, as according to Mussulman ideas they are unclean, and they are rarely fed, but are left to pick up their own living, and are consequently lean, gaunt, and half-starved. Why they should be kept at all it is difficult to understand, unless for their use as watch-dogs. Both night and day they are prowling about the walls and house-tops, and keeping the street in a continual uproar at the passing stranger. Cats, on the contrary, are petted and protected, and beautiful specimens are frequently seen, especially the graceful creatures of the Bukharan breed, with long silky hair and bushy tails. Pet birds are very common, particularly small quails, which are kept and trained to fight, and every youth of fashion carries a quail or some similar small bird on his hand or in his bosom.

In spite of what my friend the Mullah said about the dearth of amusements I found that music and dancing have their votaries in Central Asia as well as elsewhere. The Sarts are especially fond of singing, and they will sit for hours together listening to a monotonous song with the accompaniment of a two-stringed guitar, or to the half-chanted recitation of some poem, while at night, when the shops of the bazaar are nearly all shut, gayer and livelier airs are sung to the clapping of hands or the beating of a tambourine or even of a brass salver, if nothing else is obtainable. The voices are bad, and in general their music is tasteless to an European ear, for the constant use of intervals, which to us are not only unmelodic, but impossible to be expressed by our system of notation, makes it seem to us false and discordant. The notes B and E of the scale, for instance, are nearer half-way between A and C and D and F than they are with us, and there is a frequent use of fourths of a tone, so that in an octave there are far more than the regular thirteen sounds. Yet after being accustomed to this mode of music it is possible to perceive many pleasing and striking airs. The music I heard in the towns was so different in character from the Kirghiz songs of the Steppe, that I am inclined to believe that it has its origin in Persia, from which country the musical instruments were certainly brought. The chief stringed instrument, which is called *dutara* (a Persian word, from *du*, two, and *tara*, string), is of the same general shape as a guitar, and is played by the hand; the strings are usually of fine wire. The *sitara* (Persian *si*, three, and *tara*, string) has, as its name indicates, three strings, and is usually played on with a bow like a violin. The *tchetara*, or four-stringed instrument is, I am told, also used. These names show us very plainly the Persian origin of the Latin *cithara* and our guitar. I saw once or twice another stringed instrument, the *kemangeh*, where the strings proceeded from a long metal foot and are drawn over a sounding-board made of a cocoa-nut, with about one-third cut off. This is also played with a bow. Of other instruments, one of the most usual, and which is always used for dance-music, is a large tambourine covered with goat-skin, which is tossed up in both hands, and played on with the flat of the fingers. The edge is fitted with jingling bits of metal, and the player constantly holds the instrument over a pan of coals to make it more resonant. This tambourine is called *tchilmanda* in Tashkent and on the northern side of the Syr

Darya, while on the other side, in Samarkand and Bukhara, it is known by the Persian name, *daira*. The *surnai* is a pipe like a clarionet, made of apricot-wood, about two feet long, in the small opening of which there is a brass pipe called a *nil*, which has a mouthpiece of reed, and close to the mouthpiece a brass disk, which serves as a support to the lips of the player. The farther end of this pipe, when it is not played on, is stopped up with a brass rod, and two small wooden disks are attached to it by a chain, which cover up the mouthpiece. The *kornai* is a large brass trumpet six or seven feet long, swelling greatly at the farther end, and giving only one unearthly deep bass note. Two trumpets of different keys are generally used at the same time. The *nagora* consists of two drums of different sizes, made of small earthenware vessels covered with skins fastened on by a network of little straps, and joined together. The smaller drum has a thicker skin, and its sound is called *zil*, or wooden; the larger, with a thinner skin, gives a more prolonged sound, called *bum*. The drums are played on in turn with two sticks. Among the Kirghiz the favourite instrument is the ordinary Jew's-harp, which bears the very appropriately sounding name of *tchang*.

In Central Asia Mohammedan prudery prohibits the public dancing of women; but as the desire of being amused and of witnessing a graceful spectacle is the same all the world over, here boys and youths specially trained take the place of the dancing-girls of other countries. The moral tone of the society of Central Asia is scarcely improved by the change.

These *batchas*, or dancing-boys, are a recognised institution throughout the whole of the settled portions of Central Asia, though they are most in vogue in Bukhara, and the neighbouring Samarkand. In the khanate of Khokand public dances have for some years been forbidden—the formerly licentious Khan having of late put on a semblance of morality and severity, and during my month's stay in that country I saw no amusements of any kind among the natives. In Tashkent *batchas* flourished until 1872, when a severe epidemic of cholera induced the Mullahs to declare that dancing was against the precepts of the Koran, and at the request of the leaders of the native population, the Russian authorities forbade public dances during that summer, on account of the vast crowds which they always drew together. It was impossible, however, for the pleasure-loving Sarts to hold out in their abstinence for more than one year, and the mere rumour that there would be a *bazem*, or dance, was sufficient to draw great crowds to the garden where it was expected to take place. In Khodjent and Samarkand no restrictions have ever been placed on public dancing, and it is not an uncommon spectacle. These *batchas* are as much respected as the greatest singers and *artistes* are with us. Every movement they make is followed and applauded, and I have never seen such breathless interest as they excite, for the whole crowd seems to devour them with their eyes, while their hands beat time to every step. If a *batcha* condescends to offer a man a bowl of tea, the recipient rises to take it with a profound obeisance, and returns the empty bowl in the same way, addressing him only as ' *Taxir*,' ' your Majesty,' or '*kulluk*,' ' I am your slave.' Even when a *batcha* passes through the bazaar all who know him rise to salute him with hands upon their hearts, and the exclamation of ' *Kulluk!* ' and should he deign to stop and rest in any shop it is thought a great honour.

In all large towns *batchas* are very numerous, for it is as much the custom for a Bokhariot gentleman to keep one as it was in the Middle Ages for each knight to have his squire. In fact no establishment of a man of rank or position would be complete without one; and men of small means club together to keep one among them, to amuse them in their hours of rest and recreation. They usually set him up in a tea-shop, and if the boy is pretty his stall will be full of customers all day long. Those *batchas*, however, who dance in public are fewer in number, and are now to some extent under police restrictions. In Kitab there were only about a dozen, in other towns even less, and the same dancers sometimes go from place to place. They live either with their parents or with the *entrepreneur*, who takes care of them and always accompanies them. He dresses them for the different dances, wraps them up when they have finished, and looks after them as well as any duenna.

At the hour appointed for the *bazem*, the boys begin to come in twos and threes, accompanied by their guardians, and after giving their hands to their host take their places on one edge of the carpet, sitting in the Asiatic respectful way upon the soles of their feet. Bowls of tea and trays of fruit and sweets are set before them. The musicians meanwhile tune their tambourines, or rather increase their resonance, by holding them over a pan of glowing coals. When the boys have devoured enough grapes and melons the dancing begins. This is very difficult to describe. With flowing robe of bright-coloured variegated silk, loose trousers, and bare feet, and two long tresses of hair streaming from under his embroidered scull-cap, the *batcha* begins to throw himself into graceful attitudes, merely keeping time with his feet and hands to the beating of the tambourines and the weird monotonous song of the leader. Soon his movements become wilder, and the spectators all clap their hands in measure; he circles madly about, throwing out his arms, and after turning several summersaults kneels facing the musicians. After a moment's pause he begins to sing in reply to the leader, playing his arms in graceful movements over his head. Soon he rises, and, with body trembling all over, slowly waltzes about the edge of the carpet, and with still wilder and wilder motions again kneels and bows to us. A thrill and murmur of delight runs through the audience, an extra robe is thrown over him, and a bowl of tea handed to him as he takes his seat. This first dance is called *katta-uin* (the great play), in contradistinction to the special dances. The natives seem most pleased with those dances where the *batcha* is dressed as a girl, with long braids of false hair and tinkling anklets and bracelets. Usually but one or two in a troop can dance the women's dance, and the female attire once donned is retained for the remainder of the feast, and the *batcha* is much besought to sit here and there among the spectators to receive their caresses. Each dance has its special name— Afghani, Shirazi, Kashgari — according to the characteristics of the country where it is national or of the story it is supposed to represent; but all are much alike, differing in rapidity, or in the amount of posture and gesture. The younger boys usually perform those dances which have more of a gymnastic character, with many summersaults and hand-springs; while the elder and taller ones devote themselves more to posturing, slow movements, and amatory and lascivious gestures. The dance which pleased me most, and which I saw for the first time in Karshi, was the *Kabuli*, a sort of gymnastic game, where two boys armed each with two wands strike them constantly in alternate cadence, while performing complicated figures, twists, and summersaults. In general but one boy dances at a time, and rarely more than two together, these being usually independent of each other.

The dances, so far as I was able to judge, were by no means indecent, though they were often very lascivious. One of the most frequent gestures was that of seizing the breast in the hand and then pretending to throw it to the spectators, similar to our way of throwing kisses. In some dances the *batcha* goes about with a bowl of tea, and choosing one of the spectators, offers the tea to him with entreating gestures, sinks to the floor, singing constantly a stanza of praise and compliment. The favoured man hands back the bowl with thanks, but the boy slips from his proffered embrace, or shyly submits to be kissed, and is off to another. If the spectator is generous he will drop some silver coins into the empty bowl, and if he is a great lover of this amusement he will take a golden *tilla* in his lips, and the *batcha* will put up his lips to receive it, when a kiss may perhaps be snatched.

The songs sung during the dances are always about love, and are frequently responsive between the *batcha* and the musicians. These will serve as specimens:—

'Tchuyandy, my soul! what has become of thee? Why didst thou not come?' 'An ill-natured father kept me; but I was in love with thee, and could not endure separation.'

'Tchuyandy, my soul! why didst thou delay, if thou wert sad?' 'Nightingale! I am sad! As passionately as thou lovest the rose so loudly sing, that my loved one may awake. Let me die in the embrace of my dear one, for I envy no one. I know that thou hast many lovers; but what affair of mine is that? The rose would not wither if the nightingale did not win it; and man would not perish did not death come.'

The *batchas* practise their profession from a very early age until sometimes so late as twenty or twenty-five, or at all events until it is impossible to conceal their beards. The life which they have led hardly fits them for independent existence thereafter. So long as they are young and pretty they have their own way in everything; every command is obeyed by their adorers, every purse is at their disposition, and they fall into a life of caprice, extravagance, and dissipation. Rarely do they lay up any money, and more rarely still are they able to profit by it afterwards. Frequently a *batcha* is set up as a keeper of a tea-house by his admirers, where he will always have a good *clientèle*, and sometimes he is started as a small merchant. Occasionally one succeeds, and becomes a prosperous man, though the remembrance of his past life will frequently place the then odious affix, *batcha*, to his name. I have known one or two men, now rich and respected citizens, who began life in this way. In the old days it was much easier, for a handsome dancer might easily become *Kushbegi*, or Grand Vizier. More often a *batcha* takes to smoking opium or drinking *kukhnar*, and soon dies of dissipation.

It is not only boys who dance in Central Asia, girls and women do so as well; but their exhibitions are in general confined to the women's court. On one occasion, however, Asudullah Bek invited me to see a splendid *tomasha*, or spectacle —a dance of women—a thing looked on with orthodox horror by most Mussulmen; but Asudullah Bek, being a Persian and a Shiite, was rather more lax in his notions than the rest, though even he was desirous that the fame of this should not be much noised abroad among his patients. Still, when the performance came off the noise of the tambourines and pipes was so great that a large portion of the city crowded to his garden, so that we had to have Cossacks there to keep them away. We went about sunset, and soon several women made their appearance, to whom we of course gave a share of the fruits and sweets which were provided for us, and had tea served to them. One of these women was a sister of the wife of Malla Khan, the former ruler of Khokand, and had here been married to some distinguished Khokandian official. It was curious to notice the deference with which she was received by the other women, who always rose to salute her or pass her a bowl of tea; even in her fallen state she seemed to have claims to their respect. After a while a girl of thirteen, with a pretty dark face and bright black eyes, though her beauty was spoiled by an indiscreet use of cosmetics—for her eyebrows were turned into one dark line, and the rouge was very prominent on her cheeks—came out to dance. Her dress was a loose bright red silk robe, and her hair hung about her neck in a dozen small braids. Her head was covered with a long silken scarf hanging behind like a veil, fastened with ornaments of silver, and she wore earrings filled with torquoise and coloured glass. Her feet were bare. She slowly circled on the carpet, bowing first to one and then another, and as the beats of the tambourine became faster her motions became more rapid, and after whirling round a dozen times she sank to the ground, much to the delight of the spectators. Then rising again she commenced a slowly swaying movement, and with arms swinging in cadence completed the circle of the carpet three or four times, again whirled about, and once more sat upon the ground. She was succeeded by others, and the dances were very similar to those danced by boys, though less vigorous and less graceful; and there was little variety in style until a little girl of eleven—for the most of them were very young, a girl of eighteen being already an old woman—began to perform a dance much more passionate than the rest. At intervals she would kneel before one of the spectators, swing her arms as if in invitation, and, as it were, make motions of enchantment, each time leaning nearer and nearer to him, until finally, when the enchantment was supposed to be at its height, he was expected to give a kiss, and the dance was ended. Though the enchantment might be practised upon many the kiss was reserved for only one, for the girl would extricate herself like a snake from the proposed embrace and immediately be on her knees before another.

I have said that the Mussulmans in general disapprove of the dancing of women, yet they do not refuse to witness it if they get an opportunity; and many a one slipped through the guards at the gate and came up and joined our circle, and from these the applause was perhaps the loudest.

A very common attendant of a *bazem*, is the exhibition of a *maskarabush*, or comedian, who, with whitened face and the addition of a rug or some rags, and the help of a bystander, will represent various scenes of native life, such as doctor and patient, *Kazi* and suitor, teacher and scholar, or will mimic dogs, cats, and other domestic animals. The most of these representations are of a very obscene character, though they are often very vivid as well as witty, and are approved with rounds of laughter.

One of the last days of my stay in Tashkent was given up to the festival of *Zang-ata*, the great festival of the year for Tashkent and its vicinity. Zang-ata himself was a shepherd who belonged to the religious brotherhood of *Khodrié*, and died in the odour of sanctity in 1097. What his real name was the worshippers at his shrine were unable to tell me, but he is said to have been dark like a negro, and thus to have got the name *Zang-ata*, 'dark father.' He is the patron saint of Tashkent and of all the country round about, and his tomb is on the way to Samarkand, about eight miles from the town. The shrine, which is built over his grave, is very shabby, rendered all the more so by the rams' horns and long bits of dirty rag which every pilgrim has felt it a necessity to tie there on some stick or tree. Old trees, especially old mulberry trees, seem throughout Central Asia to be in great veneration, and the older and the deader they are the more bits of rag they have on them. The bits of rag are symbols of sacrifice, and the custom is probably a survival of the primitive tree-worship. Cannot the *Arbor secco*, which Marco Polo and the other Asiatic travellers of the Middle Ages mention so often, be referred to some tree similarly venerated? Near by is the tomb of the mother of Zang-ata, who especially patronises the women, and while the crowd of men about the tomb of the son is large a row of women may be seen weeping and wailing near the lattice of the mother's shrine. The shrine of the saint, however, is of very minor importance; there is a large college, with arched portal and small rooms, for the accommodation of the Mullahs; and more than this, there is a fine garden, with orchard, ponds, and canals, suited to the pic-nics and out-of-door feasts which necessarily accompany pilgrimages of piety into the country.

The festival fell last year among the first days of September, and lasted three or four days. Everybody goes there, and Tashkent is deserted by nearly all except the women and a few young men whose love of intrigue determines them to remain in such company. As I was very anxious to see this feast we made up a little party of friends, including Jura Bek, and drove out there. The dust was something frightful, for the road was filled with *arbas* and equipages of all kinds, and men on horses and donkeys; nowhere have I seen such a throng, unless perhaps on the Derby-day. The nearer we got the thicker it became;

people were returning as well as going, having perhaps already spent two days there, and got to the bottom of their holiday purses. At last we came to the gate, and the native policeman, who recognised us, could with difficulty force an opening through the crowd of talking and gesticulating pleasure-seekers. We at last got safely to the corner of the college, where we found our friend Mirza Yusuf, who had invited us to join his party. Some friends of his were Mullahs of the college, and we were made to feel at once that we were at home. We found our friends occupied the extreme corner of the arcade, which was cut off from the rest by awnings and curtains. Here we reclined on cushions, after getting rid of the dust and dirt of the drive, and took tea, and our Mussulman friends were neither astonished nor shocked to see us bring out a bottle of red wine, though each stood somewhat in awe of the rest, so that no one was willing to share it with us. When we were a little rested we went beyond the college into a large grove, where was a very singular sight; almost every available spot was occupied by tents and booths, the ground having been parcelled out beforehand, each person erecting a tent and running curtains about his little plot of ground, or several parties taking plots together and throwing them into one. *Samovars* were smoking everywhere, and all along the brook were pots where *pilaf* was preparing. In almost every booth there was some one playing on the guitar and singing, and in very many could be heard the rapid beating of a tambourine and the measured clapping of hands, showing that there dancing was going on. All about us was an immense crowd of people who had no places for themselves, and had merely come to be amused, buying their melon or their bread from the itinerant vendors, or taking a bowl of tea or some *kumys* at one of the tea-houses. More solid food was provided by the kitchens, for it seemed as if every native *restaurateur* had come from the bazaar to fix himself here for a week. In the centre of all was a large pavilion which had been erected for the use of the authorities, and here I found the chief officials of Tashkent, who had come to amuse themselves with the native sports. In front of this was a large enclosed space, where boys were constantly dancing to the music of a large native orchestra, while at intervals the Russian military bands scattered through the grounds struck in with airs from the 'Grande Duchesse' and other operas of Offenbach's. The carouse was kept up until late that night; but by nine o'clock, in spite of a proffered supper with the officials, we had had enough, and were glad to take our dusty ride home again.

Later on, to amuse the officers, the Russian prefect of the district had some women dance, much to the horror of the Mussulmans that a religious festival should be so profaned. It was one of those little things shocking to native feeling which not all Russian officials are careful enough to avoid. Such a dance was once before arranged on a public festivity when the Governor-General was present, but he was deceived by the story that the women who danced were the wives of the chief natives, who did this in his honour, and he even presented them with some silver cups and souvenirs, which were found the next day in various brothels.

Perhaps the most important event in the life of a Mussulman is circumcision. Before this he, of course, is born, washed, fed, and has received his name, but he does not form one of the body of orthodox believers until this necessary rite has been performed upon him. The birth and early life of the child are accompanied by some curious practices. When a boy is born the midwife does not inform the mother of the sex until the afterbirth, on account of a tradition that out of joy it would be harder for her to endure the pain. The father, who may always be present, and usually is if he be fond of his wife, then buries, in case of a boy a mutton bone, and in case of a girl a rag doll, under the floor of the room where the birth took place, in the corner opposite to the door. The midwife then congratulates the parents and receives presents. No shirt is put on the child until the fifth day. On the ninth day the grandmother of the child brings a cradle, which, with its belongings, she has prepared in advance, and the child is strapped in it on a bed of barley. It continues to use the cradle, and to be nursed until the birth of a second child. Until this ninth day, when it is placed in the cradle, a light is kept burning near it to ward off the evil eye. On this same day the mother rises from her bed and there is a great feast, varying according to the circumstances of the family. This is the only feast given for a girl. In order to escape evil influences the child should not be carried into the street until the fortieth day. When the hair of the child is cut for the first time, the locks are weighed against gold or silver, and the money is given to the poor. In Tashkent, and in general throughout Central Asia, boys are circumcised when they are between seven and ten years old, although it may be done at an earlier period, and sometimes through poverty it is deferred until later. As the circumcision feasts—*tui*—are very expensive, and all the friends of the family have to be invited, it usually happens that two or three men have their sons circumcised at the same time, in order to avoid expense. If the father is rich he naturally gives the feast himself. The boys' friends gather at some place and come in procession, all disguised and decked out with paper caps, wooden swords and paper shields, and masks made of melon-rind, and the boy who is to be circumcised is carried on the back of one of the elder boys, in case the feast is not in his own house; if, however, it takes place at home, the boy is taken from the house through the streets in triumph and then back again. He is, however, in a state of unconsciousness, having had administered to him early in the morning a powerful narcotic, *gul kan* (literally flower-sugar), which is made of sugar-candy mixed with the sifted pollen from hop-flowers and reduced to a hard paste. When the guests are all assembled there is usually a grand banquet, with *pilaf* and all possible delicacies, and sometimes with sheep roasted whole. After this there are either dances or, what is more usual, the native comedians come in and perform a course of farces and impersonations for the amusement of the boys. This being over, the guests walk round the performers in a circle, throwing to them for their pay money or handkerchiefs or whatever they can afford with their right hand over their left shoulder. During the time of this feasting the boy is in the women's court, where he is dressed in his best clothes, and when the proper time arrives he is brought back to the men's court and laid upon the cushions—his father having collected all the best pillows and cushions which he has and spread them over with the richest materials in his possession. This bed is prepared in the guest-room, and the most distinguished of the guests sit about it. The operation is performed by a sharp razor, and gunpowder or fine wood-ashes are immediately placed on the wound, which heals in the course of two or three days. The cries of the boy are drowned by shouts of '*Ai Musulman bulgan Kaffir!*' 'Hail, Mussulman! Thou wert an unbeliever.' He is now a member of Islam, and nothing short of flagrant apostasy can prevent him from entering the paradise of the blessed.

When a boy reaches the age of fifteen or sixteen, or sometimes when he is even younger, his parents think it is time for him to get married, and look about them for a suitable match. Misalliances are greatly disliked among the Sarts, and it is desired that the family of the bride should be equal to that of

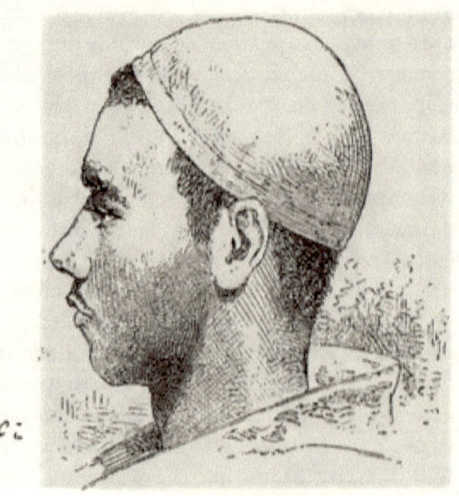

A BOY OF TASHKENT.

the bridegroom. A Hodja, or descendant of Mohammed, for example, can marry only a Hodja's daughter, and among those of good blood it is rare—for the first wife at least—that any great inequality of birth is allowed. Girls are considered marriageable between eleven and fifteen, and although according to the strict letter of the law, a girl of nine can be married, it is not well looked upon in Tashkent. Development is quick in these countries, and a woman of twenty-five or thirty is already old and ugly. The mother, or sister, or some female relative of the youth who is to be married, after having found what appears to be a suitable match, or at all events a girl who pleases the boy himself or his parents, goes to the girl's family and discusses the advantages of the marriage. The matchmaker is at once asked how much *kalim* will be given, and she in her turn is anxious to know the amount of the dowry, as it is desired that the *kalim* and dowry should be nearly equal. It is commonly believed that the *kalim*, or money given by the husband, goes to the father of the wife, and that it is in the nature of purchase-money, but this is not correct; the *kalim* is given to the wife herself, and it remains her property, so that in case of divorce from her husband she may have something to fall back upon. When the friend of the young man has carefully looked at the bride and found out all about her, she returns to the young man, and tells him about the appearance and manners of his future wife. In Tashkent the young man is then allowed to look at her without her veil, but only on giving his solemn word that he looks at her with the intention of marrying her, and not simply out of curiosity.

After the consent has been obtained the *kalim*, in the quantity agreed upon between the families, is sent to the wife and with it the wedding presents. The *kalim* may be either in money, or in anything which may be lawfully considered property. It is not, however, absolutely necessary to pay the *kalim* before the marriage actually takes place, but the wife has the right to refuse all intercourse with her husband until it is paid; and if, after the conditions of the marriage have been fixed, the husband withdraws from the contract, he is obliged to pay to the wife one-half of the amount agreed upon as *kalim*. The wedding presents are usually given by nines, which is looked upon as a sacred number, nine times nine being usually the largest number that is given. The number nine is used with regard to other presents, as those given to guests or in exchange of hospitality. After the presents have been given and received the wedding-day is fixed. The bride then gives a feast to her friends, and the young man also gives a feast to his comrades, each at their own houses. On the day of the marriage a grand feast is held at the house of the bride's family, and all the friends and relations of both parties are invited, the women being in one court and the men in the other. The Mullah from the nearest mosque, or in particular cases some distinguished saint or *Ishan*, is invited to perform the ceremony.

The bride and bridegroom are not present at the actual marriage ceremony, which is conducted for them by their witnesses, who are in all cases male relatives. The witness on the part of the woman is her father or uncle, or some one of that generation, no other person being allowed to act for her without special power of attorney to that effect. If the bride should be a slave—in those countries where slavery is allowed—it is her master who acts as her witness. The Mullah, who is in the same room with the witnesses, asks them if the persons whom they represent consent to marry each other, and then enquires what the *kalim* and dowry are, and if they have been properly given; he then recites a prayer giving praises to the Prophet and his descendants, draws up the marriage contract, and repeats a prayer, which is placed at its head: 'Praise to God, who has allowed marriage, and has forbidden all adulterous crimes; let all heavenly and earthly existences praise Mohammed and his pure and honourable posterity.' He then pronounces the words, 'I have accomplished the marriage between a man and a woman, a woman and a man, according to the power given to me by their witnesses, and in accordance with the conditions set forth in this contract.' Immediately after he again says: 'On behalf of the husband and wife I declare consent to this marriage according to the commissions given to the witnesses, and the conditions expressed in this contract.' The Mullah and witnesses then place their seals on the contract, ask the assistance of God, and recite the *fatha*, or first chapter of the Koran. The marriage contract is given to the wife or her witnesses. The marriage fee is given by the husband, and cannot be demanded from the wife. The bridegroom then goes to the apartment of the bride, but is met at the door by her brother or some relative, who does not permit him to enter until he gives him a piece of money or some small present. When he has thus succeeded in obtaining admission he joins the bride, and remains with her and all the other women. On his entering, the bride is concealed amidst a group of women, among whom he must find her hand before she can come out. As he has perhaps never seen her, it is a somewhat difficult matter. When a feast is held it usually lasts all night; bonfires are lighted, and refreshments are served. The women go away in the morning after having received their presents. The feast of the men takes place in the outer court, and they stay there until half of the night is passed, when they receive their presents and retire. It is necessary at the same time also to give alms either to the mosque or to poor persons. At any time the day after the husband is allowed to take his wife to his own house, if he has one, and this done the marriage is entirely consummated.

In most Mussulman countries, especially in Persia, a temporary marriage is allowed, but this is not known in Tashkent. Marriage with a slave is permitted, though it is not well regarded, but it is strictly forbidden to a Mussulman to marry an infidel. There are also certain degrees of blood-relationship in which marriage is forbidden, nor is it allowed with persons similarly related to a nurse. A man cannot marry the relations of his wife in the ascending or descending lines, nor can a son marry the wife of his father, or *vice versâ*. It is not allowed to marry two sisters at one time; the first must be divorced before the second can be espoused; but if the consent of his wife be obtained, a man may marry his wife's niece.

By Mussulman law every man is allowed to have four wives at one time, but more than this he cannot legally possess without divorcing one he has already; it is, however, the practice among rich men to have various concubines, either as servants or otherwise. The wife is obliged to obey her husband in all things, and to avoid everything that is unpleasant to him, and cannot without his consent make any contracts. She has, however, a right to food, clothing, lodging and servants, and to money for those expenses which are usual among persons of her rank, such as for baths, for visitors, and for the entertainment of friends; if these be not allowed by the husband she can complain to the *Kazi*, or judge, and he can allow her to borrow money on account of her husband, or can even order the sale of some of her husband's property in order to provide her with the money which is necessary. She is obliged also to preserve her beauty so far as she can, and to try to please her husband; and for this purpose she is allowed by law to use various cosmetics. Besides his wife a man is obliged to support his children, and even his father and uncles, if they be unable to support themselves. The marriage may be dissolved if either of the parties abandon the Mussulman faith, or if the husband be absent for a certain time without news being heard of him, or in case of a minor who on reaching his majority refuses to consent to a continuance of the marriage; as well as if madness or certain diseases be discovered, or if it be discovered that the marriage was not properly solemnised. In addition to this the husband has always the right of divorcing his wife whenever he chooses, without giving any reasons. He is obliged in this case to give back to his wife all her own property, as well as the amount of *kalim*, if he have not already paid it. Such a divorce, however, must be given before witnesses, and with the observance of a certain form. The husband may also divorce the wife by her own consent, and is obliged to do so if she tell him she wishes to marry another man who is better than he. But if the husband refuse to divorce his wife at her request, and she be able to give a sufficient reason why such a divorce should be had, the *Kazi* will compel him to divorce her. In case of her adultery the husband not only divorces her but curses her, and in this case she is prevented from re-marrying, though he may re-marry her after having given her a divorce once or twice, but never after the third time. There are certain contemptuous expressions which if used by a husband to his wife give her the right of divorce, and allow her to prevent him from having access to her, unless he buy this right by a gift called *kefforet* and the recital of certain prayers.

The position of a wife who is regarded by her husband merely as an instrument of his pleasures, or as an obedient servant to manage his house, cannot be a very pleasant one, liable as she is at any time to be divorced at his fancy or his desire to replace her by another. Still, if she be a person of ability, or even a coquette, she may be able to hold her husband completely under her control, quite as much as wives manage their husbands in more civilised countries. As the wife has the privilege of visiting her friends she naturally is able to pick up much gossip and scandal, and by means of her stories and talk she may cause her husband to pass far more pleasant hours in her society than he does in the outer court. Besides this she may through her husband be able to obtain influence over many people, and to meddle in affairs of various kinds; and if he be placed in high position, she may even have great influence over the politics of the country. I have known, for instance, cases where women who have shown capacity have been consulted by their husbands on almost every subject, but these are exceptions. Enquiry into these matters is difficult, for it is quite contrary to Mussulman etiquette for one person to speak to another of his wife unless they be on extremely intimate terms; the most that can be said is a mere allusion to the hearth of one's friend. The different wives seldom live in the pleasantest relation to one another, not so much from jealousy—for I doubt if either jealousy or love be greatly developed—as from envy of the privileges that another enjoys or the presents she receives. Every husband tries as far as possible to keep his wives separate. Wives have a peculiar expression for each other: *kün-dash*, day-companion.

The Sarts are not only attacked by the usual maladies to which our frame is heir, but they have besides two or three which are peculiar to the country, or at all events very common there. One of these is the *reshta*, or 'Guinea-worm' (*Filaria medinensis*), which is known also in several other parts of the world where the climate is hot and the water bad. It is probably produced by infusoria, from bad water being taken into the system, which in about a year develop into a white worm that passes through the body and makes its appearance usually in one of the legs. The part affected begins to swell, and the native physicians, to whom the symptoms are well known, immediately make an incision, and dexterously catching hold of the worm, slowly wind it off on a stick. This is an operation which has to be done with great care, as should the worm be broken each part would become a separate worm, and would be the cause of innumerable ulcers. There are often many such worms at the same time. The disease is accompanied by severe pains in the bones and internal heat and thirst. It is rarely met with in Tashkent, but is very common in Jizakh, Bukhara, and Karshi. In Samarkand it is less common, and at the time I was there I was unable to meet with a case. At the three places first named the rivers and canals come to an end, and most of the water for drinking is taken from the large pools and tanks, where it has remained in a stagnant state for many months.

Leprosy is common throughout the whole of Central Asia, and the lepers are obliged to live in separate quarters of the towns, where they have their own bazaars and prepare their own food, and are as far as possible cut off from intercourse with others, though in Samarkand numbers of these hideously disfigured beings were near the gates, and especially near the Mosque of Shah-Zindah, asking alms from the passers-by. The constant ablutions performed by the Mussulmans in the water of the canals and ponds no doubt contribute greatly to spread diseases of various kinds, especially those of the skin. One of these, which is known in Tashkent among the Russians by the name of the 'Sart disease,' is clearly traceable to the use of water; for if a person use boiled water, or water from a well for washing, he is not liable to have this malady. On the contrary, those who live nearest to the native towns, and who use the water from the canals for washing purposes, are nearly always attacked with it. It is known by the natives as *Yarra-Afgani*, 'Afghan sore,' or *Pasha-harda*, literally 'worm-eaten,' and is especially common among children. It is a very disagreeable ulcer, which breaks out on the face or hands, spreading constantly, and eating deeper and deeper. The native physicians are very skilful in curing it, though the Russian physicians have only of late been able to do so. A child of an acquaintance of mine, a chemist, was cured by an application of acetate of lead, and no trace was left, though usually ugly, indelible scars remain.

In the year 1872 the cholera appeared at Jizakh, and spread with great quickness to Samarkand, Shahrisabs, Hissar, and the Amu Darya, on the south; to Bukhara, both from Katta Kurgan and from Nurata, and even as far as Khiva, on the west; to Ura-tepé and the Khanate of Khokand, on the east; and northwards to Tashkent, branching off in one direction to Lake Issyk-kul, and in the other to Fort No. 1. It raged with violence, and the mortality was very great, especially at Bukhara and Khokand. In Tashkent measures were taken by the Government which gave some relief, though the terror was extreme. From the best information that could be obtained from the natives the cholera had appeared in Central Asia but twice before—once in 1832, and again in 1848 and 1849—the periods of the appearance of this great epidemic in Europe. Since 1849 it had not been known in Tashkent. In 1871, however, there was a disease prevalent in Bukhara which was so horrible as to cause many persons to die of fright. This was probably the cholera, and was in all likelihood brought over from Persia, where it was raging in consequence of the famine. From Bukhara it probably spread to Jizakh, where it remained dormant during the winter, and broke out in the spring, returning to Bukhara with renewed violence. It was so bad in the district next to Katta Kurgan that the Beks applied to the Russians for medical assistance, which was readily given. It is noticeable that the cholera on this occasion travelled along the high roads and postal routes, while in the depths of the Steppe the inhabitants were free from it.

The parasites which are known all over the world, such as fleas and lice, are exceedingly common through the whole of Central Asia, but it is strange that the bed-bug was unknown there until introduced by the Russians. It is now very common at Tashkent and at all the post-houses, but is not yet known either in Bukhara or Khokand.

The first care of the Sart physician is to study your general appearance and ask you about your temperament. He has learned in the *Tukhpatul Muminin*, the most common medical book here, that you must belong to one of four classes, and his treatment of your malady is governed accordingly. When he has combined your symptoms with your temperament he will pull a bag out of his pocket, or untie the scarf which serves him for a girdle, and open an assortment of drugs in twisted bits of paper, perhaps tasting and smelling to find the right ones, and having chosen the proper medicine, will give you the usual directions about doses and diet. The medicaments employed by Central Asiatic physicians are, in general, very simple, being in most part vegetable substances, but few animal matters and minerals being used. They are usually taken simply in the form of powders or decoctions, and when a mixed medicine is used the physician delivers the substances to the patient and allows him to mix them for himself. This not only saves the physician trouble, but, in a certain way, soothes the suspicious feelings of the patient, who might imagine, in case he did not immediately improve, that he had been poisoned by the doctor. Professor Dragendorff[1] says that the

[1] 'Ueber den jetzigen Zustand der Volksmedicin in Turkestan.'—*Russisch Revue*, vol. ii. p. 331.

medicine of Turkistan is of the same general nature as that of all Mussulman countries, having been introduced by the Arabs at the conquest of the country. Of 226 vegetable medicines which he examined at least 210 were known to the contemporaries of the great Arabic physician Ebn Baithar, and certainly 172 to Dioscorides and Galen. The remaining substances replace others which were used in the old times, but which are either with difficulty procurable or entirely inaccessible, and they are usually externally similar to them, though their properties may be very different. Professor Dragendorff lays it down as a general rule that in all Mussulman countries the few medicines in use which seem to be of native origin, and to be brought down by tradition from the old times, are simply used to replace others which could not be had. Of the 226 drugs mentioned by him 12 were stated to have been brought from China and 62 from India, but these statements refer, in general, only to the places where they were bought, and not to their origin. Seventy-one of them grow wild, or are cultivated in Tashkent, fifty in Samarkand and Bukhara, and some are brought from Khiva, Khokand, and Afghanistan. Seven were said to be of Persian origin, six from Arabia and Turkey, one from Egypt, and four from Europe. The medicines imported from Europe are not new to the country, but have been long well known there. The Russian merchants sell them cheaper and better than they can be otherwise procured.

As soon as a man dies his body is washed by a woman called *kiranda*, whose special business it is to take care of the dead, and to weep and wail during the funeral ceremonies. The burial takes place as soon as possible, usually the same day. The body, after being washed, is dressed and covered with a shroud, and placed in a reclining position, with the hands straight down by the sides, and is then tied round and round with a long bandage, which, among the richer classes, is usually of silk. In Tashkent a form of prayer is recited in the house by the Mullah, but in Shahrisabs and Bukhara the body, which lies on a bier, provided at times with a top made of matting and even covered with rich cloths, is carried to the mosque, and the funeral service is performed there. Though a woman, when alive, cannot go to the mosque, she has no distinction made against her after death. When the body is borne to the cemetery the women follow it, weeping and uttering various cries in praise of the deceased and in lamentation at his death. The body stops at every mosque on the road, the Mullah of which is asked to come out and recite prayers. The grave has been prepared beforehand, and consists of a deep ditch, at one end of which an underground chamber has been hollowed out. As the bier is brought to this ditch, the body—which of course is without a coffin—is tumbled down and shoved into the hollow chamber, together with the jug used in washing it; the ditch is then filled up with earth, and a mound raised over it. In many cases this is all that is done, a stick being perhaps stuck in the mound to mark it; in others the chambers are made of bricks plastered over with clay, in different forms, usually square or oblong, and sometimes with a pavilion or temple over them. A small lamp is frequently placed on the grave, and sometimes objects belonging to the deceased—especially the cradle in case of a child. The cemeteries of the cities are for the most part within the walls, and present a very lugubrious appearance, as no pains are taken to render them attractive, and there is no verdure whatever about them. Feasts called *ash* (literally 'food') are given to the friends on the day of the funeral, and on the seventh day, the fortieth day, the half-yearly, and the yearly anniversary of the death, and women come to the tombs to weep and wail. The first day of mourning goes by the name of *gap*, i.e. commemorative talk. For a year the women are obliged to wear dark clothes, as signs of mourning, but the men do not express their grief in this way.

It is curious that these periods of commemorative mourning for the dead are the same as those observed in Russia among the Christians, from which it would seem either that they had been adopted by the Russians during the epoch of Tartar ascendency, or that they had both come down from the early times when Russia and Central Asia were inhabited by much the same races. There are other resemblances in the funeral feasts, and in Russia the funeral processions also stop at the churches which they pass for the sake of having prayers read.

In Tashkent, when the mourners leave the grave they take with them a handful of the earth which they have just thrown into it. The same practice exists in some parts of Russia. A friend of mine at the burial of her child was advised by the old nurse to take some of the earth home and rub her breast with it, so as to mitigate her grief. Instead of the water jug, in Russia the scraps of the material used for the grave clothes are buried with the body, as well as the wine glass with the wine and water used in extreme unction, and the ashes of the incense.

I had, until my visit to Central Asia, believed with Soloviëf and others that the influence of the Mongol conquerors on Russia was very slight and superficial. Russia, it is true, was only a vassal, and there was no Mongol and Tartar population scattered through the country, but the Russian princes had frequently to pay their respects at the Mongol court, even at Karakorum, in Mongolia; there were Mongol ambassadors and tax-collectors stationed in Russian towns. Still, the Mongol domination lasted for more than two hundred and fifty years, and must have left some traces on customs and language. I could not but be struck in Central Asia with many little things, such as these customs about funerals, and I was led to believe, not only that the Mongol influence was much greater than I had supposed, but that much in the history of Russia could not be thoroughly understood without a careful study of Asiatic life as it now is in Bukhara and Tashkent. Deductions of this sort, however, must be cautiously made. Two things, for instance, are often mentioned as consequences of the Mongol domination—the severe and cruel punishments formerly in use in Russia, and the retired life of the women up to the time of Peter the Great. Yet it is now clearly shown that the severe punishments were introduced from Constantinople with the ecclesiastical law, which by degrees spread its influence over the civil law; and we well know from contemporary authors that the Mongols by no means secluded their women, who, on the contrary, appeared in public on all state occasions. The Asiatic influence was most visible on the Russian rulers and their court, for it was the princes and the aristocracy who had the directest relations with their Mongol suzerains. The style and ceremony of the court were modelled after Asiatic forms; among other things the word 'above' (*verkh*), which was constantly used of the residence of the Tsars in the Kremlin, and is even now-a-days a not uncommon expression for the Winter Palace, is to this day used in Bukhara (*yukhari*) to denote the residence of the Amir. The Russian Grand Prince Ivan Kalitá, the first consolidator of Russia, received his surname from *halta*, the Turki for bag or purse, a word now habitually used in Central Asia. The Russian nobles shaved their heads and dressed in the fashion set by their conquerors. They wore little skull-caps exactly like those now worn in Central Asia. That of the murdered Tsarevitch Dimitri is still preserved in the cathedral of the Kremlin; and the crown called the 'cap of Vladimir Monomakh' is nothing but a Kirghiz cap ornamented with precious stones. Even the names for many common articles of dress, such as shoes (*bashmak*), boots (*itchetof*), belt (*kushak*), are Tartar. Asiatic stuffs were common in Moscow under their original names. The stables for the best horses of the Tsar were, even in the seventeenth century, called those for the *Argamaks*—still the best breed of horses in Central Asia. As one of the most evident and most galling relations of the Russians to the Mongols was the tribute which was exacted, it is but natural that the word for 'treasury' or 'crown property' still in use (*kazna*) should be a Tartar word coming from the Arabic, and that *kaznatchi* (treasurer) should be a purely Tartar form. This same word has come to us in a very different way—through the Spanish, in the form *magazine*. In spite of this it seemed strange to me to find that the Russian word for money, *denga* or *dengi*, in the form *tenga*, meant everywhere in Central Asia a coin of twenty kopeks; the smaller coin, *pul*, appears in the Russian *pul* and *polushka*; and *altyn*, originally six *tengas* (Tartar *alty*, six), remains in the word *pyataltyn*, five altyns or fifteen kopeks, in frequent use with the cabmen of St. Petersburg. Asiatic weights and measures can be seen in *batman* and *arshin*; and *ambar*, *sarai*, and *tcherdak* (garret and storehouse), are Eastern words. It would be a curious subject of enquiry whether the Russian laws regarding taxes and real estate do not also show the effects of Asiatic influence.

Islam, as we all know, means 'submission (to God),' and is founded on the Koran, which the Mohammedans believe to have been delivered to Mohammed in separate chapters, called *suras*, by God himself through the Archangel Gabriel. The great principle of the religion is the unity of God, as distinguished from the idolatry of the Arabians, the mysticism of various sects, or the trinitarian teachings of the Christians. But in the Koran we find, beside merely religious doctrines reiterated in many forms, a series of rules with regard to daily life and practice, and even to political relations. Mohammed had advised his followers to learn all his regulations by heart, promising them on so doing a reward in the future life. This was done, and is still often done; but the *suras* of the Koran were never collected together into one book or placed in order during the lifetime of Mohammed, and were preserved by his followers in various forms, written on materials of all kinds. After his death the Khalif Abu Bekr ordered Seid Ibny-Sobit to collect all these scattered papers, and in the thirteenth year of the Hegira the Koran was published in its complete form, divided into 114 chapters or *suras*. Other collections were made, and there came at last to be seven different versions, varying probably chiefly from the different dialects in which they were written, several of which laid claim to special authority. In the time of the Khalif Othman, in the thirtieth year of the Hegira (650 A.D.), a revision of the Koran was undertaken in one dialect, and when this was completed copies of it were sent to the different parts of the Mussulman world, and previous obscure and incorrect copies were destroyed. This is the form in which the Koran has come to us. As the Koran contained the basis of legislation and various rules and laws, with special directions for their application, it was necessary in many cases to have recourse to certain annotations, so that in the early days of Islam there arose three supplements to the Koran, *Hadis, Ijma-u-Ummet,* and *Kias.* The *Hadis* was a collection of remarks and orders of the Prophet, as transmitted by oral tradition, and examples from his private and public life. Although these orders, not coming from the Almighty, did not have the force of the Koran, yet as they had come from the lips of the Prophet himself they served for deciding cases which were not mentioned in that book. But in the collection of these traditions there were certain differences, especially between the traditions collected by Ali, the nephew and son-in-law of the Prophet, and those handed down by others of his friends and followers. The *Hadis,* or traditions as recognised by the Sunnite sect, consist of six books, called

Sikhokhe Sitte, or six books of regular traditions compiled by the most eminent doctors, the chief of whom was the celebrated El Bukhari. The *Ijma-u-Ummet* is a collection of the decisions of the first four Khalifs, and their orders and explanations of the Koran with regard to civil and religious matters. The *Kias* is a collection of decisions and judgments founded on the Koran and *Hadis* by the Khalifs, other than the first four, and by the Imams and highest spiritual persons.

Mohammed himself had predicted that Islam would have seventy-three different sects, as the religions of the Magis had been divided into seventy sects, that of the Jews into seventy-one, and that of the Christians into seventy-two. Certainly, many sects were formed soon after the death of the Prophet, and many now exist, the principal of which are the sect of *Sunni* and that of *Shii*. The chief differences in the dogmas of these two sects spring from the doctrine of *Imamet*, the hereditary right of the descendants of Ali to rule over the Mussulman world. The Sunnites do not admit any Imams except the first four Khalifs, and believe that on the death of the Prophet the spiritual and worldly power was confided to the worthiest persons on the choice of the society or people. For the Shiites the *Imamet* is the chief doctrine of religion, and they consider the first three Khalifs, as well as those of the houses of B'ni Ummie and B'ni Abbas, as infringers on the lawful rights of Ali and his descendants, and that all done by them is not only unlawful but deserving of contempt and curses. The Sunnites consider Ali as a lawful Khalif, but only as the fourth after Abu Bekr, Omar, and Othman, and respect his descendants as those of the Prophet, but do not believe that the Khalifate was legally confined to Ali and his descendants alone. Another difference is that the Shiites believe it possible and allowable to abjure their religion in case of danger to their life, which is not permitted by the Sunnites. Besides having many differences in the rites of ablution, prayers, pilgrimage, and various laws and rules of civil and domestic life, the Shiites accept the *Hadis*, or traditions, as a proper supplement to the Koran in so far as they do not contradict it, but deny many traditions that are received by the Sunnites.[1] The Shiites, who chiefly

[1] See Baron Tornau's 'Basis of Mussulman Law,' St. Petersburg, 1850.

inhabit Persia, and are nearly always of Persian race, recognise the Sunnites as Mohammedans, though considering them heretical. In the same way the most of the Sunnites consider the Shiites merely as heretics; but owing to the decision of the Mullah Shems-eddin Mohammed of Samarkand, the Sunnites of Central Asia look upon the Shiites not as heretics but as infidels, and therefore believe it right to make slaves of them. On both sides the fanaticism is so great that heretics seem almost worse than infidels, and it would be difficult to find a parallel for it among Christians of the present day.

The Sunnites are divided into four chief sects, named after saints or eminent religious men,[1] who have sketched out certain rules for the external rites of Islam, or for the decision of certain judicial questions. These are the *Hanifeh*, or *Azem*, the *Shafi*, the *Malik*, and the *Hanbal* sects. Of the inhabitants of Central Asia the majority are Hanifeis, and a much smaller number Shafiis; but there are no others. The recent revival of pure Islamism by the *Wahabis* never extended to Central Asia, though it has so many votaries in India and Afghanistan.

It is the duty of every Mohammedan not only to believe in the doctrines of Islam but to perform all the external rites, prayers, fasts, &c. which are laid down by the spiritual teachers, and especially to attend prayers in the mosque on Friday, or *Jumma*. As in most Oriental countries, and as seemed to be the case in the early Christian Church, a day extends from sunset to sunset. The 300 mosques in Tashkent were always filled on Thursday evening and Friday morning, especially for the 11 o'clock prayer, while after that there were only the few habitual attendants who might be seen there every day, for it is an act of merit to attend the mosque daily; and then besides one has the chance of meeting one's friends and having a little gossip. The mosques here are for the most part small oblong buildings, with one side open to the air, in front of which is a large portico, the wall facing the entrance being in the direction of Mecca, and the *kibleh*, or point, which marks the direction of the *kaaba*, being placed there. The interior is generally destitute of ornament, save perhaps rude lithographs or prints, coming probably from India, which represent the holy buildings at Mecca,

---

[1] The Imam Azam-Abu-Hanifeh, 699-767; Imam Shafi, 767-819; Imam Malik ob. 795; and Imam Hanbal, who died in Bagdad, 855.

with written descriptions and explanations. At times, too, there are pasted on the wall in ornamental writing certain texts and sentences from the Koran. In the grounds of every mosque is a small pond for the use of those worshippers who have not had an opportunity of performing their ablutions at home. Every mosque has an *Imam*, or parish-priest, who says the prayers, and a *Sufi* or clerk. The Imams receive voluntary offerings from the inhabitants of their parishes at *Ramazan*, but the Sufis receive nothing except the remnants after a feast, and gowns as pay for washing the dead. One cannot but be struck with the appearance of good Mohammedans going to the mosque in their holiday clothes, one end of their turban floating over their shoulder, and all the elderly men with long heavy canes. Leaving their overshoes at the door, they go to their places and spread on the floor the praying-carpets, which they have brought with them, if the mosque does not provide any, for at prayers the worshipper must stand on a perfectly clean substance, and if possible on something owned by him. When prayer is once commenced they are all attention, and they must think of nothing else whatever. The postures and prayers are the same here as in other Sunnite countries, with some slight variations in the position of the hands or the manner of bowing; and one notices here, even perhaps more than elsewhere, the deep religious earnestness which seems to pervade all. It is customary for the worshippers to stand and kneel in regular lines in the mosque or portico, and not in any place that may please individual caprice; and should any person put himself forward he is contravening the principle of equality which rules among Mussulmans, and his conduct is severely blamed. I remember one instance which caused some little talk. Said Azim, of whom I have already spoken, one day at the mosque took a position in advance of all the rest, as perhaps he had noticed that high Russian dignitaries did in their church, for many natives have attended the Russian service out of motives of curiosity. He was reprimanded by the Imam, but still refused to stand in the line; and when the service was over, being censured in more severe terms by the Imam, he told him that he would do as he pleased, and that if such remarks were made to him he would have him expelled from the parish. The parishioners took the side of their Imam, and since that time

Said Azim has been obliged either to absent himself or to take an equal position with the rest.

Islam admits of many religious orders, both monastic and unmonastic, who, though subjected to a less strict discipline, are superior in numbers as well as in influence on the popular mind to the monastic brotherhoods of the Christian Church. To some one of these various orders belong the *Duvanas*, or Dervishes (called also *Kalendar*), who are so frequently seen in the towns of Central Asia. In Tashkent the dervishes are prohibited as dangerous to public order, their sermons and exhortations being often of a seditious character. In Hodjent and Samarkand they are freer. In the monastic fraternities, or *Sulhuk*, there are persons of all conditions of life, who adopt the mystic principles of the order, as the surest way of reaching salvation. Such fraternities exist at Tashkent, and the most prominent ones are the *Nakshbandi*, *Hufiá*, *Jahriá*, *Khodrié*, and *Tchistia*, the last, however, being chiefly followed in Hodjent and Khokand. It is very difficult to ascertain the origin and foundation of these orders, each having its separate legendary history, in which it strictly believes, and each being protected by some saint, the *Nakshbandi*, for example, by Baha-uddin, the celebrated saint of Bukhara; the *Jahriá* by Hazret Yasavi, the eminent saint who is buried in Turkistan; and each has its method for obtaining the eternal blessing of the Almighty, for exalting the soul, and for arriving at a state of perpetual happiness. The *Hufiá* believe that this spiritual exaltation is to be obtained by silent prayer, while the *Khodrié* prefer gaining it by exertion of the voice and loud cries. The *Nakshbandi* differ much from the others in their rules, and live more like monks. The brotherhood of the *Jahriá* has daily services in various places in Tashkent, as, for instance, every Sunday until Monday morning in the mosque of Ishan Hodja, and on Monday from eight o'clock in the morning until two o'clock in the afternoon in the mosque of Hodja Akhrar; while from nine o'clock on Thursday evening until five or six o'clock on Friday morning the service is held in the mosque of Ishan Sahib Hodja, near the *Urda* bazaar, where I had an opportunity of witnessing the ceremonies.

At about ten o'clock one Thursday evening, in company with several friends, we went to this mosque, and were at once admitted. I may remark here that Russians have not the slightest difficulty in entering any of the mosques in Tashkent, and are not even requested to take off their boots; and, what seems to me to be a great stretch of politeness, there is no objection made to their smoking in the precincts. Some thirty men, young and old, were on their knees in front of the *kibleh* reciting prayers with loud cries and violent movements of the body, and around them was a circle two or three deep of men standing, who were going through the same motions. We took up a position in one corner and watched the proceedings. For the most part the performers or worshippers had taken off their outside gowns and their turbans, for the night was warm and the exercise was violent. They were reciting the words *Hasbi rabi jal Allah* ('My defence is the Lord. May Allah be magnified'); *Mo fi kalbi hirallah* ('There is nothing but God in my heart'); *Nuri Muhammed sall Allah* ('My light, Mohammed, God bless him'); *La iloha ill Allah* ('There is no God but Allah').

These words were chanted to various semi-musical motives, in a low voice, and were accompanied by a violent movement of the head over the left shoulder towards the heart, then back, then to the right shoulder, and then down, as if directing all the movements towards the heart. These texts were repeated for hundreds and hundreds of times, and this *Zikr* usually lasted for an hour or two, though it depended upon the will of the *Ishan* who was leading. At first the movements were slow, but continually increased in rapidity until the performers were unable to endure it longer. If anyone failed in his duty, or were slower, or made less movement than was required, the Ishan who regulated the enthusiasm went up to him and struck him over the head, or pushed him back out of the circle and called another into it. Occasionally persons got so worn out with their cries, and so wet with perspiration, that it became necessary for them to retire for a few minutes' rest, and their places were immediately taken by others. When their voices became entirely hoarse with one cry another was begun, and finally the cry was struck up of '*Hai, Hai! Allah Hai!*' ('Live, Allah, the immortal'), at first slowly, with an inclination of the body to the ground; then the rhythm grew faster and in cadence, the body became more and more vertical, until at once they all stood up; the measure still increased in rapidity, and each one placing his hand on the shoulder of his neighbour and thus forming several concentric rings, they moved in a mass from side to side of the mosque, leaping about, and always crying '*Hai Allah Hai!*' Hitherto there had been something wild and unearthly in it, but now to persons of weak nerves it became positively painful, and two of my friends were so much impressed as to be obliged to leave the mosque. Although I was sufficiently cold-blooded to see the ridiculous rather than the horrible side of this, I could not help receiving an impression that the devotees were a pack of madmen, whose motions were utterly independent of any volition of their own. Finally, as their strength gave out the mass gradually found its way back to the *kibleh*, and standing in a half-circle, moved their bodies from right to left with the same words, *Hai Hai! Allah Hai!* or with a slight change, *Hua Allah!* moving forwards and backwards. At last several of the worshippers came forward to the centre of this ring and began a wild frenzied dance, the accompaniment being constantly changed. They seemed entirely to have lost their senses, and often rushed against some of those who surrounded them, pulled them violently into the midst and forced them also to dance. Then, when all their physical powers were exhausted, the brethren of the order again sat down in a circle and devoted themselves to contemplation, while the *Ishan* recited a prayer. After the prayer there was a pathetic recitation by a *Hafiz* (the word *Hafiz* is employed here to denote one who recites the poems of *Hafiz*, or generally any religious verses) of some touching episode in the life of one of the saints, or of reflections on the mortality of man or the fires of Gehenna. The intonations of the voice were very remarkable, and were often accompanied by most singular gestures, the hands or a book being often held to the side of the mouth, in order to throw the voice as far as possible. Often these recitations are merely collections of meaningless words, which always seem to produce the same effect on the hearers, and are constantly interrupted by cries of *Hi, ho, och och, ba ba,* and groans and sobs, and the hearers weep, beat their breasts with their fists, or fall upon the ground. When one *Hafiz* has finished a second begins, and another prayer by the *Ishan* follows, interrupted from time to time by the regular chant of the brethren, *Ya hai ya*, *Allah*, or *Allah akhbar*, or accompanied by gestures and the stroking of the face and beard, while the words themselves are silently recited. The cries and movements then begin again, then follow the dances, until finally everything seems to be done at once, each one endeavouring to drown the voices of the others, until fatigue again intervenes, when silence prevails, and so over and over again the performance goes on until the morning. There is no regular rule as to the sequence of different acts of devotion, the whole matter being regulated by the order of the *Pir* or *Ishan*. After a while we retired from the mosque, and were taken to the chief *Ishan*, who was too unwell to preside at the performance, but feasted us with some tea and fruit; and on our return his assistant, knowing that he would receive at least a ruble on our departure, did his best to make the performances more interesting, changing them more rapidly and devoting more time to dancing and less to recitation. When the cries were the loudest and the motions the most violent he seemed quite content, and even asked if we were pleased by it; yet this is the most fanatical sect of Muslims in Central Asia.

I do not know whether it be a wish to please their Russian masters, or whether it be a sign of gradual liberalism which has crept in, that the Mussulmans are so willing to show Christians their religious rites. I am inclined to think, however, that it is owing to a gradually increasing spirit of indifferentism. It has been found necessary in all Central Asiatic countries to keep up the observances of religion by severe penalties; both in Khokand and Bukhara there exist officials called *Reis* whose duty is to compel the attendance of the inhabitants at the mosques, even driving them if necessary from their shops and occupations. Should religious laxity become known to this official, he, or one of his assistants, quickly punishes it by blows administered by a broad strap fastened to a handle, which he carries over his right shoulder; he is required, however, not to remove his hand from his shoulder in giving the blow, though this does not prevent it from being severe. When the Russians occupied Tashkent they abolished the office of *Reis*, and since that time there is much laxity of observance; the mosques are much more thinly attended. The *Kazis* say that not half so many go to daily prayers as formerly, and many persons, especially those who are much occupied, never think during the day of making their ablutions or of saying their prayers. Much has been said of the fanaticism of Central Asia, but the fanaticism seems to me more apparent than real. The Mullahs and Dervishes are fanatical partly from a spirit of caste, and partly because it is their interest to be so. The rest of the population are often religious only when in public. They will let pass many observances and commit many sins if they think no one knows it, but will be the loudest in their cries against one who is found out.

There has not been the slightest hindrance offered by the Russians to the full exercise of Mohammedanism, which is professed by many Russian officials, and is one of the state religions, the most of the Mussulman subjects of the Empire being under the control of the *Mufti*, who resides at Ufa, and who by-the-by is a Russian nobleman and an accomplished gentleman. General Kaufmann has refused to allow any missionary enterprises among the natives, and one or two persons who have come from St. Petersburg with this idea have been compelled to quit Tashkent sooner than they at first intended. This action of the Russian Administration is very praiseworthy, and is sure to be followed by very excellent results. The natives are content in seeing that their religion is not oppressed, and that there are no martyrs is perhaps one reason why there is less religious enthusiasm. During the cholera of 1872 the *Kazis* and chief inhabitants of Tashkent made a representation to the Government requesting that they would prohibit dances of boys and various other customs which they said were not in accordance with the strict rules of their religion, and they desired the Russians to compel attendance at the mosques. It was impossible to grant the last request, but upon this representation the public dances of boys were for a time all stopped, not so much on account of the religious feeling, as because by gathering large crowds together they might be instrumental in propagating disease.

Education in Tashkent, as in general throughout Central Asia, is entirely religious. In one sense it can be said to be in the hands of the clergy, for although the teachers are not generally speaking parish priests, yet they belong to the learned class which is instructed only in religion and religious law, and nothing is taught which does not have some bearing upon religion or law. Schools are of two kinds, the *makhtab*, or primary school, of which there is usually one in every parish attached to the mosque; and the *medressé*, or college, where the higher religious and legal studies are prosecuted, of which there are seventeen in Tashkent, six of them large and flourishing. Of these the college of Kukol Tash was founded 450 years ago. The college of Barak Khan, founded some 320 years ago, has 100 students. It was at one time almost reduced to ruin, but Khanayat Shah, one of the generals of Malla Khan, gave it a large property during his lifetime, and on his death left it much more, which was confirmed by the Khan. The college of Beklar-Bek, which was built only about forty years ago, is one of the largest and richest. It owns many shops and houses, besides mills and lands, and supports 200 students. The teachers of the *makhtabs* are paid by voluntary contributions from the parents of the pupils of from twenty to forty kopeks a year, and a special gift or a gown before the holidays, which occur twice a year, before the feasts of Ruza-ait and Kurban-ait. Besides this they receive a loaf of bread or some small gift every Thursday. The pupils in the *medressés* pay nothing, but they, as well as their professors, are supported from the revenues of the college derived from *vaqf*, or lands and property given for religious uses. The endowment of mosques and colleges has for centuries past been looked upon as a work of piety and glory, and many even during their lives devote their fortunes to such good ends. I remember visiting one evening the college of Seid Abdul Kasim, a man who is universally regarded as a saint in Tashkent. At first he would have no intercourse whatever with the Russians, but since then, not finding them so bad as he expected, he has altered his opinion. Seid Abdul Kasim is no doubt a very learned man in Mussulman law, but what he and his family are chiefly celebrated for is their ability to recite the whole of the Koran by heart. A person who can do this is called here *kari*; in the Levant, *hafiz*. His two sons, a grandson, and two daughters—though the latter I did not see—are said to be able to accomplish this feat; and what is more strange, scarcely one of them is at all acquainted with Arabic, and the effort therefore is entirely one of memory, they not having the slightest idea of the meaning of the words which they repeat. They of course know the contents of the Koran from illegal translations in the Persian and Turki, but would be unable to translate it verse for verse. The college of Seid Abdul Kasim is supported entirely by him. At one time his revenues were considerably diminished by the forced closing of his *sarai* on the bazaar in consequence of the opening of the Tashkent fair. Upon the advice of some friends he proposed to the Russian Administration to introduce into his college courses of the Russian language and of modern sciences, on condition that the prohibition against his *sarai* should be withdrawn. As the coal sold in his *sarai* could not be brought with advantage to the fair, his request was acceded to; but whether the authorities forgot this proposition, or whether their ideas changed, no steps were taken either to co-operate with Abdul Kasim or to provide him with teachers, and the proposed courses have not yet begun.

Boys begin to study in the primary schools at about five or six years of age, and continue through a course lasting at least seven years. They commence with the alphabet, which is followed by parts of the Koran, and then study six or seven books, among which are 'Tchar Kitab,' 'Mantyk,' and 'Farsegain.' These seven books they must be able to read and copy with ease, but after that the course is not fixed, and they read various books in Persian or Turki with no special sequence. The first few books they are obliged to read aloud all at one time, and they learn to write, with the usual Indian ink, on wooden slates like small spades. The teacher, with huge spectacles on his nose, sits on one side, with a pile of books near him, and round him is a circle of boys, all kneeling and bending over their books, which are upon the floor. A spectator wonders how the teacher is able to distinguish anything, but he is so used to it that should one boy be for a moment silent he is immediately reminded of his duties with a long rod. With the exception of one or two books, the boys understand nothing of what they read, though it is perhaps better for their morals that this should be the case. The attendance is from sunrise till about five o'clock in the evening, with occasional short intervals during the day for rest and refreshment. Holidays are very few. When a boy begins to read the Koran it is customary for his father to present the teacher with a gown. As soon as a boy has finished the course of the primary school he may begin that of the college, where he is instructed in religious law. The course at the college, which is divided into three classes, includes at least twenty-eight books, though it may extend to 137, and lasts about fifteen years. But few ever finish the entire course; if they do so, they are then qualified to be Imams, or parish priests, teachers of schools, or Muftis, and secretaries of the Kazis. The revenues of the college are looked after by the steward, or *mutevali*, who collects them and pays the regular amounts to the professors and pupils and to the various servants of the college.

The pupils of the college usually prepare their lessons beforehand, either in their rooms at home or in the grounds of the *medressé*. I was present at several recitations or lectures held by a professor, or *mudaris*, who first read a passage of the textbook and then commented on it, his hearers showing that they were paying attention by groaning from time to time *Ach, ach*, and nodding their heads. They then made remarks and disputed over the passage, one interrupting the other when his opinion was different, to which the professor likewise assented with *Ach, ach*. Bystanders are also allowed to join in the discussion, and one or two of the Mullahs who were with me did so, and the conversation became very animated. The question was, I believe, about some peculiarities of the law of divorce. When the pupils have ceased their disputes, the professor states what is the true doctrine with regard to the matter and passes to the next paragraph. The manner of teaching is not without advantage, though the prolonged discussions over very trifling matters are apt to waste the time of the students, and consequently extend the number of years during which they will have to study. Besides the regular *medressé* there are some special schools, such as *Saliavat Khana*, where nothing but prayers are taught; *Karikh Khana*, where the pupils do nothing but learn the Koran by heart, so as to become *Kazi*; and *Masnavi Khana*, where the works of the poet Masnavi are studied.

Education is not confined to the men; girls also are taught to read and write in special schools, and study for three or four years, after which for the next year or two, up to their marriage, they are occupied in learning to sew.

Among my most interesting acquaintances in Tashkent were

the Kazis, or native judges, two of whom I remember with great pleasure. The most able and honest of them was Mukaneddin Hodja, son of the former Kazi Kalian. One of my earliest visits in Tashkent were made to him, and with him and his brother and cousin, all equally learned and pious, I spent a very agreeable evening. Conversation was of course chiefly on education and on Mussulman law, but I found that they did not disdain occasional jokes and jests, though these were said somewhat under their breath, as if they were contrary to the spirit of the place, for there was a mosque and a small college close by, where the Kazi had his students of law.

The law courts among the native population of Central Asia are of two kinds: among the settled population there are the *Kazis*, who administer justice on the basis of written laws,—the *Shariat*, founded on the Koran, and introduced together with Mohammedanism; and among the nomads,—Kirghiz, and others,—the *Biis*, who judge according to the unwritten traditions and customs, *adat*. Though these traditions are unwritten and unformulated they are none the less generally known, and are a pure product of national life, altered by no importations from a foreign civilisation, and in many particulars directly contrary to the doctrines of Mussulman law. One prominent characteristic of this traditional law is, that no difference is made between civil and criminal offences, all crimes being viewed only in their relation to others, and being punished by damages in favour of the injured party. A *bii* is, properly speaking, an arbitrator, versed in the national traditions, but bound by no formalities. The proceedings are therefore entirely oral; no record is kept, and no appeal can be taken. The *biis*, up to the time when the Russians introduced changes into the government of the Steppe, were not permanent officers, but were chosen for the occasion, although naturally a man distinguished for his probity and his justice would be the more often called upon to fill this office; but disputes were often referred to the first comer. A Russian Cossack, who went yearly to fish in Lake Issyk-Kul, acquired such a reputation among the Kirghiz of that region that he was frequently asked to be *bii*, and was paid the usual fees; many affairs were even purposely deferred until his yearly visit.

The Russians retained the court of *biis*, believing that

there was nothing in this institution opposed to the spread of Russian influence, but introduced certain changes, in making the *biis* permanent officers elected by the people, and in establishing appeals from a single *bii* to councils of *biis* in two instances, and from thence to the Russian courts. For the purposes of appeal, the very idea of which is opposed to the theory of a court of arbitration, it is necessary to have written records of the proceedings of the courts and of the judgments. As the Kirghiz are generally uneducated, they are thus thrown into the hands of clerks and copyists, chiefly wandering Tartar Mullahs, whose influence has already proved very harmful.

In the settled portions of the country the courts of the Kazis, judging after the *Shariat*, or written Mussulman law, were brought in with Mohammedanism, and have gradually got the upper hand of the traditionary procedure, which was more in accordance with the national spirit. Some of the Uzbek clans, however, still preserve their custom law—*uzbektchilyk*— especially for family matters, in spite of their Kazis; and in Shahrisabs the Mussulman code was only permanently introduced by the Amir Nasrullah on his conquest. When at his death Shahrisabs became again independent under Jura Bek, the Mussulman code was retained, as being best adapted to the country.

Under Mussulman rule in Tashkent—as is now the case in the independent Khanates—the Kazis, who were appointed for life by the Khan or Bek, after a long and careful examination in the rules of the Shariat and the decisions of learned Mullahs by a special commission of learned men, were unlimited in number. The court was small, with but a single Kazi; and, as there were no fixed districts, the suitor had recourse to that one in whom he had the greatest confidence. In the larger places there was the Kazi Kalian, who was as it were the presiding justice. The proceedings in all these courts were oral, but the judgment and the documentary evidence were copied into special books kept for this purpose by the *mufti*, or secretary, and sealed with the official seal of the Kazi. Citations of similar cases were often made by the *alyamas*, who acted as advisers to the Kazi. The Kazi had jurisdiction in all civil suits, but only in small criminal matters, the larger being reserved for the decision of the Bek himself. Persons who were dissatisfied with the decisions of the Kazi could lay an appeal before the Bek, who in some cases left such appeals without attention, in others he called a session of all the Kazis of the place for investigation of the matter. The Kazi Kalian was the president of this session and kept order there, which gave him a great influence, for the other Kazis usually considered it a duty to agree with him in everything, not only on account of his experience and learning, but also from a desire to stand well with him. The more important criminal cases were sent by the Bek to this session of Kazis for decision, but capital and heavy punishments could not be inflicted except with the confirmation of the Bek.

When the Russians occupied Tashkent and prepared regulations for the government of the country it was considered best not to touch the principle of the native courts. The Kazi, besides deciding all ordinary suits, had special charge of marriages, divorces, and all family matters, which were governed by rules coming from the Koran, and it would therefore be impossible to abolish his jurisdiction without hurting the religious feelings of the Mussulmans. As this was very undesirable it was thought best to retain the Kazis. The Russians had the examples of the Caucasus and the Crimea, where the Kazis had been retained, and where by giving a right of appeal or choice, on consent of both the parties, to the Russian Court, the importance of the Kazis had gradually diminished, and the jurisdiction of the Russian courts had greatly extended among the Mussulman natives, except for family matters. The Russians, too, might have learned something from the English in India. In 1864 the Kazis in India were abolished, a step which caused great discontent among the Mussulmans, as it was found impossible without them to have legal marriages or to settle divorce or abduction cases. The English finally saw the error into which they had fallen, and lately revived the Mussulman courts of the Kazis. Though the Russians had every right and reason to follow the example of the previous Central Asiatic rulers and appoint the Kazis, yet, from a curious devotion to the principle of popular election, which in a country like this, accustomed only to arbitrary rule, was of very doubtful application, established that they should be elected for a limited term by the best men of the community, in the same manner as the aksakals and police officials. This elective system has turned out very badly, bribery and corruption having become prevalent in the elections, and direct pressure being at times exerted by the authorities for their favourites, certain persons being excluded from the lists as being fanatical, and the choice of certain candidates almost commanded. The importance of individual judges was somewhat diminished by abolishing the office of Kazi Kalian, appointing each Kazi to a separate district, and rendering it obligatory for the inhabitants of the district to have recourse to his judgment, and by making all the Kazis equal among themselves. The Kazi had final decision in all civil matters of less than a hundred rubles, but in suits for sums greater than a hundred rubles, and for the lesser criminal affairs,—the more important criminal cases being reserved for the Russian courts,—there was arranged a session of all the Kazis of a district. At the same time the privilege was given that on the appeal of both parties, either before the session of the Kazis or after it, the dispute could be referred to the Russian courts. There was no qualification required for the office of Kazi except that the candidates should be in good repute among the community, over twenty-five years of age, and not accused or condemned by any court. No salary was fixed by the Government, but it was allowed to the community in which they lived, before electing them, to give them a salary or to permit them to receive fees on affixing their seals. In the city of Tashkent there are four Kazis, whose decisions have in general given satisfaction, and there have been as yet few appeals to the Russian courts; but during the last three years there have been instances where several of the Kazis have been accused of having taken bribes and of having been influenced in their decisions, so that some of them have been removed. In one instance the Kazi, being hand-and-glove with certain of the officials in some land speculations, was retained for a long time against the popular will, and he was only removed when an outbreak was threatened.

The whole Mohammedan legislation is based on the Koran, the traditions and books which interpret it, and the decisions and examples of the first Khalifs in accordance with it. This code of law, contained, with all its glosses and commentaries, in numberless volumes, is called the *Shariat*—the road for reaching heavenly bliss.[1] It is impossible to give in a few words any idea of Mussulman law, but I cannot help laying stress on the principle which is its foundation, namely, that in the actions of Mussulmans good faith is always to be supposed. The judge is never to suppose either deceit or malice in the action of anyone until that person has admitted it or it has been shown by proof. If in a suit before the Kazi a defendant do not admit the justice of the plaintiff's demand he is obliged either to bring witnesses on his side or to take an oath that the complaint is unjust. If he take this oath the case is at an end. In some cases it is possible for the defendant to demand that the plaintiff take an oath that his complaint is correct. If he swear to it, the matter is decided in his favour; if he be unwilling to do so, the matter is decided in favour of the defendant. If the defendant absolutely demand that the plaintiff take an oath, and refuse himself to take one, and after the demand—three times repeated—of the Kazi should still refuse, the matter is decided against him. The repugnance to taking an oath is so great that it is considered a great insult to be requested to do so, and often a suitor, though he may have a perfectly just claim, will prefer to lose it rather than lower his dignity in the eyes of himself and his friends by swearing to his complaint or defence. It is but fair to say for the Mussulmans that they show great good faith in their transactions with one another, and suits-at-law are much less common than in many more civilised countries.

Sometimes, in default of evidence, resort is had to superstitious means for discovering the truth. In a certain case of theft suspicion fell on several persons of bad reputation, although there was no plain proof against them. Finally the Aksakal gave an order to the inhabitants of the neighbourhood to 'pile earth,' which meant that each one had a fixed time in which to bring in the corners of his gown some handfuls of earth and place it carefully in one heap. When the heap was afterwards examined the stolen money was found, and thus the loser recovered his property without the thief being known. In another case I was told of, the suspected persons were ordered each to swallow a small piece of bread. The guilty party, excited

---

[1] In Turkistan the Shariat is chiefly expounded from the 'Mukhtessr-ul-viksiyat,' and the 'Sheriaul-Islam.'

probably by the commotions of his conscience, was unable to swallow it, and immediately made confession and restored the stolen property. Another way is to write the names of all the accused on small pieces of paper and shake them up in a washbowl. Each of the accused is then obliged to poise this bowl on the fore-finger of his right hand. If after a little the bowl begins to revolve, it shows that the name of the thief is there. Several of the names are then taken out and the experiment is again tried until only the name of the thief is left in. This method, I am assured, is certain, and I presume most believers in spiritualism would agree to it.

The original legislation of Mohammed being made for the Arabs of the desert, it was necessarily narrow in its scope, and there is some difficulty in applying it to the wants of more developed and civilised communities. To accomplish this it has been necessary to call in tradition, casuistry, and special pleading; but there are too few broad principles, and too many practical applications and petty details in the Mussulman code to make casuistry an easy matter. For instance, its provisions are too strict as regards trade and inheritance to suit modern civilisation; it is impossible by Mussulman law to purchase or sell articles which are not in existence, such as future crops, or to take interest on money. But these restrictions are somehow successfully evaded by legal fictions, and business goes on much the same in Mussulman countries as in others, although the spirit of speculation and credit is less rife there. Up to the present time the Mussulman code answers well enough the needs of Mussulman communities, and in the hands of skilful lawyers it is capable of still greater development.

We should make an error did we, as is often done, compare the strict theory of Islam and of Mussulman law as laid down in the Koran and in the Shariat, with the practice of Christianity and civilisation. A comparison of the theory—the strict letter—of the Bible with that of the Koran is not so much to the disadvantage of the latter. Were the precepts of the Scripture to be carried out to the letter, as has been attempted at many times and places, civilisation would be almost impossible, and life would be at least as restricted as it is now in Mussulman countries. Christianity, as expounded by the Puritans and the literal believers, constantly inculcates separation from the world, exclusive devotion to religious life and religious ceremonies, heedlessness of the temporal future, and the sundering of every tie which unites man to the world whenever it be contrary to the development of the conscience and the spiritual life. This is hardly better than the strict regulations regarding food, dress, posture, and prayer, which are found in the Mussulman code. But in the development of Christian civilisation the letter has been disregarded, and Christian sects nearly all preach the Gospel according to a far more liberal interpretation of it. Science is as strictly precluded by the Bible as it is by the Koran, and yet science flourishes. Science and art both flourished once under Mussulman rule as well. When Islam first arrived on the civilised soil of Europe and Asia, it yielded enough to outside influences to permit of an extraordinary development of learning and civilisation, where art, science, and philosophy all found their votaries. Since that time it has been expelled in great part from Europe; waves of barbarism have passed over Asia, which effectually destroyed civilisation and enlightenment there, and threw nations into a state of torpor and stagnation from which they have never recovered. This, however, was not the effect of Mohammedanism, though that religion has had its part in keeping up this state of things. Relieved of external influences, fanaticism and ignorance had full play. Yet the present state of Mussulman countries seems hardly worse than that of Europe in the dark ages preceding the Reformation, if we take into account the difference of races and national character. Unfortunately, the contact of Christian civilisation with Mohammedan nations has, thus far, only served to develope faults and vices under a gloss of civilisation. Reform and progress, to be stable, must come from within. But one great attempt at reform has yet been made—the Wahhabi movement—which, in misdirected zeal, corresponds so closely with the Puritan movement in England. There is reason, however, to believe that another great revival of Mohammedanism is at hand. How far it will be beneficial to the world, the future alone can tell.

CHAPTER V.

THE BAZAARS AND TRADE.

The Tashkent bazaar—Sunday bazaar—Silversmiths—Brassworkers—Cutlery and arms—Iron-foundries—Tea-houses—Barbers—Apothecaries—Cosmetics—Oils—Dyes—Shoes and Leather—The Kirghiz bazaar—Caravanserais—Hindoos—Money-lending and its subterfuges—Pottery—Embroidery—Cotton goods—Silk and silk culture—Legendary history of silk—Weights and Measures—Money—Duties and Taxes—The Fair and its results—Statistics of Central Asiatic trade—Transportation—Trade routes—Proposed railway.

ACCORDING to Central Asiatic ideas, a city, to be really such, must have a *Jumma* mosque, that will hold all the inhabitants at Friday prayers, and must possess all of the thirty-two guilds or trades (*kasaba*) which are thought to comprise the whole world of commerce. Possibly there were thirty-two guilds originally, although there are many more now, but probably this number was chosen because the human body is supposed to be made up of thirty-two members, for which reason, the body of merchants must be made up of thirty-two guilds. Moreover, each branch of industry, such as shoemaking, silk-weaving, &c., must have at least thirty-two subdivisions. All of these trades are to be seen in full working in the bazaar, and it is the bazaar of Tashkent that we must now visit.

As we pass along the great street which divides Tashkent nearly into equal parts it becomes straighter and wider. Finally, we descend a little hill over the rough stones, and cross a rude bridge over one of the canals which water the city, with a large mill-pond at the left. Then begin little shops, with close by an iron foundry, and a cotton-printing establishment, walls with skeins of freshly-dyed cotton hanging out to dry, and before us is the great *medressé* of Beklar Bek, which is the real beginning of the bazaar. We pass through the gate and go up the steep path to the platform of the mosque, whence we can overlook the whole bazaar, and yet we see only three or four shops. We look over what seems to be a flat clayey plain toward the hill beyond, crowned by another mosque, near which rises the domed roof of a bath. The bazaar lies in the winding valley between these hills, and we see merely the flat mud roofs of the houses and shops, overgrown sometimes with grass and poppies. It is only when in the very bazaar that we have any idea of it, and it is only by walking there day after day that we can begin to realise its size, for the streets are so crooked and so thronged with people that there is no vista whatever. The foot-passenger must keep carefully to the raised paths by the side of the shops, or he will run the risk of being trampled on by the Kirghiz and Sarts riding heedlessly along on horses and asses. Each street is devoted to a single trade; here are the silk shops, there the jewellers, here the brass workers, while occasionally a large gateway with a court beyond marks the place of a caravanserai for the accommodation of guests and the storage of goods. Here and there are open spaces, in the centre of which are small booths sheltered for the most part by umbrellas and mushroom-like awnings of woven reeds, while all about perambulatory vendors collect in groups. Here is a small kitchen with cabobs and patties cooking over the coal-fires, here a tea shop, there the stand of a baker, and next perhaps a man, sitting crosslegged on a high platform, deals out spoonfuls of snow and sugary syrup to the boys at a *tcheka* each. The sun pours down in the streets and makes the bazaar intensely hot, for there are few awnings spread over the street as in many other Asiatic bazaars. Each shop is merely a small square room with perhaps a still smaller one behind it, quite open to the street, as the boards which compose the front of the shop are all taken down in the day-time. The merchant sits crosslegged on a rug or bit of matting, while his wares either occupy the rest of the floor, or are placed on shelves behind him. Most of the shops are so small that there is rarely place for a friend or two inside with him. The customers either stand in the street, or sit on their horses, or take their positions on the threshold of the shop.

The whole bazaar is old and primitive, looking as though it had seen no change nor improvement for a century. General Tchernaief proposed to make two wide boulevards through the old town, crossing each other at right angles, and the Prefect of the city has long desired to improve the bazaar by making through it a wide straight street, well paved or macadamised, connecting it with the Russian quarter of Tashkent. This would lead to the reconstruction of some portion of the bazaar, and would be of great benefit, not only to trade, but to health. This project, however, has been three times rejected by the Governor-General on the ground that it would be detrimental to trade, that is, that it would increase the trade of the native bazaar and draw people away from the newly started fair on the other side of the city, of which I shall speak presently.

The chief day for the bazaar in Tashkent is Wednesday; not that there are not always customers and that the shops are not open on every day, but on Wednesday there is far more trade, and people come in from the country bringing in what little things they have to sell. The throng is then so great that it is difficult to move about with comfort. I am speaking only of the great bazaar, for there are besides this several smaller ones near the gates, and especially one called the Urda bazaar at the edge of the Russian town near the former citadel (*urda*).

A new bazaar has of late grown up in the Russian town, chiefly for the sale of bread, fruit, meat, vegetables, and small wares, being in fact a market devised for the Russians. This is chiefly frequented on Sundays, and thence takes the name of 'Sunday bazaar.' The name of 'Drunken bazaar,' which has been given to it by the Russians, is probably owing to its being full of drunken soldiers, for in Tashkent these are not kept under the strictest discipline, and it is found that imprisonment is of no avail as a cure for intemperance.

I often used to stroll about the bazaar alone, or with the Mullah or other friends, either bargaining with the shopkeepers, or sitting on the thresholds and looking at the labours of the artisans, or watching the trade that was going on. The shopkeepers were always ready to trade, although with a certain methodical slowness, never showing you more than one or two articles at a time, bringing down one or two more, if these did not suit you, and never seeming eager to induce you to purchase. If you told them that you did not want to buy anything, but had merely come for *tomasha,* or amusement, they were always ready to explain and show you everything you wished to see. Their commercial calculations seemed to be peculiar, for they always objected to selling their whole stock of any article at once; and if they did so, always asked a higher price in consequence. As one man said, 'Why, I have enough goods now to trade for a week, and if I sell them all to you, what shall I busy myself with?'

I was particularly interested with the jewellers. Their shops are all collected in one small street, and it was amusing to sit and watch them by turns. Upon every new occasion they produced to me a few articles which they never seemed to think of before. Their stock-in-trade was always very small; a few silver rings and earrings, belt clasps and amulets to be worn on the shoulders or in the hair, and sometimes necklaces and bracelets set with pieces of coloured glass. There were few precious stones to be had, and none that seemed of value. Everywhere were great quantities of turquoises, but nearly always of very bad quality, chiefly used for decorating bridles, the horns of saddles, and the handles of sabres, where they are all thickly set together in silver, and then filed and polished down to one uniform surface, looking then much like shagreen leather. Their instruments were very simple: a small hand-furnace which a boy blew with a bellows, a few forceps and rods, and thin silver strips and wires which they made into filagree work. Very little of the work seemed to be done in gold; all that I saw consisted of very thin leaves of gold, which were cut into small pieces, hammered together, and then stamped in a mould. Among the silversmiths were one or two watchmakers, principally Tartars, who were occupied in repairing watches of European make, or sometimes in making rude imitations, with Arab numerals on the dials. The trade in watches must be considerable, for most of the richer natives have one or two, which they usually keep in a small leathern pouch and produce with great delight. In Bukhara one can buy a good Swiss or English silver watch almost as cheaply as in Moscow.

The brass-workers occupy another street on the south side of the bazaar, and the whole neighbourhood is deafened with the sound of their hammering. The Russian *samovars*, which they are mending, first strike the eye. These are never made here, but are all imported from Russia—as was the case long before the Russian occupation. But they manufacture in great numbers the native teapots and ewers (*kumgan*), usually of very graceful shapes, and often of very delicate workmanship, being covered with fine ornament cut with a chisel; sometimes portions of the surface are covered with a thin coating of tin, which is chiselled so as to show the decoration in two metals. There seem, however, to be no very skilful master workmen, or else there is something greatly lacking in their taste, for these jugs are seldom completely finished, a beautifully decorated vessel often having a rude and clumsy handle, which has not even been filed down smooth. For purposes of washing they also make a large basin surmounted by a platter, pierced with delicate arabesques, to receive the water poured over the hands. Here, as elsewhere, the manufacture is divided into several branches, one shop making nothing but the bottoms of the ewers, another soldering them on, another producing the handles, another the covers, while others are occupied in chiselling the ornamentation on the sides. At the end of this row are heaps of large iron kettles for cooking purposes, brought from Russia. All the iron which is used is imported, and the natives work it but little, except for making knives and sabres. The greater part of the knives, razors, and scissors offered for sale are made of iron, although many knives have steel edges welded on, while some are made entirely of steel,—usually out of old sabres—and are sold at a much higher price. Knives being so necessary to the life of every Asiatic, this trade occupies a large number of persons, both for the manufacture and the sale. The handles are usually made of bone, often richly ornamented, and nearly every knife has a case, generally of horse leather dyed green. This is fastened to a piece of skin or leather, frequently with ornamented tassels, which is hung on the belt.

Few good sword-blades are made now-a-days, as the art in this part of Asia appears to be lost. The really fine ones are brought from Persia, and are handed down in families from father to son. They are therefore considered very precious, and are rarely to be bought even at high prices. I was offered two or three sabres, which seemed fair, at prices ranging from 10*l.* to 20*l.* There are not many good cutlers now in Russian Turkistan, and even in the native states there is no call for blades except when a war is imminent, and then the smiths have more than they can do; but in times of peace they devote themselves to the manufacture of knives, razors, and small instruments. Sword blades are sometimes re-made from good Damask blades which have become broken, and this branch of industry is carried on to a great extent at Hissar, and to some extent at Samarkand, but the more ordinary method of making a blade is to forge it from good iron or soft steel, and then weld upon it a thin edge from English needles. The native likes this blade because it will not break, as its method of manufacture makes it elastic and tough. Another method, similar I believe to that practised at Toledo, is to make a blade out of horse-shoes, or horse-shoe nails, and to put it between two very thin steel blades—those made of English needles being preferred—of equal curvature, and then to weld the whole into a solid mass, the edge being made by the union of the two steel blades. Most of the blades here are very much curved, few are straight. The wheel used in sharpening them is of wood, covered with leather thickly spread with emery powder. A strap is passed twice around its horizontal axle and pulled in alternate directions by one man, thus giving the wheel a motion first to right and then to left, while another applies to it the edge of the knife.

As to fire-arms, almost the only kind manufactured in Central Asia is the matchlock, the barrel being chiefly of rough European make or of old pattern, brought principally from India and Persia. In Tashkent there are a few iron-foundries, which are mostly occupied in making small articles for household use, such as lamps, which resemble very much the old Roman lamp in form, but are of far grosser workmanship; for, owing to the imperfect liquefaction of the iron, the surfaces are always rough. The whole process of casting is very primitive. A foundry consists of a court, with a shed at one side open always to the south, so as to give the sun's rays full play for drying the moulds. Fragments of iron mixed with charcoal are placed in an open iron pot lined with clay on a rude forge, which is fed by bellows worked by hand. When the iron is melted the pot is lifted off by hooks, and the contents are either ladled out, or in case of large articles poured into the moulds, which are sometimes skilfully made. The technical terms and the very name of the trade (*dig-rizi*, kettle-casting) being Tadjik would seem to show that this branch of manufacture was brought from Persia.

Weary with the heat we take refuge in one of the teahouses (*tchai-khana*),[1] where a group of natives is discussing the latest local gossip, or the rumours from the Khivan expedition. We sit down on a silk mattress, and the boy—these houses seem to be always kept by boys—throws a handful of

A BAZAAR-COOK.

green tea into a brass jug, fills it from the great Russian *samovar*, which stands at the entrance, lets it simmer a moment on the coals, and sets it before us, bringing us at the same time a small china bowl. We give a bystander a few small coins and he buys us a few lumps of sugar, some *kishmish*, or raisins, some small round cakes of hot bread, and some delicious apricots. If we wish for them we can have some meat patties from the cook-shop round the corner. Nothing but tea is sold in these tea-houses, and the natives bring their own bread and raisins

[1] Although both parts are native words, this compound expression was introduced by the Russians, and has now obtained the rights of citizenship. In speaking to each other Sarts usually say 'the *samovartchi's*,' using a word derived from the Russian—but long ago.

tied up in the folds of their girdles, which when spread out serve as their table-cloths.

We wind up with cigarettes, while our neighbours who are discussing the gossip of the day over their bowls of tea, take each a puff at a huge gourd pipe. On leaving the tea-house we find close by a barber in the act of shaving a customer's head. He uses no soap, but wets the scalp thoroughly from a small brass basin, and with admirable skill takes the hair off with a most uncomfortable looking iron razor stuck in a handle like a pen-holder. He then washes the head again, dries it on a towel, and with one turn of the razor takes an inch from the middle of the moustache. God forbid that he touch the beard or the ends of the moustache, but all laws of Mussulman propriety demand that the part immediately under the nose should be shaved clean. The barber, as in all primitive countries, is a surgeon as well, and will let your blood or operate on you as best he can, but he has no connection with the apothecary's shop over the way.

The little drawers, the round boxes with coloured labels, and the bunches of dried herbs, leave no doubt as to which that is. Here you can find all the drugs known to the Asiatic pharmacopœia. You can get, too, Persian dried lemons of the size of a nutmeg, but which when broken and soaked in your tea leave a decided flavour, small mirrors, and Russian paper; and here, also—as the very name of the shop, *attar-khana*, would indicate —you can find all the cosmetics used by the women, although these have but a small sale, as any garden will furnish the articles commonly used.

The most necessary is, perhaps, *usma*, a species of woad (*Isatis*) which furnishes a black colour for painting the eyebrows. The juice of the fresh leaves is squeezed into a tea-cup, and is applied with a small piece of reed instead of a brush, or with the finger. Fashion demands that not only the eyebrows, but also the space between them, shall be painted so as to make one long line. The colour is at first a dirty green, but in a few moments it becomes a bluish black, though it soon disappears, and has to be renewed every two or three days. This custom is so prevalent that even children of less than a year old are thus decorated. *Surma*, a black powder of antimony, is used for painting the eyelashes, even by men, and is thought to relieve the inflammation of the eyes caused by dust and wind. *Upa*, or white lead, brought from Russia, and rice-powder are the most common preparations for whitening the face, but they are used only by women whose complexion is very yellow. The clear olive complexion, which is sometimes seen among the pure Tadjiks of Samarkand, is not defiled with powder, as it is thought very beautiful of itself. Rouge (*iglyk*) is prepared by soaking cotton wool in an infusion of the root of some boraginous plant. Henna, for colouring the nails, is replaced by the common garden balsam. The leaves and flowers are bruised, mixed with a little alum, and at night bound about the nails of the fingers and toes, which in the morning will have a yellowish red colour. It was formerly the custom for the women, especially the old ones, to paint their teeth black with a powder composed of the gall of the pistachio tree mixed with the scales from a blacksmith's forge, but this has in great measure gone out of fashion. There are no pomades for the hair, which is cleaned solely by being thoroughly rubbed with sour milk and then washed in warm water. I do not know whether it is the result of this practice or not, that the women all have wonderfully thick and long, although coarse hair. They perfume their persons either by carrying a bunch of some sweet-smelling plant, usually basil, or with rose-water, which is used to such an extent as sometimes to make the society of women very unpleasant. Baths and houses are frequently perfumed by burning gums or roots, the most expensive and most esteemed of which is *sumbul*, the real nature of which was for a long time a puzzle. Mr. Fedtchenko managed to obtain a living root of it, which was successfully planted in the Botanical Gardens at Moscow, and proved to be an umbelliferous plant, to which the name was given of *Euryangium Sumbul*.

Two kinds of cosmetic soap are made, but usually the soap is very dirty and ill-smelling, being made by boiling together the ashes of a species of *Salicornia*, lime, and the lowest quality of tallow. Oil for cooking, lighting and other purposes is pressed from various kinds of seed, the most common being that from the *kunzhut*, or sesame. This is used chiefly in the preparation of food, but it frequently has a bad odour and a disagreeable taste, in consequence of being mixed with *indau*, (*Eruca*) and cotton seed. As the *indau* grows among the sesame, it is very difficult to prevent this admixture, but the cotton seed is used principally to increase the bulk of the residue, which brings a high price as food for animals. A special oil is also made from the *indau* for use in veterinary practice. Linseed oil is most common after sesame, and is used partly in food, but chiefly for lighting. Oil from walnuts, sunflower-seed and poppy-seed, is made in small quantities for use by the better classes. Hempseed oil is little used in cookery, because it acts on the head in the same way as *hashish*. From the seeds of the caper-plant an excellent oil is prepared, which burns with a clear bright flame without smoke. Candles are also manufactured from ordinary tallow, both candles and oil being sold in separate shops.

In similar small shops are sold the dye-stuffs in use. Besides indigo imported from India and Brazil, and other dye-woods coming from Russia, and madder, which grows wild and is also much cultivated in the gardens, there are some dyes, the use of which is perhaps peculiar to the country. One of these, *isparuk*, is a sulphur-yellow larkspur (*Delphinium sulphureum*) which grows in great abundance on the Steppes.[1] An infusion of its flowers gives a beautiful and permanent bright yellow dye. Another yellow dye is *tukhmak*, the flowers of *Sophora Japonica*. *Pugak*, a fungus growing on the mulberry tree, especially in Khokand, is used for dying skins a greenish yellow colour. Pomegranate peel is greatly employed for dying black. Another and the most common black dye is *buzguntch*, which is not a fruit, as some have supposed, but the gall-nut of the pistachio tree. Cochineal is frequently used for dying silk red. It is chiefly brought from Bukhara, although the insect is found in abundance in the spring in Tashkent and the neighbourhood, on the young leaves of the ash, mulberry and other trees. Since the introduction of *fuchsine* from Russia the use of cochineal and of other native dyes have fallen off. For that reason in Khokand the Khan prohibited the importation of fuchsine, as being an inferior dye-stuff. A kind of Indian ink is prepared for painting as well as for writing, by boiling together with rice and water the soot obtained by burning linseed oil. When it has reached a sufficient thickness it is allowed to dry in cakes.

[1] This plant would be very pretty for gardens, and might be of use in commerce. Unfortunately the seeds I brought did not germinate.

One whole street is taken up with the shoemakers, some giving their whole work to galoshes, some to the soft morocco boots so much in vogue, others to riding-boots with their soles studded with nails and with small sharp heels, each shop being devoted to a specialty, if it be only cutting out the leather for the soles. The methods of the tanner are very primitive, his vats being merely large holes or pits in the ground, although he has four different ways of preparing leather. In the first method the skins are soaked in a mixture of alum and soda, then well cleaned from the hair and washed, covered with a mixture of barley meal, and then dried and rubbed with tallow. Calf, goat and sheep skins are prepared in the same way, but instead of being rubbed with tallow they are tanned with the bark of the sumach (*Rheum Emodi*). They are coloured black with pistachio galls mixed with green vitriol. Yak and buffalo hides, after being subjected to the mixture of alum and soda, are salted and finally smoked. A kind of chamois-leather, chiefly used for riding-trousers, is made of goat and sheep skins in the same way and coloured red with madder, and yellow with *isparak*. *Saura*, a sort of shagreen, which is especially used for boots and galoshes, is made from horse and ass hides in much the same way; but, instead of smoking the skins, the tanners cut cross-lines in them by means of a sharp instrument, and after scattering over them millet seeds, spread felt over them and then trample on, or beat them. When the surface is well indented the skins are dried; the seeds are then removed from them and copper-filings mixed with a little arsenic and some substance, the composition of which is not known, are placed on them, by which they obtain a bright green colour.

Passing through rows of saddles, bridles and harness, leaving on our left the shops where carts with their large rude wooden wheels are made, we come to what is called the Kirghiz bazaar, where are to be found the productions of the nomads, especially camel's hair cloth, ropes, carpets and rugs, tent-frames and felt. The manufacture of felt is a specialty of the Kirghiz women. Placing on the ground a mat of reeds, they cover it with a thin layer of wool, which they beat with rods until it is even. They then sprinkle it thoroughly with water, or better with water in which oil cake has soaked for some time, and then tightly roll up the matting together with the wool, tying it at the ends and in the middle, and roll it along the ground, sprinkling it from time to time with water, and tightening the cords with which it is bound. After it has been sufficiently pressed in this way, they untie it and roll it without the matting for several hours, sprinkling it at times with water. It is then dried in the sun. Some of the finer kinds of felt are of wonderful lightness and beauty. The best is the white felt, brought from Kashgar, on which the native rulers are elevated on their accession. The rugs and the carpets made by the Kirghiz are coarse. The best are made by the Turkomans near Karshi and Tchardjui, and are to be found in any quantity only at Bukhara. Here also are the shops for selling the various kinds of grain and flour, and cotton, both cleaned and in the pod; and near by are booths, where one can procure all the garden and flower-seeds known to this country.

In going through the bazaar we frequently see large gates, inside of which are courts filled with merchandise. These are caravanserais, partly used for the storage of goods by wholesale merchants, and partly also for the accommodation of foreign merchants who come for a short time to trade. Three of them are occupied almost exclusively by Hindoos, of whom there are large numbers in every considerable town of Central Asia, there being some 140 in Tashkent alone. They come chiefly from Shikarpur, and although engaging in many kinds of commerce, devote themselves pre-eminently to money-lending and usury. With their tight trousers, their peculiar coats, and the red or black caste-marks on their foreheads, apart from their race-characteristics, they are easily distinguished. As soon as they saw that I was a stranger, they received me most hospitably, and each wished to be my entertainer. I tried in vain to find one who spoke English, although some could repeat the alphabet and the numerals, and say some common phrases. A little room at the corner was fitted up as a temple, and on a sort of altar were arranged numerous small idols, curious stones, and similar little objects. I was obliged to remove my shoes to enter, but, once inside, the acting priest took great pains to explain to me everything, and it was with great difficulty that I could persuade him to accept a small offering for the benefit of his shrine. My companion had given himself out as an Englishman, although he found some difficulty in expressing himself in that language.

On leaving the caravanserai one of the Hindoos asked if he could accompany us for a short distance. He then suggested to us to avoid the crowd, and with an air of mystery, took us along a retired path by the side of a small stream. Apart, however, from praises of the English, and complaints against the Sarts, he had no confidences to give us. His whole action, however,

A HINDOO.

was so peculiar, that my companion concluded he must have some secret mission from the Indian Government to report on the conditions of things in Tashkent.

These Hindoos live in little *ménages* of one or two exclusively in the caravanserai, partly in order to be near the business centre of the town, and partly for safety, as they thus have greater protection against the possibly murderous designs of insolvent debtors, than they would have in remote houses or gardens. Their chief occupation, as I have said, is usury, although they are not the only money-lenders, for Jews, Afghans, and even native Mussulmans, also engage in this lucrative business, it being estimated that there are at least a thousand usurers in Tashkent. The Hindoos usually lend sums for twenty-four weeks, to be paid in weekly instalments of one *tenga* to every *tilla*, that is, one nineteenth, making a gain as interest in the course of the transaction of five *tengas*, or about twenty-six per cent., which would be fully fifty-six per cent. per annum. The rate of interest is sometimes much higher, although among Mussulman capitalists four per cent. a month is considered fair. As the money is thus paid back in instalments, it is evident that a money-lender with a very small capital can make a large yearly profit. Lending out money at interest is forbidden by Mussulman law, and tradition says that lending money freely to the poor is a more worthy action, and will have a greater reward from God than giving alms. But while the Mussulman is strictly forbidden to make a contract for the payment of interest, it is perfectly allowable for him to receive interest which is voluntarily given by the borrower. Casuists, however, have without much difficulty discovered what are called 'paths,' that is, methods of evading the strict letter of the law, which, from the places where they were invented, or are most customary, are known as the Bukharan, Samarkand, Tashkent, and other 'paths.' For instance, the Tashkent 'path' is this. In order to receive the interest of twenty rubles on one hundred, the hundred rubles are lent without interest, and some small article, as a whip, is nominally sold to the borrower for twenty rubles more. This article is called *shari*, i.e., lawful, and must always be the property of the seller. The Bukharan way is similar, but here, instead of a nominal sale, some article, usually a book, is handed to the borrower for safe keeping, and for keeping and using this book he pays the sum constituting the interest on the principal lent to him. Another method is for the lender to buy of the borrower some piece of property, as a house, or a horse for less than its value, paying him at the same time the amount of the loan. A paper is then drawn up before the *Kazi*, in which the lender promises to resell the property to the borrower for a sum that will equal the money lent with the interest added. Mussulmans, however, perfectly well understand that these methods are evasions of the direct religious command, and among the traditions as to future punishment is one that the usurer will be sealed up in a metallic box, which will then be heated in a fire. When the usurer cries out in his torment, asking the reason of such punishment, the Almighty and All-blessed will answer him, 'You are punished because you took usury.' 'But I did not take usury;' he will reply, 'I sold a thing lawfully.' 'Well,' the All-highest will reply, 'I do not burn *you*, I only heat the box.' Where the borrower is a person of property and known for his probity, the lender merely makes a note in his account-book, and gives the debtor a similar note to remind him of the payment. In other cases, however, the receipt of the debtor is taken and witnessed before the Kazi, and frequently large security is demanded.

The shops of the dealers in china and earthenware cannot fail to attract the attention of anyone fond of pottery. The ware is coarse and is always rudely, and often carelessly made, but the freeness and spirit in design, and the harmony in colour, are very pleasing, and render the better-made plates worthy of being used for decorative purposes. The designs are usually in blue and white, though occasionally a faint bluish green tinge is given to the ground, and sometimes yellow or dark violet is sparingly used. Chinese porcelain is greatly esteemed by the Tashkentians, and brings absurdly high prices. The best class of native ware is therefore called *tchini* (Chinese) and bears a clumsy imitation of a Chinese mark. The productions of Mohammed Shakyr of Hodjent are considered the best, and good things are also made at Samarkand, and especially at Andijan. The villages are supplied with the ordinary kinds of glazed and unglazed ware by potters from the large towns, who, during the summer, make a tour through the country, and work from the clay found on the spot—an easy matter, as the tools and belongings of the trade are few and simple. Common pottery and glazed tiles have long been known, but it is believed that the manufacture of *tchini* was very recently introduced into the country by a certain Usta-Kasim of Samarkand, who had learned it at Meshed, from which place he returned about

1857. The ingredients used for *tchini* are a felspathic white clay (*gil-buta*) found in the Karnan mountains, south of Kermineh, and near Ablyk, between Tashkent and Khokand, quartz (*ak-tash*, white stone, *tash-kum*, stone sand) obtained from the mountains on the upper Zarafshan, or in the shape of pebbles from the gravelly bank of that river near Samarkand, and lime and soda (*ishkar*) derived from the ashes of a species of *Salicornia*. The glaze is made from a mixture of *ishkar* and oxide of lead, with occasionally an admixture of tin, which gives the iridescence so much admired in Moorish ware. If a greenish glaze is desired, a little verdigris is added. In case the vessel is to be ornamented, the colours, which are mixed with water and a little cherry or apricot gum, are applied with a goat's-hair brush on the dry surface of the glaze before firing. Blue is produced by lapis-lazuli, violet by *mag'l* (manganese?), yellow by ochre, and green by verdigris. Recent excavations at Samarkand show that glass was once made there,[1] but its manufacture had been forgotten for ages until a Russian company started some works, which proved a failure from the defective construction of the ovens. A Siberian glass manufacturer, Isseief, then opened some works at Digmai, near Hodjent, which was in successful operation when it was sacked and burned by the Khokandians during the summer of 1875.

Leaving on one side booths where men are dexterously turning spindles, reels and other small wooden objects by means of a chisel and a small lathe set in motion by a bowstring, passing round corners where black-veiled women are selling embroidered skull caps and belts, we come to the street where gowns are sold, from those of Russian printed calico to those of many-coloured Bukharan silk, or even velvet and cloth of gold,—these last imported of course from Moscow. Here too are the embroiderers. Embroidery here is a trade practised chiefly by the men.[2] The cloth, on which the pattern is roughly marked out in chalk, is stretched over a hoop, and the workman with a

---

[1] Lui Yu, a Chinese envoy sent to Hulagu in 1259, says: 'The doors and windows are provided with glass.' Tch'ang Tch'un, writing a few years earlier, tells us that the vessels for wine were made only of glass. Curiously enough, this passage is omitted by Dr. Bretschneider in his translation.

[2] Evidently an old practice, for a Chinese envoy sent to Tchinghiz Khan, in 1220, says: 'Sewing and embroidery are executed by men.' Bretschneider's 'Notes on Chinese Mediæval Travellers to the West,' p. 105

needle, in shape somewhat like a crochet needle, set in a wooden handle, pulls the silken thread through in a sort of chain-stitch with the greatest rapidity. The labour is so light and the materials so inexpensive that prices for embroidered articles are comparatively low. The natives use embroidery principally on their caps and their wide leather riding-trousers, but since the Russians have come, there has been such a demand for pillows, table cloths, &c., as to give a great impetus to the business and to raise the prices.

Whole rows are filled with cotton goods, among which it is impossible not to notice in every shop the large quantity on sale of Russian printed fabrics. The native goods are all of coarse texture. The most important is *buz*,[1] which is undyed and generally unbleached, and is especially used for making shirts and drawers. It is commonly known among the Russians by the name of *mata*, a name long ago given to it by some mistake. *Mata* is properly a measure of about eight yards, and is the name given to the piece of goods, and not to the fabric itself. *Daka* is a much thinner material, a kind of muslin, of which the coarser sort is used for the lining of gowns, and the finer kind for turbans. The best turbans, however, are of English muslin imported though India. As this is of a quality not manufactured in Russia, no effort has ever been made to prohibit its importation. *Alatcha* is a striped material on a blue ground, dyed in the thread. *Kalama*[2] is of a somewhat better quality, the stripes usually being on a white ground. The natives also print cotton goods, sometimes in three colours, by means of wooden stamps, which are applied by hand.

In 1869 an endeavour was made to see how far the supplies for the army could be obtained from the country itself, and it was resolved to use the native *buz*, instead of Russian white cotton cloth, for the blouses of the soldiers. Red tape, however, was too strong, for the army regulations, which for some reason it seemed impossible to change, required material

---

[1] The Russians have corrupted this word to *biaz*, but its pronunciation is evident from the proverb:

Suz birar,
Buz birmas.

Words he gives, but *buz* he gives not.

[2] The origin of this word is interesting. It is an abbreviation of *kala-mal*, city, or Russian, wares—*kala*, a fort or city, being commonly used to denote Russia.

of a width of fourteen inches, while *buz* was never made wider than eleven inches. The contractors, therefore, found it impossible to procure in Tashkent the desired material, and were obliged to have recourse to Bukhara, where cotton production is carried on more largely, and even here it was necessary to start special factories at Hazhduin [1] for its manufacture. The result is, that while the industry of Tashkent was not in the slightest degree benefited, the price of the *buz* specially manufactured for the army was as high as that of the Russian goods brought from Moscow, including the cost of carriage, and the latter had the merit of being heavier and far more durable.

The best silk goods are those of Bukhara, next come those of Khokand and Hodjent, and then those made in Khiva, the least prized being those of Tashkent. In consequence of the prohibition of the Koran, the use of pure silk fabrics is confined chiefly to women and children, stuffs of mixed silk and cotton being principally employed for the men's gowns. Silk goods are woven in narrow stripes, or in broad splashes of colour, especially red, green and yellow, forming an irregular design, or are sometimes quite plain. Much, however, is now made in more regular patterns to suit the European market. The colours are durable, and the silk has a firmness and brightness which it retains after several washings. Of the half silk fabrics, the best and most known are *bikasab*[2] and *adras*, both being usually made in narrow stripes. The gloss is given by beating them with a wide flat wooden instrument.

Owing to the importance of the silk trade in Central Asia, I shall perhaps be pardoned if I enter into some details concerning it.

The manufacture of silk was, as tradition tells us, introduced into Khotan from China, and probably spread to a certain extent throughout the whole of Central Asia; but in Tashkent, Hodjent and Samarkand it had entirely died out until it was revived after the capture of Merv by Shah Murad Khan in 1785. He transferred all the inhabitants of this city to Bukhara, where they continued the silk culture, which was one of their favourite occupations. During the reign of the Amir

---

[1] Or Hizhduan.

[2] I was told that *bika-ab* was derived from *bi* outside, and *kasaba* trade guild—an evidence of its recent origin.

Nasrullah, the descendants of these colonists were allowed to live in Samarkand, and from that time silk culture began to flourish, and is now the chief occupation of many villages of the districts of Zarafshan, Hodjent and Kurama.[1]

[1] Every trade guild has a written tradition called *resala* or 'message,' with mythical stories of its origin and directions as to the proper manner of work. In the following tradition translated from the Turki and Persian originals, the beginning is borrowed from the life of the prophet Ayub or Job in the widely-spread book *Kassasi-el-Anbia* (Lives of the Saints).

In the name of God the Merciful and the Compassionate! Praise to God the Universal Lord, and eternal blessedness to him who fears him, Reverence and peace to his messenger Mohammed, and to his family, and to all his companions! After praise to God and reverence to his messenger, honour to the princes of the World, the children of Adam and his descendants! The sun in the brilliant sky! The nightingale in the gardens of knowledge! One who has attained the secret of the spiritual world! The translation of universal Right! The parrot in the gardens of truth! The fulfilment of business is before everything! In the gardens there is grass, and on the grass is a peacock! He who feeds on what exists in heaven and on the earth and who satisfies all! The unexpectedly-giving!

All that I have said above I say in the name of the chosen prophet Mohammed, may God be merciful to him and keep him! With regard to him the great God ordered thus:—'But thou, oh Mohammed! wert sent only to preach and to warn this world. We sent thee, oh Mohammed, as a witness who will give proof against them, as an apostle who calls and warns them.' The highest prophets with their companions teaching, said:—'Every prophet has left witnesses to his people; of our brothers Job left the worm.' These worms were created on the tree *Syr*, and God gave them for food its leaves; through these leaves they received strength and crawl on this tree. All this good thing came from the patience and mildness of the prophet Job, for, as is related, the great God said to cursed Satan: 'Thou hast not fulfilled My command, thou hast not thanked for that which has been given to thee, and thou hast fallen under my curse and thy name will remain cursed, but there are people who bow down to me and fear and thank me for their happiness.' And Satan answered, 'Show me these people.' Then the great Almighty God said to the prophet Job, 'Show thyself to Satan, and let Satan take an example from thee.' But Job wept and said, 'Oh, thou pure one who keepest and givest life, do not be angry with me!' But the Lord God Almighty then said, 'Oh Job, show thyself, and look at my might after that.' Then the prophet showed himself to Satan. Satan said to God, 'Thou gavest to this man much riches and much of everything, for which he prays to Thee and obeys Thee.' Then God said to His Archangel Gabriel, 'Take all the riches from this man.' The Archangel Gabriel came down from heaven with a hundred thousand angels, and took all the wealth from the man who was pleasing to God; but notwithstanding this the prophet of God ten times increased his prayers. After this God said to Satan, 'Oh cursed one! now hast thou seen that I have taken away all his wealth and he has increased his prayers ten times.' Satan answered, 'His body is sound, and for that he praises and thanks Thee.' Then God said to the Archangel Gabriel, 'Send disease into his body.' By the order of God the Archangel Gabriel sent to Job disease, so that his body, pleasing to God, was covered with worms, All these ills and worms the prophet Job endured and lifted up his spirit to God,

The annual production of silk in Central Asia is estimated, after careful calculations, at about four and a half millions of thanking, praying, and weeping. After some days these worms increased still more and ate up the whole body of Job, so that there was not one spot healthy, and all was covered with sores. Being very ill and covered with sores he nevertheless did not cease praying to God; but once he was so weak that he could not lift up a worm which fell from his wounds to place it back again, and he therefore begged his wife to pick up the worm and place it in the wound, saying: 'If God have ordered me to feed worms with my body it would be sinful to deprive it of food.' The wife of the prophet fulfilled his command and placed the worm on the body of her husband. But patient Job remained in his place and praised God. 'I have seen all this,' said Satan to God, 'Job prays to Thee because his heart and his tongue are still sound.' Then God commanded the Archangel Gabriel to smite the ground, and from under the ground where there is the sea, called the 'sea of light,' to obtain water. By the command of God the Archangel Gabriel with several thousand angels went down to the earth and smote it with his wing, and from under the earth there arose a spring of water; and there was a command to the Archangel Gabriel to hurl the prophet Job into the water and see the wisdom of God. By command of God the prophet Job threw himself into the spring and in that minute made himself whole. The worms fell from him, his body became sound and his rotting places became whole.

This spring so remained under the name of 'the sea of light,' and all believers who bathe there become whole in body and soul. The worms which were in the body of Job crept up into a mulberry tree there and began to eat its leaves, and then knitted themselves a covering and shut themselves up in this covering. The nest where they remained was called, as it is now, *pilla*, a cocoon. [According to other traditions the worms which fell into the water became leeches and those which flew away became bees.]

The Imam Jagaffar Sadyk being asked the question, 'Who was the first silk-winder and inventor of this trade?' said: 'Daud-darai came to that tree where were the worms, and taking a cocoon in his hand said to God: "Oh pure giver of all creatures on the land, these worms have come away from the body of Thy friend and have placed themselves on this tree, and they feed themselves on it, and here they spin cocoons which serve as a covering for their bodies; wouldst Thou open to me how cocoons were formed, and how the worms proceeded from the body of Thy friend, so that people should profit by them and remember him?" He had not yet finished these words when he opened his eyes and saw a man who said to him, "Dost thou know me?" he answered, "No." The man said, "Thou hast asked of God, and I am God's treasurer and fulfil thy wish. Tell me what wishest thou?" Daud-darai said, "My wish is that it should be shown to me what cocoons are?" Then the man began to teach him. "Throw this cocoon into hot water and beat it with a stick, and see the power of God." Daud-darai did so, and the cocoon was found to be silken.' After that the Imam Jagaffar said, 'Young men, carry on your trade.' And by his order they wrote all in this book so that the people of the Prophet should avail of this knowledge of the Prophet and should wish them well.

Daud-darai learned from Hazyr thus: 'First throw the cocoons into the water and seizing in the right hand a crooked stick say: "In the name of God the Merciful and the Compassionate!" and strike the cocoons; then on this stick there will be a thread which is called silk.' The learned Talus Hakim took and pounds avoirdupois, of which one million and a half is from Bukhara, and the same quantity from Khokand. Khiva pro-

turned it about, and from him learned Akhmet Khayan and many other saints and masters of this art. Profiting by this business give alms and do good for them. All who engage in this business should fulfil the following rites; wash themselves and make two *rakaat*; after the obeisance read three times the *Sura Ikhlas*, and this prayer will serve God for an offering for the teachers, and through it help will be asked for their souls. He who fulfils all that has been here said will have success in business and will never need for his daily bread. For this business there are still some rites and some precautions; the workman ought to fulfil them. He should wash before beginning to work, should make two obeisances, should be pure in spirit and thought before beginning work, and remember that all this business is the gift of God, should be clean in his eating, and sleep purely, should be affectionate and not malicious, should always use good words, should be obedient to his teachers, and during the time of his work should not have intercourse with those people who speak badly of others. He should always receive from his companions blessing and praise to God, that is, should say *Allah Akhbar*, and have constantly on his tongue the name of God. [Then follow other good counsels of a similar sort as to the conduct of workmen, and finally some special advice.]

If the teacher should be asked what should be recited while going from home to the shop where cocoons are worked, he should answer: 'In the name of God the merciful, our God, we have done ill, pardon us!' If he should be asked what the workmen should recite when they take the stick in their hands, he should answer: 'Oh God, Thou hast made us unendingly happy.' If he should be asked what the winders ought to recite when they lift up the stick, he should answer: 'By His pure wisdom may God cleanse us from our sins.' If he should be asked what the winders should recite when they take the end of the silk from the stick, he should answer: 'We thank the God of Paradise!' If he should be asked what the winders ought to say when the thread is applied to the reel, he should answer: 'They should think of the way to paradise and should recite the verse, "Direct us into the right road."' When the pupil regulates the fire he should remember that fire is of hell, which burns people and even stones. 'When they shut the shops what ought they to do?' he should answer: 'They should take up from the ground all that has fallen on it during the time of work and recite, "May all our voluntary and involuntary sins of this day be forgiven us."' Then the workmen ought reverently to rise from their seats with their left foot and go out backwards. In this way for every operation of the art there are certain pious sentences which should be recited and meditated upon. If one who is truly wise wish to occupy himself with this business, he should learn from a teacher, and should keep his thoughts and eyes from sin, his hands from uncleanness, his feet from wickedness, and his mouth from sinful food. He should trust his teachers, and not speak nor listen to bad words. If anyone say what is bad, answer him with good, and speak the truth and do not lie. Do not know one who speaks untruth and acts badly. If anyone do not fulfil the rites which are here written, and do not believe his teachers and the saints saying, 'I do not trust them,' he speaks untruth and considers the saints as his enemies. If anyone shall be constantly pure, and shall constantly magnify God, he will receive the reward of God in this book and also from the four prophets, Adam, purified of God;

duces about a hundred thousand pounds, Kashgar four hundred thousand, and the Russian possessions nearly a million more.[1]

The climate of Central Asia is in the highest degree favourable to silk culture. There is almost no rain nor hail during the summer, while thunderstorms and violent winds are infrequent, and it is therefore possible to do without artificial heat and ventilation. At the same time there is abundance of the indispensable food of the worms,- the mulberry tree. The causes which limit the quantity and quality of the silk production are in the methods of breeding and in the mode of life of the inhabitants.

The rearing of silk-worms is not considered a particularly honourable occupation in which rich and well-to-do people engage to pass the time, and except in those localities where the culture is greatly developed it is almost solely the employment of the women of the family. Being thus confined to the women's court it is difficult to study it and to devise measures for its improvement. It is evident from the differences in the colour, form and size of the cocoons, that there are several varieties of silk-worms reared in Central Asia, but they are so unscientifically treated, and have been allowed to cross so much, that it is difficult to get at the typical characteristics of each variety. The natives distinguish two kinds, the common one of a milky white colour, which is simply called silk-worm, *ipek-kurt*, and another of a dark colour, called Arabian (*arabi*). Yet the cocoons of these two varieties do not seem to differ, both having the variations just mentioned. Some silk-worms, however, have four periods and others five, the eggs of the first kind being said to be somewhat larger. By careful breeding the original types of these different varieties could probably be recurred to, and some of them would perhaps prove valuable. The eggs of silk-worms are kept in small cotton bags hung to the ceiling. In places where silk culture is prevalent they are sold in the bazaars, in the apothecary's, or in the provision shops. The bazaar price in spring of a small thimbleful, in which are about two thousand eggs, varies from twenty to

---

Noah, the prophet of God; Abraham, the beloved of God; and Mohammed, the chosen. Reverence and peace to them all!

[1] See the excellent 'Report on Silk Culture in Central Asia,' by N. F. Petrofsky, Agent of the Ministry of Finances (pp. 120, xi. Tashkent, 1873), to which I am greatly indebted.

thirty kopeks. Their soundness is tested by putting them into water, those which sink being considered good. At the beginning of April the women put the eggs into small bags and tie them next to their body round their waist, or under their arms, turning them over every day. The heat thus obtained may be a natural one, but it is accompanied by exudations which cannot but prove injurious to the worms. After about a week the worms begin gradually to appear. The bags are then opened every day and the worms that are hatched are placed on a large tray, which is covered with a clean cloth and set in a sunny place, although sheltered with gauze from the sun's direct rays. If the days and nights be especially cold, these trays are placed on the *sandal*, or brasier used for warming the room. During the first two periods the worms are fed with mulberry leaves carefully picked off, and as they grow care is taken to give them more room and better places. After the second period the worms are transferred to shelves placed along the sides of the room in which they are kept, and which is half darkened, having no light save what comes in at the door, and they are then fed three times a day with small mulberry twigs. The old twigs are never removed, but the new food is placed on the top and the worms gradually crawl upwards out of the dirt and refuse, which is perhaps the only reason why this careless method of feeding them does not kill them. Finally, small branches, and especially of a dry plant with a bright pink flower, named *ming-bash* (thousand heads), are placed on the shelves so that the worms can crawl into them and there spin their cocoons. The life of the silk-worm from the egg to the cocoon varies, according to circumstances and nourishment, from forty to seventy days.

No one with sufficient botanical knowledge has accurately studied the different kinds of the mulberry, which is by far the most common tree in Central Asia. Of the varieties distinguished by the natives, the four most important are the *hassak*, which is the wild mulberry cultivated from the seed and used greatly for silk-worms, and also serving as the stock on which other varieties are grafted; the *shah-tut*, brought originally from Persia; and the *balkhi*, introduced from Balkh, the largest and most beautiful variety of all, and the most common tree in the Zarafshan valley; and the *khorasmi*, from Khorasm, or Khiva. The large white, almost seedless, berries of this last, both when fresh and dried, are greatly used for food. They are sometimes made into a flour, which mixed with water is a refreshing drink, and with wheat flour makes a paste called *tut-halvah*.[1]

Mulberry trees are raised from the seed, which is planted in May and June. In a year's time the young trees will be five feet high and as thick as the little finger, when they are thinned out and transplanted, all not required being used for feeding the worms. In the second or third year they are grafted and the next year produce fruit. When used for silk-worms, it is common, instead of stripping off small twigs, to cut off huge branches, reducing the tree to a pollard. Healthy grafted trees three years old of good size sell on the bazaars for from twenty to fifty kopeks, according to the variety. The cut branches of a tree, according to its size and the demand for the leaves, bring from one to four rubles. In 1871, the prices of mulberry leaves in Hodjent, on account of the over-production of silk, stimulated by speculation, rose from sixty kopeks to over two rubles for an ass-load of five bundles.

As soon as the cocoons are spun, they are taken into the court, stripped from the twigs to which they are fastened, and in order to kill the worms, spread on a mat exposed for several days to the full power of the sun, being gathered together in a heap at night and covered up. For the purposes of breeding, the largest and best cocoons are picked out, particular attention being given to the form and none to the colour, except that they should have a watered or *moiré* appearance. Some thirty of these are strung on a thread by passing a needle under the outside layer. The strings are left for three days on the cool clay floor of the hut and are then put into cotton bags which are hung by long nails to the walls or ceilings. On the fourth day the butterflies come out and immediately begin to lay eggs, it being from ten to fourteen days from the spinning of the cocoon to the appearance of the butterfly. Coupling goes on

---

[1] An analysis of leaves of five kinds of mulberries from Central Asia was made by Dr. Reichenbach, who found an average of 37·36 parts of azote in 1000, corresponding to 233 parts of proteine, their leaves being fully as rich as those of China and Japan. Unfortunately the quantity of leaves sent was too small for a more minute analysis.—*Turkistan Gazette*, No. 42, 1873.

from about nine in the morning till noon; and about three in the afternoon the female begins to lay her eggs and continues till midnight.

The butterfly lives but a day and a half and lays about 450 eggs, of which a quarter are unfruitful. In the Caucasus, with the same conditions of climate and nourishment, a butterfly lives three days and lays fully 600 eggs. It is a custom sanctified by tradition, to exchange silkworms' eggs every three or four years if possible for those of some distant place, or at least for those of one's neighbours. Cocoons are usually sold in the bazaar in their fresh state before they are dried, and during the whole month of June the trade in them is very brisk, the prices ranging from seven to twelve rubles a pud.[1] The prices for dried cocoons, which are not sold on the bazaar, are far more variable, sometimes rising to forty or fifty rubles a pud.

In Khokand it was formerly the custom to present the first cocoons to the Khan, who in return gave a *sarpai*, or complete suit of clothes (from Persian *sar*, head, and *pai*, foot). When Shir Ali Khan, Khudayar's father, who had lived all his life among the Kirghiz, came to the throne, he was as usual presented with the first cocoons, and, supposing them to be some rare fruit, ate them with the greatest composure.

A family of four persons can raise on an average about three puds of undried cocoons, for which it uses nearly an ounce of eggs that were received from a pound and a half of cocoons, and twenty mulberry trees of medium size, costing about fifteen rubles. Thus, without counting the insignificant expense of apparatus and the cost of personal labour, the expenses for this quantity of cocoons reach about eighteen rubles. The receipt of an average price of nine rubles a pud would be twenty-seven rubles, leaving a profit of nine rubles, although in most cases the profit is much greater, because people usually have mulberry trees of their own and are not obliged to buy the whole amount of food consumed by the worms.

The natives have noticed four different diseases of the silkworm, which they ascribe either to the cold, to wet mulberry-

[1] The pud (a Russian weight) is 40 pounds Russian or 36 pounds English. The ruble I have taken as equal to $30\frac{5}{12}$ pence or 61 cents, thus making 7·30 rubles to the pound sterling, and about 5 rubles to 3 dollars.

leaves, or to the presence of persons who have not performed all the ablutions demanded by their religion. Mr. Fedtchenko, in his microscopic observations, discovered the presence of *cornalia*, or the corpuscules causing the disease called *pebrine*, which has made such havoc among European silkworms. Some cocoons from which he got no butterflies were filled with quantities of these corpuscules, and they were also found in small numbers on the wings of butterflies that had come from the cocoons. As silkworms in Turkistan were entirely cut off from those in Europe, his observations led him to believe that the disease caused by these parasites existed everywhere, and was only noticed by breeders, and became epidemic, in case of a very great development of the parasites, while a small number of them had no influence on breeding; and further, that the multiplication of the parasites, and the infection and death of all the worms, was directly affected by the number bred in a given place, and by the care taken of them, as he proved that caterpillars coming from sound eggs become infected by the excremental matters of a few diseased worms becoming mixed with the food.

The method of silk-winding is of a piece with that of breeding. Numbers of unsorted cocoons are thrown into a pot of boiling water, and are stirred with a stick, and when the ends of the threads are fished up in proper number, they are wound on a large reel until all the cocoons are used; then the water is changed, new fires are lighted, and the process begins again. The silk wound directly from the kettle, and then reeled off in skeins to be sent for dyeing, is called *kaliava*, and is chiefly intended for home consumption. It sells at from 122 to 127 rubles a pud. A better sort, to which more attention has been paid in reeling, called *homiak*, has been sold during the last eight years prepared exclusively for export, and costs from 180 to 190 rubles a pud. Of late it has been also prepared in Khotan. Silk of two threads reeled from spools ready for woof is called *tokhfil*, and brings from 178 to 212 rubles a pud. A Bukharan variety, *tchillya* warp, is exported through Kazala, but has been brought to Tashkent and sold at 240 rubles the pud. *Sarnak*, the floss or *bourre-de-soie*, when uncleaned, sells at 15 to 20 rubles a pud, and when cleaned, sometimes brings as high as 40 rubles. It is largely exported to Russia. In Tashkent it takes from 8 to 9 lbs. of good dried cocoons to produce 1 lb. of reeled silk; while in Samarkand, where the workmen are more skilful, 1 lb. of silk can be obtained from 16 lbs. of fresh, or 5 lbs. of dried cocoons. Russian silk-winders, with their machinery, have got a pound of silk from $14\frac{1}{2}$ lbs. of fresh, or 3·9 lbs. of dried cocoons. In Europe, 12 lbs. of fresh, or 4 lbs. of dried cocoons will give 1 lb. of silk.

Rude as are its methods, the silk manufacture of Central Asia, owing to its importance to the country, is relatively more developed than other branches of industry. Its faults are connected with the whole structure of the native life, and to remedy them entirely in a short time would be beyond the power of any government.

The Uzbek is by nature pre-eminently an agriculturist, and all his industries are in their nature domestic, but the breeding of silk-worms, and the winding of silk, are two entirely different branches, which can with propriety be separated. Successful breeding demands an amount of personal, and, so to speak, loving care, with great attention to details; while it is essentially a domestic employment, and the smaller the number of worms raised, the more care can be given to them. Silk-winding, on the contrary, is a mechanical trade demanding chiefly good order and discipline. It can therefore be best performed in factories, and it will be by founding filatures on the spot that the Russians will improve the silk culture in Turkistan. Silk culture can be improved in part by teaching the natives better methods, but principally by the demand for the sorted cocoons of the better class. An increased demand for a better article will at once bring out an increased supply. From 1867 to 1872, not counting minor attempts, seven important filatures were established in Turkistan, but with one exception they, for various reasons, were soon closed, in spite of the pecuniary assistance which they received from the government, without having had any effect upon the native silk manufacture. One filature still existed at Hodjent when I was there, belonging to a company of Moscow merchants. It had been founded, with a capital of 200,000 rubles, on the earnest personal solicitation of the chief of General Kaufmann's chancery. It was put under the charge of incompetent men,

and its affairs were greatly neglected owing to the great
distance from the owners, and lately (November, 1875), a
notice has appeared announcing its liquidation with a loss of
four-fifths of the capital. One great reason of the failure of
these filatures was that Central Asia was considered one of
those countries where money was sure to be made in any undertaking,
and persons rashly engaged in silk-spinning, who
had not the slightest acquaintance with that business, or in
some cases, indeed, with any other. Another reason was the
high prices that had to be given for cocoons. The natives of
Central Asia have a keen commercial instinct, but they are so
inexperienced in anything out of the ordinary run of life, that
the slightest additional demand, the starting of any new trade,
or a call for new articles, increases the price to an absurd
extent. There was a curious example of this in 1869, when
for a tannery which had been started, there was a demand
for the root called *taran*. The purchases in the bazaars immediately
raised the price double and triple. People living in
Britch-mulla, and the neighbouring villages where the *taran*
grew, hearing of the rise in prices, immediately abandoned all
their husbandry, ceased cultivating their fields, and devoted
themselves exclusively to gathering this root, and sending it to
Tashkent, selling their cattle, and buying horses and asses to
transport it. When it arrived at Tashkent, however, the immediate
want of it had passed, and the poor people were obliged
to sell it for almost nothing, and were nearly starved in the
winter. In the same way, when, during the early days of the
Russian occupation of Tashkent and Samarkand, there was
a speculation in silkworms' eggs, several Italians, Barbieri,
Adamoli and others, visited Central Asia for the purpose of
studying silk, and of buying silkworms' eggs for Italy. Barbieri
succeeded in raising about a thousand pounds of eggs, and the
price of dried cocoons immediately rose from thirty to forty
and fifty rubles a pud, while fresh cocoons were very difficult
to obtain as people refused to sell them, reserving them for the
purpose of raising eggs. To meet what was imagined would
be the increased demand, so many were prepared, that the
following spring they were offered in the Tashkent and Hodjent
bazaars for three rubles a pound without purchasers. Owing
to the opinions prevalent in Tashkent that the export of silk-

worms eggs was destructive to the industrial interests of the country, it was forbidden by an Imperial order in the spring of 1871. In the same year the government founded a school of silk culture with a laboratory. This institution, by investigating the different breeds of silkworms, and the causes of their diseases, and by experimenting on the food, and teaching more rational methods of breeding, cannot fail to be of great use, but it can hardly succeed if it attempts to improve merely the methods of silk-winding among the natives themselves. The best it could do in that direction would be to start a small pattern filature, in which native workmen could be educated as masters for some larger factory.

The Sarts, in all their dealings with each other, and most commonly in their dealings with the Russians, use their old systems of weights and measures, which vary not only with every country but almost with every town. No such thing as dry or liquid measure exists, but everything is sold by weight. The unit of weight is the *batman*, or rather perhaps the *tcharik*, usually $\frac{1}{64}$ of a *batman*. The *batman*—which was a weight known to Russia in the middle ages, and still exists not only in the half-Tartar Caucasus and Crimea, but in the purely Russian province of Tver, there equal to 36 pounds—varies greatly in different places.[1] In Tashkent the *batman* is about 374 lbs. avoirdupois. The *tcharik*, $\frac{1}{64}$ part of a *batman*, or rather more than $5\frac{3}{4}$ lbs., is, disregarding the various subdivisions which are of only local interest, divided into 80 *paisas*, each a little more than an ounce. The *miskal*, which is more especially used in Bukhara and Samarkand, is the smallest weight of all, being only a quarter of an ounce. In Khokand the *tcharik* is more frequently used than the *batman*, and varies from 162 to 180 lbs., being divided into 16 *tchaksas*, and each of these into 200 *paisas*, weighing each $\frac{3}{4}$ of an ounce. In Hodjent the *batman* is very large, weighing 432 lbs., and is divided into only 12 tchariks of 36 lbs. each. At Ura-tepé a *tcharik* is 9 lbs., and a *batman* of 64 *tchariks* is 576 lbs. In several towns on the border between Tashkent and Khokand there are still other

---

[1] A different use of the *batman* for silk—the large of 9 pounds, and the small of $4\frac{1}{2}$ pounds—seems exceptional. Cocoons are sold only by the *tcharik*, and reeled silk only by the skein. The *batman* is used only in calculating with the workman for the quantity he has wound.

variations. In Samarkand and Bukhara there are two *tchariks*, the large and small, the large weighing 9 lbs., and the small half as much. A *batman* of 64 small *tchariks* is therefore 28½ lbs. The same *batman* prevails at Jizakh, while at Zamin, between that place and Ura-tepé, it is only half as large—144 lbs. In Khiva it is still smaller, being only 142 lbs. Here a quarter of a *batman* is called an *anser*, or *ansyr*, meaning ten *syr*, an imaginary weight which exists in various combinations there as well as Bukhara and Samarkand.[1] The *ansyr*, as well as the *batman*, was known to Russia in the sixteenth century, and was apparently a recognised Russian weight, as it frequently appears in the records. It was at first equivalent to 1¾, and finally to 1 Russian pound. Going eastward, at Aulié-ata the *batman* is about one-third larger than at Tashkent, and when we come to Kashgar we find several systems, including Chinese, in use. Here a *batman* is nearly four times as large as at Tashkent, and includes eight *galvers*, each as large as a Khokandian *tcharik*. Besides this there are two kinds of *tchariks*, the smaller of 17 lbs., and the larger of 21½ lbs.

The *batman* (a Turkic word, and probably unconnected with the Arabic *menn*) was originally a dry measure, probably for grain, which has now come to be used as a weight. It is only in this way that its variations throughout Mussulman Asia can be explained. The weight of a measured *batman* of the staple article of each locality, wheat, rice, millet, or whatever it may have been, was probably taken as a standard.

In the bazaars rented from the government, and not always then, the use of the legal Russian weights is obligatory. Owing to the high price of metal, stones of approximate heaviness are usually substituted for the native weights. They are seldom correct, and make much cheating possible. Under the native rule a religious officer, the *reis*, whose duty it was to look after the morals of the community, verified the weights, but his office is abolished, and these stone weights are never compared with the standard.

The most common measure of length is the *giaz*, which is equal to seven fists, the last with upturned thumb, making about

---

[1] The *syr* is never used alone, although we have the expression *du-nim-syr*, two half-*syr*.

twenty-seven inches. In measuring the *giaz-kirbuz*, which is rarely used for measuring cotton stuffs, each thumb should be held up, making about forty-two inches. A *kari* is twice the length of the extended arms, or pretty nearly twelve feet. The measure *altchin*, of twenty-eight inches, of which the Russian *arshin* is a corrupted form, is also in use. For measuring long distances the *tash*, or *farsang*, is used. This is considered to be equal to 12,000 paces, or about $5\frac{3}{4}$ English miles. It derives its name from the *tash*, or stone, put up to mark the distance. *Sang* is a Persian word for stone, and *farsang*, the ancient *parasang*, means probably only the Persian stone as distinguished from the measure of some other country. There is only one measure for land, which is the *tanap*, equal to 60 *giaz* square, or about $\frac{3}{4}$ of an acre. At Kazala and Perofsky, as also at Vierny, the Russian weights and measures have quite crowded out those of the natives; but at Tashkent and Samarkand the Russian authorities have thus far made no efforts to enforce the use of the Russian system. It is greatly to be regretted that they have not taken occasion to introduce here the decimal system, which they could easily have done at the beginning, and for which it may still be not too late.

The monetary unit in Central Asia is a small silver coin called a *tenga*, or in Khokand and Tashent *tenga khokand*, or simply *khokand*, the real value of which is about $16\frac{3}{4}$ kopeks, or $5\frac{1}{2}d$. It bears on one side the name of the sovereign, and on the other usually the name of the town or the date of the year in which it was struck. There is also a gold coin, smaller and much thinner, called the *tilla*, the value of which varies with the rate of exchange, and probably with the amount of precious metal in the coin. The Khokandian *tilla* is valued at nineteen *tengas*, and the Bukharan *tilla* at from twenty-four to twenty-eight *tengas*. In Khiva there are two kinds of *tillas*, the large, worth eighteen *tengas*, and the small, worth nine. The only other coins in use are of brass or iron, called *pul*, or *tcheka*. Of this they count in Tashkent sixty to a tenga, and in Khokand forty. In Bukhara there are from forty-four to sixty four *puls* in a *tenga*, and in Khiva from thirty-five to seventy, according to their abundance. By a decree of the Ministry of Finance in 1869 the value of a *tenga* was fixed at twenty kopeks, although now it is found to be worth, as I have said, only 16¾.¹ At this rate they have been in frequent use for small money, and have been received by the treasury for the payment of taxes and other indebtedness. In this way the government by the autumn of 1874 had accumulated 3,750,000 *tengas* for the purpose of recoining at the value of 750,000 rubles, while they were really worth only 628,906 ¼ rubles, thus losing on the operation more than 121,000 rubles. To be sure, as they will be recoined into Russian small money, which passes for twice its real value, the government will be able in a certain way to make by them, but the operation still remains a loss to the treasury, for it could have made this much more by having previously ascertained the actual value of the coin, and taken it at that value. At present Russian money passes freely in Tashkent, and last year appeared to be at one per cent. premium in Khokand, a circumstance which greatly gladdened the hearts of the administrators, but which was entirely fictitious owing to the fictitious value given to the *tenga*.

At the time of my visit commercial operations were very much impeded by the absence of any banking facilities, not even a private bank being in existence, nor was it easy to procure a bill of exchange, and money had to be sent to and from Russia by post. This has now been remedied by the extension of the telegraph to Tashkent, and by the opening there in 1875 of a branch of the Imperial Bank.

When Tashkent was occupied by the Russians, and it became necessary to seek for sources of revenue, it was resolved to maintain for a while the native taxes, one of the most important of which was the *zekat*, or tax on trade. Originally by Mussulman law the *zekat* was a tax obligatory on all believers, for the support of the poor, and for carrying on of all wars against the infidels, and was levied on gold, silver, dates, oxen and sheep. In modern times this came to be chiefly a tax on caravans or commercial transactions, and in most countries of Central Asia it is for Mussulmans, one fortieth part or 2½ per cent.

---

¹ According to one analysis by the Mining Department at St. Petersburg the Bukharan *tilla* is 44⁷⁄₁₆ proof, and contains 1 zolotnik 5¼ dolia (4·5098 grammes) of pure gold; the Khokandian *tilla* is 82⅔ proof, and contains 77¾ dolia (3·4454 grammes) of pure gold; the Bukharan *tenga* is of 59 proof, and contains 44 dolia (1·9536 grammes) of pure silver; and the Khokandian *tenga* is of 87⁷⁄₁₆ proof, and contains 60 dolias (2·664 grammes) of pure silver. There is evidently some error with regard to the Bukharan *tenga*. A typical coin could not have been chosen.

Before the recent commercial treaties with Russia Christians were taxed double that amount on every caravan. Besides the ordinary or external *zekat*, the Russian administration invented an internal *zekat*, which is a tax on the trading capital, and is collected once a year. Until 1874 it existed in all parts of the district of Syr Darya with the exception of Kazala and Perofsky, which were subject to the Russian commercial code, and in the district of Zarafshan. The internal *zekat* was imposed only on the native merchants and not on the Russians, and was estimated according to the amount of capital declared by the merchant on the day of assessment, or by the valuation of goods which he had in his possession. This latter was the more usual way. The merchant then received a certificate which gave him the right of trading for one year upon that capital. It sometimes happened that articles on which he had paid *zekat* for one year, and had not been able to dispose of in the course of that year, were assessed again the ensuing year, so that the same article was taxed two, three or four times. The external *zekat* is in the nature of a customs duty, and was imposed upon all goods entering or leaving the limits of the district, whether Russian or native, but there was a difference between the *zekat* imposed upon Russian subjects, no matter what their origin, and that imposed upon the subjects of foreign states. Foreigners were obliged to pay *zekat* amounting to $2\frac{1}{2}$ per cent., or one fortieth part of the value of goods, on every importation or exportation made. Russian subjects, on the contrary, paid $2\frac{1}{2}$ per cent. on the value of an importation or exportation which allowed them to traffic freely for one year on that amount of capital. Thus, for instance, if a merchant had imported goods from Russia to the amount of 10,000 rubles, he would pay a tax of 250 rubles and would obtain a certificate which would enable him to trade with this 10,000 worth for a whole year, no matter how many times the capital was turned over in the meantime. If, for example, he were sending a caravan to Russia, he would hardly be able to receive the returning caravan within the year, and at most would turn his capital over but once. If, however, he were trading with Khokand, he might turn it over four or five times, but would pay only one *zekat*. It will easily be seen that the system was productive of many difficulties and afforded considerable opportunity for deception.

A commission was therefore appointed to study the subject, and it was finally decided entirely to abolish the *zekat*, and to introduce the Russian code of taxes and duties on trade with all its complicated system of guilds, tickets and licenses. Certain modifications were made by the Ministry of Finance, allowing the trade in articles of domestic or household manufacture without a tax, and the system went into force on January 1 (13), 1875, for a trial of four years. Objections to the introduction of this system were made by Russians in the interest of their trade, on the ground that by placing the natives on an equality with them, and by enabling the larger merchants to trade with fewer taxes than before, the whole trade of Central Asia would fall into native hands and the Russians would be crowded out of the market. There was a certain foundation for this fear, for, with the exception of one or two firms, all the solid houses trading in Tashkent are either natives or Tartars. At first there was some dissatisfaction among the natives, as pains had not been taken to translate the law, and even had it been translated it would have been difficult for them to understand its complicated provisions. As this system presses much more hardly on small traders than on large, the great native merchants found themselves by the payment of the first guild tax of 265 rubles a year in a much better position than before, and able to trade freely in all parts of the empire. Even the taxes on the smaller merchants, though high, were not so oppressive as they at first seemed, because under the *zekat* system the traders were in the habit of concealing a great part of their capital. Before the tax collector came round, they removed from their shops the greater part of their goods. The collector, when dissatisfied, said: 'This is too little, I shall charge you so much,' and the sum was usually paid without a murmur, as it was even then less than the amount really due. The new system brought in during January 1875, when most of the tickets and licences had to be taken out, 157,565 rubles, or 90,000 more than had been obtained in previous years from the Russian traders and from the natives in those districts where this law had been applied.

As under the new system the external *zekat* is also abolished, and as the customs frontier of Orenburg and Southern Siberia was abrogated in 1868-9, foreign goods can now enter the

Central Asiatic provinces duty free. Thus, if the letter of the commercial treaties with the neighbouring states be adhered to, it will leave the Russians in the position of admitting all goods free and still of paying the old $2\frac{1}{2}$ per cent. duty to their neighbours. It must not be supposed, however, that all goods are allowed to pass the frontier; for in 1869 the Governor General issued an order keeping out nearly all articles of European manufacture, and—in order to benefit the Kiakhta merchants—tea introduced by the way of India. In addition to this the order which I mentioned on page 48 was given to keep European merchants from entering the country.

Little more than this has been done by the Russians for the benefit of trade. Various manufactories, some of which I have already mentioned, have been started, but with the exception of the distilleries, they have nearly all failed. These distilleries seem to be doing a prosperous business and afford a considerable article of the revenue derived from the country. Most of the Russian merchants who ventured into the Central Asiatic trade, ruined or greatly crippled themselves,—Khludof and Pervushin, for instance,—and the recent failure of the silk filature at Hodjent, which I mentioned above, will, probably, for some time bring commercial enterprises in Turkistan into complete discredit.

There *is* one thing more, the fair.

In one of the happiest sketches of the Russian satirist Stchedrin, there is the characterisation of a Tashkentian. The type to which he gives the name 'Tashkentian,' is a civiliser, an enlightener—'an enlightener in general, in every place and in every way, and an enlightener too, free from science, but not confused by that, for science in his opinion was created not for the spread, but for the hindrance of enlightenment. A scientific man first demands alphabets, then syllables, the four rules of arithmetic, multiplication tables, &c. The Tashkentian sees in all that nothing but chicanery, and says up and down that to stop over similar trifles is to stumble and to waste golden time.' One of his characters develops the advantages of the Russian *telega* as a means of civilising the Kirghiz. 'Don't interrupt me, *mon cher*, because I must express my idea fully. Thus, as I said before, the original mode of locomotion was on foot, but as man began to conquer nature and tame animals, the means of locomotion became more complicated, and instead of confining himself to pedestrianism, man now begins to ride on four-footed animals. Thus arises a notion of property, which, on the basis of the rule *omnia mea mecum porto*, is placed on the same animal with the rider. This is already a step in advance, but you will agree with me a very limited step. (I nodded and winked a little, as though I wished to say, *Oh, comme je vous comprends, mon général!*) The property is insignificant, the means of transport are also insignificant; there is the key for explaining the existence of pastoral and nomadic nations. They wander about, move from one place to another, and never can settle in one place—*enfin tout s'explique!* At last appears the *telega*, that uncomfortable and jolting equipage; but see what a revolution it produces! By its very uncomfortableness it compels its possessor to avoid superfluous movement, and in this way fixes him to the land. Thus fixed, he begins to get an idea of manure. Seeing the gradual accumulation of this fertilising material, the simple shepherd asks himself, what is manure? For the first time he begins to think about it, for the first time the idea comes to him, that manure, like everything else in nature, does not exist without a purpose. He begins to appreciate manure, he sees in it *ses pénates et ses lares*. He constructs his dwelling near it, and imperceptibly to himself he enters into the period of settled life (*Oh, comme je vous comprends, comme je vous comprends, mon général!*) Do you understand? Man invents a *telega*, and this simple fact, which almost every day passes unnoticed before our eyes, is quite sufficient for him to obtain elementary ideas of manure, and to leave for ever the habits of the nomads. But more than this, having a *telega*, he understands the basis of a sound civilisation (*Oh comme je vous comprends!*) Don't you see what a radical reform we at once make in the life of these unhappy vagabonds, risking nothing, even bringing nothing with us except a simple Russian *telega! Aussi, je leur en donnerai . . . . du telègue! Ah!*'

It must have been a man of this kind that projected the Tashkent fair.

Considering the part which fairs have played in the history of Russian commerce, it was perhaps natural for persons unaccustomed to mercantile life to imagine that trade could not possibly be carried on without them, and that to start a fair meant to create trade. It was forgotten that trade seeks its own channels, and cannot be arbitrarily increased at the command of the authorities. It was forgotten too that commerce is very delicate and susceptible, and cannot be interfered with with impunity. Nevertheless plausible arguments full of fine phrases were made to the Governor-General, a petition was drawn up, to which the signatures of the merchants were easily obtained—for when will Russian merchants refuse to sign a petition, or an address brought to them by an officer of the government?—and the authorities resolved on the establishment of a fair, and a commission was appointed in 1870 to study the details, and prepare the organisation. In the order appointing this commission the reasons are thus stated : 'The exchange of the manufactures from the internal provinces of the Empire for the raw material (cotton and silk) of the Asiatic countries has up to this time been chiefly carried on at two fairs: those of Irbit and Nizhni Novgorod. Closer relations between consumers and producers, and the consequent permanency of price and of commercial relations, would doubtless be greatly facilitated by bringing the centre of exchange nearer to the Central Asiatic markets.'

It is curious that at the first session of the Commission the merchants who had just petitioned for the fair unanimously declared that the fair of Irbit, the remoteness of which had been a cause of complaint, had not the slightest influence on the trade of Central Asia, while the fair of Nizhni Novgorod had so great an influence that it was useless to found a fair at Tashkent, as the prices there would inevitably be governed by those at Nizhni. The views of the non-commercial members prevailed, and the commission established two fairs, one in spring and the other in autumn, and ordered the erection of suitable buildings. The site chosen for the fair was at about two miles south-east of the Russian town, and fully five miles from the bazaar of the native town. This place was chosen in order to draw native commerce away from the native influences which prevailed in the old town, to subject it to close governmental supervision, and to render it amenable to governmental control.[1]

[1] See also page 175.

Buildings were erected on a large scale and at great expense. There were offices for the administration, large caravanserais, and many rows of shops. The projectors intended to transfer the entire wholesale trade of the region to this locality. The work was pushed on as fast as possible, although the troops, the real sinews of Russian strength in Asia, were suffering from the want of suitable barracks. Yet in spite of all their efforts, when the fair was opened in October 1870, it was found that, with the exception of the Russian merchants, no persons came to buy or to sell, and the natives could not be persuaded to leave their shops and establish new ones in the bazaar, even though they were offered accommodation free of rent. Consequently it was necessary to issue an order that during the whole duration of the fair, two months in the year, all the native merchants, with the exception of the sellers of provisions, should close their shops at the old bazaar, and remove their trade to the shops of the fair. Many traders, however, sooner than transport their goods such a long distance, resolved to abandon commerce entirely for the duration of the fair, or carried it on secretly in their houses. In consequence of this it was proposed to impose fines on persons who did not appear, and, I am told, they were even hunted up and driven to the fair by Cossacks. These measures were, however, found to be useless, and the Russian merchants, who sold goods to the natives on credit and received weekly or monthly payments from them, were unable to collect their accounts, and petitioned the government to allow the natives to trade as before in the old town, as otherwise they would themselves be ruined. The Russian merchants also themselves found it disagreeable to be compelled to keep warehouses for their goods at the fair as well as in their private establishments. The buildings are therefore empty, and, according to good information, the fair, while not officially closed, has in reality ceased to exist. The whole enterprise has therefore been a complete failure, and up to the end of 1873 had cost the government 377,247 rubles; of this sum 29,631 rubles were spent in the purchase of private buildings and land, 245,676 rubles in the erection of the fair buildings, 56,863 rubles in salaries and administration, and 15,726 rubles in the expenses of collecting the revenue of the fair, and the remainder, about 30,000 rubles, for various expenses. The receipts of the fair to cover these expenses were 32,395 rubles. The only advantages known to have been derived from it were the opening breakfasts and dinners, the cost of which was defrayed by a subscription extorted from the merchants.

The business done at these fairs is thus stated in the official reports in rubles:

			Brought	Carried away	Total dealings	Sales by brokers
1870	Autumn fair[1]		3,890,828·63	2,335,050·35½	6,225.888·98½	680,323
1871	Spring	„	2,520,316·73	1,393,356·02	3,913,702·75 }	not stated
„	Autumn	„	4,742.858·	2,042,521·	6,788,379· }	
1872	„	„[2]	1,849,749·89	1,538,583·32	3.388,325·21	252,292·94

		Brought	Carried away	Transit trade	Brokers' sales	Total
1873	Spring	735,985·72	907,827·27	160,213·	472,198·90	2,285,244·89
„	Autumn	1,260,297·32	860,169·62	131,628·20	190,692·35	2,442,787·39

I quote these figures to show the minuteness with which the details of the fair have been studied, even to the fractions of a kopek, and at the same time as an example of the difficulty of using statistics which have been made to order. The fair grounds are not like a country where the exports and the imports are different. Nothing can be carried away from the fair but what has at some time been brought there, and much is brought and taken away without being sold; while the same goods are sometimes brought several times, goods being taken from the fair to the native town, then brought to the Russian quarter and entered again at the fair. It is only the amount of actual sales which shows the dealings of a fair. Here the amounts for goods brought in are added to the amounts for goods taken away to make the total dealings; and in 1872 the amount of the transit trade, 159,889·34, is added to both sides, so that it appears twice in the total; while in 1873 not only the transit trade but the sales by brokers are added, the same transaction thus appearing in three different ways. Besides this the figures are made up in part from estimates, and in some cases, from fear lest the amount should not be large enough, 20 per cent. has been added to it. Sometimes transactions are included which have nothing to do with the fair, as for instance the cattle trade. Cattle are brought to Tashkent in large numbers on every bazaar day, twice a week, and the numbers driven and sold

---

[1] This fair lasted two months instead of one.

[2] I have been unable to obtain the returns for the spring fair of 1872.

during the months of the fair are no greater than at any other time; in fact, the figures are intended rather to show the total trade of Tashkent during the months in which the fair is held; for it is so arranged that all imports and exports have to pass through the office of the committee of the fair, and I find by comparison that these amounts are not proportionately larger than those of the other months. The only positive data are the amounts of sales by brokers, although these by no means cover the total actual sales. The fair committee tried to establish the rule that nothing should be sold at the fair except by brokers licensed by the government, and this was called a measure for encouraging trade!

The causes of the failure of the fair are easily intelligible. Tashkent is not a manufacturing nor an agricultural centre, nor is it really a trade centre; it lies on the road from Khokand to Orenburg and Troïtzk, and that is all. The trade of Tashkent with Bukhara and the Zarafshan valley is very insignificant, as that trade follows the old route direct across the steppe from Bukhara to Kazala. Articles of prime necessity—such as sugar and candles—are sometimes cheaper in Samarkand than Tashkent, being imported too through Bukhara, where they have to pay duties. Tashkent is a halting place for the Khokand trade, simply because, as the seat of government, the chief merchants find it convenient to live there, and to store the goods forwarded to them until they have occasion to send them on. It is not a place where great purchases are made. Were the capital transferred to Tchimkent, no one would ascribe any commercial importance to Tashkent.

The transit trade through Tashkent with Khokand in 1872 was 1,162,738 rubles, and with Bukhara 22,669 rubles. In the year 1871, the only one for which we have exact, detailed statistical returns, the imports into Tashkent from all parts of Russia and from the independent Khanates were 8,992,320 rubles, the exports 6,112,495, making a total of 15,104,815 rubles; of this 4,094,291 was with Khokand, and only 337,854 with Bukhara. In 1873 the trade of Tashkent is stated to have been: Imports, 10,938,159; exports, 6,299,182; total, 17,237,341; transit, 954,289.

Some idea of the trade of Tashkent may be formed from the transportation statistics for 1872 and 1873.

	Pack-camels	Pack-horses	Carts
1872 Arrived	55,658	7,279	6,624
,, Departed	26,792	1,539	761
1873 Arrived	46,294½	2,663¾	2,436
,, Departed	36,208	1,632½	1,212

The average load of a camel is 576 lbs.; that of a horse 288 lbs., and that of a cart 990 lbs. From this we see that there were brought to Tashkent in 1872 40,713,120 lbs. of merchandise, and there left it 16,628,814 lbs., while in 1873 there were brought 29,845,388 lbs. and taken away 22,525,848 lbs.[1]

It is very difficult to arrive at the exact figures of Central Asiatic trade. The Orenburg-Siberia frontier customs line was abolished in 1868, and the collection of statistics has consequently ceased. The only materials which exist for determining the amount of trade consist in the declarations of the Russian and the native merchants, of the kind, quantity, and value of the wares which have been imported or exported by them, as delivered to the economical *bureaux* of the districts for the payment of duty or *zekat* on such goods, and of the *zekat* receipts, which show the amount of duty received. These receipts, which are chiefly written in the Turki language, have enabled the agent of the Ministry of Finance to publish 'materials for the statistics of the Asiatic trade.' It is a matter of considerable difficulty, however, to collect such data with any pretence to accuracy, as the *zekat* system did not exist in all parts of the country, and the full amount of the trade is not indicated there, the *zekat* receipt for the goods brought by caravan allowing the merchant to trade on the capital represented by those goods for a whole year without paying other *zekat*, and consequently, where it was possible to turn over the capital more than once a year, the full amount of the transactions is not shown. So far as it is possible to ascertain, making allowances for the places where the full returns are not given, the imports into the district of the Syr Darya from all quarters in the year 1872 amounted to 13,400,000 rubles, and the exports for the same time amounted to 9,185,000 rubles, making a total of 22,585,000. Of this, however, at least 10,000,000 rubles must be

---

[1] These figures are too large. A camel-load, as a standard of weight, is 16 puds or 576 lbs.; the load carried by a camel—especially in long distances—is usually far smaller.

deducted for trade with the Kirghiz Steppe, leaving 12,585,000 rubles as the actual trade with the Khanates. But this does not include the direct trade between Khiva and the Caspian littoral, which is small, and that between Kashgar and Vierny, of which I shall speak further on. Allowing for the trade on these two routes the highest estimates, we would have for the present trade with Central Asia proper, both exports and imports, the total of about fifteen million rubles (2,000,000*l.*).

By the customs returns on the frontier in 1867, we have the following:

Exports to Tashkent (including Khokand)	.	5,478,000 rubles
„ Bukhara	.	4,910,000 „
„ Khiva	.	487,000 „
Making a total of	.	10,875,000
The imports were as follows:—		
From Tashkent	.	868,000 rubles
„ Bukhara	.	6,215,000 „
„ Khiva	.	1,421,000 „
Making a total of . . .	.	8,504,000

The total trade consequently amounted to 19,379,000 rubles (2,650,000*l.*). It would seem therefore that the trade with Central Asia has diminished rather than increased since the year 1867, unless the figures for that year were exaggerated.

The trade of Bukhara through Kazala was in the year from September 1868 to September 1869, 4,193,000 rubles imports and 1,793,000 rubles exports, and through Tashkent in 1872, 8,643 rubles imports and 14,000 rubles exports. The trade of 1869 was, however, much larger than usual, as can be seen from the amount of *zekat* received, which in 1869 was 114,000 rubles; in 1870, 36,000 rubles; in 1871, 33,000 rubles; in 1872, 24,000 rubles. The probable trade with Kazala therefore in 1872 was not more than one third of what it was in 1869; but, counting it at one half, we would have the total trade with Bukhara in 1872,—inclusive of both exports and imports,—as not more than 3,000,000 rubles. In 1869 the total trade with Bukhara was more than 11,000,000. We cannot ascribe this falling off in the trade to the separation of the Zarafshan district from Bukhara, for we find that the whole trade of the Zarafshan district, as represented at Samarkand for 1872, was only 2,000,000 rubles. It is of course possible that the *data* from which these statistics are made are not full, and it is possible that the disturbance in the Kirghiz Steppe, and the crisis in the cotton trade, had considerable influence on the commerce with Bukhara, but in any event the result is not favourable.

For the trade of Khokand the statistics are tolerably full, and we find that in 1872 the imports from that country amounted to 2,189,836 rubles, and the exports to 1,273,520 rubles. The chief articles of import from Khokand are cotton and silk, and in much smaller quantities fresh and dried fruit, coarse native half-silk and half-cotton materials, and native clothes. The exports are chiefly Russian prints, cotton yarn, cloth, and Russian shawls and handkerchiefs, which are used as girdles.

The chief statistics for the present trade with Khiva are those taken in Kazala. From September 1868 to September 1869 the exports from Russia to Khiva were 112,045 rubles, and the imports from Khiva 294,887 rubles. The exports to Khiva in that year were entirely confined to the winter months from January to April. Most of the Khivan trade passes through Kazala, although a small portion of it goes through the Caspian Steppes.

As to the special articles of import, those of the greatest importance are cotton and silk; cotton having been imported across the Orenburg and Siberia customs line, in 1863, to the amount of 2,933,248 rubles; and in 1864, to the amount of 6,583,229 rubles; in 1865, 3,394,267 rubles; in 1866, 4,326,145 rubles; in 1867, 5,513,422 rubles: all of course coming from Tashkent, Khokand, Bukhara and Khiva. In 1872 there was imported from Khokand, in transit through Tashkent, cotton to the amount of 208,568 rubles. From Tashkent there was sent to other parts of Russia, as well as to other towns of the Turkistan district, 1,953,860 rubles' worth. In 1872, from Tashkent, the district of Kurama and from Samarkand, there was only 785,089 rubles' worth exported. In 1869 the cotton imported from Kazala amounted to 1,943,860 rubles, and from Khiva 60,002 rubles. If we take the highest figures of the export from Tashkent, the total amount of cotton imported into Russia during 1872 would come to only 3,606,356 rubles (500,000*l.*), a considerable falling off from former years.

The silk trade, which began to increase after the occupation of the country by the Russians, makes rather a better show. In 1867 it amounted to 75,643 rubles; in 1869 to 1,181,967 rubles. In 1872 there was exported, in transit through Tashkent, silk to the amount of 200,360 rubles. In 1871 there was transported from Tashkent to Russia 471,188 rubles' worth. In 1872 from Tashkent, Kazala, and Hodjent, it amounted to 762,468 rubles. The import of silk from Kazala in 1869 came to 1,095,667 rubles; from Khiva 86,300 rubles. Should we take the highest figure, which would be unfair, as the import of silk from Bukhara in 1872 was by no means equal to that in 1869, we should have the total of the silk trade 2,134,795 rubles (300,000*l*.).

Fully one half of the silk sent to Russia comes from Bukhara, and nearly all the other half comes from Khokand, but a very slight quantity coming from the Russian provinces. Thus in 1871 there was brought to Tashkent from Khokand 929,537 rubles' worth; from the cities of the Syr Darya, a province, only 70,523 rubles' worth. The trade in horse-hair, which in 1872 amounted to only 10,113 rubles, could probably be easily increased.

The chief articles sent from Russia to Central Asia are prints and cotton goods. Of these there were sent, in 1869, from Russia to Tashkent, 3,857,207 rubles' worth; to Bukhara 2,810,060 rubles' worth; and to Khiva 284,522 rubles' worth; the total amounting to 6,951,789 rubles (952,000*l*.). Of such goods there were sent to Tashkent in 1872 4,470,723 rubles' worth; to Bukhara, in 1872, 1,054,717 rubles' worth; to Khokand, in 1869, 240,630 rubles' worth; to Khiva, in 1869, 55,829 rubles' worth: the total being 5,821,902 rubles (800,000*l*.). These figures will also show a falling off in the Central Asiatic trade, although the market is reserved almost exclusively to the Russians, very few English goods getting farther than Bukhara. Tea is also sent in large quantities, the amount imported into Turkistan in 1872 being 1,048,508 rubles, of which but a very small quantity (about 100,000 rubles) came from China through Siberia, the rest being sent from Moscow. During the last half of 1868, the whole of 1869. and the first half of 1870, there were 635,273 lbs. of tea imported. Of this 174,772 lbs. were sent to Khokand, while 18,533 lbs. were brought back from that country, not being saleable. In 1871 141,597 lbs. were sent to Khokand, and in 1872 only 21,970 rubles' worth. In general the tea trade with the Khanates is not flourishing, as green tea in very large quantities is imported from India by way of Bukhara. Its passage through Turkistan is prohibited, but, nevertheless, most of that used in Khokand passes through Russian territory close to Samarkand by what is called the 'robbers' road.' Much also is smuggled for sale in the country. For instance, in the Zarafshan district no one buys Russian tea except the Russians, and in 1872 but 11,900 lbs. of tea were imported from Bukhara through the Custom House (the prohibition not being then applied to this region), which for over 200,000 inhabitants is less than half-a-pound a year each. Now tea is universally drunk, and the consumption of each man is much nearer half-a-pound a month. Fully 500,000 lbs. of tea must have been smuggled. The import of sugar in 1872 was only 171,700 rubles.

Very exaggerated notions have been held with regard to the amount of trade to be derived from Kashgar. The country, however, is poor, the population scanty, and there is little demand for foreign goods, and there are almost no native goods that can be exported with advantage, the chief article of export being *daba*, a coarse kind of native cotton goods, which is sold to the Kirghiz, who pay in sheep, at the rate of a sheep for a piece of *daba*. As the sheep is worth 3 rubles, and the *daba* 40 to 50 kopeks, Kashgar gains by the traffic. The trade with Russia is principally carried on by the roads from Vierny, Tokmak, and Naryn to Kashgar, though there is some trade also by the routes of Aksu and Karakol, and through Khokand. The only statistical materials of this trade are those which have been kept at the fort of Naryn. In December 1868, and the whole of the year 1869, the total trade of Kashgar with Russia, passing through Naryn Fort, both exports and imports, amounted to 274,665 rubles (37,628*l.*). In 1870 the imports from Kashgar were 184,182 rubles, and the exports to that country 39,843, making a total of 224,025 rubles (30,688*l.*). In 1871 the imports from Kashgar amounted to 473,338 rubles, and the exports to Kashgar 140,372 rubles, in all 604,710 rubles (82,837*l.*). In 1872, up to the first of May, the imports from Kashgar amounted to 50,539 rubles, and the exports to 53,564 rubles, making together 104,103 rubles (14,260*l.*). These figures are small, because most of the trade is in the latter months of the year. Mr. Kolesnikoff, who was the commercial agent of the Russian Embassy to Kashgar in 1872, estimates the total exports from Kashgar to Russia from 1st of June 1871 to 1st of May 1872 as 1,100,000 rubles (150,685*l.*), including those sent viâ Khokand. During 1874, according to published returns, there were imported from Kashgar, through the Naryn pass, about 1,662,000 lbs. of merchandise, including 721,729 pieces of *daba* worth about 324,000 rubles. During the same year there were exported to Kashgar 1,678,000 lbs., and 85,382 sheep worth, at 3 rubles each, about 256,000 rubles. In 1875, up to the 22nd of July, the imports were 1,111,000 lbs., including 881,560 pieces of *daba* worth about 396,000 rubles, and the exports were 402,000 lbs. of goods, and 54,049 sheep worth about 162,000 rubles.

To a country separated so far from the rest of the world, not by water, but by arid wastes, the question of trade routes and of the means of transportation becomes of prime commercial importance. Goods are chiefly transported in Central Asia in pack-trains, or on the *arbas*, or two-wheeled carts of the country. This last method is, however, principally employed in the south between neighbouring towns, as between Bukhara and Samarkand, and Hodjent and Tashkent, while for longer routes transportation by camels becomes a necessity. The use of carts has greatly increased since the Russian occupation and the construction of passable roads. As the method of harnessing is very burdensome to the horses, the maximum load of a cart is not more than 2 camel-loads, or 32 puds (1,152 lbs.), but the ordinary load is only a camel-load and a half, or 24 puds (864 lbs.). The ordinary load of a horse is 8 puds (288 lbs.), and of an ass half that amount. These animals are chiefly used for rocky and mountainous roads, where hard hoofs are necessary, as on the short road over the mountains from Tashkent to Khokand.

By far the most common and most useful beast of burden is the camel, which carries ordinarily 16 puds (576 lbs.), and which can travel over almost any soil, can find his pasture as he goes, and, except in cold weather, does not need the care which must be bestowed on a horse. As his gait is twice as slow as the horse, the latter, though carrying only half as much, can with advantage be used for short distances. The fact, however, that a camel kneels down to his load renders it much easier to load and unload him at the halts, thus relieving the attendants of much labour. In unloading the camel the ropes or straps connecting the two bales which make up the load are untied, the bales remain standing on the ground, and the camel walks away from them. In loading he kneels down between them, and they are fastened on with a very small expenditure of manual labour. Attempts have been made to use camels harnessed to a cart, it being found in this way that they can carry from 50 to 60 puds (1,800 to 2,100 lbs.).

The chief trade route to Bukhara is from Orenburg through Kazala, varying according to the road chosen, whether directly across the steppe, or by way of Orsk, from 1,060 to 1,160 miles in length, and requiring about 47 days. The caravans cross the Syr Darya at Kazala, or a short distance above, on the Russian ferries, or on the reed bridges made by the Kirghiz. Freight cost formerly only from twelve to fifteen rubles per camel, but owing to the rise of prices cannot now be had for less than twenty-one rubles. The Bukharan caravans occasionally, but of late years less frequently, go to Troitsk, about 1,000 miles, needing 52 days. As this route falls in with the wanderings of the Kirghiz, from whom the camels are hired, freight is often half less than that to Orenburg. The road from Bukhara to Samarkand, 150 miles, is very much frequented, but very little of the trade goes farther on to Tashkent, about 340 miles in all. A small amount of trade with Siberia goes over another road from Bukhara, which crosses the Syr Darya near Turkistan. The total cost of a pud of goods from Moscow to Bukhara would be about 2·75 rubles (7s. 1d.), or 2$\frac{1}{2}d$. per pound.

For the Khokandian trade there are two routes from Tashkent, one, as I have said, directly over the mountains through Telau, 140 miles, occupying five or six days, and the other, which is possible for carts, by the way of Hodjent, being over 200 miles, and taking eight or ten days.

Formerly nearly all caravans from Tashkent went to Petropavlovsk and Troitsk. The greater part of them now go directly to Orenburg, following in general the post road, a distance of

1,300 miles, or 60 days. From Tashkent to Orenburg freight costs from 14 to 25 rubles per camel, or 90 kopeks to 1·69 rubles per pud, return freight being dearer. The route from Tashkent to Petropavlovsk, after passing through Tchimkent, skirts the northern slope of the Kara-tau to Suzak, and then goes straight through the Bek-pak-dala Steppe to Akmolinsk and Petropavlovsk, about 1,200 miles. Propositions have been made to establish postal communication on this road. Freight is now from 90 kopeks to 2 rubles per pud, or from 14 to 32 rubles a camel. The route from Troitsk to Tashkent requires about 39 days, and is considered to be about 1,200 miles. Freight is from 11 to 17 rubles per camel, or 20 kopeks to 1·30 rubles per pud.

The Kashgar trade usually follows the road through the Naryn pass to Tokmak and Vierny, but a certain portion of it goes over the Terek-davan and through Khokand, the distance from Kashgar to Khokand being estimated at over 300 miles, requiring from 12 to 20 days for a caravan.

The trade with Khiva, when it flourished, went by three roads; from Orenburg through Kazala and Irkibai to Khiva, 54 or 55 days' journey of 1,140 to 1,230 miles; or from Orenburg through the Emba Post, and skirting the west shore of the Aral Sea, 43 days and some 880 miles; or from the Caspian through Mangyshlak, directly across the Ust-urt—a difficult road, on account of the scarcity of water, and almost unused since 1855. The price of freight from Orenburg to Khiva is about 16 rubles a camel, or 1 ruble per pud. Since the Khivan expedition Colonel Glukhofsky, who seems greatly impressed with the possibilities of trade with Khiva, has devoted his energies to establishing a caravan route and regular commerce between Krasnovodsk on the Caspian and Khiva. One of his caravans, during the summer of 1875, went from Krasnovodsk to Khiva by the shortest road in seventeen days, but as there were wells only at distances of two or three days' journey, it is not the most advantageous. Taking advantage of specially favourable circumstances, he paid a freight of ten rubles for every $12\frac{1}{2}$ puds of merchandise. The caravan also made the return journey to Krasnovodsk in seventeen days. In the autumn of 1875 another of Col. Glukhofsky's caravans was pillaged by the Turkomans.

From Khiva to Bukhara the usual route is to ascend the

Amu Darya in boats as far as Ustyk, and then, loading on camels, to proceed to Bukhara through Kara-Kol, some 350 miles, or a journey of about 17 days. The current of the Amu is so strong that the return journey is much shorter.

The road from Bukhara to Balkh, by the way of Karshi, is estimated at about 300 miles, and demands 13 days. To Kabul is 350 miles more, needing another 13 days. Should the caravans go direct to Kabul through Khulum, without touching Balkh, the journey could be accomplished in 20 days. The freight from Khulum to Bukhara is 25 to 30 *tengas* for a camel load of 12 puds (432 lbs.), and 50 to 60 *tengas* for a camel load of 16 puds (576 lbs.), while from Bukhara to Khulum it is much dearer. From Khulum to Kabul freights are from 25 to 40 rupees per camel load of 12 puds. From Kabul to Peshawur caravans go in 12 days, a freight of from 15 to 20 rupees being charged for a camel load of 12 puds. This makes the total cost of freight of a camel load of 432 lbs. from Bukhara to Peshawur about 34·49 rubles or 4*l*. 14*s*. 7*d*., without including the customs duties or transit dues, or the great exactions of the Amir of Kabul,—nearly the same as from Moscow to Bukhara.

From Bukhara to Herat, through Maimena, is a journey of about 600 miles, which can be accomplished in 25 days; a camel load paying about 36 Bukharan *tengas*. From Bukhara to Merv is a journey of 11 days; and to Mashad of some 10 days more. The price of freight for the whole distance is about 3 Bukharan *tillas* per camel load.

The commerce of Central Asia, which passes through Petropavlovsk, goes to Ekaterinburg and Perm, and so down the Kama to Nizhni Novgorod; that through Troitsk takes either the same route, or goes across the Ural to Ufa and thence to Nizhni. The caravans for Orenburg usually stop at that place, and the goods are then generally placed on carts and taken to Samara on the Volga; a railway is now being built between Samara and Orenburg, which will greatly facilitate communications. Krasnovodsk, on the Caspian, is connected with Astrakhan and thence with Nizhni by occasional steamers.

Communications being so difficult, the Russians have naturally considered what could be done to improve them, and various plans have been suggested. It was at first thought that there could be water communication by the Sry Darya, and that this would be the main line of trade for the region about Tashkent, but, as I have shown in a previous chapter, the difficulties in the way have thus far proved too great. For the Khivan trade it was also desired to run steamers from Kazala through the Aral Sea and up the Amu Darya. Some of the obstructions which impede the navigation of that river at the delta were removed, and in 1874 a steamer did succeed in reaching Nukus, but by a round-about route through the *Dau Kara* lake, and with the greatest difficulty. Explorations have been made of the old bed of the Oxus, partly with a purely scientific aim, and partly to investigate the possibility of turning the water of the river once more into its old channels. It has been found that a well defined bed exists in what is called the Uzboi, debouching in the Caspian near Krasnovódsk, and it is believed that if the dams on the Laudan were removed, the water would flow along the old beds for some distance, at least as far as Sary Kamysh; but there seems to be this difficulty in all the schemes for the improvement of river navigation in Central Asia, that the amount of water in the rivers is not so great as formerly, owing no doubt in a great measure to the destruction of forests on the mountains along their upper courses. In order to have sufficient water for navigation it would seem to be necessary to destroy the irrigation systems, and this by diminishing, if not putting an end to the productive power of the countries of Central Asia, and thus destroying the commerce, would remove the only reason for which navigation is considered requisite.

The idea of a railway has therefore been mooted. There were frequent suggestions of the possibility of a railway; and in 1873 General Beznosikof, an official who had served a time at Semipalatinsk and who still needed two or three years of active service in order to receive a pension, was assigned to the duty of investigating the feasibility of constructing a railway to Tashkent. He has made a voluminous report, but from what I saw of his methods of enquiry, and from what was told me at Semipalatinsk, I should not be inclined to place much confidence in his reports or in his projects. The idea, however, of a Central Asiatic railway made no great head until it was taken up by M. de Lesseps in his letter to General Ignatieff of May 1, 1873. M. de Lesseps laid stress on the fact that over the route from Calais to Calcutta by way of Orenburg, 7,370 miles, railways had already been constructed as far as Orenburg on one side and Peshawur on the other, making together 5,100 miles, and that it was therefore necessary in order to complete the line to construct less than half that amount, namely 2,270, of which Russia should make 1,470 miles from Orenburg to Samarkand, and England the remaining 800 from Samarkand to Peshawur. For the preliminary surveys he considered that there would be necessary two years of time and three millions of francs, which could be collected by a public subscription, the subscribers to form the 'Grand Central Asiatic Railway Society.' In a subsequent letter to Lord Granville, M. de Lesseps dilated on the advantages of his plan, and stated that he intended to send his son and another engineer to India to make the preliminary studies. According to *The St. Petersburg Exchange Gazette* of April 5–17, 1874, this idea did not originate with M. de Lesseps, but he owed it to M. Cotard and M. Yanitzky, the latter a Russian engineer who succeeded to M. Lavalet, one of the chief constructors of the Suez canal. These gentlemen were in St. Petersburg at a time when various societies there were busying themselves with Asiatic trade routes, and entered fully into their ideas, and procured from them statistics on the subject. However this may be, it was not until after M. de Lesseps' letter that the idea of a Central Asiatic railway took any strong hold on the Russian public. Immediately numerous projects were brought forward, some of them of an even wilder nature than that of M. de Lesseps: Mr. Bogdanovitch, for example, seriously proposed to construct a railway from Saratof on the Volga to Gurief at the mouth of the Ural, and then across the Ust-urt to Khiva, Bukhara and Samarkand, with one branch to Tashkent and another to Peshawur.

Subseqently it was proposed, instead of M. de Lesseps' railway to Tashkent, Samarkand, Kabul, and Peshawur, to turn it eastward from Tashkent to Khokand and Kashgar, and then over the Karakorum to Ladak, a work which would demand more engineering skill than any railway yet constructed. The divergence in views of the Russian and English Governments, with regard to Asiatic affairs, and the character and political condition of some of the countries through which a railway to India must pass, will probably for a long time prevent the construction of any such railway, and therefore, so much of it as concerns India may be left out of the question. So far, the projects for a direct railway to Central Asia have not received much encouragement from the Russian Government —the scheme having been rejected in a special ministerial council held on the subject of a letter of M. de Lesseps to the Emperor—although the Tashkent authorities have considered them more seriously. The engineering difficulties of a railway from Orenburg to Tashkent, Samarkand, and even as far south as the Amu Darya, through Karshi, would be trifling ; but the cost of construction, and more than that of running, on account of the lack of water and fuel, would be immense. Besides this the greater part of the country which would be traversed by this railway is now almost uninhabited, and utterly unfit for colonisation. That such a railway could be built I have no doubt, if the Government for military reasons considered it necessary; but what I have before said with regard to the trade of Central Asia—which, including everything, amounts to barely three and a half million pounds sterling a year—will show in some measure what returns such a railway could expect. If Tashkent be ever connected with Russia by rail, it will probably be by means of a branch from the Siberian railway which will sooner or later be built. Although the route has not been actually fixed, it is practically determined to build a railway which will connect Moscow with Tiumen in Siberia, and ultimately with Omsk and Irkutsk. It is even possible that the railway from Samara to Orenburg may be the beginning of the Siberian railway, and in that case it would naturally pass through Troitsk and Petropavlovsk. From Petropavlovsk to Akmolinsk the country, although steppe land, is fertile, well watered, and suitable for colonisation. A railway here could be as easily constructed as was the Pacific railway in the United States; and were lands along the line to be granted to the railway company, sufficient colonisation might be attracted from the northern and inclement parts of Russia, to go a great way towards paying the expenses of the railway When a railway shall have reached that distance, it will be comparatively easy to extend it to Tashkent, should reasons of state render it advisable or necessary.

CHAPTER VI.

SAMARKAND.

The Mullah—Tchinaz—The Famished Steppe—Assafœtida—Murza Rabat—Jizakh—Gates of Tamerlane—Rock inscriptions—Tchupan-Ata—First view of Samarkand—Hafistas—Early history—The Græco-Bactrian dynasty—Chinese travellers—Clavijo—Baber's description—The Russian conquest—Siege of the citadel by the natives, and its heroic defence by the Russians—Mosque of Shah Zindeh—Bibi Khanym—Shir-dar—Tomb of Timur—The *Kok-tash*—Hodja Akhrar—Koran of Othman—Bazaars—Dervishes—The Jews—Abdul Rahman Khan of Affghanistan—Russian adventurers—Russian soldiers—Russian administration.

It was on a lovely May evening when, with my interpreter the Mullah Hair-ullah, I set out for Samarkand. Driving rapidly over a good road, which led out of the town, and between the high clay walls of the many gardens, we came suddenly on the magnificent villa of the Governor-General, which is almost as well fitted up as his town house; then passing through more gardens and open fields, we reached the little station of Niazbash, when it was already dark. The Mullah is a Russian Tartar from Kazan, who had been educated in the medressé there, and had come out to seek his fortune in Tashkent, where he had relations, being a nephew of my friend Alim Hadji Yunusof. He had been employed as an interpreter and as an assistant in the custom office, but had preferred to leave the service, being disgusted with the corruption which he saw about him, and had set up a small shop at the Sunday bazaar where he sold prints and cottons; not that he contented himself with that entirely, for he had decided literary tastes, knowing Persian and Arabic as well as Russian, Tartar, and Kirghiz, and remembering enough of his Latin to be able to translate for me half of an ode of Horace. His great regret was that he had never gone to the University. His leisure he occupied with reading the Koran and theological and legal books, and with translating the 'Arabian Nights,' for the supplement to the 'Turkistan Gazette,' that being considered probably by the authorities the most innocent and improving reading which could be given to the natives, as it is utterly devoid of political tendencies. Mullah Hair-ullah was a very pleasant companion, and, although he had never visited Samarkand before, had been about the country, and knew the traditions of various places, although, as I afterwards found, it was hardly necessary for me to have taken an interpreter, as in Samarkand I got on well enough without one.

The road now became very bad, being over the high ground which bordered the river Tchirtchik, and the clayey soil was worn into large holes filled with the finest dust. Passing the remains of Old Tashkent, a pretty and rather picturesque, though tumble-down place, we arrived at Tchinaz, on the bank of the Syr Darya, at five o'clock in the morning. Here is a large fort to guard the ferry over the river, and close by a Russian settlement of a few houses, the native town being several miles off. In the first flush of occupation it was expected by the Russians that Tchinaz would become a place of some importance, as it was the head of steam navigation on the Syr Darya, but the steamers of the Aral flotilla being so irregular in their visits, and the navigation of the river being so bad as to discourage any private companies from starting vessels there, the great commercial future of Tchinaz has not yet arrived, and it remains a little Cossack settlement. The river here is about two thirds of a mile wide, and I found a rapid current in the muddy yellow water. The ferry boat is a large rude scow, which is rowed over the river by eight or nine men working two large oars in the bow, but the Kirghiz who keep the ferry are such bad watermen that it takes a long time to cross, and even then the boat has been taken by the current far below the landing place, and all the men have to get out and tow it with ropes up to some place where passengers and their horses can be landed. This operation took us more than an hour.

From the river almost to Jizakh,[1] eighty miles, extends an arid Steppe called by the Russians the 'Golodnaya' or

[1] This name, which means *key*, is also spelled Dizakh. I give the usual pronunciation.

'Famished Steppe,' which is now a parched and barren waste, although at one or two places there are wells and cisterns of brackish and unpleasant water. Near the river there are traces of old canals and ditches, showing that there at least the land was at one time cultivated; and it is known that some portions of the Steppe near to the mountains were formerly inhabited and worked, by means of a canal which was brought from the river Zarafshan through a small mountain pass. The cultivated districts were, however, probably always small, for we know from the Chinese traveller Tch'ang-Tch'un, who in 1222 passed through this region on his journey to the camp of Tchinghiz Khan, that the most of it was then, as now, a bare Steppe, and he speaks of the great difficulty and discomfort which his party had in crossing it.[1] The fact too that stations and cisterns were erected on the road,—the legend says by Abdullah Khan (1597)—shows that this road did not lie through an inhabited district. The canals which lie near the Syr Darya were probably filled by the water from that river, possibly pumped into them, as is sometimes done even now by the Kirghiz. There is a project at Tashkent to irrigate this Steppe by the construction of a large canal from the Syr Darya above Hodjent, and engineers who have examined the spot declare this to be feasible, the Syr Darya falling about a foot in a verst; still no careful survey for such a canal has been made, and it is declared by many that such a canal is impossible, and that all money spent before a survey is made is simply thrown away. The work on the canal has, however, been already begun.

Near the bank of the river the uneven ground was thickly covered with high reeds, affording, as I was told, lurking places for numerous tigers. Beyond, the Steppe was still of a bright green, interspersed with scarlet patches of poppies, as far as the station of Malek, about fifteen miles from the river. Here there were once wells, but they are now choked up, and the water used at the station, which is a little underground hut, is brought from the river. Mr. Zemtchuzhnikoff, the contractor for this

---

[1] In the memoirs of Hiouen Thsang, six hundred years before (629-645) it is said: 'One enters into a great sandy desert, where neither water nor grass is to be found. . . . It is necessary to look at some high mountain in the distance, and seek for abandoned bones, to know how to guide oneself and recognise the path to be followed.'—*Voyages des Pèlerins Bouddhistes.* Stanislaus Julien.

post route, whom I met at Malek while I was detained for want of horses, told me that he believed it would be possible to clean these wells, and have a sufficient supply of water to cultivate enough corn and barley for the whole route to Jizakh. He had made a proposition to the government, offering to do this on condition of being given the waste land which he should reclaim; but after nearly a year occupied in negotiations, he was informed that the government would gladly see him reclaim the land, but would be unwilling to give him the title to it. This was sufficient to deter him from taking any steps in the matter. The canal, which will necessitate the handling of large sums of money, seems to be the favourite project with the authorities. Beyond Malek, the Steppe, so noted for its tortoises and venomous spiders, while without grass, was covered with very small herbs, and occasional flowers. The most characteristic vegetation was the Assafœtida plant (*Scorodosma fœtidum*), which grows here in great profusion. The leaves had fallen to the ground and died, but there rose a tall round stem, a foot or more high, branching off at the top, like the spokes of a wheel, into small heads of insignificant flowers. The peculiar odour of the plant was very perceptible, though I am told that it disappears after boiling, and that the young shoots and heads are considered by the Kirghiz as a great delicacy. I did not try them.

Twenty miles from Malek are the ruins of an old caravanserai called Murza-Rabat, supposed to have been built by the famous Abdullah Khan, who did so much in this way for travellers. The building is made of large square bricks, and consists of a central room surmounted by a dome and surrounded with small vaulted rooms, each having its little cupola. Originally it must have been very large and it was certainly a handsome building; but now the outside walls are shattered, though it can still afford a shelter, and is occupied not only as a post station, but by a small guard of Cossacks. Opposite this is what is called a *sardoba*, or cistern, which is a large underground chamber, covered with a flat roof, built of burnt bricks, with large arched windows on a level with the ground. At one side there is an entrance down a steep incline to the bottom, but the brick staircase has long since disappeared. It is said that this cistern was at times full up to the window sills with water, but the inside is now quite bare, though there is a well of brackish water in one corner. Inside of this it was delightfully cool after the hot Steppe. At the next station, Agatchly, there were formerly similar buildings, but the caravanserai has disappeared, leaving nothing but some hillocks of earth and bricks, in which underground rooms have been hollowed out for the use of the Cossacks. I found the water to be disagreeable to take much of, and the tea which it made was thick, muddy, bitter and salt. The horses do not like it, but the Cossacks drink it without disagreeable consequences. It is very probable that if the wells in this Steppe were cleaned and deepened, pure water could be obtained in large quantities, even sufficient for irrigating the surrounding land, as the subsoil is of gravel and conglomerate, and similar experiments at Tashkent have resulted successfully. It would be necessary to line carefully the sides of the wells, to prevent the water dissolving out the saline ingredients of the soil.

As we approached Jizakh we saw a slight range of mountains, which further on grew higher, as they enclosed the Upper Zarafshan valley, extending away to the left in the direction of Ura-tepé. At last the Steppe grew more and more fertile, trees and fields began to appear, and we saw before us the walls and houses of Jizakh. Passing round through the now almost deserted bazaar, for it was near sunset, and turning a sharp corner we brought up at the post station. Jizakh itself, now a very insignificant town, of importance only from its bazaar, was formerly an important frontier fortress of Bukhara. General Tchernaieff advanced toward it in 1866, hoping to take it by a *coup-de-main*, and thus cause the release of his envoys, who were then imprisoned in Bukhara, but found, however, that the fortress was too strong for him, and returned to Tchinaz. In the autumn of the same year, after the capture of Ura-tepé, Jizakh was taken by the Russian troops under command of General Kryzhanofsky. Several thousand men had worked during eight whole months to render the fortress as strong as possible, and the city was surrounded by triple walls of increasing height,— the outside one being eight yards high and nine yards thick,— and by a triple ditch in some places twenty-five feet deep. There were many barbettes and towers, and the citadel was the acme of native engineering. The works were carried on even to the last minute before the storm, when the gates were walled up, and the Commander, Allayar Bek, resolved to perish if he did not save the town. The garrison consisted of at least 10,000 men, with 53 guns, and was composed of the remnants of best troops of the Amir, strengthened by bodies of Afghans, Persians and Turkomans, who had not only the usual matchlocks, but also muskets of European form, and many pistols.

The defence was well managed, and the natives did not open fire at long range as usual, but waited until the Russians had come close to the city. After several days spent in reconnaissances, and in placing the batteries, the fire opened on the city on October 28, and on the 30th at noon an assault was ordered. In an hour the fortress was in the hands of the Russians. The enemy for some time refused to give in, and, massed in front of the gates, were actually slaughtered there, very few escaping. A small part of the garrison, seeing the impossibility of further resistance, threw themselves into the powder-magazine and blew themselves up. Of the eighteen Beks who were present, sixteen—among them Allayar, the commander of the garrison—fell in hand-to-hand fight. Nearly 6,000 of the garrison are supposed to have perished, and some 2,000 were taken prisoners. The Russians lost 6 killed and 92 wounded. Just after the capture of Jizakh, the cavalry left to defend the Russian camp were attacked by a Bukharan force of 2,000 men with 18 guns sent to reinforce the garrison, but on meeting with resistance, and learning the fate of the city, they fled. A great portion of the town was destroyed at that time, and since then Jizakh has lost its importance. It is noted for its great unhealthiness, and especially for the prevalence of the *reshta* or guinea worm. Owing to the unwholesome quality of the water, which is principally obtained from ponds, it became necessary to place the Russian garrison about three miles off, where there were some springs of fresh water; and about this little fort a small village has grown up, which in its turn is beginning to be deserted, since the transfer of the greater portion of the garrison to the healthier locality of Ura tepé It is supposed that the great numbers of dead, who were but slightly buried, have had some effect in causing the fevers which rage there; though these are also ascribed to the winds which blow up the defile of Jalan-uta, laden with miasma from the rice fields near Yany Kurgan. The Russian troops have to change their quarters constantly, and one-third of them are always in the hospital, while the cemetery grows apace.

From Jizakh the road leads through what is known as the defile of Jilan-uti,[1] a somewhat narrow valley between the low hills, in no place, I think, wider than 100 yards. The small stream which runs through it toward Jizakh takes such a zig-zag course that it is necessary to cross it eight or ten times before being well clear of it; occasionally the road follows its bank, but sometimes we were obliged to climb a hundred feet up the hill side. This pass, serving as it did for the entrance of the Mongol and Turkish hordes into the fertile valley of the Zarafshan, has been the scene of many bloody struggles, two of which are handed down to us by inscriptions on one of the high pyramidal slaty rocks known by the name of the 'Gates of Tamerlane,' though neither inscription nor legend speaks of that conqueror. The rock to the right, some 400 feet high, standing out quite alone in the valley, has deeply cut on a smoothed square place, about 40 feet from the base, two Persian inscriptions. The mullah, with the aid of an opera glass, was able to translate for me both inscriptions, the first of which says: 'With the help of God the Lord, the Great Sultan, conqueror of kings and nations, shadow of God on earth, the support of the decisions of the *Sunna* and of the divine law, the ruler and aid of the faith, Ulug Bek Gurugan (may God prolong the time of his reign and rule) undertook a campaign in the country of the Mogols and returned from this nation into these countries uninjured, in the year 828.' (A.D. 1425.) This Ulug Bek was the famous grandson of Timur, so well known for his patronage of learning, for the observatory and college which he founded at Samarkand, and for his astronomical tables.

The second inscription relates to one of the victories of Abdullah Khan, a century and a half later. 'Let passers in the waste, and travellers on land and water, know that in the year 979 (A.D. 1571) there was a conflict between the army of

---

[1] The natives explain this as meaning—'a serpent has passed'—on account of the turns in the defile; and Mir Izzel Ullah says that he was told that the defile was greatly infested by serpents.

the lieutenant of the Khalifate, the shadow of the Almighty, the great Khakan Abdullah Khan, son of Iskender Khan, consisting of 30,000 men-of-war, and the army of Dervish Khan, and Baba Khan, and other sons of Barak Khan. In this army there were 50 relatives of the Sultan, and 400,000 fighting men from Turkistan, Tashkent, Fergana, and Deshta Kiptchak. The army of the sovereign, by the fortunate conjunction of the stars, gained the victory, having conquered the above-mentioned Sultans, and gave to death so many of them that, from the people who were killed in the fight and after being taken prisoners, during the course of one month blood ran on the surface of the water in the river to Jizakh. Let this be known.'

On emerging from this defile we are again on the Steppe, with before us a distant view of the snow-covered peaks south of Samarkand, and passing the town of Yany Kurgan, we come at last to Tash-Kupriuk, or 'Stone Bridge,' where hills begin once more. The bridge over the little stream, which runs between two steep banks, is now only a wooden one, in a very bad state of repair. A small Russian fort at the top of the hill guards the passage. Here, though fortunately before coming to the bridge, the stupid sleepy native driver was unable to manage the horses, letting them climb up the steep hill side and overturn our carriage. I was asleep at the time, but managed at last to undo the curtains and crawl out, as the horses luckily stood still. We had some difficulty in righting the heavy carriage, but discovered that nothing was broken but the top, and that the wheels were all right. It was but a few rods to the station, to which we now preferred to walk. After that accident I was never able to sleep with comfort while travelling, which was a great annoyance, as it necessitated my stopping for sleep at least one night out of three. From here we descended into the lower valley of the Zarafshan, where the road constantly led through gardens and fields, and over and along numerous canals. At Jambai, a large village, the country people were already thronging to the bazaar. From here we had to take a side road through fields, as the new *chaussée* was still unfinished. This is one of the improvements of the prefect of Samarkand, and will be an excellent thing over this clayey soil. The road is macadamised, and has a double row of trees on each side. At last, after crossing two or three small branches, we came to the main stream of the Zarafshan—the 'gold-strowing,' —above the dyke built to divide the waters and send the proper contingent to Bukhara. The water was then so high as to compel us to put all our luggage on a high native cart, which was piloted over by the guardians of the ford, and the empty carriage was dragged through the water and arrived soaked. On our left rose a high, bare hill called Tchupan-ata, the top of which is crowned by the small tomb of a saint of the same name, who is the patron of shepherds as well as of the city of Samarkand. There is an old legend, that when the original Arab missionaries were journeying to preach the religion of Mohammed, they stopped on this hill, and cutting up and boiling a sheep agreed to decide by lot the direction of their future journeys. One put his hand into the pot and drew out the head, which gave him the first choice, and he decided to remain at Samarkand; another drew the heart and chose to go back to Mecca; while the third got the hind quarter and preferred Bagdad. Hence Samarkand is called the head, and Mecca the heart of Islam to this day. The one who remained at Samarkand received the name of Tchupan-ata, Father Shepherd. It was on this hill that the celebrated observatory of Ulug Bek stood, where the astronomical tables that bear his name were calculated. At its foot are what seem to be the remains of a very ancient bridge, built of stone and brick, two complete arches of which are still standing disposed at right angles to each other, with apparently the ruins of a tower at the corner. I could get no information nor even hear of a tradition about the origin of these remains, which are called the Bridge of Shadman-Malik. We now skirted along the base of the hill, till, as we came to the highest point of the road, we saw before us the clay roofs, crowned with large blue domes and lofty towers, and knew that we had reached the famous Samarkand.

Lovely as the view was, it did not last long, for we speedily descended into a narrow valley between houses and gardens, and soon passed the base of a high clayey hill, hollowed out into countless caverns, where saints are said to have lived in hermitage. By the side of the road ran a little rivulet, which, passing through a green field, was somewhere lost under the wall of the town. On our right were the high towers and domes of the mosque Shah Zindeh, and on our left the immense dome of Bibi Khanym. Passing the cemetery, full of mounds and ruined brick tombs, assailed at every step by lepers and beggars, we entered the gate of Shah Zindeh, and found ourselves on the new boulevard, with its good pavement and shady trees, which the Russians have made from this gate to the fortress. We had to go to the end of this road and pass round the fortress to the post-station, which lay on the other side, in what will be the Russian town.

There are no hotels in Samarkand, and I had been recommended to put up at the house of a Mussulman, a Hodja, where I would probably have facilities for best seeing the native life. He lived on the boulevard, but was absent from home, and I therefore resolved to stay, for the time at least, at the post-station, which proved to be a large, new, and clean building. Having refreshed myself with a bath and some tea, I found a droshky—for even in Samarkand there are droshkies—and drove to the citadel to call on General Abramoff, the Governor, to whom I had letters. He was at home and received me most cordially—a short, amiable man, with grey hair, though still young, and a black skull-cap which he is allowed to wear on account of a wound received in his head. Finding I had no place where I could live, he requested the Prefect of the city to give me a lodging, and I accordingly had my luggage transferred to his house that afternoon. After leaving the General's I could not resist the temptation of driving about the town, and taking a hasty view of some of its wonderful ruins. From the citadel itself there was a magnificent view. The whole town lay spread out before me, with the columns and domes of the three great mosques standing up just opposite to me. From the middle of the market place on either side, melon-shaped domes rose above the flat-roofed houses, and the background was closed in by a range of high mountains, their tops then covered with dazzling snow. I went first to the bazaar to get an idea of the wealth of blue and white mosaic which still bedecked the ruins of the splendid mosques. Here I saw a large crowd on the steps of one of the mosques, and the platforms of the booths, and even sitting in a great circle on the pavement Inside the circle two boys were reciting verses. 'They are *Hafistas*,' a bystander said to me, meaning that they were reciters of religious poems. Each of them had a book, though they made no use of them except to put them at the sides of their mouths, so as to throw the sound to different parts of the audience. Their declamation was occasionally so loud and shrill that they placed both hands on their ears in order not to deafen themselves with their own cries, while at times they spoke in a low, well-modulated voice. These cries and monotonous chants seemed greatly to affect the audience, and there were continual sighs and smothered exclamations. The person who first spoke to me, seeing that I was greatly interested, again addressed me, asking me if I did not think it all very beautiful, and seemed much pleased at my agreeing with him. I then told my driver to take me to the tomb of Timur, but he having slight acquaintance with Samarkand drove me instead to the mosque of Shah Zindeh. I paid but little attention to the tomb of the saint, my curiosity being attracted by the proceedings of the Jahria brotherhood in the little mosque at the entrance. The rites were much the same as I had seen at Tashkent, but there seemed far more excitement, and the mosque was crowded with worshippers, all looking intently at the struggling crowd of devotees, who were pushing each other from side to side of the mosque, with continual shouts of '*Hasbi rabi jal Allah!*' 'My defence is the Lord, magnify Allah!'

With vivid impressions of all that I had seen—for Samarkand is very different from Tashkent, and seems, as it were, a remnant of a far-off world—I gladly went to the Prefect's, and passing through a large court with its square water-basin in the centre, surrounded with old trees, I entered the house, a native one of considerable beauty, altered by the insertion of windows to suit Russian convenience, and found dinner waiting for me, which after two days and nights of dusty travelling was particularly agreeable. I could not, however, keep quiet, and before sunset wandered out again to take in once more the beautiful view from the citadel, where, fortunately, I met a cousin of some old friends in Moscow, who took me home with him to tea, and to a delightful evening. I saw much of him on this occasion, and in the two subsequent visits I made to Samarkand I was his guest, and I owe so much to his kind hospitality, and to the sensible talk of himself and his friends, that I look back to Samarkand with feelings of special pleasure, and consider it one of the places in the world to which I would gladly return at any time or under any pretext.

There is no place in Central Asia, the name of which has so impressed the imagination of Europe as Samarkand. Surrounded by a halo of romance, visited at rare intervals, and preserving the traditions of its magnificence in a mysterious impenetrability, it long piqued the curiosity of the world. The local traditions ascribe its foundation to Afrosiab, a mythical hero, whose conquests and victories are legendary in Persia and Turkey, as well as in Central Asia. A hill just outside the walls covered with ruins and mounds is called Kalai Afrosiab, and is said to be the original site of the city.[1] However this may be, Samarkand came into history as Maracanda, the capital of Sogdiana when it was conquered by Alexander the Great. The meaning of the name is uncertain; the termination *kand*, signifying a town, is frequent in Central Asia, but as to the derivations of *Mara* or *Samar* one cannot give more than very ingenious, but scarcely plausible guesses.[2] In Alexander's time it was a large and flourishing city. Quintus Curtius says that its walls were seventy *stadia* in circumference, and that the citadel was then, as now, surrounded by another wall. It was here that Alexander killed his old friend and comrade Clytus in a fit of drunken passion; and Samarkand was his head-quarters during the contests with the mountain tribes and the expedition against the Scythians across the Syr-Darya, which was confounded with the Tanais or Don—a mistake which was kept up by later geographers out of flattery for Alexander, who thought that he had made the circuit of Asia

---

[1] During the spring of 1875 some unsystematic excavations were made in this place, resulting in the discovery of broken pavements, ruins of houses, and of an ancient pottery. The explorers found many perfect jugs and bowls, glass-ware, from its decoration apparently made by Chinese workmen, glazed tiles, and coins.

[2] Ye-lü Tch'u-ts'ai, the minister of Tchinghiz Khan, in describing his travels to the west in 1219, calls it Sün-sze-kan, and adds: 'Western people say that the meaning of this name is 'fat,' and as the land there is very fertile, the city received this name.' Chinese authors now frequently write the name Sie-mi-sze-kan, which would correspond to Semiscaut, as the Nestorians and others called it in the Middle Ages. In fact *semi* or *semiz* in various Turkic languages means 'fat;' but this is probably only an explanatory adaptation, such as made Tashkent from Shash. The original name is probably of Persian origin. Hiouen-Thsang writes it Sa-mo-kien.

and had returned to Europe. The city of Alexandria, which he founded, is usually placed at Hodjent, and was probably a mere collection of mud huts where a few infirm soldiers were colonised. The exploits of Alexander, or Iskender Dulkarnain (the two-horned), in this region have been preserved by legend, and are known to every inhabitant. Many of the petty princes in the mountain countries of the Upper Oxus claim to be descended from him. The generals to whom he entrusted these provinces of Bactriana and Sogdiana did indeed found dynasties —called Græco-Bactrian—which lasted until about a hundred and thirty years before the Christian Era, and introduced a certain degree of Greek culture (among other things the Macedonian calendar) of which no traces now remain, except the numerous coins and medals bearing the effigies of Demetrius, Euthydemus, Antimachus, and others, which are now often found on the Steppe and in the ruins about Samarkand. It is curious that these coins were rudely imitated by the contemporary rulers of the surrounding states, as well as by later sovereigns.[1]

The Græco-Bactrian dynasty had its day, and passed away; and was succeeded by the Yuetchji (as we are told by the Chinese general Tchjan-Tsian, who visited the country of Samarkand in 125 B.C.), apparently a nomad tribe living in the Steppe, whose capital was near the present Khiva.[2] The country was probably still under their rule when it was attacked by the Arabs, who after many plundering expeditions succeeded in 710 in forcibly introducing Mahommedanism. Persian and Turkish princes in their turn put down the Arab dynasty, and at last Tchinghiz Khan, the great Mongol conqueror, took and plundered the city in 1221. The Arab and Persian historians speak much of the barbarities of the Mongols, and represent Samarkand as having been completely destroyed. That this was not the case is evident from the account of the Chinese traveller Tch'ang-Tch'un, who visited Samarkand in the following year (1222) and spent the winter there. According to him,

---

[1] The most complete account of the present state of our knowledge of the Græco-Bactrian dynasties is found in an article of Prof. Grigorief in the 'Journal of the Ministry of Public Instruction,' (Russian) for Nov. 1867.

[2] 'Collection of information about the peoples inhabiting Central Asia in ancient times,' by the monk Hyacinth (St. Petersburg, 1851), Part III. p. 6–10, 15, &c.

out of 100,000 families but one-fourth remained, and there was much brigandage, but the city seemed to be in good preservation, and the fields, orchards, and vineyards were still cultivated and fruitful.¹

For centuries after the Mussulman conquest Samarkand was a Christian see with a bishop; Prince Sembat, High Constable of Armenia, in a letter written about 1246 speaks of the flourishing state of the Christians, and of the privileges conferred on them by Tchinghiz Khan; and Marco Polo, although he did not himself visit the city, tells us that the church of St. John the Baptist still existed, the central pillar of which was miraculously supported in the air, the stone which had been its foundation (a sacred stone of the Mussulmans) having been removed by order of the authorities. There are of course no traces of any ancient Christian church now; since the Russian occupation a small modern one erected in the citadel replaces it.

The dynasty of Tchinghiz was overthrown at last by Timur or Tamerlane. This chieftain, who was born at Kesh (now Shahrisabs), to the south beyond the mountains, was so attracted by the beauty of Samarkand that he made it his capital and spared no pains in embellishing and beautifying it, in which he was imitated by his successors. It was the beloved resort of the great Baber, a hundred years later, who, after having several times been driven out of the city, and after having several times recaptured it, was obliged at last to abandon it with a sigh, and soon afterwards made himself the Emperor of India. What Samarkand and its surroundings were under Timur, and what magnificence was shown there, we know from the account of the good knight Don Ruy Gonzalez de Clavijo, who was there in 1404 on an embassy from King Henry III. of Castile. Hans Schiltberger, of Munich, was there as a captive at about the same time, but he tells us nothing regarding the city.²

---

¹ A Russian translation of the journey of this Taoist monk was published by Father Palladii in the 'Labours of the Members of the Russian Religious Mission in Pekin,' vol. iv. p. 261: St. Petersburg, 1866. An abridged and imperfect French translation was published by the late M. Pauthier in the 'Journal Asiatique,' 6ᵐᵉ Série, t. ix., and there is an excellent English translation by Dr. Bretschneider in his 'Notes on Chinese Mediæval Travellers to the West,' (Shanghai, 1875).

² Clavijo's 'Life and Acts of the Great Tamerlane' was in part translated by Markham for the Hakluyt Society. Schiltberger is accessible in Neumann's edition, Munich, 1859.

MEDRESSÉ OF HODJA AKHRAR, SAMARKAND.

In Baber's time Samarkand must have retained much of its former beauty. He says in his 'Memoirs' under the year 903 (1497): 'In the whole habitable world there are few cities so pleasantly situated as Samarkand . . . . I directed its wall to be paced round the rampart, and found it was 10,600 paces in circumference. The inhabitants are all orthodox Sunnis, observant of the law, and religious. From the time of the Holy Prophet downwards no other country has produced so many Imams and excellent theologians as Maverannahr.' Baber speaks of many palaces and gardens built by Timur and his grandson Ulug Bek, at that time still in their glory, though many had been ruined. In the garden of *Dilkusha*, or 'heart's delight' was a large palace with a series of paintings representing the wars of Timur in Hindustan. The great mosque near the Iron Gate, he calls a very grand building, and says that the verses of the Koran inscribed over the portico were in letters of such a size as to be read at more than a mile off. The college of Ulug Bek, and the other colleges, were still in their glory; and the observatory erected on the hill Kohik, or Tchupan-ata, Baber describes as being three stories in height, and provided with astronomical apparatus. He also says:—
'At the foot of the hill of Kohik, on the west, there is a garden, named *Bagh-i-meidan* ('the garden of the plain'), in the middle of which is a splendid edifice, two stories high, named *Chehil-Situn* ('the forty pillars'). The pillars are all of stone. In the four turrets on the corners of this building they have constructed four *Guldestehs*, or open minarets, the road up to which is by these four towers. In every part of the building are stone pillars curiously wrought; some twisted, others fluted, and some with other peculiarities. The four sides of the upper story consist of open galleries, supported by pillars all of stone, and in the centre is a grand hall or pavilion likewise of stone. The raised floor of the palace is all paved with stone. Towards the hill of Kohik there is a small garden wherein is a great open hall, within which is a large throne of a single stone, about thirty feet long, fifteen broad, and two high. This huge stone was brought from a great distance. There is a crack in it which it is said to have received since it was brought to this place. In this garden there is another state pavilion, the walls of which are overlaid with

porcelain of China, whence it is called the Chinese house. It is said that a person was sent to Khita (China) for the purpose of bringing it. Within the walls of Samarkand is another ancient building, called the *Laklaka* (or echoing) mosque; because whenever any person stamps on the ground in the mosque, an echo is returned. It is a strange thing, the secret of which is known to nobody.'

'In the time of Sultan Ahmed Mirza, many of the greater and lesser Beks formed gardens, some large, others smaller. Among these, the *Chehar Bagh* of Dervish Mohammed Tarkhan, in respect of climate, situation, and beauty, is equalled by few. It is situated lower down than the *Bagh-i-meidan*, on a small eminence that rises above the valley of Kulbeh, and commands a view of the whole vale, which stretches out below. In this *Chehar-Bagh* there is a variety of different plots laid out one above another, all on a regular plan, and elms, cypresses, and white poplars, are planted in the different compartments. It is a very perfect place. Its chief defect is that it has no great stream of running water.'[1]

'Samarkand is a wonderfully elegant city. One of its distinguishing peculiarities is, that each trade has its own bazaar; so that different trades are not mixed together in the same place. The established customs and regulations are good. The bakers and shops are excellent, and the cooks are skilful.'

It was probably about this time that the couplet was written, 'Samarkand is the face of the earth: Bukhara the marrow of Islam: were there not in Mashad an azure dome the whole world would be merely a ditch for ablution.'

From the time of Clavijo, Samarkand was unvisited by Europeans until the journey of Khanikoff and Lehmann in 1841, except by the Russian envoy Khokhlof in 1620, and by the Russian non-commissioned officer Yefremof toward the end of the last century. Traditions of its past glories were preserved, and especially of the great library of Greek authors which Timur had carried off from Brussa; and the news of its capture by the Russians in 1868 excited a glow of interest, like the awakening of some half-forgotten memory, far different

---

[1] *A propos* of these gardens of Samarkand Tch'ang Tch'un says: 'Even Chinese gardens cannot be compared with them; but the gardens of this country are very quiet: no singing of birds is heard there.'

from the feeling called out by the other successes of Russia in Asia. At last, we thought, the curtain is to be drawn aside.

After the capture of Jizakh in 1866, the Amir of Bukhara was more disposed to peace, and a treaty was sent to him by General Kaufmann, which he kept for a very long time under consideration. According to this treaty one part of the boundary line between Turkistan and Bukhara was to run along the highest part of the mountain range of Nurata, the Russians supposing that there was but one range of mountains. It turned out, however, that there were two, and that the important Bekship of Nurata lay between them. The Amir was in great trouble to know which mountain chain was meant; *Kara-tau* the northern, or *Ak-tau* the southern. The Russians found it impossible to come to any agreement with him, and laid this misunderstanding entirely to his disinclination for peace, which was partly true. After the discovery by the Russians of the existence of the two chains of mountains war had already begun.

At this time in Bukhara there were two parties against the Amir, that of his eldest son the *Katta-Tiura*, and another desirous of placing on the throne Seid Khan, the nephew of the Amir, then living in Shahrisabs, under the leadership of Jura Bek of Shahrisabs, Abdul-Gaffar Bek of Ura-tepé, and his brother Omar Bek of Tchilek. Jura Bek said afterwards, speaking of Seid Khan: 'The more stupid he was, the better for us. We should have been more independent.' The conspirators, knowing the position of affairs between the Amir and the Russians, ordered Omar Bek to advance from Tchilek, and fall upon the Russian forces near Jizakh, so as to make them believe that it was an onslaught of the army of the Amir. Omar Bek did so, and being easily repulsed immediately fled to Shahrisabs, lest the Amir might punish him. But a few days before the Afghan Prince Iskender Khan with about 2,000 followers had abandoned the Bukharans in consequence of a quarrel with Omar Bek, and had surrendered to the Russians. The Russians naturally thought that the attack of Omar Bek was one of revenge against the Afghans, which may indeed have been partly the case. General Kaufmann, who was still in hopes of coming to a peaceful arrangement with the Amir, and who had no idéa of beginning a campaign,[1] was on the point of starting for St. Petersburg, and when the courier arrived with the news of the attack on Jizakh, his carriage was already at the door. Supposing from this attack that the war had been begun by the Amir himself, General Kaufmann postponed his departure, and immediately marched to Jizakh and thence towards Samarkand. The bands of the enemy retired before him as he advanced, and he arrived at the banks of the Zarafshan without having had recourse to arms. Embassies, however, had constantly been sent to him asking for longer and shorter delays, promising that the Amir would then sign a treaty, and explaining away the massing of the troops. On the very banks of the river, while the enemy were full in sight drawn up on the hill of Tchupan-ata, a fresh ambassador brought him a treaty signed by the Amir, which purported to be the same General Kaufmann had sent him. It was found, however to be totally different. Again time was asked, but only two hours were granted for the troops on the hill to retire. Instead of retiring they kept up a desultory fire, and at last General Kaufmann ordered the attack. This affair can hardly be called a battle—though it was made much of, and gained for one general the cross of St. George—for the Russian troops no sooner forded the river and advanced up the heights than the enemy withdrew, leaving several guns as trophies. The next morning (May 14) a deputation came from the city of Samarkand, saying that the troops had left it, and asking the Russians to occupy it, expressing at the same time their desire to be taken into subjection. The city was accordingly occupied, and most of the neighbouring cities sent delegations to express their submission. There were, however, two exceptions, Tchilek in the north, which had been a nest of marauders, and from which the small expedition had started which had attacked the Russian garrison near Jizakh, and Urgut in the mountains to the left of the road to Shahrisabs. Two detachments were therefore sent against these

---

[1] In the memoirs (unpublished) of Kamal-eddin, the late Kazi Kalian of Samarkand, it is stated that a letter from General Kaufmann demanding the surrender of Samarkand had some weeks ago been addressed to the Bek and other influential persons. This would seem to show that the campaign was premeditated.

places. Urgut was taken, though the Bek Hussein and the garrison escaped, and Tchilek was brought to submission. The main body of the troops was sent on to Katta Kurgan in pursuit of the Amir's army, and that town was taken by General Golovatchef, while a small detachment under General Abramof was sent southward to Kara-tepé against a detachment of troops from Shahrisabs which had appeared there. There was a small engagement but the Shahrisabs troops after beating off the Russians retired into the mountains where it was impossible to follow them, and the action was therefore without much result.

In the meantime the position of the Russians had become very critical; the Amir had recovered his hopes and was making a stand near Katta Kurgan, threatening the troops of General Golovatchef with greatly superior numbers. Communications with Tashkent had been for some time cut off, and the nephew of Abul Gaffar Bek had again collected at Tchilek 15,000 cavalry to fall upon the small Russian garrison left at Yany Kurgan. The lack of intelligence from the army at Samarkand was leading to much excitement among the natives at Tashkent, and in fact in all towns under Russian rule, and a great disaster might have been ruinous. At the same time 20,000 troops from Shahrisabs were threatening Samarkand from the mountains twenty miles to the south. It was impossible to attack them, for they would merely retire again through the mountain passes, and the movement would result in nothing. General Kaufmann therefore decided—leaving a small garrison at Samarkand—to advance to the support of General Golovatchef, thinking that possibly he might be able to have a decisive battle with the Amir which would end the contest and force a peace. After having gone only a few miles from Samarkand, General Kaufmann received a direct report from General Golovatchef that he was entirely surrounded by the enemy who were attacking him in overwhelming numbers, and he therefore advanced by a forced march.

General Kaufmann and his forces were no sooner out of sight than the troops of Shahrisabs appeared in the outskirts of Samarkand, where many of them had been for some time secreted. The motives which actuated the leaders of Shahrisabs were peculiar. I have spoken before of the conspiracy to overturn the Amir. When General Kaufmann had advanced on the road to Samarkand as far as Yany Kurgan, messengers reached him from Jura Bek and Baba Bek promising to give him secret assistance if necessary against the Amir, and agreeing in case this were not necessary to remain neutral in the contest, on condition that when Samarkand should be occupied he should not demand their presence in that city. General Kaufmann expressed his great pleasure at this message, but said that active assistance would be unnecessary. Nevertheless, after he had taken Samarkand he sent for Jura Bek and Baba Bek, despatching as his messenger Kamal-eddin, the chief Kazi of Samarkand. According to Kamal-eddin's account, Jura Bek at first disbelieved his story, and had him imprisoned, but subsequently, finding the errand was a true one, thought that the Russians were playing him false, and consequently resolved to break with them and make his peace with the Amir. He therefore sent a letter to the Amir promising to take the field for him against the Russians; and the Amir, in gratitude for this, offered to transfer to him the frontier town of Tchiraktchi, about which there had been a constant dispute. It was in consequence of this arrangement of the Amir that the troops of Shahrisabs had been massed at Kara-tepé—even before General Kaufmann's departure—and had now marched on Samarkand.

The garrison of Samarkand consisted of 762 men including officers and camp followers and 450 sick and wounded men in the hospital. They were well provided with ammunition, but the citadel itself was very difficult to defend. It measured nearly two miles in circuit, and was full of houses, barracks and narrow streets, and in some places the houses outside were built up against the walls, so that there was easy access from their roofs. In many cases, however, the walls were very high and steep, so that it was thought unnecessary to specially guard them, and it was possible to concentrate the defence at the two gates and at the weaker parts of the *enceinte*. Before the departure of General Kaufmann some efforts had been made to put the citadel in a better condition, but not much had been done. On the evening of June 13, the Aksakals from the Hodja Akhrar Gate came to the Commandant with a request for troops, saying that there was an attack of the enemy on the gate. Major Albedil was sent there with one company of men, but found the gates open and no enemy there, and the people who lived near the gates said that no hostile forces had been seen. A little later, however, large masses of armed men were seen on the heights of Tchupan-ata. At three o'clock on the morning of the 14th the Aksakals at the same gate came again to the Commandant to say that the enemy was attacking the city. The Commandant, Major Stempel, went himself to the gate with a company and a-half of men and two guns. He met some armed bands whom he dispersed, and further on in the gardens he saw a crowd of men who fired one or two shots, and then ran in the direction of the Bukharan Gate. The Aksakals begged him not to fire on them as they were inhabitants of the city who had armed themselves to fight against the enemy. On returning to the citadel Major Stempel was nearly cut off by a large body of men who had intended to take easy possession of the citadel while he was in pursuit of an imaginary enemy. Measures were at once taken for an active defence. Soon after the citadel was attacked on all sides by the troops of Shahrisabs, the Kiptchaks, Karakalpaks, and the citizens, with beating of drums, blowing of trumpets, and loud cries. The garrison, though suffering much from the fire of the enemy, which was directed against them from the tops of the mosques and minarets, beat off the assaults made on various portions of the wall, and succeeded in defeating the attempts which were made to set fire to the gates. Every man who could possibly leave the hospital volunteered in the defence, and Lieut.-Col. Nazarof, who was suffering from a wound, waived distinctions of rank, and placed himself under command of Major Stempel. The fire was severe during the whole day, and the Russian loss was great, two officers and twelve soldiers being killed, and four officers and fifty-four men wounded.

The next day the attack was still continued with the utmost vigour, and the Samarkand gates were set on fire, and would have been completely destroyed, had not bags of sand been placed against them. Toward evening, Jura Bek—who had difficulties from the insubordination of the other Beks under his command, twenty-two in number, having received intelligence of the victory of General Kaufmann at Zera-bulak, and being misled by a false report that he was advancing on Shahrisabs, withdrew his troops. The others, however, still kept up the siege. The Russian loss that day was seventy killed and wounded. The attack continued until the 19th, though weakened of course by the withdrawal of the troops of Shahrisabs. The Russians were reduced to their last point. It had been found impossible to give attention to the wounded in the hospital, and those who were active in the defence were almost worn out by fatigue and hunger. The garrison had resolved to transfer everything to the great central building in the citadel—the Amir's palace—and abandoning the walls, to defend that to the utmost, and if fate should be against them, to blow up the magazines and to perish, when on the evening of the 19th they received the welcome intelligence that the troops of General Kaufmann were on their return, and had reached the gardens of Samarkand. Out of seven messengers who were sent to him, only one had reached him, the others having been intercepted and killed. The whole Russian loss during the siege was more than 180 men; 30 more than had been lost by the army in all of its seven engagements with the enemy from the time of entering the Zarafshan Valley. This defence of Samarkand against overwhelming numbers is one of the brightest and most glorious pages in all the history of the Russian advance in Asia.

Had Jura Bek not abandoned the siege in consequence of being misled by the false report that General Kaufmann was advancing on Shahrisabs, he would almost without doubt have taken the citadel on one of the following days. He would then, without paying attention to General Kaufmann's army, have at once marched in the direction of Tashkent, falling on that city contemporaneously with the insurrection of the inhabitants which had been planned, and would probably for the moment have entirely annihilated the Russian power in Central Asia. Communications having been cut off, the army of General Kaufmann could not have maintained itself in the midst of the hostile population. The Khan of Khokand was prepared to join the movement, but his envoy Mirza Hakim had been taken on the campaign by General Kaufmann, to keep him out of mischief, and his reports did not give his master the encouragement he desired.

This attack on Samarkand has been often called an act of base treachery, but it seems to me that it is impossible to consider it in that light. The inhabitants of Samarkand gave up their city to save it from pillage, as their own army had retreated, and they knew perfectly well that it would be occupied. The attack of the people of Shahrisabs was certainly not an act of treachery, and proceeded from what was supposed to be a breach of faith on the Russian side. It was through the influence of the Beks of Shahrisabs that the city was induced to revolt. They were acting from policy to preserve their independence, and though for a moment taking sides with the Russians against the Amir, it is absurd to suppose that after the misunderstanding with General Kaufmann, they would not have taken advantage of an excellent chance entirely to annihilate the infidels.

But to return to the city as it now is.

The day after my arrival an Aksakal and several *jigits* were ordered to show me all the ruins, and, as friends went with me, and we looked at everything carefully, it kept us well occupied the whole day. We drove first to the mosque of Shah Zindeh, which has been wrongly called by some travellers the summer palace of Timur. Kasim Ibn Abbas, tradition tells us, came to Samarkand in the early Mussulman times and preached the Koran to the infidels with great success, till finally on this very spot he was overcome by the enemy and beheaded. But the infidel was not destined to triumph : adroitly seizing his head, Kasim leaped into a well near by, where he even now remains, ready to come forth at some future day as the defender of Islam. From this circumstance he is called Shah Zindeh (the living king). There is a prophecy, said to be five hundred years old, that he was to appear in 1868 to defeat the Russians; but Samarkand was occupied, and Shah Zindeh appeared not, so that his fame has of late somewhat fallen off. The mosque on the site of his martyrdom was erected in 1323 by Timur, and was without doubt originally very splendid. Even now its ruins are—with perhaps one exception— the finest in Central Asia. In front is a large arched portal built of brick, faced with porcelain tiles, of white, light blue, and dark blue, arranged in mosaic patterns, and in many places forming in Cufic letters verses from the Koran. On each side are small mosques, now almost ruined. From the arched door a long staircase leads up the hill side. These steps were once covered with slabs of marble, but with one or two exceptions these have been destroyed, and nothing but the uneven brickwork now remains. At intervals along the sides are small mosques for tombs; and on the right, in a little court under a dome, is shown the famous well in which the faithful can still see, especially at night, the form of Shah Zindeh. Of course a draught of the water is healing and healthful. At the top are several domed buildings, one covering the tomb of the saint, and others the tombs of famous mullahs and citizens of Samarkand. One of these mosques has a melon-shaped dome, from which the tiles have nearly all fallen. The outer building, however, is still well preserved, and the inscription surrounding the dome is nearly perfect. Once the walls along the staircase were all covered with mosaic tiling, but this in most cases has fallen off, and quantities of fragments are to be picked up. Sometimes there is real mosaic of porcelain-faced bricks; in others the brick wall seems to have been covered with a sort of veneer of enamel, for the designs do not follow the divisions of the bricks, and where patches of it have fallen off, it is easy to perceive that it was subsequently applied. The interior walls of the buildings are also covered with mosaic work, sometimes in bricks, and sometimes in stone, while the various arches and domes are full of pendent alabaster work, with arabesque designs, always very beautiful. The pillars which hold up the domes and the ceilings are all of wood, larger at the top than at the bottom, and beautifully carved. The glazed bricks used in this and the other buildings in Samarkand were originally brought from Kashan, in Persia, where this art was cultivated, and all the great edifices in Samarkand—as is evident from inscriptions—were erected by Persian architects, or by their pupils.[1] The majority of inscriptions on the walls are merely

[1] According to M. Lenormant the peculiarities of Persian and Arabic architecture were inherited from Babylonia and Assyria. 'Les toits des édifices assyriens étaient plats, en terrasse, bordés de tous les côtés par un feston de créneaux en gradins, dont la disposition a été conservée par l'architecture arabe du moyen âge pour le couronnement des murailles extérieures des édifices, ainsi qu'on peut le voir aux belles mosquées du Caire. Cette particularité charactéristique est nettement indiquée dans toutes les représentations de monuments que contiennent les bas reliefs; aussi Mr. Thomas a-t-il été pleinement en droit de l'introduire dans ses restaurations. Mais ce n'est pas le seul emprunt que l'architecture de l'Arabie et de la Perse ait fait aux traditions de l'art assyrien. Lorsqu' on voit les dessins dans lesquels l'habile architecte adjoint à M. Place a restitué l'aspect extérieur des diverses parties du palais de Khorsabad, on se croirait en

texts from the Koran; occasionally there are epitaphs, but few of importance. The *mazar* or mosque, which covers the tomb of Shah Zindeh, is divided into two or three rooms. We found a number of persons prostrating themselves in front of a niche, in which behind a grating was dimly seen some object covered with cloths, looking like a sitting mummy well wrapped up; these cloths are small offerings which have been placed in it at different times, consisting of prayer-cloths on which Mussulmans have knelt, and which in fulfilment of some vow, or in gratitude for some favour, have been bestowed on the saint. The mullahs, the guardians of the tomb, quickly informed us that the saint was willing to receive offerings of money, and took our Russian silver and paper with alacrity. In the adjoining room there was a large Koran, about three feet by two, magnificently illuminated in antique letters.

Directly opposite the mosque of Shah Zindeh is a little brick building constructed in the ancient style, once a mosque, but now used as the city prison. Not far from Shah Zindeh, but within the city walls, is the beautiful *medressé* of Bibi Khanym. This college was built, it is said, in 1385 by Bibi Khanym, the favourite wife of Timur, and the daughter of the Emperor of China, and is remarkable not only for the immense span of the entrance, but for the gigantic dome with which the chief building is crowned. This dome is double, and the inner lining, though half broken away, still holds on its top the heavy column which supports the external dome, through which there is also a large hole. To enter the chief mosque it is necessary to pass through two courts, around which were the cells of the mullahs. Owing to the constant dilapidation, caused in great part by earth-

présence d'un édifice arabe. Le rôle si considérable des revêtements en faïence émaillée dans les monuments persans du moyen âge tire son origine de l'Assyrie. L'emploi des coupoles dans l'architecture arabe et persane a la même origine.' *Manuel d'Histoire ancienne de l'Orient*,' par François Lenormant. Paris, 1869, vol. ii. p. 193. Even the building materials are of very old date: ' Les Assyriens . . . . préférèrent à la brique sechée ou cuite une espèce de pisé particulier dont ils semblent avoir été les inventeurs, composé de briques encore molles, qui adhéraient intimément les unes aux autres sans ciment, de telle façon que chaque muraille, chaque voûte, une fois sechée, constituait une seule masse compacte. C'est là l'unique élément de la construction de tous les édifices assyriens que l'on a fouillés jusqu'à présent.'—*Id.* vol. ii. p. 189.

quakes, the *medressé* was disused some twelve years ago, and since that time has been converted into a market for cotton, and is full of mules and horses (which are stabled there), and of carts placed there for safe keeping. In the interior of the mosque is a large marble reading-desk supported on nine short thick pillars, on which formerly lay a large Koran. It is believed by the Mussulmans that diseases of the spine will be cured by crawling under this desk in all directions. On each side of the exterior entrance is a slender minaret, from which the mosaic work is fast peeling off. Tradition says that Bibi Khanym was once told by a Dervish that she would die by the bite of a tarantula, and that she therefore requested Timur to have her buried not in Mussulman fashion under the ground, but above it in a coffin. It was in consequence of this that Timur built this *medressé* and the mosques adjoining it. The clay which was necessary for making the bricks he had dug from beneath the building so as to leave large vaults. When the *medressé* was finished and Bibi was inspecting it a large serpent came from out of the vaults, and warmed itself in the sun. Her attendants wished to kill it, but Bibi prevented this and caressed it. On her death Bibi was decorated with all her jewels, laid in a coffin studded with golden nails, and placed in this vault. Hearing of this, some robbers one night broke into the vault and dismantled the body of its ornaments; but before they could get away this same serpent came out and bit them all to death. The next day people were astonished to see the dead bodies, and at once understood the crime and its punishment. At first no one dared to replace the jewels. At last one old man carefully put them all back on Bibi's body; but before he could leave the vault the door closed of itself, and shut him in for ever. A short time ago the Russian authorities, in cleaning the courts of the *medressé*, found a small mosque which had been entirely concealed by the surrounding buildings and was almost forgotten, and which they were told contained the tomb of Bibi Khanym. A short time after, the roof of this building fell in and broke through the floor, when it was discovered that there was indeed here a large vault containing many gravestones with inscriptions in ancient characters; but these were only prayers and contained neither names nor dates. The vault was no sooner opened than the belief spread in the neighbourhood that the old serpent came out every day to warm himself for an hour in the sun.

In the centre of the bazaar on three sides of the great square, called in imitation of that at Bukhara, the *Righistan*, are the *medressés* Shir-dar, Tilla-Kari and Ulug-Bek. The *medressé* Shir-dar, which occupies the eastern side of the square, is said to have been built about 1648, by Yalang Tash Bahadur, an Uzbek hero, vizier of Imam Kuli Khan, from the spoils of the shrine of Imam Riza at Mashad. The front contains two stories of cells, with arched windows on the square, on both sides of a large arched portal. On each corner are cupolas surmounted by melon-shaped domes. The sides of the *medressé* have no windows, and both front and sides are covered with inlaid tiles. Passing through the portal we come to a large court around which are the cells, 64 in number, for two students each. Even at the late day when this was constructed, the Persian architectural style prevailed, and though Samarkand was then independent of Persia, the upper corners of the portal over the arch are filled with rude representations in blue and yellow tiles of the lion and the sun, the Persian arms, although in fact the lion is far more like a tiger. Those mosaics have evidently given the *medressé* its name of *Shir-dar*, lion-bearing. In front of the building is a square raised platform, on one corner of which is a small conical tomb, like an ant-hill, where I frequently saw lighted candles and other votive offerings. On the opposite side of the square is the *medressé* Ulug Bek, built by the sovereign of that name about 1420, but one story high and containing only twenty-four rooms. It is now in a very ruinous state, though once the home of mathematics and astronomy. At each corner there is a large minaret about 150 feet high, which seems to lean, though this is an optical delusion, as one side of the tower is perpendicular, and the other is at an angle, and it is possible to get a point of view where it appears perfectly erect. Added to this, the sides of the portal are not parallel to each other, which increases the illusion. During the siege of the Russians in the fortress, a mullah did very good service with a falconet from one of these towers. After General Kaufmann returned, a mullah was brought before him as the guilty party, and his immediate execution was ordered. It is difficult to see why, especially without trial. On the north side of the square is the *medressé* Tilla-Kari, built like Shir-dar by Yalang-Tash. The exterior, with its large arched portal and domes and corner minarets and two stories of windows, is in ruins, but the court is in a better state of preservation, and it is on the whole one of the finest. On the left side of the court is the mosque. The pulpit has very handsome carved wooden steps, and the space about the *kibleh* is covered with rich gilt ornament, which seems to be gold foil under a thin layer of transparent enamel. It is probably from this that the *medressé* is called *Tilla-Kari*, or gold covered.[1]

On the top of a slight hill to the south of the fortress, is the most interesting monument of Samarkand, the *Gur'-Amir*, or tomb of Timur. It is an eight-sided building, surmounted by a melon-shaped dome, and with two ruined minarets. Passing through a broken mosaic portal and a court, we come to the steps leading into the mosque. Over the gates is an inscription in Persian: 'The weak slave Mohammed, son of Mahmoud, from Isfahan, built this.' The inside of the dome is full of the usual alabaster work, and the walls are covered with hexagonal plates closely set together of finely carved transparent gypsum, which is often supposed to be jasper. On the side turned to Mecca there is a pillar and a large ancient standard with floating horse-tail. The tombstone of Timur occupies the exact centre of the mosque, and is a slab of greenish black stone, six feet long, fifteen inches wide and about fourteen inches thick, which is flat on the top and not pyramidical as has been represented. It has been broken or cut in the middle into two parts, and one of the lower corners has been broken off and subsequently polished down, as is shown by a part of the inscription being missing. Around the edge is a very complicated inscription in antique letters, giving Timur's name and titles, together with those of all his ancestors, and the date of his death, 807 (1405). To the right of this slab is another of grey marble, of nearly the same size, with an inscription showing that it is the tomb of Mirza Ulug Bek, grandson of Timur, who died in 853 (1449). The back and part of the top are covered with plaster. On the other side of Timur's tomb, is a grey marble slab in memory of Abdullatif Mirza, son of Ulug

---

[1] Literally, covered with *tillas*, or gold coins.

Bek, who died in 854 (1450). There are slabs to three other sons of Ulug Bek; and beside these, between the tomb of Timur and the standard, is a grey marble slab dedicated to Mir Seid Belki Sheikh, the teacher of Timur, who died two years after him. The walls of the mosque are covered with various inscriptions, some texts from the Koran, and others religious

THE TOMB OF TIMUR.

verses; while in the adjoining room was one which my mullah translated to me as meaning, 'If I were alive people would not be glad,' without date or name. Passing into this room on the left of the main mosque we went down a narrow staircase into the vault below, and found the tombs of Timur and his descendants placed exactly under the slabs above. The tombs are beneath the ground, and nothing is visible but slabs of grey marble covered with complicated inscriptions. The vault itself, which is of a very wide span, is of light grey burnt brick, and is still in a perfect state, being a beautiful piece of workmanship. This mosque, and even the tombs, were found in a very dilapidated condition by the Russians on their occupation, and it is owing to them that repairs have been made and everything put in order, and a guardian appointed to the mosque. The beautiful carved stone railing which surrounds the monument in the upper room, was found badly shattered, but has now been completely restored. In a small building near by are the tombs of Timur's wives.

The citadel contains several mosques and tombs, of which one with a very beautiful melon-shaped dome is dedicated to a local saint Kutf-i-Tchirdani, and is noticeable from the fact that the mosaic inscription running round the dome is, for the sake of symmetry in the letters, merely the beginning of the great article of faith repeated over and over again, the words being 'La Allah, La Allah, La Allah,' ('There is no God, there is no God'). Pious Mussulmans, however, supply the rest, never once thinking that the inscription seems profane.

In the citadel is also the former palace of the Amir, containing the famous *kok-tash*, now used as a Russian military hospital, an insignificant building of unburnt bricks covered with clay.

The court, which was used by the Amir on all occasions of ceremony, is enclosed on three sides by a verandah raised three or four feet above the ground. All is very simple and plain. The slim rudely carved wooden columns support a brick cornice. In the middle is a large octagonal stone three or four feet high, with a square top, in which is a cylindrical hollow, perhaps a water-basin, but looking for all the world like a baptismal font.

The *kok-tash*, which is placed on the verandah opposite the entrance, is an oblong block of whitish-grey marble, polished at the top, carved in arabesques on the sides, and with small pilasters at the corners. It is ten feet four inches long, four feet nine inches wide, and two feet high, without the base of brick and plaster nine inches high, on which it stands. It has been common to speak of this stone as a blue or green

MEDRESSÉ SHIR-DAR AT SAMARKAND.

stone, the word *kok* usually meaning one of those colours, and Lehmann (if it be not a remark of the editor) in his travels speaks of the stone as being of *lapis lazuli*, evidently from hearsay. *Kok* however is an indeterminate word for colour and even means grey, as in the sport of *kok-büra*, 'grey wolf.' The term might thus be applicable to marble. It is probable that the name of this stone had another origin. Baber speaks of the palace which Timur constructed in the citadel of Samarkand as being stately, and four stories high, and famous by the name of *kok-sarai*, just as the palace of Timur in Kesh was called *ak-sarai*, or 'white palace.' The *kok-sarai*, Baber says, 'is remarkable on this account; that every prince of the race of Timur who is elevated to the throne, mounts it at this place, and so one who loses his life for aspiring to the throne loses it here. Insomuch that this has passed into a common expression, that such a prince has been condemned to the *kok-sarai*, a hint which is perfectly well understood to mean that he has been put to death.' The *kok-tash*, we are told, served as the foundation for the throne of Timur, and probably received its name from being the famous stone which was in the *kok-sarai*. The elevation of the sovereign on the *kok-tash* passed into a custom, and a legend arose that the stone had fallen from Heaven, and would not allow a false Khan, or one not of genuine descent, to approach it; and as late as 1722, in the rebellion against Abul Feiz Khan, the complaint was made that he had never fulfilled the formality of sitting on the *kok-tash*, and the rebels proclaimed in his place Rejen Khan, who was consecrated in the usual manner. When the Russians took the city, there was a decorated slab of hard plaster which formed a back to this stone and made it appear like a throne. This, which has now fallen off, and rests against the wall of the building, is evidently of very recent date. The Russians have erected a neat and ornamental bronze railing about this stone to keep it from injury. Behind the stone itself is a large arched niche, decorated with alabaster in the prevailing style, and on one side of this is affixed an oval piece of metal looking like half of a cocoanut; this bears an Arabic inscription, showing that it had once marked the tomb of a saint. The inscription runs: 'This is the tomb of the Sheikh Imam, the Hermit Hodja Akhmet Rodoveri Ishak El Khivi. May Heaven forgive him and his parents and all

Mussulmans who have died. Dated the 22nd day of the month Moharrem in the year 550 (1155) of the hejra of Mohammed.'

There are other remains of the flourishing era of Samarkand in the suburbs of the city. Among them is the *Ishrat-Khana*, said to have been built by Timur's wife for her tomb, but which was turned into a palace on account of a sudden embrace which he gave her on seeing it, so impressed was he by its beauty. The finest of these ruins is the mosque of Hodja Akhrar, a large square building, with a lofty portal and arched doorway, still retaining its mosaic tiling in very good preservation. The Persian lions appear again here over the archway. Inside of the court are the rooms for students, and opposite the entrance a good sized mosque, where, at the time of our visit, we found the pupils and their teachers reciting the evening prayers. Beyond this is a large garden, as well as a cemetery, where rest the remains of Hodja Akhrar himself, once celebrated not only for his sanctity, but for his immense wealth. According to tradition, Hodja Akhrar lived about 400 years ago in Tashkent, and was originally named Ubeidullah, but was called Akhrar (consecrated to God) from his piety. He devoted himself to religion from early youth, and became a member of the religious order of Nakshbendi, and, after the death of the *Pir*, its head. It is said that when several of the younger brethren were making their pilgrimage to Mecca, one found himself in Rum, and cured the Khalif of a great disease by prayer and by reading a benediction which his master had given him. In gratitude the khalif offered him anything he liked to choose, and he asked for the Koran of Othman, the third Khalif, which was preserved in the Khalif's treasury. This Koran was said to have been written by Othman himself; and he was engaged in reading it in his house when he was murdered, and his blood spurted over the book, where traces of it still remain. The Khalif was obliged to fulfil his promise, and the celebrated Koran was taken to Tashkent, where it added still more to the celebrity of the saint. Subsequently Hodja Akhrar removed to Samarkand, taking the Koran with him, and after his death it was preserved in this mosque, lying on a large stone reading-table. It is a most beautiful manuscript, written entirely in Cufic characters upon parchment; and when the Russians occupied Samarkand there was not a single learned native who was able to decipher it.

THE DERVISHES.

Seeing the value which the Russians set on this relic, some of the fanatical mullahs thought to remove it to Bukhara, but this was forbidden by General Abramoff; and the Imams of the mosque of their own accord offered to sell it for 125 rubles, saying that before it had brought them in money, because people came and paid for the privilege of kissing and touching it, but as this would no longer be done they might as well dispose of it. The money was accordingly given, and the Koran is now in the Imperial Public Library at St. Petersburg.

The bazaar of Samarkand is comparatively insignificant, much smaller than those at Tashkent and Hodjent, although large enough for the 30,000 inhabitants that Samarkand now contains. The chief portions of the old bazaar are the *Timi*, a large octagonal covered building, where the smaller things are sold, and one or two wooden houses for silk and cotton goods. Besides Hindoos and Jews, there were many Afghans to be seen there, and it was not an uncommon thing to meet Dervishes, or *Kalendar*, as they are there called. They are permitted to frequent the city and to ask for alms, though they are forbidden to preach or to recite prayers. I went one morning with my Mullah to the *Kalendar Khana*, situated just outside one of the gates. This, which belongs to one of the few orders of Dervishes remaining at Samarkand, is a large garden containing one or two mosques, and a number of small cells. We found some seven or eight wretched-looking devotees, and on paying our respects to their *Pir* or chief, and accepting the tea which he offered us, they proposed to sing. It was, however, some little time before a sufficient number for a chorus could be collected, as many of them were in the town, and the rest were lying asleep in different parts of the garden, or were half stupid from smoking *nasha*, or hemp. Finally several of them were induced to appear, and after taking a friendly pipe of *nasha* together, to give them the necessary inspiration, they donned their oldest robes of rags, slung their wallets over their shoulders, and put on the high conical caps, which are a requisite to their religious toilette. They then stood in a row and began to sing, now in Persian, and now in Turki. The chant was not unmelodious. One or two lines were sung by the leader, and then the whole band broke out into the refrain. As they warmed up, they went faster and faster, and the leader however much he might strain his voice, was almost inaudible on account of the cries of the others, who, without waiting for the response, sang, or rather shouted, continually. Their song, in praise of the founder of their order, ran something like this:

> A wild beast cries in the waste: Thou Mighty One!
>   (*Refrain*) O God, our friend!
> Than Thee there is no other,
>   O God, our friend!
> We have no other protector than Thee,
>   O God, our friend!
> Our head is Nakshband Durana,
>   O God, our friend! &c. &c.

When we were tired of one hymn, another was begun, and finally they started one very wild and quick, with numerous boundings, prostrations and whirlings, but the exercises, except those of the voice, were by no means violent. Fanatics as they were, they made no objection to exhibiting before me, as they felt sure of a *sillau*, or present, at the end, and they made no scruple about accepting the offered money. The whole affair, as they themselves very well know, is a comedy played for lucre. There are few of them that trouble themselves about piety or religion, except so far as it can be made profitable. When I was about to go, the chief addressed me a petition, saying that this establishment of Dervishes had been founded long ago for pious uses; that it was devoted to the reception of the poor, the sick, and the blind, and of persons who had no other refuge, and that the only means they had to support it was, by taking contributions from the faithful throughout the city. They begged me therefore to represent to the authorities the religious and charitable objects they had in view, and to request that they might be allowed as before to recite their prayers and to preach their sermons in public. I replied that I had heard that this was prohibited because many of them had been in the habit of inveighing against the Russians, and of preaching hatred and hostility to the infidel. This they denied vigorously, saying that they had no ill feeling whatever to the Russians, who treated them well. I told the Prefect afterwards of the request which they had preferred, and which he was not at all astonished to hear; but he said, that, however they might deny it, instances of their treasonable language were only too well proved, because officers frequently, in passing by unobserved, had heard parts of their sermons, which usually consist of the narration of some old legend where the people were enslaved by the infidel on account of their irreligious life and practices, and end with an appeal to repentance, saying that thus the infidel may be driven away. Islam is frequently depicted under the form of a white she-camel which is oppressed by a heathen tribe.

Not the least interesting of the inhabitants of Samarkand are the Jews, who, under the rule of the Russians, have here at least equal rights with the rest of the population. In old times they were obliged to live in a separate quarter, to which indeed they now chiefly keep, and were forbidden to ride within the city walls, or to wear any other girdle than a rope. Such is the contempt of Mussulmans for the Jews that they do not think them even good enough for slaves. Having expressed a wish to buy some antiquities, a Jew one day presented himself to me with some Greek coins and engraved gems. He was in his way a curiosity. He was the son of Mamun, a noted Hebrew dealer in *lapis lazuli* at Bukhara, who befriended Dr. Wolff when he was there to inquire into the murder of Stoddart and Connolly. He and his father went to India on a trading expedition, and then resolved to go to Europe; but in order to do so they were obliged at Bombay to make themselves British subjects, and to take out British passports. After staying for more than a year in London, the father returned to Bukhara, where he now is, while the son went to Paris, where he remained three or four years, and then found his way to Samarkand. He speaks English fairly, and French very well. It was amusing to see him in his little Paris coat a thorough European among his countryman in their caps and long gowns. The Jews shave their heads, as do the Mussulmans, leaving two long locks on the temples, curled if possible, and in other respects adopt the native dress. Mamun offered to take me into the Hebrew quarter, and one morning we started off together. We went first to the new synagogue, which was built by a rich Jew named Mushti Kalanter. On each side of a broad portico was a large room with a desk for the Rabbi, simply but prettily decorated. In the back were a number of pigeon-holes, where were placed the rolls of the law, none of them of great antiquity. The Rabbi and his assistant were engaged in teaching two classes of bright and merry children in smaller adjoining rooms. The Rabbi, a very intelligent man, had come there from Morocco in the old Bukharan times, for even then a synagogue existed, although concealed with the greatest care from the eyes of the authorities. From the synagogue we went to the house of Kalantar, and we sat for a long time in the garden under the trees, while a pretty girl with unveiled face picked and brought us bunches of fresh roses. It was only after some time that Kalantar himself, a venerable man with a grey beard, came in and took tea with us. The Jewesses, though unveiled at home, have their faces covered in the street like the Mussulman women, to avoid disagreeable and insulting remarks.

I made the acquaintance at Samarkand of Abdur Rahman Khan, the former ruler of Afghanistan and the nephew of Shir Ali, the present Amir. Dost Mohammed Khan left sixteen sons, and on his death there was much contention for the succession, until finally Shir Ali succeeded in establishing himself at Kabul, and was recognised as the lawful Amir by the Indian authorities. Several of the brothers, however, were unwilling to submit to him, and raised rebellions; among these was Afzul Khan, or rather, his son Abdur Rahman Khan, for Afzul himself played but a passive part in the struggle. On being ordered to come to Kabul, Abdur Rahman Khan fled for refuge to Bukhara, while his father was immediately imprisoned by the angry Shir Ali. This was in the end of November 1864. The next spring there was another rebellion. Azim Khan rose in insurrection, but was defeated by Shir Ali, and driven to Kandahar. Abdur Rahman Khan then collected some Bukharan troops and appeared in Afghanistan with great success. He gained possession of Balkh, and moved directly on Kabul, which was given up to him; and on March 1, 1866, he entered into the city and freed his father from imprisonment. Shir Ali was beaten twice more, and at the end of 1867 fled to Herat. The conflict continued for two years more. Afzul Khan died, and Abdur Rahman Khan was proclaimed Amir. Finally Kabul was taken in 1868; Abdur Rahman Khan and Azim Khan were thoroughly defeated, and fled to Mashad. In July 1869, Abdur Rahman Khan sent messengers to Samarkand to ask if he could be allowed to seek a refuge in the Russian territory, and was answered that if he could go nowhere else he would be permitted to come. He accordingly arrived in Tashkent in March 1870, and was well received. The Russian Government allows him about 25,000 rubles a year, and insists on his remaining in Samarkand. He has several times asked for permission to go to St. Petersburg, but it has always been refused. About four years ago he asked General Kaufmann to give him 100,000 rubles, saying that with that he would be able to raise an insurrection against Afghanistan, which he hoped would turn out to his profit. This sum General Kaufmann refused to grant him, saying that the Russians did not wish to be mixed up with the affairs of Afghanistan. As, however, he lives very quietly in the Amir's garden in Samarkand, and can hardly spend, even with all his messengers and secret correspondents, more than 5,000 rubles a year, he must now have nearly enough to prepare the proposed expedition.

I was very desirous of seeing him, and accordingly sent him word asking when I could call. He replied that he would do himself the honour of coming to me first, and appointed the next day. About one o'clock a messenger came in, and said that the Afghan Prince was on his way. With the respect due, even to fallen royalty, we of course went to the door to receive him. Abdur Rahman Khan is a tall well-built man, with a large head, and a marked Afghan, almost Jewish, face. He wears long locks of hair at the side, and a full, curly black beard. He carries himself with much dignity, and every movement denotes a strong character, and one accustomed to command.

He was dressed in a semi-military dress— a long dark *caftan* ornamented with wide silver galloon, and frogs of silver braid, with a highly-wrought silver belt, and silver mounted sabre. On his head he had a white turban striped with blue. Our conversation was naturally chiefly about Afghanistan, and the Prince had much to say about the reports which were then rife, that an army had been sent by Shir Ali to Seistan. He was unwilling to believe the story that Iskender Khan, now living in England, had made peace with Shir Ali, and had been put in command of the expedition. Another report had just then reached us that the English were making an attack upon Herat, and we were even told the numbers of troops which had been despatched from Shikarpur and other points on the Indus. Abdur Rahman explained that this would be impossible without previous operations on the Persian Gulf, of which we would inevitably have heard, and asking for a pencil and sheet of paper, drew a rough outline map of Afghanistan and the roads leading from India to Kabul, Herat, and Kandahar. His conversation was interrupted from time to time, according to Eastern custom, with enquiries after the health of the persons to whom he was talking, and good wishes for them. Although usually reserved, he was very ready to talk with me, and while saying nothing especially ill of Shir Ali, plainly showed his enmity to him. He spoke of the story that Shir Ali had forbidden his name to be mentioned in Kabul under pain of death, laughingly saying that it would not much matter, because people would only think twice as much of him. He felt sure that he need only declare himself to have the population entirely on his side, because Shir Ali was detested by all the Afghans for his complaisance towards England. I asked him if the subsidy given to Shir Ali by the English had any effect upon the feelings of the Afghans. He said to make them well-disposed to England it had no effect at all, though it possibly might have an effect upon Shir Ali personally. If the English were to give Afghanistan the whole revenues of India, the people would not love the English the better. I then asked him whether, in case of a war between any other country and England, an attack were made on India, the Afghans would be willing to join in it. He said that if word were given to the Afghans that an attack was to be made against the English in India, and they were convinced the war was not against India, but against the English domination there, they would willingly join in it without any subsidy, or the necessity of much urging. During his stay in Samarkand he had learned considerable Russian, so that he occasionally answered questions without waiting to have them put into Persian for him; once notably to the confusion of the friend who was interpreting for me, as my question was one which did not exactly please him, and he was unwilling to translate it literally. The Prince stayed with me for over an hour, and on taking leave said that he would send to me when he would be able to receive me, but I never heard any more from him, and on my

subsequent visits to Samarkand I did not see him. I was told
that he was living so quietly and economically that he did not
wish to show his household arrangements to strangers. He
does not seem to be quite contented with his treatment by the
Russian authorities, who certainly do not use him as a tool for
intrigue. He said once, rather bitterly, that the first time he
came to Tashkent a carriage of the Governor-General was
placed at his disposition, that on his second visit he had an
ordinary carriage, but that when he came the third time he was
left to go a-foot.

The Russian occupation of Central Asia has brought to
light many adventurers, chiefly Russians, who had fled from
Siberia, or from Orenburg, and had played various parts in the
native States. Some such men are still in Bukhara and Khokand, while others made their peace with the Russian authorities and remained in the districts occupied.

Of one of these men I had heard much, but unfortunately
he died of the cholera before my arrival at Samarkand. He
was a Pole of the name of Gerburt von Fulstein, who, when
quite a young man, had for some political offence been sent
to Orsk.

At this time there was great commotion among the Kirghiz,
and there was much talk about the son of the Sultan Sanjar,
who, it was said, had been carried off by the Russians and
educated by them. Gerburt was surrounded on the road by
a party of Kirghiz, who immediately professed to recognise
him as the missing man, and took him with them into the
Steppe and finally to Turkistan. The Khan of Khokand had
married a daughter of Sultan Sanjar, and for greater surety she
was admitted to see him, and immediately declared him to be
her brother. He was then received in a manner befitting the
Khan's relative, and was appointed Bek of Namangan. Here he
led such a debauched and dissipated life, being constantly
drunk, that the Khan found it necessary to remove him and
keep him with him. When the Amir of Bukhara took Khokand
he carried Gerburt with him, and appointed him to a considerable post at Court. He was in Samarkand when the Russians
took it, and, on account of his acquaintance with the natives
and their languages, was given a small position, where he made
himself useful. In relating his story, he said that he was him-

self at times confused to know whether he was really a Pole or a Kirghiz.

An adventurer of a different kind was twice in Samarkand during my stay there. He gave himself out as the Khan Zadeh Arash Kul, a Persian prince, who was desirous of proceeding to Bukhara for some business relating to his property.

For some reason or other his conduct aroused suspicion both in Tashkent and Samarkand, and it was thought that he might possibly be a dealer in counterfeit money. He was not allowed to proceed to Katta Kurgan, on the ground that his road pass was only to Samarkand, and was turned back. He went back therefore as far as Jizakh, procured another road-pass to Katta Kurgan, and went directly there. The frontier at Katta Kurgan is very closely watched, and the Prefect is very particular about all suspicious characters. As this man had no letters from the authorities, orders were given that he should not be allowed to go to Bukhara, and all his efforts to run away at night were unsuccessful. After complaint was made against him that he had been living in the post-house for a long time to the discomfort of other travellers, he was ordered to leave the place. On returning, he abandoned his post-carriage at one station from Tashkent, and proceeding on foot, took another at one station on the other side, in order better to escape observation. When this was discovered suspicions against him were even stronger, but all traces of him had disappeared. A year after it turned out that he was a criminal named Babaef, who had been sentenced to Siberia for falsely assuming the title of Prince Goktchaiski. He succeded in escaping from Russia, but was arrested at Vienna and sent to Moscow, where he soon after died in prison.

At Samarkand I made my first real acquaintance with the Russian soldier in Central Asia. Of course I had seen many at Tashkent and elsewhere, very frequently indeed drunk in the street; but it was here that I first saw them in barracks, in camp, at exercise, and at work. On my two later visits to Samarkand I lived with my friend T——, in the camp, of which he was the Commander. This camp was situated outside of the walls, in several large gardens, the one we were in being that of the mosque called Namazga, used chiefly during the great festivals. In the centre was a large square pond, and by its side a grassy platform surrounded by high elm trees. Here our tents—large, commodious, and well furnished canvas houses—were pitched, with the servants and kitchen in the rear; while at a little distance on either side were long rows of barracks, with canvas roofs and sides—for here in summer it seldom if ever rains. The mosque was turned into a dining room and billiard saloon for the officers. Here we lived in the open air, looping up the sides of our tents to let the breeze through, and changing our rugs and cushions from one side of the pond to the other as the shade required. A new camp was then being made, further out on the plain, where the troops can drill and parade with more ease, but unfortunately the place is utterly bare of trees, although probably in two years there will be a grove immediately about the barracks, which are permanent, and built of unburned bricks. In different places through the town, soldiers could be seen at work digging clay, mixing it in water, stamping it in moulds, and placing the bricks to dry in the sun. The soil is so peculiar here that such bricks may be made everywhere, and when a person wishes to build a wall about his garden, or even to erect a house, he either digs in his own grounds, or scoops a ditch along the side of the street for the required material. The warm climate demands a suitable uniform: and the soldiers here wear white cotton or linen blouses, and loose trousers of sheepskin, dyed crimson with cochineal or pomegranate juice, and tucked into their high boots. It is not only a picturesque uniform, but one well suited to the soldier; for his movements are entirely free, and he looks far more robust and manly than when he gets on his ill-fitting winter uniform, badly made of coarse dark cloth.

I used to be waked up in the morning by the *reveillé* of the drums and bugles; and as soon as the tea-urn of my friend was seen on the table in the shade, and he was known to be up, the serjeants brought in their reports. I went once to see the soldier's mess, and found everything very orderly, and the food—white bread and cabbage soup, or mutton broth—excellent.

In the evening the battalion bands usually played, or the choruses of the soldiers sang; for each battalion has its own chorus of select singers, who sing various songs, either composed by themselves, or written by some officer, celebrating the fights in which they have been engaged. Some of these songs are very spirited, and occasionally they speak more truth than pleases all of their commanders. At nine o'clock the songs always ended with the evening prayer, and after that there was quiet in the camp, though not necessarily sleep. The soldiers here lead an active enough life, and apparently a comfortable one. In their campaigns they certainly have shown great energy, and a wonderful capacity for enduring fatigue and hardship, and are always cheerful and good-natured.

Once or twice a year those whose terms of service have expired are sent home with their wives and children at the Government expense, camels being provided for their transport. I saw the departure of one of these caravans on the night I myself left Tashkent. It was exceedingly amusing; almost all the men were drunk, for had they not been taking leave of their comrades? and it was with great difficulty that their wives or some sober fellows were able to keep them on the uneven backs of the camels, where they lay or sat amidst the piles of luggage. Occasionally one fell off without seeming to be injured by the fall, and could with difficulty be re-seated. It is strange that no effort seems to be made to induce the soldiers and their wives to remain as colonists. Many would be glad to remain, at least for a time, but they are influenced by the privilege of free transportation home, of which they must avail themselves immediately, or not at all.

The Russian society of Samarkand is very small, and there are, as yet, very few new houses. A new quarter is, however, laid out on the further side of the citadel, in which streets and houses are gradually springing up. During my visits, this whole region was a scene of dust and confusion. There are but two or three merchants, and the population is made up of the officers and officials, and of the camp followers; and as but two or three of the officers have wives, Russian society is almost as masculine as that of the natives. In these remote regions the marriage ceremony is not regarded as of the utmost importance, and society cannot afford to be too punctilious.

It is impossible not to be struck with the difference between the administration in Samarkand and that in Tashkent. Nearly all the officials seem to have at heart the welfare of the country, and to be earnest in their work. They are, for the most part, the remainder of what are called the 'Tchernaief men,' many of them having been with that General in his first

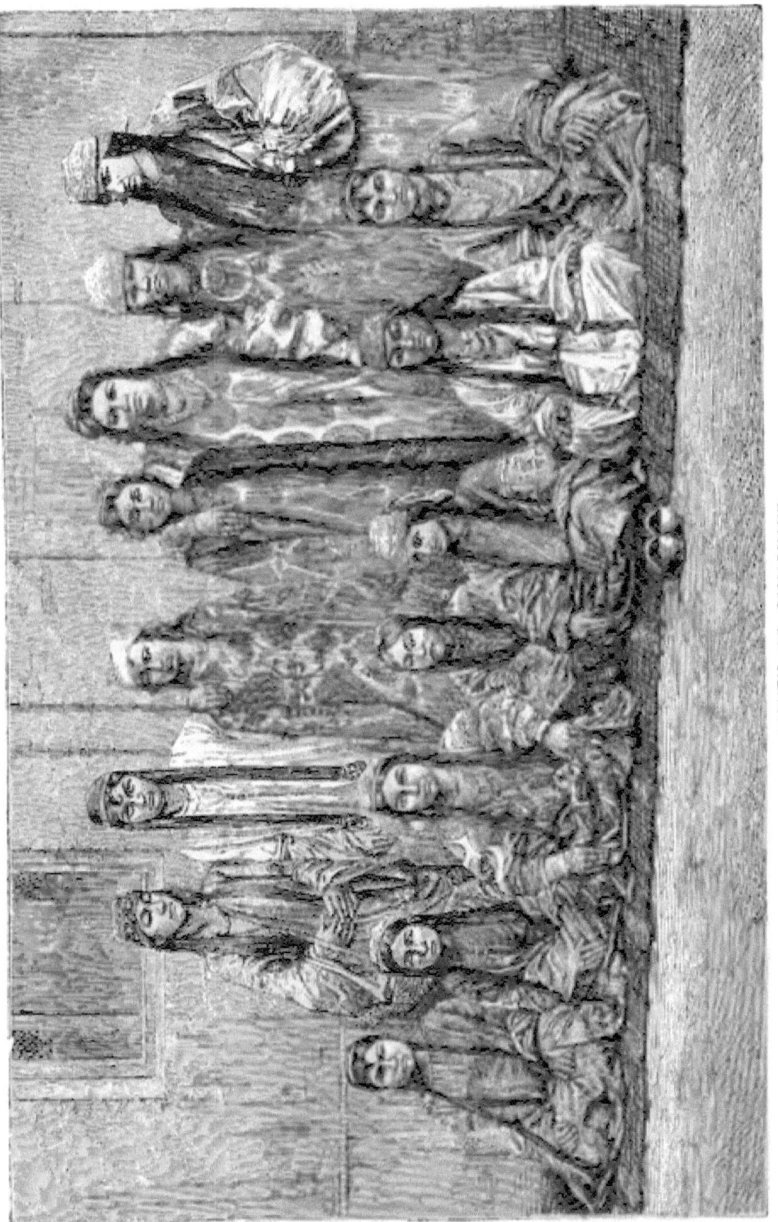

WOMEN OF SAMARKAND.

Central Asiatic campaign. General Abramof, the commander of the province, began as a sub-captain, but by his great bravery and dash in all his fights has succeeded in winning for himself the grade of Major-General with numbers of orders and decorations. He is a most active man, and knows well the whole of the country. I do not believe that there is a village under his rule which he has not visited. He endeavours to keep himself thoroughly informed of all that goes on, and, although his will in Samarkand is law, as the administrative regulations for the rest of Turkistan have never been applied to that province, he is most anxious to act always with justice, and in the spirit of the Russian law. He is ably seconded in his administration by men who know well the people with whom they have to deal. The Prefect of the city was, at that time, Captain Syrtlanof, a Mussulman gentleman of Bashkir origin, speaking Kirghiz, Turki, and Persian with great fluency. While I was living in his house I had an excellent opportunity of seeing the manner in which he administered the affairs of the city. The inhabitants were well pleased with him, not only because he was a Mussulman, but because he was able to listen himself to their complaints and to decide their disputes, and was, what is rare enough to deserve mention, thoroughly honest. Having at heart the interests of the population, he established in Samarkand an excellent public hospital, and was instrumental in founding there a school for Mussulman children, which is meeting with great success. So far it has attained the object of inducing many leading Mohammedans to send their children there for the purpose of learning Russian. Unfortunately both for the population and for the best interests of the Russian Government, Captain Syrtlanof is no longer there. The Governor-General got an idea into his head that he was a fanatic, and removed him.

CHAPTER VII.

THE ZARAFSHAN VALLEY.

Urgut—Our idyl—A second visit—The mountain ranges—The glacier—The Upper Zarafshan—Kohistan—The petty Beks—Iskender Kul Expedition—Annexation—Small extent of arable land in Central Asia—Irrigating canals—Regulation of irrigation—Water supply of Bukhara—Methods of irrigation—Systems of husbandry—Rotation of crops—Cereals—Famines—Lack of statistics—Cotton—Gardens—Price of Land—Land tenure—Proposed land settlement—Land taxes.

My friends at Samarkand urged me to prolong my stay for two or three days in order to visit Urgut—twenty miles off in the mountains. Accordingly we made up a little party, and attended by a number of *jigits*, we started from Samarkand one bright afternoon. We drove through lanes made fragrant by the odour of caper plants, and by the spicy scent of the yellow-flowered *jidda*, or wild olive, and after we had got clear of the gardens and fully into the plain, I found that my friend the Prefect had prepared a surprise for me in the shape of a *baiga*, the great national sport of Central Asia, known also by the name of *kok-bűra*, or 'grey wolf.'

In an open field along the side of the road fifty horsemen were waiting, one of whom had a dead kid slung from his saddle bow. As we came along this man rode up to us and asked if we would like to see the sport. Of course we willingly assented, and we started off with everybody else in full pursuit. The object of the game was to succeed in bearing the kid away from its possessor and in bringing it up to me as the judge of the contest. Away they went, through canals and over the plains, up and down hill, sometimes forwards sometimes backwards, the possessor of the kid skilfully dodging and holding on by main force to the animal with which he was charged. Men often approached him, but it was seldom that they could catch hold of the kid, and still more seldom that they could retain the hold sufficiently long to make a struggle. At one place, in order to get rid of his pursuers, Ish Jan—for such I believe was his name—had to plunge into a pond, or rather the enlargement of a canal, where the water was much deeper and swifter than he had thought, and soon there were a dozen men there struggling and plunging, all up to the necks of their horses in water. All got out without accident and the kid was still safe, but just as Ish Jan was going up the bank one of the men, who had not plunged into the water and who was lying in wait, quickly pulled the now slippery animal away from him and brought it in triumph to my carriage, for which of course I had to give him a *tenga* and pass the animal on to another. The next time they went almost out of sight across the gravelly plain and rapidly returned with another as the victor. The sport lost much by not being played, as it should be, on a grassy steppe where the vista would be large enough to take in the whole position and with a throng of enthusiastic spectators on horseback, but even as it was it was extremely exciting. I saw it again on the occasion of a Kirghiz feast, though at a long distance, but with my field-glass I was able almost to see the intense expression of the faces, and even then was so much interested that, although I was hastening on, I made my driver wait for nearly half-an-hour that I might look at the game. Fully a hundred men were surging backwards and forwards over a broad hill-side, their horses so close together that it seemed as if some of them must get smothered. Sometimes half a dozen separated from the rest, a struggle followed, one bearing the kid dashed off in triumph, when all rushed at him and the *mêlée* began again, reminding me then of nothing so much as of a good game of foot-ball.

Since then I have seen *polo* played, a game of a similar nature. When I first saw it, Hurlingham, the royal guests, the ladies and the officers all faded away, and I was again on the steppes of Asia amid a throng of Uzbeks.

After travelling about fifteen miles we came to a village, or rather a farm, called Yangy Kishlak (new village), belonging to one of the native officials who accompanied us. He insisted that we should take some repose here, and we were conducted into a large garden where on the side of a square pond a kibitka had been erected, and where we found a bountiful lunch.

The further we went the barer and more desolate and gravelly the valley became, and the nearer the foot hills of the great range seemed to us; although even then Urgut was seen only as a black patch on the mountain side. As we approached, the black patch grew green and turned into a broad grove of trees, and soon the clay house-tops appeared amid the gardens. The road led for some distance along the shelving bank of a mountain stream, and at last over a stony plain which seemed almost the moraine of some old glacier.

Under a large spreading tree surrounded by a platform of earth, about two miles from the town, we were met by the Kazi and various officials, who told us that every preparation had been made for us, and who accompanied us to the town.

It was now getting quite dark, and as we entered Urgut the whole population met us in the street, all bearing lamps and torches to show us the way. We had expected to be obliged to leave our carriage long before and to proceed on horseback, as we were told that the road was in a bad state, and we had sent on our horses in advance of us to Yangy Kishlak, but we found that the road was quite good, although very narrow and steep, and we were able to go beyond the town quite to the grove of *tchinars*, or Oriental plane trees, where we were to stop. Here were a mosque and the tomb of some local saint, as well as small huts for the devotees at this tomb. On a broad terrace in front of the mosque, and close to a running stream, two large kibitkas had been erected for our accommodation, and a welcome supper was also spread out for us. It was very late, but the mountain air was so fresh and exhilarating, and so different from the sultry heat of the plain, that we were betrayed into lingering long in the starlight and felt for some time no inclination to sleep.

The next morning we awoke to find ourselves in a beautiful shady retreat, with a fragrant scent coming down from the heavy branches of the plane trees. The mountain stream which ran past us was the clearest and purest that I had ever seen, and, as we found when we bathed in it, one of the coldest, but it put us into a nice glow.

We were still at tea when the Aksakals of the city came to pay us their respects, and to ask if there was anything that we desired. We told them that we were anxious to see the town, and at once ordered our horses. T—— stayed at home, but M—— and I accompanied the Aksakals back to the town down the mountain road, whence we got a beautiful view over the valley of the Zarafshan, Samarkand and the hill of Tchupan-ata being at once recognisable in the distance. We passed the citadel, which was entirely in ruins and now un-inhabited, just as it had been left after it had been stormed by General Abramof, much, we presume, to the delight of the inhabitants, for in none of these cities did we find that they had loved their Beks too well.

It was bazaar day, and the bazaar was crowded, not only with the inhabitants of Urgut, which is a town of 10,000 people, but with men who had come there from the mountain Bekships, and even perhaps from Hissar and Karategin. The shopkeepers sitting in their stalls looked cool and comfortable in their robes of pink Russian calico with roses and sprigs of mint stuck under their skull caps over their ears, while the crowd of purchasers on horseback seemed sweltering in their heavy robes and sheepskins. They made way for us with their good natured smile of curiosity, as the Aksakals touched them with their whips, but the dust and the heat were so great that we soon left the bazaar, and asked for some place where we might rest. Going a little distance further along a small stream we were shown into a large garden, with a square pond in the middle, where there were a number of tea booths, and there in the shade of some tall elm and plane trees a carpet was spread for us at the side of the pond and a bright looking boy in a silk robe was quickly handing us bowls of green tea.

We soon entered into conversation with some friends of the Aksakal who joined us, and we then found that the boy was a dancer as well as a tea-seller, and on hinting that we should have no objection to a little amusement, another boy was produced, and soon three or four musicians appeared with their clumsy tambourines, at the first sound of which the garden began to fill, for every Asiatic is only too glad to find an excuse for pleasure. Shops were shut up, the bazaar became empty, and in a short time our garden was filled with eager spectators, who seated themselves in long rows all about the pond and covered even the tops of the walls and the roofs of the surrounding buildings. The sight was certainly very picturesque. One dance succeeded another; occasionally beggars came for alms; and the crowd, perhaps to show their gratitude to us for the unwonted spectacle in the day time in such a crowded place, pelted us with roses. The hated heat of the sunny street, combined with the attractions of the spectacle, made us the more willing to linger, and two or three hours elapsed before we were inclined to rise from our cushions under the elm trees, remount our horses, and go back to our grove.

When at last we started, we were respectfully accompanied half way up the mountain side by fully half the population, but no one was admitted to our garden save our immediate attendants and Madamin, the son of the chief Aksakal, a boy of about sixteen, with an immense pair of boots on his feet, which his father had probably lent him in honour of the occasion, who lolled about wonderingly all day, and shyly began to make acquaintance with us just as we were about to leave. Later on we followed up the course of the brook under vines and creepers, and at last climbed the steep bare peak that stood out over us with its jutting crags, until on its top a wonderful vista of mountain and plain and river opened up to us. When we had filled our eyes and souls with the sight, we slowly descended the peak, mounted our horses, and bade good-bye to Urgut. We rode as far as Yangy Kishlak, where we found our carriages, which we had sent on earlier in the day, and late in the evening we were in Samarkand again, feeling gladdened and refreshed as though we had been in some far off unreal world.

Once again I was in Urgut, on my return from Bukhara, but this was a visit of state and ceremony, for I went with the General and a dozen officers, and we were escorted by a troop of Cossacks. This visit was in many respects hardly less interesting than the former, though very different. There were carpets and tents and banquets at the halting places, deputations met us at every mile, and by the time we reached the town we had formed a grand procession, the dust caused by which did not add much to our pleasure. We stayed in a different and larger grove, and had with us the

General's kitchen and cooks, forming a great encampment.
Here we stayed three days, devoting the morning to long
walks and mountain climbing, the afternoons to happy indolence
and the evenings to talk and cards. The first day we were
long kept from our dinner by the arrival of the deputations
from the town and neighbouring villages bearing trays of

A YOUTH OF URGUT.

sweets, nuts and fruit, and many written addresses. The visit
of the Hindoos gave us perhaps the most pleasure, for apart
from their interesting countenances and figures, with a delicate
instinct of what would be pleasing to us, they brought us as their
gift—a large sack of excellent potatoes. Each deputation, after
it was received, retired a little distance and took seats on the
ground, while the rest of the population gradually came up and

stood behind them. This gave to our dinner a certain solemnity, for when one is closely watched by several thousand people, all preserving a profound silence, one eats as though one were performing a high function. We had with us on this trip two bright little boys, sons of the prefect of Tashkent, who, speaking Turki, soon made acquaintance with the youth of Urgut, and easily persuaded them to accompany us on our hill-top excursions, show us all the curious places, and relate to us the legends of the neighbourhood, and delighted them by allowing them to fire off our pistols.

The mountains on the side of which Urgut stands are prolongations of the great Alpine region of the Tian-Shan, which, forming the ranges of the Alai, collect into a sort of knot at Kok-su, between Khokand and Karategin, and a little to the east of the meridian of the city of Khokand, that is long. 71° E, and then divide into three separate mountain ridges forming the watershed between the basins of the Syr Darya, the Zarafshan and the Amu Darya, to which the Russians have now agreed to give the names of the Turkistan, the Zarafshan and the Hissar ranges. In spite of certain high peaks in the Turkistan range, the general elevation of the ground is toward the east and south until we reach the top of the Hissar range, the ground descending on the other side into the basin of the Amu Darya. Not only the valleys are at a higher level as we go east and south, but the mountain passes and the ranges themselves. The Turkistan range, which forms the northern side of the Zarafshan valley, extends from Kok-su nearly due west, until a little above Urmitan it separates into two branches, one following the river to a little below Penjakent, although continuing somewhat further as a slight elevation of ground, and finally reappearing as the Godun-tau or Ak-tau mountains some distance beyond Katta-Kurgan. The other branch goes more to the north-west, and, cut at Jizakh by the defile of Jalan-uta, continues in the Kara-tau or Nurata mountains in little ridges on the south-western boundary of the Kyzyl-Kum, until it disappears in the Bukan-tau, about long. 63° East.[1] Some of the peaks in the eastern parts of this range are

---

[1] It is impossible to rely upon the native nomenclature of mountains, lakes, or rivers, in Central Asia, as frequently they have no names, or are known to different villages by different appellations. Those ranges of mountains on which the snow

estimated at 20,000 feet in height, but the highest measured are one near Paldorak of 15,000 feet, and another near the village of Tabushin of 14,500 feet.

Of the twenty passes in this range east of Urmitan the two highest are Yany-sabak, which is 13,270 feet above the level of the sea, and that of Autchi at 11,200.

The Zarafshan range, which forms the southern side of the Zarafshan valley, and separates it from the valleys of the Yagnau and the Kashka Darya, has a direction nearly due west, gradually lowering in height to Djam, where it terminates, reappearing a little later in the low range of Karnan and Kiz-bibi to the south of Ziaueddin and Kermineh. It is cut by three narrow and precipitous defiles, through which run the Fan Darya, the Kshtut Darya, and the Magian Darya, the three affluents of the Zarafshan. The most accessible pass from the valley of the Zarafshan to that of the Yagnau is that of Darkha, at a height of 13,000 feet. The range here varies from 12,000 to 15,000 feet in height. The southern, or Hissar, range, starting from Kok-su, and separating the waters of the Zarafshan from the Surkh-ab and other affluents of the Amu Darya, has in general a south-westerly direction, ending in the neighbourhood of Khuzar. Several of the passes leading into Karategin are at an elevation of 12,000 feet, and the great Mura pass, near Lake Iskender Kul, is 12,200 feet above the sea. Many of the summits rise to a height of from 16,000 to 18,000 feet, and near the glacier of the Zarafshan still higher. In the branches of this range,

lies for a long time are called *Ak-tau*, 'white mountains,' while others are called *Kara-tau*, or 'black mountains,' and if there be any diversity of colour they are *Ala-tau*, 'striped or mottled mountains.' This accounts for the constant reappearance of these names. In the same way lakes are frequently called *Kara-kol* or *Kara-kul*, 'black lake,' with no idea of referring to the colour of the water, but merely because any considerable body of standing water receives the epithet of black; while streams, especially rapid, clear streams, are named *Ak-su*, or 'white water.' In fact *Ak-su* is a common term for water in general, and a Kirghiz, in apologising for his hospitality, will frequently say that he has nothing to offer you but *Ak-su*, white water. Both *Kara-kol* and *Ak-su* are indefinite names for lake or river, and therefore their frequent appearance should be no puzzle to geographers. In this way explorers frequently put names on their maps through misunderstanding. I remember an amusing instance. A Russian officer in one of his journeys asked the name of a certain mountain ridge, and on repeating the question two or three times the native replied. *Khudai-biladi* (God knows!), and the Khudai-biladi mountains were immediately put down in the officer's note-book and appeared on his chart.

which near Magian and Kshtut seem to unite it with the Zarafshan, there is to the south of Magian the group of peaks, Sultan Hazret, over 15,000 feet in height, and in the meridian of Urmitan the peak Tchabdara, 18,300 feet.

The general aspect of these mountains, the northern slopes of which are longer, less precipitous, and with more streams than the southern, is that of bare, rocky crags, above which are everywhere snowy summits, the snow line on the northern sides coming down to 11,000 feet, and on the southern sides receding to 13,000 feet. Very little vegetation is visible, and that little seems lost in the great extent of bare surface. The chief trees are juniper and cedar, the birch being found only near Lake Iskender-kul and in the Pasrut defile. *Taran*, a root used in tanning, and the fragrant *sumbul* are almost the only vegetable productions of value. Except along the upper regions of the Zarafshan and the Yagnau there are no mountain valleys, but the river courses are mere defiles and ravines, through which it is exceedingly difficult to pass.

The Zarafshan takes its rise in a large glacier, situated about long. 70 deg. 32 min. E., at a height of 8,500 feet above the level of the sea. This glacier presents the form of a mountain of ice blocking up the valley of the river. Its length is about 35 miles. Baron Aminof, who ascended it, says that its surface, which rises and falls in a wide plain, is covered with stones and gravel, and full of cracks and pools. He was able to make only 200 paces in the course of an hour and a half, as at every step he was in danger of being crushed by large stones, which, in consequence of the melting of the surface, rolled down from every little eminence, bringing masses of gravel with them. Five miles was the extent of his view in an easterly direction, the glacier then turning to the south and being concealed by the neighbouring peaks. All the side ravines, not only of the glacier, but below it, are filled with smaller glaciers.[1] From this glacier the Zarafshan issues in a

---

[1] 'Military-Topographical Sketch of the Mountain region of the Upper Zarafshan,' (with an excellent map) by Baron Aminof, in Part iii. of 'Materials for the Statistics of Turkistan,' St. Petersburg, 1874. See also 'Geological Observations during the Zarafshan Expedition,' by D. K. Myshenkof, in the 'Memoirs of the Imp. Russ. Geog. Soc. General Geography,' vol. iv. p. 267, St. Petersburg, 1871. 'Geographical and Statistical Information about the Zarafshan District,' by L. N. Sobolef, in 'Mem. Imp. Russ. Geog. Soc. Statistics,' vol. iv. p. 163, St. Petersburg, 1874.

strong stream seven yards wide. After taking in numerous
small streams, its average width where it has one bed is twenty-
one yards. Its length, including all its windings from its
source to the village of Dashty Kazy, where the valley first
begins to widen, about twenty miles above Penjakent, is 134
miles, in which it falls 4.700 feet, or about 35 feet in a mile.
During the winter the river becomes shallow, and where the
current is slow becomes covered with a thin crust of ice, which
is not strong enough, however, to bear a man. The river is
subject to three risings; in early spring and autumn from the
rains, and in the summer from the melting snow, during which
it rises from ten to fifteen feet. Near Varsaminor it receives
its largest affluent, the Fan Darya, which is formed by the Yagnau Darya,[1] a stream rising in a glacier about long. 69 deg. 30
min. E., and flowing parallel with the Zarafshan until it is met by
the Iskender Darya, a small stream flowing out of the mountain
lake Iskender Kul. This lake, which is at an elevation of 6,770
feet above the sea, was found to be of far less importance than
had been supposed, being only five or six miles in circumference.
At 340 feet above there is evidently what was the previous
level, from which, owing to some volcanic disturbance at least
a century ago, the lake has sunk. The only fish found in
this lake is the *Barbus fluviatilis*, well known for its poisonous
roe. At one end of the lake is a fine waterfall, and the whole
surroundings are wonderfully picturesque. It was first visited
by Lehmann, who called it Kul-kalian (large lake). The name
of this lake, as well as the descent which the petty mountain
princes of the upper Amu Darya claim from Alexander, show
the permanence of the traditions about the great Macedonian
conqueror. These legends are, however, most vivid far up
in the mountain valleys among the Galtchas; in the plains
they are overlaid and replaced by stories about Tamerlane or
about Mussulman saints. With regard to Lake Iskender Kul,
there is a legend in Bukhara that once the site of that city was
a marsh overflowed by the Zarafshan. Alexander, wishing to
drain it, went to the source of the river, and shut it up with a
golden dam, thus forming the lake called after him, and making
the valley habitable. The water, however, rubs off particles of

---

[1] Written also *Yagnauh* and *Yagnau-ah*.

gold, which are found in the river, and give it the name of Za-rafshan (gold-strewing). This golden dam, the Bukharans say, is inaccessible, for it is guarded by a race of centaurs; water-spirits also entice into the lake and drown all who come to it. The Kshtut and Magian are small mountain streams, affluents of the Zarafshan, flowing nearly north.

This mountainous region, which is known under the name of Kohistan (mountain country), is inhabited chiefly by Tadjiks or Galtchas, who have from time to time been driven from the valleys by the influx of the Uzbeks. But one eighty-fifth of the whole extent of territory is cultivated and settled, and yet 36,000 people live in wretched villages, and manage to procure for themselves a scanty subsistence by cultivating the soil and by pasturing their flocks on the mountain sides. The valleys are so narrow that it is difficult to irrigate them; the rain-lands are of small extent, and insufficient grain is raised for the needs of the population, the remainder being brought from Ura-tepé, Penjakent, and Hissar. During the summer the people abandon their habitations, and go to the still more elevated mountain regions, where there is good pasture for their sheep and goats. Horses are rare, asses being used for burden. The acquaintances made during the pasturing season of summer are not interrupted by the difficult communications over the mountain ranges, and there are villages separated by passes 13,000 feet high, where all the inhabitants are connected with one another by ties of blood or of marriage. Besides the flocks of the inhabitants, many wild sheep and goats are to be found, as well as bears, wolves, and foxes. The most common game is a species of mountain partridge, which is found in the other ranges of the Tian-Shan and also in the Himalayas. The naturalist Fedtchenko, in speaking of these and other birds, as well as of certain fish and plants which are found everywhere in the Tian-Shan, and of which the same or similar species are also found in the Himalayas, states that the result of his studies points to a relationship between the fauna and flora of the highest mountain systems of Asia, and leads us to suppose that here is a natural zoographical region. On the Yagnau and the Fan Darya there are large deposits of iron-ore and of coal. Gold is found in insignificant quantities in the Zarafshan, and only the poorest class of the population try to work it. Four men in a day can wash out, under favourable circumstances, an amount worth 60 kopeks, or 1s. 7d. Alum is obtained in some of the villages on the Fan in much greater quantities, four men in three months being able to work out 1,800 lbs., worth on the spot from 22l. to 27l., for which they were formerly each obliged to pay certain dues to their Beks. Silver, which is found on the upper Fan, was a monopoly of the Bek, who collected the inhabitants three times a year to work it.

Politically, up to 1870, Kohistan was divided into the seven bekships of Farab, Magian, Kshtut, Fan, Yagnau, Matcha, and Falgar, which were nominally subject to Bukhara, but were secured from the interference of that government in their affairs by the payment of a small tribute. Magian, Kshtut, and Farab, always more or less acknowledged the supremacy of Urgut, the Beks of which (Uzbeks of the tribe Ming) had long before succeeded in making themselves nearly independent and in maintaining the right of hereditary succession. In the early part of this century the Amir of Bukhara, Seid Mir Haidar, subdued Urgut and sent its ruler, Yuldash Parmanatchi, to Bukhara, where he died in prison. Magian, Farab, and Kshtut, then gave in their submission to Bukhara. In subsequent troubles, Katta Bek, one of the sons of Yuldash, established himself in Urgut and placed his brother, Sultan Bek, in Magian and Kshtut. He was driven out by Mir Haidar, but in a subsequent rebellion he not only re-established himself but even tried to get possession of Samarkand. Defeated in this, he made peace by giving his daughter in marriage to Nasrullah, the eldest son of the Amir, and was allowed to retain his hereditary dominions as a fief. In the troubles attending the accession of Nasrullah, Katta Bek succeeded in having his hereditary right to the country acknowledged, and on his death his sons entered peaceably upon the government.

During Nasrullah's long reign affairs continued in this peaceful condition; but shortly before his death he called these Beks to Samarkand, arrested them, and sent them with their families to Tchardjui—where the greater part of them died— and appointed new beks to the mountain districts. One of the younger men, Hussein Bek, soon succeeded in escaping from his exile, and took refuge in Khokand and subsequently in

Shahrisabs. When, after the capture of Samarkand the Bukharan Beks ran away from the mountains, Hussein Bek took possession of Urgut, and, being driven from there by the Russian troops, fled to Magian, where he established himself and recalled his brother Shadi and his cousin Seid, and appointed them rulers in Kshtut and Farab.[1] The annals of Eastern Kohistan are full of the internecine struggles of the various chiefs, of occasional visits of Bukharan emissaries for the forcible collection of tribute, and of incursions from the neighbouring countries on the other side of the mountains. The memory is still green of one Bek of Falgar, Abdush Kur Datkha, who in the beginning of the present century united all the districts under his rule and built roads and bridges through some of the hitherto inaccessible defiles. During the reign of Mir Haidar, Bukharan Beks were established and forts were built, but the country was again nearly forgotten until towards the end of the reign of Nasrullah. When the Bukharan Beks had all run away after the capture of Samarkand, the country was for a time left without rulers, and then Abul Gaffar, the former Bek of Ura-tepé, occupied Urmitan and made himself Bek of Falgar. The inhabitants of Matcha turned to Mozaffar Shah of Karategin, who sent there his nephew Rahim Khan. He drove Abul Gaffar out of Falgar, defeated Shadi Bek of Kshtut, who had come to its assistance, and after subduing the provinces of Yagnau and Fan, made an expedition against Hissar; but before he had reached the stronghold of that country his troops rebelled and drove him from the throne, choosing in his place a native named Patcha Hodja. The Falgarians, who considered themselves more civilised and superior in every way to the inhabitants of Matcha, recalled

[1] I have already spoken of some of these Beks on page 87. Perhaps the following genealogical table may prove useful.

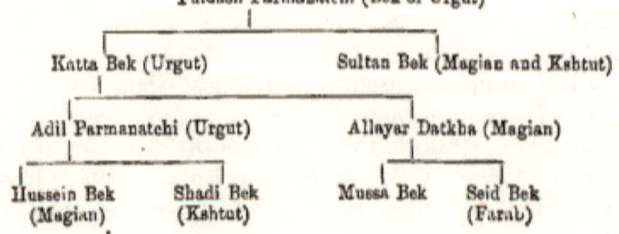

Abul Gaffar, but he was beaten and had to fly to Samarkand, where he gave himself up to the Russians. The disordered state of the mountains, and the constant predatory incursions into the valleys occupied by the Russians, were the chief causes of the so-called Iskender Kul Expedition in 1870, which had also the purpose of exploring the head waters of the Zarafshan, and which resulted in the permanent occupation of these regions.

This expedition, composed of two *sotnias* of Cossacks, a company of sharpshooters, a rocket battery, and a *peloton* of mountain guns, under the command of General Abramof, who was attended by several scientific officers, started from Samarkand on May 7, and on the 12th occupied Urmitan, and on the 21st Varsaminor, both in the bekship of Falgar, with the acquiescence and to the delight of the inhabitants, many of whom had previously fled to Samarkand, offering their submission and requesting to be delivered from the tyranny of the Bek of Matcha. This Bek, Patcha Hodja, retreated, and contented himself with sending threatening letters. As the expedition approached the boundary of Matcha, on a cornice road in a narrow defile, stones were rolled from above on the troops, and they were obliged to retreat. General Abramof at once sent a company of sharpshooters to climb the mountains and dislodge the mountaineers, but without waiting for that he himself with his staff rode along the road notwithstanding a shower of stones, and this bold action produced a great impression on the natives, and was perhaps one reason why they offered no further opposition. Oburdan was occupied on May 28, where the expedition was met by a detachment composed of a company of sharpshooters, fifty Cossacks, and a surveying party, who had crossed the mountains through a different pass from Ura-tepé. On pursuing his march General Abramof received a letter from Patcha Hodja who offered his entire submission ; but instead of waiting to receive the presents sent in return by the General, he fled from the country. After ordering the destruction of the forts at Paldorak, a work in which the inhabitants engaged with evident pleasure, the General with a small party proceeded to the Glacier of the Zarafshan, which was reached on June 6. Meanwhile, Lieutenant-Colonel Dennet with his surveying party attempted to return to Ura-tepé through the pass of Yany-Sabak,

13,400 feet above the sea, but after crossing the pass he was attacked in a narrow defile by the mountaineers, who rolled huge stones down on his command, killing and wounding many men; and after a vain effort to find some means of ascending the mountains he was obliged to retreat. On the news of this Baron Aminof was sent to meet him and to keep the pass clear. On the night of June 12 the surveying party succeeded in re-crossing the pass, which was so difficult that they were obliged to carry everything by hand, and to drag the horses and mules across by lassoes. On his return down the valley of the Zarafshan General Abramof placed various citadels at the disposition of the inhabitants, who immediately levelled them with the ground. From Varsaminor the expedition turned southward to the fort of Sarvada and to Lake Iskender Kul. Reconnaissances were undertaken of all the neighbouring passes, and Baron Aminof with a small surveying party went up the valley of the Yagnau. From Sarvada it was proposed to return to Samarkand through the bekship of Kshtut. Although at the start of the expedition Shadi Bek of Kshtut had sent messengers to General Abramof with his compliments, he seriously objected to having his dominions invaded and had prepared for resistance. While the troops were at Sarvada a *jigit*, who had been sent from Samarkand through Kshtut, arrived saying that his comrade had been retained prisoner, that the letters and despatches had been seized, that a sutler's clerk had been killed, and that he himself had barely escaped with his life. At the same time Shadi Bek wrote to General Abramof that he personally would be glad to allow the expedition to pass through the country, but that he could not rely upon his people, and that therefore he advised him to go back by the road by which he had come. In answer the General threatened him with severe punishment if he made the slightest opposition to his movements, and on the next day, July 6, reached the top of the pass of Kshtut, 10,000 feet above the sea. From this place the road descended into a deep basin surrounded by almost inaccessible crags; and it was the intention of Shadi Bek to draw the Russian troops into this defile, and then overwhelm them by an attack from above. Suspecting this, General Abramof, before descending, gave orders to occupy if possible the heights of Kuli Kalan on both sides. A severe fight resulted, which lasted all day, and in which, although they defeated the mountaineers, the Russians lost 37 men in killed and wounded, a large proportion of the small detachment. Kshtut was occupied and destroyed without further opposition, and the next day the detachment returned to Penjakent and Samarkand. The scientific results of the expedition were the exploration of all the upper waters of the Zarafshan as well as of its glacier, the barometrical and instrumental determinations of a large number of passes and peaks, and a careful map of the whole region.

When this expedition was undertaken, the Russians had no intention of annexing the mountainous districts; but shortly after another expedition was made by General Abramof to Shahrisabs, which resulted in the capture of the cities of Kitab and Shaar, and their transfer to Bukhara. From Shahrisabs a part of the troops returned to Samarkand, while another detachment went up the valley of the Kashka Darya to Farab and Magian, the Beks of those places having been implicated in the attack on the Russians at the Kuli Kalan heights, and having refused to present themselves when summoned to Samarkand. The forts of Magian and Farab were destroyed, and Seid and Shadi Bek surrendered to the Russians. Hussein Bek, of Magian, secreted himself, and was not captured for some months after. The districts of Farab and Magian were immediately annexed to the Russian district of Urgut. The decision to annex the remaining mountain districts was taken the following year, 1871.

In the winter of 1874 one of the former ruling class managed to establish himself in the mountains, from which he could not be driven out by the Russians until the spring. Soon after there were disturbances in the neighbourhood of Urgut, caused by the conduct of the natives put in authority by the Russians. In the summer of 1875, during the rebellion in Khokand, there were again disturbances in the mountains in consequence of the action of the ruler of Karategin, which immediately ceased on the appearance of a Russian force, but at the end of November matters became somewhat serious. The inhabitants of Matcha, influenced, it is said, by emissaries from Khokand, threw off its Russian allegiance, and endeavoured to occupy the neighbouring district of Falgar. A small Russian force, consisting of 100 infantry, one gun, and ten Cossacks, was sent to put it down, but it was driven back with the loss of its commander, two officers, and one-fourth of the men. Additional reinforcements were sent from Samarkand, as well as across the mountains from Ura-tepé, and after another severe fight the Russians succeeded in compelling the insurgents to lay down their arms. But the condition of the mountain districts cannot yet be considered in all respects perfectly satisfactory.

From Penjakent the Zarafshan loses its mountain character, and enters into a wide valley, where it flows along in a broad shallow stream, dividing into several branches, and carried off in every direction by irrigating canals; yet through this most fertile part of Central Asia it is possible to ride long distances without so much as seeing a bit of verdure, so small is the extent of country irrigated by the river. A map of Central Asia, on which the arable lands were carefully marked, would be at once instructive and curious, so narrow would be the green strips along the rivers and at the foot of the mountains. In that part of the valley of the Zarafshan under Russian rule there are estimated to be 10,187 square miles, about half of which is covered with mountains. In and along the mountains about 1,200 square miles are arable, but in the valley itself only 1,615 square miles; that is in all only 18 per cent. of the surface is at present cultivable, while even if we include that part of the Zarafshan valley which belongs to Bukhara, we have altogether but 3,000 square miles of arable land, of which only 1,793 is watered by the Zarafshan. If we look at other parts of the country, the result is even worse. If we add to the Zarafshan the districts of Hodjent (excluding Jizakh) and Kurama, thus including almost all the cultivable land in the country, we find that but $7\frac{7}{10}$ per cent. of it is arable. If to this we add the other districts of the province of the Syr Darya, Jizakh, Tchimkent, Aulié-ata, Perovsky, and Kazala, the most of which is steppe land, amounting to over 164,000 square miles, and to cover all mistakes allow for that half as much cultivable land as in the three districts first mentioned, we shall find that of the whole of Russian Central Asia (excluding the late-annexed Kyzyl-kum desert) only $1\frac{6}{10}$ per cent. is cultivable, a result which speaks plainly as to the value of the recently-acquired

Russian possessions. After the capture of Tashkent, it was thought that, as the Russians had now come to the granary of Central Asia, the army would be independent of any other base, and that forage and provisions could be procured at even less cost than before; but the addition of even this small number of Russians has so raised the prices of all grains that in many places the culture of cotton has been abandoned for the more advantageous grain crops; and more than that, owing to the actual insufficiency of the local production, most of the grain for army use has to be brought from Vierny, Kopal, and Southern Siberia.[1]

Cultivable land in Central Asia is of two kinds; that which lies along the mountains, and is fertilised by the spring and

[1] The table immediately following of the average prices for ten years at Katta Kurgan, was compiled by Captain Grebenkin, expressed in rubles:

Year	Wheat per batman	Barley per batman	Rice per batman	Mutton per pud	Mutton Tallow per pud
1862	1 60	1 40	7 0	2 20	3 30
1863	2 40	2 0	6 40	2 40	3 60
1864	2 80	2 0	6 80	2 40	4 0
1865	2 80	2 40	7 20	2 40	4 0
1866	3 20	2 20	7 60	2 40	4 40
1867	3 20	2 40	8 0	2 40	4 40
1868	4 0	2 60	9 20	2 40	4 40
1869	3 20	2 40	9 60	2 50	4 80
1870	14 40	11 20	18 0	7 20	25 60
1871	8 0	4 0	11 20	2 80	7 20

The average prices at Samarkand for 1869, 1870, and 1871, according to Colonel Sobolef, expressed in rubles were:—

	1869	1870	1871
Wheat, per batman	4 20	0 0	8 75
Barley ,,	2 60	7 0	5 20
Flax ,,	5 40	9 20	12 80
Rice ,,	4 20	5 60	5 80
Sorghum ,,	2 60	6 40	3 80
Millet ,,	2 20	6 0	3 80
Cotton ,,	8 0	12 0	10 0
Mutton, per pud			2 73
Mutton Tallow, per pud			6 76

It must be remembered that 1870 was a year of famine in Bukhara on account of a short harvest. In Tashkent a small cake of bread which at the conquest cost one *tcheka* now costs three.

autumn rains, called *lalmi*, and that which is watered almost solely by irrigation, called *obi* or *abi*. Although the *lalmi* lands, which are the most extensive, produce, especially in favourable years, large crops of grain, and are the main reliances for feeding the population, yet the irrigated lands, on account of their richness and fertility, the constancy of their harvests, and the variety of their produce, are by far the most important to the well-being and civilisation of the country. The proper regulation of irrigation is, therefore, a matter of the greatest consequence, especially in the valley of the Zarafshan, where every drop of water has value, and where without more water there is hardly room for another inhabitant. The worth of land is estimated chiefly by the amount of water to which it has a right, and most of the law suits about lands arise out of disputes concerning water. Between Penjakent and Lake Kara-kul, where the Zarafshan terminates, there are eighty-five main canals, or *aryks*, drawn from the river, the length of which, taken together, is estimated at over 1,570 miles, without speaking of the numerous branches, smaller canals, and ditches, by which the water is drawn from the main canals for the actual irrigation of the districts and fields.

A few words will, perhaps, explain the general system. Near Penjakent a large canal, called Bulungur, turns to the right, and waters the districts of Shiraz, Sugut, and Tchilek on the northern side of the valley, being in all about seventy-five miles long. It is one of the oldest, having been dug more than 300 years ago, as legends state, by Abdullah Khan. From this another canal, called the Tuya-Tartar of which I have before spoken,[1] flowed as far as Jizakh. This was also constructed by Abdullah Khan; but as, although it made a garden in this region, it left Bukhara almost without water, it was abandoned on his death. Further down, the Dargam canal goes off to the left, watering Samarkand and the country to the south, being with its continuations nearly seventy miles long. At the base of the hill Tchupan-ata, near Samarkand, the river is divided into two parts, the Ak Darya (Darya Safit) and the Kara Darya (Darya Siya). The Ak Darya, which constitutes the main stream of the Zarafshan, and through which the most water passes, is to the northward, and after going a short

[1] On page 227.

distance is on a considerably lower plane than the Kara Darya. After about seventy miles these two branches, which are never more than eight or nine miles apart, reunite, forming an island of the greatest fertility, known under the name of Miankal—a term also extended to the whole middle course of the Zarafshan. Above Katta Kurgan the Kara Darya gives off a large canal, Nari-pai, which, after about fifty miles, flows again into the Zarafshan near Kermineh. On the Kara Darya and the Nari-pai the whole eastern part of Bukhara is entirely dependent for water.

The city of Bukhara and the districts lying north of it are watered by the Shahri-rud and other canals taken from the Zarafshan below Kermineh; nearly all that remains of the water of the Zarafshan is dissipated by other smaller canals, very little finding its way into Lake Kara-kul. If we may believe legends and chronicles, the region about Kara-kul three hundred years ago, strange as it may seem, was irrigated by water brought from the Syr Darya, and was one of the most flourishing parts of Bukhara. It is said that Abdullah Khan, annoyed by the constant wars which he had with the nomads to the north of Bukhara, resolved to free himself from their neighbourhood, and collecting an army, marched to the lower Syr Darya, or to the Yany Darya, and dammed up the canal.

At present most of the irrigated land is on the northern side of the Zarafshan valley, although a century ago the southern side was more cultivated. Owing to political revolutions one hundred and fifty years ago the northern side of the Zarafshan became almost depopulated, the inhabitants emigrating to Tashkent, Khokand or to the mountains. Those who settled in the neighbourhood of Urgut began to draw off the water for their use in that direction, and the southern side of the valley became the more populous, but with the restoration of order under Mir-Haidar the abandoned lands on the north were again cultivated, new canals were opened, and the diminished population on the southern side being unable to manage the quantity of water sent to them, some large canals were entirely closed up and nearly all the water was sent again to the north.

As for certain crops the seed must be sown in the spring, (*bogari*), and for others in the autumn (*teremai*), it is necessary to have water on the lands at several different times in the year, especially during the months of March, June, July, August, and September.[1] When the whole valley of the Zarafshan was under one rule, the distribution of the water was carefully looked after by the government, in order that the inhabitants of the upper parts, by a too plentiful use of the water, might not injure those living lower down. After the occupation of Samarkand by the Russians great complaints were received from Bukhara, especially from the districts of Ziaueddin and Khatyrtchi, that on account of the failure to renew the dams the inhabitants of these localities received no water, and were unable to cultivate the lands. A commission composed of Russians and Bukhariots was therefore appointed in the winter of 1872 to consider the question. It was found that the natives distinguished in an indefinite way three states of water in the river: high, low and middling. When the water is high there is always sufficient for Bukhara; when the water is low no precautions or measures are of any avail; but in its middle state it is necessary to take certain measures to allow the water to go on to Bukhara. To this end it is necessary, for the benefit of the inhabitants of Khatyrtchi and Ziaueddin, to keep up the practice of constructing a dam on the Ak Darya near its beginning to raise the water sufficiently high to allow it to flow through the Kara Darya; and another dam in the Kara Darya, near the mouth of the Nari-pai canal. These dams will not prevent water from going on to Bukhara; but to give the city of Bukhara and its suburbs sufficient water at the two periods of the year, May and September, when it is especially necessary, it was resolved to half-close the gates of all the canals leading from the Zarafshan in the Russian province: completely to close them would be for the Russians to ruin their own agriculture for the benefit of the Bukhariots. These dams,

---

[1] *Bogari* from *bogar*, spring, means properly the crops, for which the seed is sown in the spring; and *teremai* from *terema*, autumn, the crops produced by seed sown in the autumn; but as on *lalmi*, or rain lands, nothing but spring crops, wheat, barley, and millet, can be sown, *bogari* is sometimes used to denote the crops raised on rain lands, and *teremai* those raised on irrigated land, although including many, such as cotton, which are sown in the spring. *Ak*, white, and *kok*, green, are also used for autumn- and spring-sown crops, *ak* being also a general germ for early crops, those which have become white and ripe while others are still green.

however, are to be kept in repair at the expense of the Bukharan Government, and for that purpose the Bek of Ziaueddin with his workmen comes to Samarkand to repair them about the first of June in every year.

Most of the canals are looked after by a special officer, called a *mir-ab* (*mir* ruler, *ab* water) chosen and paid by the inhabitants who are specially benefited by him. Other subordinate officials, *banman*, are appointed to take care of the dams. The engineering skill of the natives in constructing their canals seems very great, when we remember that they have but the most elementary knowledge of hydraulics, and are totally destitute of levelling and surveying appliances. The water is brought upon the fields either directly from one of the subordinate canals, or by means of water wheels or scoops. These water wheels, which are turned either by the rapidity of the current, or by means of a water-fall, or, as frequently happens, by the labour of an ox or a horse, have fastened to their rims a large number of wooden or earthen jars, which fill from the canal, and as they reach the top pour the water into a pipe leading to the reservoir. The scoop is a large wooden shovel with a long handle, suspended by a rope to a pole leaning over the canal, and is worked by hand, the leverage of the swing being sufficient to throw the water up five or six feet. It is exactly similar to the scoop used in Russia for baling out barges. There are three methods of applying the water in tillage. For such plants as cotton and tobacco it is brought through the fields in small ditches and allowed to filter through the soil; for rice, the fields must be kept submerged for a considerable time at different periods. For lucerne and grains, where an even distribution of water is necessary, the field is usually divided into squares by small walls of earth a few inches high. When these squares are filled with water the opening from the canal is closed and the water is left to soak in.

Systems of husbandry differ somewhat with the size of the estate; small farmers, possessing only four or five acres, aiming by careful cultivation to get as much out of their land as possible, without allowing it to lie fallow too long. In general, the larger farmers pursue a modification of the three-field system. The field, after lying fallow for a year, is sown with winter wheat or barley. The next year after this crop is reaped, the land is again ploughed up and sown for the second harvest with either millet, sesame, lentils, carrots or poppies. The third year a summer crop of rice, sorghum, cotton, flax or vegetables is raised. It is usual, however, when the land has been prepared either for rice or for cotton, to sow it for two years with the same crop. Other than this general order of summer and winter crops there are no commonly received rules for the rotation of special crops. Lucerne, *jenushka—Medicago sativa*—is usually sown on the same ground for ten or twelve years, producing an abundant crop. The first year it is cut twice, yielding an average to a *tanap* of 200 to 220 bundles of an average weight of nine pounds each. The second year there will be four harvests of 200 bundles each, and from then until the eighth year the field will yield 1,000 bundles a year to a *tanap*, or about five tons to an acre. After the ninth year the lucerne is cut only three times a summer, giving each year less and less; and after the twelfth year the field is allowed to lie fallow for four years, and is then planted with sorghum, then with melons, and then for two years with winter wheat, after which it is good again for lucerne. When wheat or barley is to be sown, the field is ploughed from five to ten times by means of a rude plough composed of a small pointed share tipped with a small piece of iron. The pole is fastened so close to the root of the share that the ground is penetrated to the depth of only seven or eight inches and is very slightly turned up. Ploughing is usually done by a pair of oxen (*kosh*), and the amount of ground which one pair of oxen can work has become the unit of husbandry, so that land and estates are frequently measured by the *kosh* instead of the *tanap*, a *kosh* being generally equal to forty-eight or fifty *tanaps*, that is thirty-six or thirty-seven acres. Each *tanap* is enriched with forty or fifty loads of manure, which is ploughed in, and at each ploughing the furrows must run at right angles to the previous ones. Winter wheat and barley are sown about the middle of September and worked in with a rude harrow. Winter wheat is irrigated two or three times, barley but once, and the harvest ripens but once, about the end of May. The grain, instead of being thrashed, is trodden out by oxen or horses, and then cleaned by being tossed into the air.

Sixteen *tchariks* of wheat are used for sowing a *tanap*, and yield ordinarily a harvest of four to five *batmans*, that is fifteen or twenty fold: in most cases about thirty bushels to the acre.[1] Four kinds of wheat (*budai*), are known; of which the best are the white, similar to that of Europe, and the red, which is the most esteemed, and of which the best bread is made. The wheat of this region is frequently rendered dangerous by the admixture of some seed called *mastak*, the exact character of which has not yet been determined. Oats will not grow in Central Asia, and rye has never been cultivated until of late, when it has been raised in very small quantities for the use of the Russians. Oats, and in a great measure barley, are replaced by sorghum (*jugara*), which is considered less heating for horses, and the green stems of which are good fodder for cattle. The leaves are given to sheep and the dry stalks are used for fuel. Two to three *tchariks* of sorghum sown on a *tanap* will produce from two to three *batmans*, that is from fifty to one hundred and sixty fold. Maize is cultivated, but only in very small quantities. Millet (*taryk*), of which there are three varieties, ripens very soon, and which is for that reason used for the second crop, after winter wheat, will produce two *batmans* from five *tchariks* of seed, or about thirty fold. The culture of rice demands much more care, patience and hard labour, on account of the irrigation, than any other grain, and is generally sown only on low swampy land, or at all events in places where water is very abundant. Its ordinary return is thirty fold. In general the production of grain is hardly sufficient to support the inhabitants, and, as I have said before, will by no means feed the Russian population and troops.

About 25 per cent. of the irrigated land is sown with wheat, and about 6½ per cent. with barley. The whole produce of wheat—which is the chief staple of the food of the inhabitants on the irrigated lands in the valley of the Zarafshan, as well as in that of the Kashka Darya, in which Shahrisabs is situated—is estimated at 6,708,500 bushels, which, for the population in those valleys of about one million and a half inhabitants,

[1] Mr. Brodofsky agrees with me in this in his 'Agriculture in the Zarafshan District, Russian Turkistan,' vol. ii. p. 240, but the tax returns quoted by Soboleff give only half as much. The wheat crop in England in 1874 which was better than the average, was 32 bushels to the acre.

would be a little more than half a pound for each per day. The rain-lands in the same regions would with fair average harvests produce 31,190,000 bushels, or a little less than three pounds each per day.[1] It is therefore evident that the inhabitants of the country must depend chiefly for food on the rain-lands, and should there be little snow in winter or no rain in spring, so that the harvests on these lands should be seriously affected, the population would suffer from hunger. Experience shows too that the harvests on the rain-lands are exceedingly variable. Thus, for example, in 1862 the extensive rain-lands to the south of Katta-kurgan, called Tchul, produced 1,106,000 bushels of wheat; in 1868, 155,620; in 1870, 486; and in 1871, 12,430. In 1870 there was a very bad harvest and a famine, and although in 1871 all the conditions were propitious, the small harvest was due to the lack of seed for sowing. A bad harvest is especially felt in that part of Bukhara lying on the Zarafshan; Shahrisabs and the districts of the Kashgar Darya can always take care of themselves. In Bukhara the population is at least twice as great as that of the Russian Zarafshan district, and the amount of cultivated land, which must limit the production of wheat, is only about one quarter as great. Consequently, in the most favourable years, Bukhara is unable to feed herself, and is obliged to import grain from other districts. It is not surprising then that famines are of not infrequent occurrence. The great famine of 1770 is still remembered. In 1810-11 there was no winter, and no rain fell in the spring, wherefore the harvest on the rain-lands failed entirely, and there was such a famine that men sold their children, their sisters and mothers, and killed the old people or left them to starve. In 1835 there was another famine from the same causes, but less disastrous in its consequences, as there had been a remarkably good harvest in the preceding year. In the winter of 1869-70, there was no snow, and very little rain in the following spring, so that the wheat on the rain-lands had no sooner sprouted than it dried up. In the Katta-Kurgan district the harvest was, as I have

---

[1] I take these estimates, as well as the facts contained in the following paragraphs, from a carefully studied and highly interesting article by A. Grebenkin on the 'Causes of the Bad Harvests in Bukhara,' published in Nos. 17 and 18 of the 'Turkistan Gazette,' for the year 1872.

said, only 486 bushels, and these were collected in sheltered mountain hollows. The famine began, as the natives expected, in the province of Khuzar, where there is nothing but rain-land. Even as early as June crowds of hunger-stricken people came to Karshi and Bukhara to seek work. The price of labour fell. By August it was evident that the winter would be very severe. The *kalym* payable on marriage fell from 15*l*. and 30*l*. to 2*l*. and 3*l*., but in spite of the cheapness there were very few marriages. As the winter came on cattle and sheep began to die for want of food, for the pastures had also dried up early in the year. Two-thirds of the stock perished. The prices of grain rose to such an extent that the inhabitants of the Zarafshan district petitioned for a prohibition of the export of grain to Bukhara, on the ground that by spring there would be none left for seed, and that therefore the next year the famine would be still worse. Nevertheless the contraband export of grain continued. About January Khiva also stopped the exportation of grain, so that there was no refuge for the hungry except the upper districts of the Amu Darya or the Russian provinces. By May 1871 it became evident that there would be a plentiful harvest, and the prices of grain accordingly fell. Fortunately there were no military operations, and the deaths from starvation were therefore not so numerous as might easily have been the case.

As to the amount of grain raised in the other parts of Central Asia, I have been unable to obtain any detailed information. The reader has probably noticed that my statistics are apt to fail me at the very point where they begin to be useful and interesting. My best explanation will be perhaps to quote from a report of an official, who at one time held a high position in Turkistan.

'All that we know of the country consists of detached descriptions of different localities, and the accounts of reconnaissances made by our troops. As to the statistical information which is communicated to us from time to time by the district chiefs, it is so vague and superficial, and sometimes even so contradictory, that it would be useless to speak of it. The so-called statistical committees, instituted in the different localities of Central Asia, exist only on paper. A general Statistical Committee for Central Asia was formed in 1868, but it has not been able to fulfil its task, thanks to the perfect ignorance of the members of the local administration, who have not communicated to it the required information. In 1869, by decree of the Commander-in-Chief, statistical committees were formed in different districts. In that of the Syr Darya the committee was formed for the first time in 1870, and it addressed to the functionaries of the local administration a circular with questions on the statistics of the localities governed by them; but these questions related to details which only provoked general hilarity. The statistical information which has been presented by the district chiefs of the province of Semiretch contains, among other things, the following: "Climate, none; productive forces, unknown." Such is the extent of our knowledge about the country which we have conquered.'

Sesame, poppies, flax and hemp, are cultivated exclusively for the oil made from the seeds, although the stalks of hemp are sometimes used for the purpose of making rope. In the district of Katta-Kurgan, and in some parts of Shahrisabs, much madder is cultivated, it being found a productive and lucrative crop. Tobacco is raised in small quantities in many parts of Central Asia, but is nowhere of good quality, the best coming from Karshi and from Namangan. In the Russian possessions it is but little cultivated, except in Semiretch by the Russians.

Although, as I have before remarked, the culture of cotton has somewhat fallen off in late years on account of the rise in the price of wheat, still, as it is indispensable for the native clothing, and is in great demand for export, it continues to be one of the most important productions in the country. At the same time it is cultivated only among other things, and there is probably no agriculturist who has all of his land under cotton, few having more than thirteen or fourteen acres so planted. A field is chosen if possible with a good southern exposure, and is then manured and ploughed from six to ten times, efforts being made to turn over the ground as much as possible, as it is considered that the more the ground be worked, the better will be the harvest. After being soaked in water for a day, the seed is cast on the ground during the first two weeks of April, and then carefully harrowed, from 30 lbs. to 38 lbs. being used on an acre. If there be heavy rains after the sowing, it is usual to plough the ground up again, and resow it, as otherwise there will be no crop. When the plants are a few inches high, the ground is carefully hoed and made into hills about the plants which are carefully thinned out; and this hoeing is repeated every week or two until the flowering, two months after the sowing, when the land is watered for the first time; but then and afterwards, during the great heats, care is taken to give no more water than is necessary, as too much would injure the plants. The gathering of the bolls is done chiefly by women and children. The natives estimate the cost of the seed, of manuring, and of preparing and planting the ground, at 6 to 10 rubles a *tanap*, and of the hoeing and subsequent work at 4 to 5 rubles. As a *tanap* will yield from 1½ to 2 *batmans*, at the average price of 9 rubles a *batman*, the profit on a *tanap* will be from 5 to 8 rubles, or 18s. 3d. to 29s. 2d. per acre. The seeds are separated from the cotton by running them between two wooden rollers, moving in opposite directions. This is a primitive and very imperfect method, as, if the rollers be not very close together, many impurities and crushed seeds will pass through. To clean the cotton of dust and dirt adhering to it, it is then usually placed on mats and beaten with light rods.

At present there are about twenty-five million pounds of cotton sent every year from Central Asia to Russia, from one-fifth to one-sixth of the whole amount imported for the use of Russian manufactures.[1] It is considered in every respect to be inferior to Surat cotton, which is in still greater quantity imported into Russia. The chief reasons of the bad quality of the Central Asian cotton are the shortness (rarely two inches stretching to three), the thinness, and the weakness of the fibre, the bad way in which it is cleaned, and its admixture with so many foreign matters. No cotton-presses are used. The cotton is stuffed loosely into a large sack, and on arriving in Russia it is found that several inches of the exterior of the bale are so full of sand and dirt as to be utterly useless. The loss in this way is

---

[1] There was imported into Russia through Europe—

	1871	1872	1873
Cotton	144,083,000 lbs.	122,148,000 lbs.	122,182,000 lbs.
Twist	9,472,000 ,,	11,009,000	11,425,000 ,,

never less than 25 per cent., often 50 per cent., and on an average 35 per cent., while the loss from the worst East Indian cotton is only 18 per cent. To cure these evils it has been proposed to introduce the use of gins and presses, and the culture of better varieties of cotton. For this purpose the Government of Turkistan has proposed to establish a model cotton plantation, but the Ministry of Finance has objected to sending the necessary money until the results of the silk-school shall be known. A commission, however, has been sent by General Kauffmann to America to investigate the methods of cotton culture there employed, and to see what improvements might be introduced into Tashkent. Many efforts have already been made to ameliorate the varieties of cotton planted, and experiments have been made with American seed. The variety chosen for this purpose was 'sea-island,' but it never seemed to occur to the reformers that sea-island cotton owed its merit entirely to the fact that it was grown on islands off the sea coast, and that when sown on uplands or in the interior it lost its good qualities. The cotton planted in Tashkent and near Samarkand came up and grew beautifully, in fact it kept on growing until it reached the height of eight or nine feet, but the winter came on before any bolls had a chance to ripen.

The gardens constitute the beauty of all this land. The long rows of poplar and elm trees, the vineyards, the dark foliage of the pomegranate over the walls, transport one at once to the plains of Lombardy or of Southern France. In the early spring the outskirts of the city, and indeed the whole valley, are one mass of white and pink, with the bloom of almond and peach, of cherry and apple, of apricot and plum, which perfume the air for miles around. These gardens are the favourite dwelling-places in the summer, and well may they be. Nowhere are fruits more abundant, and of some varieties it can be said that nowhere are they better. The apricots and nectarines I think it would be impossible to surpass anywhere. These ripen in June, and from that time until winter fruit and melons are never lacking. Peaches, though smaller in size, are better in flavour than the best of England, but they are far surpassed by those of Delaware. The big blue plums of Bukhara are celebrated through the whole of Asia. The cherries are mostly small and sour. The best apples come either from

Khiva, or from Suzak, to the north of Turkistan, but the small white pears of Tashkent are excellent in their way. The quince, as with us, is cultivated only for jams or marmalades, or for flavouring soup. Besides water-melons (*tarbuz*, whence the Russian *arbuz*) there are in common cultivation ten varieties of early melons, and six varieties which ripen later, any one of which would be a good addition to our gardens. In that hot climate they are considered particularly wholesome, and form one of the principal articles of food during summer. When a man is warm or thirsty, he thinks nothing of sitting down and finishing a couple of them. An acre of land, if properly prepared, would produce in ordinary years from two to three thousand, and in very good years twice as many. Of grapes I noticed thirteen varieties, the most of them remarkably good. The Jews distil a kind of brandy from the grapes, and the Russians have begun to make wine, but all the brands which I have seen, both red and white, were harsh and strong, and far inferior even to the wines of the Crimea or of the Caucasus. Large quantities of fruit are dried, and are known in Russian commerce by the name of *izium* or *kishmish*, although the latter is only properly applied to a certain variety of grape. If the fruit were dried properly and carefully, it might become a very important article of trade, as it is naturally so sweet that it can be made into *compotes* and preserves without the addition of sugar.

The price of an acre of land of medium quality in the best parts of Zarafshan valley would be, when reduced into English currency, for gardens 7*l*. 4*s*., for vineyards 10*l*. 16*s*., for lucerne 5*l*. 8*s*., and for tillage 3*l*. 12*s*. According to the tabulated prices of 1871, such garden-lands would produce per acre a crop worth 4*l*. 6*s*., vineyards 7*l*. 12*s*., lucerne meadows 2*l*. 4*s*., and fields, if planted with wheat, 3*l*., and if with cotton, 3*l*. 12*s*. In the immediate suburbs of Samarkand, land is much dearer, an acre of garden-land selling for 14*l*. 8*s*., and producing a crop worth 7*l*. 4*s*.; an acre of vineyard-land for 18*l*., producing a crop worth 12*l*.; an acre of meadow or tillage-land 10*l*. 16*s*., producing, if sown with lucerne or wheat, 4*l*. 6*s*., and if with cotton, 3*l*.

The question of land tenure in Central Asia is one of prime

importance; firstly, because Russians are not allowed to buy land, nor is Russian colonisation permitted until there shall be some kind of a land settlement; and secondly, because in all of the projects of a land settlement which have been prepared by the Russian officials, it is openly or tacitly assumed that the fee of all the lands is vested in the State, and that therefore the government has the right to dispossess the proprietors, or to alter the tenure at its pleasure. In all this part of Central Asia there has not yet been found any trace of communal ownership, but the land tenures are governed theoretically by the same rules that prevail in all Mussulman countries, although in practice perhaps changed by certain local conditions.

By the general principles of Mussulman law, lands are of five kinds; *milk*, the property in the most absolute manner of private persons; *miriié*, public domain, or the property of the State; *mevqufe*, lands in mortmain; *metruké*, 'abandoned' land, *i.e.* land given to public uses, such as roads, streets, &c., or pastures belonging to a village or canton; and *mevat*, dead, or waste lands. *Milk*, or private property, is either *milk-ushri*, or tithe lands, lands divided among the conquerors when an infidel country has been overcome by force of arms, and paying a tax of one-tenth part of the harvest; or *milk-haradji*, lands which at such conquest were left in the possession of the non-Mussulman inhabitants, subject to the payment of an impost always more than the *ushri*, and varying from a seventh to a half of the harvest. *Milk* lands are at the entire disposition of the owner, and can be sold, given away, bequeathed, or turned into *vaqf*, or mortmain; but if the owner die without heirs, the land reverts to the government. *Miriié* lands, or the public domain, if kept by private persons, are held by them as tenants at will, the tenure passing on their death to their male descendants, to the exclusion of the female line.[1] *Mevqufe* lands, or *vaqf*, as they are more usually called in Central Asia, are such as have been given or devised to some mosque or college, or for some religious or charitable purpose either by private persons or by the State. Lands may be made

---

[1] By recent reforms the holders of *miriié* lands in Turkey are allowed to sell them with the permission of the authorities, and such lands can be inherited in the female line.

vaqf either purely for a religious or charitable purpose, or under the pretext of such purpose for the benefit of one's children or other descendants, thus forming a sort of entail. For instance, a small mosque will be built, of which the descendants of the donor shall always be the trustees, and the land will be dedicated to their support as such. *Mevat*, or waste lands, can be turned into *milk* or private property by any person who, with the consent of the government (although some schools of law think this unnecessary) reclaims, or in the phrase of the *shariat*, 'vivifies the land,' that is, irrigates, or plants it. This reclamation of waste lands, however, must take place within three years from the time of occupation, otherwise no right of property passes. Strictly speaking, the land owned by private persons in Central Asia is all *milk-haradji*, there being no *milk-ushri*, except such as under a mistaken idea was made by the Russians, because the land was not originally divided up among the conquerors, and because, as the older lawyers put it, there was no *milk-ushri* in the lands watered by the Saihun (Amu Darya) the Jaihun (Syr Darya) the Nile, Tigris and Euphrates. *Hur-halis*, another species of *milk* land, has been created in these regions, which is freed from all taxes, they having been commuted at the time of its creation, either actually, or by a legal fiction. They are also called *zar-hariti*, 'changed for gold.'

In the countries of Central Asia under native rule, the Khanate was divided into several provinces governed by Beks, who held with regard to the Amir or Khan a sort of loose feudal position. They were obliged to support part of his army, and made him large presents, and in certain matters had recourse to his superior authority, but the taxes which they collected went into their own separate treasuries, and not into that of the Khan. In every bekship, however, the Khan had lands, the revenue of which went into his own treasury, and such lands were called *amlak* lands, as distinguished from the Bek lands, and the tax-collectors subject to him, and not to the Bek, bore the name of *amlakdars*.[1] With respect to these *amlak* lands, some hold the theory that they belong to the State, and that the holders of them are only tenants of the

---

[1] The *amlak* and the *zekat* (see page 205) constituted the privy purse of the Amir.

State, and are unable without the State's permission to sell their lands. Others say that these lands are all *milk*, or the absolute property of the persons who live on them, and that they are only the property of the State in the sense that the taxes from them go to the treasury of the Khan, and not to that of the Bek; in a word, that the percentage of the harvest paid by the holder of the land is a tax, and not a rent. Whatever may be the theory, in practice these lands are the property of the persons cultivating them, for they are sold, given away, bequeathed, and turned into *vuqf* as freely as other lands, without any recourse to the government. It seems, however, unquestionable that here, as in England, the legal fiction exists that everyone in the last resort holds of the crown; but this is merely a fiction, and has no effect in practice.

The Russian officials, however, who have prepared the projects for a land settlement, advocate the view that all these lands actually belong to the State, and that the holders are all under one form and another tenants. To support this view they bring up the theory of the origin of landed property in conquest or reclamation, as laid down in the *shariat*, and the fact that when there are no heirs, the lands are claimed by the State, as well as the fact that in certain cases the enjoyment of the land is restricted. In this, however, they make an error; for they hold that the right of property is restricted or limited by certain regulations, especially those regarding irrigation. For instance, as an irrigating canal is made for the benefit of all the lands bordering it, the use of the water is subject to certain restrictions. Proprietors living near the beginning of the canal have no right to use more than their proper share of water to the detriment of those farther on. This applies particularly to rice-lands, but as it would be an expensive matter to have guards at the entrance of every man's field to prevent him from using too much water, it is found simpler to forbid the culture of rice in certain localities. This, however, is not a limitation of the right of property, it is only a limitation of the right of enjoyment, in the same way as under our laws no person has a right to maintain on his land a public nuisance, nor is he allowed to infringe the rights of his neighbours as to water privileges where there are mills, &c.; but his right of property remains intact, as he can still sell, give away, and bequeath his land as he chooses.

It is therefore now proposed, after quite ten years of occupation, during which the natives have been left in the full possession and enjoyment of their lands, and after the government has recognised this by the purchase of lands from them, that the land tenures shall be settled by the government taking possession of all of the lands, in contempt of the fact, which is admitted by all the officials, that whatever may be the theories of the law books, the customs of centuries have given to the possessors of these lands the actual rights of property in them, and by redistributing them to the inhabitants in limited quantities on the payment of a yearly rent, the non-payment of which will work the forfeiture of the lands. It is proposed suddenly to deprive a whole population of their landed property, and reduce them to the state of tenants, putting them practically in the same position as the Christian rayahs are under the Turkish government, with whose wrongs the Russian government so deeply sympathises. Absolute property is to be recognised in the land only where documents emanating from the Russian authorities have already been given for it. As to *vaqf* lands, disregarding the fact that many of them are really nothing but entailed property, and those lands which the authorities are willing to acknowledge as *milk* lands, there are two propositions. One is to leave them in the possession of the persons or institutions actually occupying them, while the lands which are underlet to other persons shall be rented to these other persons, the owners of the *vaqfs* being properly indemnified. The other proposition is that the government take all the *vaqf* lands into its actual possession, applying the revenues to religious, benevolent, and educational purposes in the districts in which the lands lie, but not necessarily to those purposes for which the *vaqfs* were created. It is claimed that the existence of so much land in mortmain is a burden on the inhabitants, and maintains a large and fanatical clerical class, which is dangerous to the peace and well-being of the State. It is also gravely proposed to found communes similar to, but not identical with, the village communes of Russia; and this in a country where communal institutions are unknown, and where they would not be consonant to the customs, feelings, or usages of the inhabitants. A forced plant like this could take no root, while its decay would poison the atmosphere. The arguments in support of these most extreme, and, as they seem to me, most unjust measures, are various and contradictory. One is that the natives would have no respect for the Russians if the government were thus to abdicate its rights, and by an uncalled-for act of beneficence grant to the natives the full right to the property which they call their own. Another is, that if the natives were confirmed in the possession of their property, they would not be willing to sell their lands to the Russians, and thus this would impede and prevent Russian colonisation; while with the same breath the supporters of the measure declare that the inhabitants will surrender all their lands for a song, and thus leave the country utterly unpopulated. Were there contests between different classes as to the ownership of lands, or were there large proprietors who had claims conflicting with those of their tenants, we might understand the proposed resettlement of the lands; but as we know that there are no large proprietors in this part of Asia, and that disputes between landlord and tenant are almost unknown, nothing as yet from the side of the inhabitants has called for any legislation on this subject, other than that which is usual in all conquered countries, of confirming to the inhabitants their rights to the property which they possess, in accordance with the laws of the preceding government. I do not know whether to ascribe these propositions to a mania for change and reform, or to an innate incapacity to understand the bases of personal liberty and of the rights of property. It is proper to say that these measures were not drawn up by statesmen, for Russian statesmen as yet have given but slight attention to the situation of affairs in the remote province of Turkistan, and all the projects for the government of that region have so far been rejected by the Council of the Empire, or have been withdrawn. They are the work of soldiers, of minor clerks who have reached responsible official positions, and of a few young men who, because they may have graduated at the Alexander Lyceum, which was founded to educate statesmen, and which is the *alma mater* of Prince Gortchakoff, imagine that from that circumstance alone they are necessarily as great statesmen as that distinguished man. The officials of Turkistan would do well to take a lesson from the land settlement of Lord Cornwallis in India, and its now acknowledged injustice and evil results, before they take such a decisive step as that proposed. Maine, in his 'Village Communities,' speaking of the English land settlements, says: 'Their earliest experiments, tried in the belief that the soil was theirs, and that any land law would be of their exclusive creation, have now passed into proverbs of maladroit management.' I am convinced that any attempt to induce the landholders of Turkistan to become tenants of the government, would be productive of the greatest discontent, and would cause the Russians such difficulties, that a far larger garrison than they have at present would be insufficient to maintain order. It must be remembered too that the appropriation of the title to the lands by the government would necessitate the intervention of another ministry, that of Crown Domains, which has as yet had little to do with Central Asia, and that although this ministry is one of the purest in Russia, a new set of officials, especially with the work they would have to do, would give additional chances of extortion and corruption.

Closely connected with land tenure, is the subject of taxes on land. At present these are of two kinds, *haradj* and *tanap*. As the *zekat*, or tax on trade, was originally a contribution for carrying on war against the infidels, the support of Islam, and the maintenance of the poor and needy, so *haradj* was a consequence of religious war, being the impost on those inhabitants who were allowed to retain possession of their lands, although now applied to all lands, Mussulman or non-Mussulman. It was of two kinds, proportional (*mekasim*), a certain part of the harvest of grain lands, and usually paid in kind; or fixed (*mudazer*), a stated sum levied on lands of fixed dimensions. In Central Asia the fixed *haradj* was usually levied on gardenlands, or orchards and meadows, and, as the unit of landmeasure was the *tanap*, it became to be known as the *tanap* tax, in distinction from the ordinary *haradj*. Under Bukharan rule the *haradj* was nominally one-fifth of the harvest, and frequently more, and it remained so in the Zarafshan valley until the spring of 1873, when just before the Khivan Expedition, in order to quiet the population, it was reduced to one-tenth, the same as it had been in the districts of the Syr Darya since the Russian occupation. Under the Bukharan administration the taxes in each of the many districts were collected by an officer called *serker*, who, with his large staff of assistants,—scribes and land-measurers,—inspected the cultivated lands during the whole summer, kept accounts of the amount under cultivation, and of the probable size of the crop, and finally after the harvest visited each thrashing-floor, and took the portion of grain falling due to the government. His salary was paid by an additional tax, *kiafsen*, which was estimated at about one-tenth of the government tax.

This system opened the way to concealment of the true harvest on the part of the inhabitants, and to a great deal of extortion on the part of the officials. The *serker* would make arrangements with the richer inhabitants, letting them off a part of their tax on receipt of a sufficient bribe[1], and exacting from the poorer proprietors much more than their due. Here is an authenticated instance which occurred under the Russian administration. On the thrashing floor of a small proprietor there were 320 lbs. of corn. The tax collector arrived and first took as his pay one quarter of it. His assistant took his usual pay,—his sleeveful,—but as he had very large sleeves for the purpose, this amounted to an eighth, or 40 lbs. The messenger of the imam also took 40 lbs., for the religious officials were by custom allowed their share. The scribe also took an eighth. The baker who accompanied the tax-collector then laid two or three small cakes on the thrashing floor and was allowed to take 20 lbs. The pipe-bearer handed to the tax collector his pipe, holding in the other a nosebag in which he was allowed to place also 20 lbs. A gipsy prostitute spread out before the *serker* a pair of new trousers and a cap, and received not only 30 lbs., but an invitation to tea as well. There remained, therefore, only 50 lbs. This was then carefully divided into five parts, one of which (10 lbs.) went to the government, while the proprietor had left an eighth of his harvest. It was remarked that in this flagrant case, the agriculturist made no complaint. In all probability he had suffered no real loss, as he had previously succeeded in concealing the greater part of his harvest.

From 1868 to 1871, as the fate of the Zarafshan valley was

---

[1] The exemption from taxes for honourable, or distinguished people—*rigaya*—is well recognised throughout Central Asia.

still undetermined, and there was an expectation of returning it to Bukhara, the native system of tax collecting was kept up. The evils of it, as carried on under Russian supervision, became at last very manifest; for it was found that the tax collectors stole a considerable part of the tax, and in 1871 they were obliged to refund more than 165,000 rubles. A change was therefore made in the method of collecting, by abolishing the greater part of the officials, and by imposing their duties on the village authorities. The receipts of taxes since that time have much improved. In other parts of Turkistan the taxes are collected by the boards of rural administration.

The *tanap* tax varied from 40 kopeks to 3 rubles and 60 kopeks per *tanap* of ground. Besides this there were some other taxes left by the Bukharan government, which continued to remain in force. The most important of these was the *kosh-pul*, a tax laid on each *kosh* of land during the reign of Shah Murad Khan, 1782-89, for the purpose of building and repairing irrigating canals.

This tax, which originally was only 40 kopeks on a *kosh*, was increased at different epochs to five and nine times that amount, and when the territory was occupied by the Russians amounted to 3 rubles and 61 kopeks.

It now goes directly into the treasury, and is no longer applied, as it should be, to purposes of irrigation. For repairs of roads, bridges, ferries, and for what in Russia are called *zemsky*, or provincial purposes, the Russians were obliged to levy another tax, which in the Zarafshan valley was fixed at 25 kopeks on each house or kibitka, amounting in all to 10,000 rubles. In the Syr Darya districts the house-tax, which is there 75 kopeks per house or kibitka, is not sufficient for the provincial needs, and it is necessary to levy another general tax, which, as I said before in speaking of Tashkent, is proportioned directly among the inhabitants.

The amounts of taxes resting primarily or ultimately on land in the Zarafshan district were in

1868	. . .	284,043 rubles
1869	. . .	408,770 ,,
1870	. . .	649,800 ,,
1871	. . .	1,190,970 ,,

In the rest of the Russian province of Turkistan, the taxes of the same character amounted to the following sums:

1868	. . .	693,970 rubles
1869	. . .	1,125,058 ,,
1870	. . .	1,416,196 ,,
1871	. . .	1,185,075 ,,

The native population in the Zarafshan district is about 281,000, and the land taxes, to say nothing of taxes of every other kind, such as the *zekat*, and trade duties, amounted in 1868 to one ruble (2s. 9d.) per head; in 1869 to one ruble and forty-five kopeks (4s.); in 1870 to two rubles and thirty-one kopeks (6s. 4d.); and in 1871 to four rubles and twenty-three kopeks (11s. 7d.). The increase in this case is more apparent than real, it being due chiefly to the better collection of the taxes rather than to their augmentation.

It is proposed, in case the land settlement should go into effect, to turn all these taxes into rent, and after dividing the land according to its returns into eight categories, to fix the average harvests and make the rent ten per cent. of their worth, which would bring in from twenty-five kopeks to five rubles a *desiatin*, or from 3d. to 5s. an acre. The *zemsky* tax would be one-tenth of that amount, and the few lands, the absolute property in which will be allowed to the natives or to Russians, being freed from the rent, will pay only the *zemsky* tax, whereby the richer portion of the community will pay no taxes at all, these all falling on the poorer agriculturists. The officials defend this arrangement on the ground of its similarity to what now exists in European Russia. They find these taxes light in comparison with those which are imposed on the Russian peasants, who sometimes have to pay in this way more than the incomes of their farms and holdings; and there is even noticeable a tone of dissatisfaction at not being able, after all the pain and cost of conquest, to grind out of the population as heavy taxes as are obtained in Russia, where the peasants are still practically fixed to the soil.[1]

One reason for this feeling is the natural annoyance felt by the Russian officials on finding that the expenditure necessary

---

[1] See the work of Colonel Sobolef, already cited, and the 'Golos,' No. 134, of 16th (28th) May, 1875.

for the government of the country so far exceeds the revenue, and that all the country which the Russians have annexed of late years is a useless acquisition, and for all practical purposes of trade and agriculture is worthless. But this subject I shall discuss more at length in the subsequent chapter.

Under all this, too, there is a lurking feeling,—which is perhaps innate in every man of a conquering race with regard to those conquered,—that the natives, even in their own country, have no rights, and that admitting and granting them are acts of a pure, if not self-injurious, liberality. Such a feeling has been very noticeable in the ideas expressed by the Russians with regard to trade.

CHAPTER VIII.

HODJENT AND KURAMA.

Rencontre at Jizakh—Zamin—Ura-tepé—Peak of Altyn-bishik—Nau—Hodjent—Its situation—Defence against the Khokandians—Coal mines—Lead—Gold—Naphtha—Exaggerated accounts of mineral wealth—Bridge over Syr Darya—Prefect's residence—Population of Kurama—Stock-raising—Climate of Central Asia—Earthquakes—The Calendars—Agricultural solar year—Zodiacal months—Their Chaldæan origin—The Kirghiz Calendar derived from the Mongol—The Twelve-year Cycle.

At last I left Samarkand one evening, and the next day at noon found myself at Jizakh, where I was told that horses were already waiting for me. I had mentioned in Samarkand, that I should be glad, if possible, to make a detour to Hodjent, and as the road thither from Jizakh was not a post road, the Prefect of Samarkand had been kind enough to send on a message that horses should be prepared for me all along the line.

While I was in the midst of an improvised breakfast, a thick-set Cossack officer dropped into the post-station, nominally to look at the wares of a commercial traveller who had fixed himself there for a day or two, but really I think to inspect me. I found out that he was the commandant of the place, but as he himself did not choose to inform me of his rank, I pretended ignorance and answered his questions, which out of politeness he addressed to me in French, as indifferently as I could. I came near laughing when he put, as he thought, some rather adroit inquiries about the movements of MacGahan, whom he evidently supposed to be an English spy, and when he tried to find out whether I had ever seen or heard of him, and whether it was not true that he had travelled in my company. I do not think, however, that he got very much satisfaction. I learned afterwards that on that very day, or the next, he started off with a troop of Cossacks in pursuit of MacGahan, having just received orders to that effect. As I had then heard nothing from MacGahan since he had left me at Perovsky, I do not think that, had I desired, I could have afforded this worthy officer any information to guide him on his road.

Turning south-east towards the mountains, we went along what seemed a good country road, through a well-cultivated region partly irrigated from the mountain streams, but chiefly composed of rain-lands on the hill slopes. The path of the moisture was visible in the steppe by the profusion of flowers, and even the drier portions were covered with capers, yellow larkspurs, and clumps of yucca. Far up on the mountain-sides we could see *yailaks*, or summer encampments of Uzbeks, and flocks and herds. After changing horses twice and driving at a fast pace about forty miles we reached Zamin, now a small town of only twenty houses, at the foot of the large dilapidated citadel which still frowns upon it from a high mound. It was formerly the residence of a Bek more or less dependent upon Ura-tepé. On this by-road travellers were evidently of rare occurrence, and I was probably mistaken for some Russian official, for all the inhabitants turned out to see me, received me with great respect, and showed me to a platform in front of one of the houses which had been prepared for my reception with rugs and pillows. I was no sooner seated than the aksakals of the village came to pay their respects, bringing with them trays of fruits and sweets. After walking up and down the one street which constitutes the town, and then dining, we set out again, but after about an hour's drive the daylight suddenly changed into darkness, and the inexperienced drivers missed their road. At first we did not notice it, but we soon began bumping over uneven ground, and finally brought up in a dry ditch, when we perceived that we were lost. Lighting our lanterns we found that no damage had yet been done, but as no one had any idea how far we were from the road, or in which direction it lay, we resolved to remain there until morning. While we were still discussing and endeavouring to put the best face on the matter some Kirghiz came up, having probably been attracted by our light, and set to work to find the road for us. How they found it I do not know, but they walked about for some time closely examining the ground, and even I think smelling it, sometimes lying flat to discover some traces. At last they told us to start, and moving on with great caution we soon came again to the road, although at a very different place from that at which we had left it. We were still reflecting on the wonderful instinct of the Kirghiz in setting us right, when we reached the hamlet of Sabat, where we waited for daylight, and arrived at Ura-tepé at 10 o'clock in the morning.

At the station some message was given to the driver, and I was taken to a large comfortable house, which, as I afterwards understood, belonged to a Russian officer who was then absent on the Khivan campaign, and which was placed at my disposition while I stayed there. At the time, however, I could find out nothing,—neither to whom the house belonged, nor who was its occupant, nor in what light I was considered. I had a vague impression that I was being billeted upon some one by superior order, and that I might be putting him to inconvenience, which made my position very awkward and caused me to hasten my departure. Soon after the commandant came in full uniform to make a formal call and invited me to breakfast, but yet vouchsafed no explanation. His official residence was on the side of a steep hill opposite the town, and above it were the crumbling walls of the old citadel, one of the strongest in Central Asia, now occupied by but a few Russian soldiers. From here I think you get the finest town view in Central Asia. At the bottom of the hill is a little stream, now narrowed, and dammed, and spanned by bridges, hemmed in on each side by walls and houses, now flowing through many channels over a wide gravelly bed. Above it the flat roofs rise terrace-like on the hill side, broken occasionally by a dome or cupola and surmounted by the long decorated façade of the college of Rustam Bek, which was built some thirty years ago in imitation of the Shir-dar at Samarkand. The town is full of gardens, and tall trees rise up everywhere between the houses, thus taking off that dead grey colour of dirt which so wearies the eye in all Asiatic towns. Gardens and green fields stretch far up the hill side, and beyond these are the ridges of other low hills, and finally the two chains of the Turkistan and Zarafshan mountains with their many snow-capped peaks. To the south-east these mountains grow higher until they culminate in the sharply outlined pyramidal mass of the Altyn-Bishik, the summit of which is always clearly illuminated by the sun. This is the highest of the three peaks of Abdu-Baisher (20,000 feet), and to account for its name the natives tell the following legend. A rich Tadjik in Hodjent had had several children, but they had all died young. At last, when a son was born, his wife consulted a witch as to the fate of the child, and was told that up to the age of sixteen the boy would be liable to die from the bite of a tarantula. The father, wishing to ward off this danger, and knowing that in high places where it is cold there are no tarantulas, scorpions, or serpents, took his son to the very top of the mountain, and set his cradle there. All went well for a time. The boy grew up strong and well in the fresh air of the mountain. At last his sixteenth birthday came, and the parents made a great feast on the mountain-top. When the festivity was at height the youth cried, fell down and died. The attendants then found an immense tarantula which had been hidden in a basket of grapes, and had thus worked the will of the fates, for the sixteen years had not yet been fully completed. The youth was buried on the mountain-top, and, in pity of the mourning parents a large cloud came and covered them and their dead child with snow, which sank down into the valleys of the mountain, while the rocky ribs stood out strong and black, as though in mourning. From that time the snow has never left it, but clouds no longer touch it, and every day, in remembrance of the past when it shone on the cradle of the boy, the sun comes to gild it with its rays.

I wandered for a long time through the curious winding bazaar of Ura-tepé, particularly attracted by the green riding boots studded with silver nails, and the large wooden *sabots*, each on three stout wooden feet, into the ends of which were driven nails. These are worn by the Galtchas from the mountains and from Karategin, who frequently come down to this bazaar. I visited the college of Rustam Bek, and the old mosque of Abdullatif, which I found without special interest, and far more beautiful in the distance than near at hand, and then returned to the bazaar, where I would willingly have lingered,—for the inhabitants were all kind and well disposed, and inclined to conversation,—had not a rain storm driven me home.

Ura-tepé, the ancient Usrushna (Oshrusene and Satrushna),[1] was in the old times an appanage of Fergana, but was frequently for a time independent, and during the present century has been a constant apple of discord between Khokand and Bukhara. Its recent history, as related by its last Bek, Abul Gaffar, was a yearly succession of broils, rebellions, campaigns, sieges, and family murders; but still, throughout it all, whether under the dominion of Khokand, Tashkent, Hodjent or Bukhara, Abul Gaffar's family succeeded, in spite of temporary disasters, in maintaining its hereditary right to rule. The battle of Irjar in 1866 broke the power of Bukhara, and led to the fall of Hodjent. It was not, however, until four months later, that in consequence of the hitch in the negotiations with the Amir, a detachment was sent against Ura-tepé, which, after much difficult work, succeeded in establishing batteries. The citadel was finally taken by assault on October 14, after a siege of eight days, and a hard struggle of an hour and a half. Abul Gaffar Bek, and most of the garrison, managed to escape to the mountains, but the retreat of many of them was cut off, and the hundreds of corpses which were found during the next few days showed how many of the defenders had perished in their flight. Besides many prisoners, the Russians took 15 cannon and 4 standards, but lost 3 officers and 200 soldiers killed and wounded. Since that time Ura-tepé has been peaceful enough, and although a town of more than 10,000 inhabitants, has required but a very small garrison.

Four hours' fast driving brought us to the little town of Nau, which, instead of being the fortress I supposed, is only an insignificant collection of houses well situated in a pretty country. At the post-station they were expecting us, and had prepared a room for us, and we had no sooner taken possession of it, than the *aksakals* presented themselves with a deputation from the town. The rain which we had met at Ura-tepé overtook us again here, lasted all night, and accompanied us to Hodjent in the morning. Everyone assured me that it was a most unusual circumstance, as in the summer there was rarely

---

[1] An interesting discussion on the primitive form of this word will be found in Mr. P. Lerch's valuable paper on the 'Coins of the Bukhar-Khudats,' p. 78, ff.

any rain at all. Perhaps the summer of 1873 was an unusual one, for this was not the only time I met with a pouring rain.

The approach to Hodjent was very pretty. The road all the way from Nau lay between gardens and fields, and I noticed here that the clay walls, instead of being high and completely shutting out the view, were low, and merely intended to keep out the cattle. This added greatly to the charm of the landscape. The fields, however,—which in the immediate vicinity of Hodjent were either cotton plantations or vineyards,—had each two or three towers or observatories, from which the guardians could see the approach of marauders. The mulberry trees along the walls had been stripped of all their branches to feed the silkworms, so that they looked like so many dead trunks. When we reached the gate of Hodjent, we were met by two *jigits*, who accompanied us to the house of the judge, on whom we were billeted. Here I was able to understand the conditions on which I was received, but they were not calculated to render my stay more pleasant, and I therefore hastened my departure. I was neither a guest nor a stranger; that is, I was never allowed to pay for my lodging or for my provisions, nor was I received as a guest of the family, but certain rooms were set apart for me, and everything which I wanted was placed at my disposition. In fact, I was quartered on the owner of the house, who in this case was the judge, and who probably was only too glad to get rid of me. Curiously enough a year later, while on an official visit of investigation to Ura-tepé, he was murdered by the officer on whom I was quartered in that place, who, it seems, saw no other method to relieve himself from the accusations brought against him.[1] The prefect, Baron Nolde, a Swede from the Baltic provinces, who had been educated at the University of Dorpat, received me very kindly, and had me shown the bazaar, under an escort of *aksakals*, interpreters, and *jigits*. I visited some mosques and some schools, made the acquaintance of some Kazis, and rode through the bazaar; but even had there

---

[1] This officer was tried and found guilty of premeditated assassination, and was sentenced to the mines in Siberia. Family influence, however, at St. Petersburg, procured a delay in carrying the sentence into execution, and General Kaufmann, on returning to Tashkent in 1875, at once released him, and the next day invited him to dine—much to the scandal of the law-abiding inhabitants.

not been a pouring rain, my suite was too large for either amusement or inquiry. Subsequently, on going to Khokand, I remained in Hodjent several days, and had a better opportunity to make myself acquainted with that place.

Hodjent has a pleasanter air than almost any other Central Asiatic city, due, I think, in part to its situation on the river bank, and in part to the sociable and pleasure-loving character of its inhabitants, for by far the majority of them are Tadjiks. In being so close to the river, Hodjent is an exception to most Asiatic cities, but the native town was never exactly on the shore, the intervening space having been since filled up by the Russians, a small colony of whom is stretched along the bank with bathing houses and washing places below. The bank being high, the river is of no use whatever to the town, which receives its water supply from the little stream of Hodja Bakargan. Towards the end of summer, this stream frequently dries up, and the city then often suffers for want of water, there being no pumping-machines to furnish water from the river for the gardens and houses. The distress from lack of water is greatly intensified by the heat. Just across the Syr Darya is a high rocky hill, called Mogul-tau, which, absorbing the sun's rays all day long, gives out heat like a furnace, whenever the wind blows from the north. In one corner of the town, not far from the river, is the old citadel, built on an artificial square mound, a hundred feet or more in height. A steep path and staircase give access to the fort, from the top of which is obtained a magnificent view of the surrounding country, and of the distant mountains. I hardly know whether the mound is even solid, on account of the hollow sounds heard in many places, and suspect that the whole thing is a wooden framework only half filled in with earth. Indeed there is a story that two or three soldiers once fell through the floor, and were never more heard of.

The bazaar is large in proportion to the size of the city (30,000 inhabitants), and although no great trade is carried on there in any specialty, it is yet an exceedingly interesting place for studying the life of the community.[1]

---

[1] Baber, in describing Hodjent, says:—' This is a very ancient city. Sheik Maslehet and Hodja Kemal were of Hodjent. Its fruits are very good, particularly its pomegranates, which are so celebrated that the apples of Samarkand and

Hodjent, being on the direct road from Khokand to Bukhara, was at one time a place of considerable commercial importance, for all the trade of the two countries passed through it. Since the Russian occupation, this trade has been in a great measure obstructed, and being in part contraband, has been obliged to seek byways, so that the importance of Hodjent has fallen off.

A HODJENT MERCHANT.

Being at the same time a city of some importance in itself, it was always an apple of discord between Khokand and Bukhara,

the pomegranates of Hodjent have passed into a proverb; but excellent as the latter are, they are greatly excelled at present by the pomegranates of Marghinan. The fortress of Hodjent is situated on an eminence, having on the north the river and although having for ages belonged to Khokand, was frequently captured and held for a time by the Bukharans. When the Amir of Bukhara assisted Khudayar Khan to remount his throne in 1864, he retained Hodjent in his possession, refusing to give it up, and still nominally ruled it, although it had been abandoned by his troops, when the Russians under General Romanofsky took it by storm on June 5, 1866, after the defeat of the Bukharan army at Irjar. As the inhabitants of Hodjent were left entirely to themselves, and had not had time to put the city in a good state of defence, and were unsupported by Bukharan troops, although bands of Khokandians were scouring the neighbourhood, and endeavouring to send in the country people to fight, its capture did not cost as much effort as it otherwise might have done. Still the Russian loss was comparatively heavy, for there were 5 killed, 6 missing, and 122 wounded.

In 1872 Hodjent was the scene of a riot, growing out of the general dissatisfaction with the Russian rule, which had to be quelled by the troops, and in 1875 it played an important part in the war with Khokand.

The Khan had taken flight, and the Russian troops were preparing to punish the rebels, but it was not supposed that they themselves would take the offensive, when on August 20 news was received of the proximity to the town of large bodies of Khokandians. This intelligence caused Baron Nolde, the commandant, to be a little more on his guard, and small detachments were stationed outside the gates and at the bridge. During the night, there was an attack upon the gardens of the District command, but it was apparently made only by marauders, who were easily driven off. At daybreak, however, the Khokandians, in great numbers, attacked the city at three points at once: on the Khokand road, at the Nau gates, on the road leading to Ura-tepé and Samarkand, and at the bridge.

Seihun, which flows past at the distance of about a bow-shot. On the north of the fort and of the river Seihun there is a hill, which is named Myoghil, where they say that there are turquoise and other mines. In this hill there are many serpents. Hodjent is a good sporting country; the white deer, the mountain goat, the stag, the fowl of the desert, and the hare, are found in great plenty; but the air is extremely noisome, and inflammations of the eyes are common; insomuch that they say that even the very sparrows have inflammation in the eyes. This badness of the air they ascribe to the hill on the north.'

The first attack was made on the Khokand road, where the Russians had only a single company of infantry, and forty Cossacks, but after the alarm, these were reinforced by two other companies and four guns, and the command was given to Colonel Savrimovitch, who immediately advanced and repelled the enemy,—who were estimated at 10,000 men,—far beyond the gardens. At the same time a large body of Khokandians appeared on the other side of the river, which they had crossed higher up, and made an attack on the bridge, of the importance of which Abdurrahman Aftobatcha, the head of the rebels, and who was in personal command at the attack on the city, was fully aware. On the other side of the bridge there was posted only a single company of sharpshooters, under the command of an ensign with no artillery; and this small detachment bore the brunt of the attack of this immense mass of the enemy for two hours and a half, until another company and two guns could be sent out. Both companies then opened front and advanced, and a few rounds of shot soon compelled the enemy to retreat from the bridge. At the Nau gate the fighting was much harder. Before the Russian forces had come up, the Khokandians, who had occupied all the surrounding heights in great numbers, had succeeded in getting possession of the gates, and it was only after a sharp hand-to-hand fight that the Russians managed to drive them off, and to retake the gate. Desultory firing was kept up all day at this point, as well as on the Khokand road, but towards evening the enemy retreated. Matters then began to look very serious, and an order was given by Baron Nolde, that the Russian families should take refuge in the fortress, he himself, it is said, first setting the example, while all the old soldiers, and all the able-bodied merchants, were armed and enrolled into a company of volunteers. That evening the besieged were agreeably surprised by the arrival of fourteen workmen from the glass works of Isaieff at Digmai, a place some nine miles off in the hills. They reported that the Khokandians, joined by the inhabitants of the village, had made an attack upon the works, and before they had had a chance of organising themselves, had captured two men and three women. The rest shut themselves up in a single room, and were intending to defend their lives to the last, when the Khokandians set fire to the building. They then jumped out of the window into the midst of the crowd, and dealt blows right and left. The Khokandians were so astonished by this sudden onset, that they gave way, and the men, by a few shots, were able to keep them at a distance, and make their way to Hodjent. The next day a company of the second battalion arrived from Ura-tepé, having kept up a running fight all the way from Nau. This place was captured by the Khokandians, and three or four Russians living there, including the station-master, were murdered outright, or carried off as prisoners. That day there was another attack on the gate, and an attempt to bring about a general fight on the Khokand road, but Colonel Savrimovitch drove the enemy back to the hills. On Monday the 23rd, the Khokandians again made an attack on the bridge from the opposite bank of the river. Two companies of infantry and two guns were sent out against them, and after a little brush, put them to flight, but could not pursue them, having no cavalry. The situation of the besieged had become very difficult. They had but few troops, and these had constantly to be moved about from one end of the town to the other, and were always in a state of alarm. They had received no news from Tashkent, although they had every reason to believe that troops were advancing. At the same time, if these troops should be slow on their march, the great masses of the enemy, although bad fighters, might succeed in tiring them all out, and they might in the end be compelled to submit to the loss of the town, and to shut themselves up in the citadel. It was therefore resolved to take the offensive, and to advance on the village of Kostakoz, where the main body of the Khokandians of 15,000 men was known to be. Two columns under Colonel Savrimovitch and Colonel Yefremof, marched at day break. Colonel Savrimovitch met the enemy's forces close to the town, and, repulsing them by a cannonade, pursued them as far as Kostakoz, where there was a severe fight, the whole contest lasting from 5 30 in the morning until noon. The enemy's loss, which was supposed to have been large, was not exactly known, as they had time to carry off their dead. Colonel Yefremof broke the retreat of the Khokandians at Ispissar, and threw them back to the Syr Darya. During the day a Russian ensign, who with a companion had been made prisoner at a station on the Tashkent road, was sent back under guard, bearing a summons from the Khokandians to the Russians to turn Mussulmans, who promised them on that condition permission to leave the country with their families and property. That night the first battalion of sharpshooters and four cannon arrived from Tashkent. This relieved the town from all danger. Everything returned to its usual quiet, and the next day the Russian families returned to their houses from the fortress.

It is a curious incident of this siege that before it began, Mullah Maaruf, the Bek of Makhram, passed a day and a night in the town in disguise. It was well known among the natives, but no one told the Russians. When General Kaufmann arrived, he reproached Baron Nolde with his cowardice, and a Commission was appointed to judge him for abandoning his post. But at the end of the campaign this was all forgotten. This Commission, as well as another investigating charges of extortion and corruption, was dismissed; and Baron Nolde received a gold-mounted sabre, with the inscription 'For Bravery,' and was presented for the cross of St. George.

Twenty-five miles to the south of Hodjent, at Kokine-sai, are some coal mines belonging to Colonel Fovitsky, which are still worked to some extent in spite of the difficulties of transporting the coal through the mountains, its consequent high price, and the small quantity which is used. The question of coal supply is one of great importance for the development of this region, as at present almost the only fuel used by the Russians is wood derived from the fruit and mulberry trees, which results in the destruction of the gardens. Even before the capture of Tashkent Lieutenant-Colonel Tatarinof was sent to seek for coal, and discovered some layers of it in the neighbourhood of Tchimkent. Since that time the Government has spared neither money nor pains to discover good coal fields. It seems however, that the ideas as to the mineral wealth of Turkistan are as delusive as are those of its agricultural or commercial importance. A small seam of coal was found near Hodjakent, about fifty miles from Tashkent, but it was difficult to work, and the coal was of poor quality. It cost, delivered at Tashkent, twenty-five kopeks per *pud*, and although seven kopeks cheaper than the Tatarinof coal, was, owing to its inferior quality, much less economical for heating purposes. An effort was made in Tashkent to accustom the natives to the use of coal by distributing it to them gratuitously; but they were either suspicious of this, or were satisfied with the small fires which they made of wood and dung, and could not be prevailed upon to use it to any extent. The Tatarinof coal field is on the upper part of the Boroldai, at fifty miles from Tchimkent, 134 miles from Tashkent, and at an equal distance from the landing on the Syr Darya at the mouth of the Arys. These mines were worked for a time at Government expense. In 1868 2,900,000 lbs. were obtained from these mines, of which 1,620,000 lbs. were furnished to vessels of the Aral flotilla. In 1869 3,216,000 lbs. were obtained, but the consumption by the Aral flotilla was less, being only 1,440,000 lbs. while 360,000 lbs. were sent to Tashkent. The consumption, and therefore the quantity dug up, from this time diminished, and the working of the mines has now ceased, after having cost the Government a considerable sum of money. The product of Colonel Fovitsky's mine increased from 100,000 lbs. in 1868 to 1,400,000 lbs. in 1871, the work being carried on only about three months during the year. The number of workmen employed varied from 1,150 to 1,750. The actual cost of the coal in 1871 was $5\frac{1}{2}$ kopeks ($2d.$) per pud of 36 lbs. Its transport to Hodjent cost twelve kopeks ($4d.$), and to Uratepé twenty kopeks ($5d.$).

In 1874, Professor Romanofsky, of the Imperial School of Mines, was sent on a tour of investigation through Turkistan. His reports to General Kaufman give a very bad show for the mineral wealth of the country. In respect to coal his conclusions are substantially the following.

In the mountains of Kara-tau, although only in the south eastern part, there appear the upper strata of the carboniferous period, that is carboniferous limestone (*bergkalk*), but there is no appearance of the lower or true coal-producing strata. The coal found in the districts of Hodjent, Kurama and Tchimkent does not belong to the oldest carboniferous strata, but to that of the Jurassic period, being brown coal, and is usually found in the upper parts of small side valleys in the mountains in small separated fields, lying in places which it is impossible to reach with vehicles. The coal is useful only for fuel and for smith work, but is utterly useless for metallurgic operations which require a strong heat, as, for instance, the reduction of iron ore. The coal fields at present discovered cannot be profitably worked for the following reasons: the friability of the coal; the difficulty of its transport through the mountains; and the small size of the coal fields, which are of a bad quality at the edges, and are much broken up by veins of rock, as, for example, the mines of Tatarinof, which on this account are not worth further working; the uncertain character of the deposit in extent and thickness. Geological investigations show that it is useless to work coal fields situated at the tops of the mountains, or in deep valleys and ravines, on account of their small size and the uneven distribution of the coal. These islands of the coal formation are probably parts of a great coal field which extends throughout the valley of the Syr Darya, and have been elevated to their present positions by the convulsions of nature which formed the mountain ranges. It is probable that the coal fields lie immediately under the tertiary limestones, the clays containing remains of fossil molluscs and the calcareous sandstones. It is likely that good localities for coal would be found (1) in the valley of Bebalma, twenty miles south of Hodjent, (2) twenty miles north-north-west of Tashkent, and three or four miles north-west of the village of Kaplan-bek; (3) in the valley fifteen to twenty-five miles north-east of the station Akjar (twenty miles from Tashkent), and (4) on the right bank of the river Sasyk opposite the limestone mountains Aktash, five or six miles north-north-west of Tchimkent. In these places the upper strata of the tertiary have disappeared, and it would only be necessary to bore through the lower tertiary strata, which are of an indeterminate thickness, in order to reach the strata which Mr. Romanofsky surmises are carboniferous.

The boring necessary to ascertain the truth of this theory of the existence of a large coal field in the basin of the Syr Darya would entail considerable expense. Reports had been made of the existence of coal and coal shales not far from Samarkand, but Mr. Romanofsky, on going to the places indicated, was unable to perceive any trace of them.

The richest mineral is lead ore; and in the Kara-tau mountains, on the Kon-kia river near Turkistan, there are lead mines which have long been worked by the natives. The most flourishing period was during the Russian advance in Central Asia, when it became necessary for the Khokandian Government to strain every nerve for defence. The work was conducted with great waste. Surface ore was taken and then only the softest and richest, and this was smelted in such a way as to leave fully thirty-one per cent. of metal in the slag. After the Russian occupation the natives found it unprofitable longer to work these mines, and sold them to the merchant Pervushin. From this ore, which is very rich, being a mixture of galena with white lead ore, Mr. Pervushin in 1869 smelted out about 11,000 lbs. while the Kirghiz by their primitive method smelted but 3,200 lbs. The work at these mines, which was somewhat difficult, has now stopped. At Karamazar, in the district of Kurama, twenty miles north-east of Hodjent, there are several parallel veins of very pure galena. An investigation of these was made by Mr. Romanofsky, and he estimated that if fuel could be obtained at not more than twenty kopeks per pud, and there could be guaranteed a yearly sale of 28,500 puds at one ruble and a half per pud for twenty-four years, it would be possible to work these mines at a profit of 48,470 rubles a year; but during the first three years it would be necessary to spend on the mines 88,500 rubles, and after that 35,500 rubles a year. Red and brown iron ores and iron ochre are often found, as well as traces of copper ore in the form of green copper in mountainous localities. It is impossible, however, to work them, in consequence of the difficulty of access to the places where the ore is found, and to the absence of any suitable fuel.

Gold is found in very minute quantities in the Upper Zarafshan, as well as on the Upper Tchirtchik, but not in quantities sufficient to pay for working. It was in consequence of the rumours of the abundance of gold on the Amu Darya that Peter the Great made his movement toward Central Asia, by sending Prince Bekovitch-Tcherkaski to Khiva in order to ascend the Amu Darya, and Captain Buchholtz through southern Siberia to Irketi or Yarkand. Buchholtz never penetrated to Yarkand, but succeeded in establishing the Russian power on the middle Irtysh.

Near the lead mines of Karamazar, as well as in one or two other localities not far from Hodjent, turquoises have been discovered, but so far only those have been found which lie on the surface and are of a greenish hue, although it is deemed possible that by following these veins to a greater depth pure turquoises of real value might be discovered. Near Samgar, to the north-east of Hodjent, there are mines of rock salt which were formerly worked. Possibly boring might lay bare new veins.

About twenty-five miles from Namangan at Mai-Bulak, (oil-spring) there are abundant springs of naphtha, which have evidently long been worked both by Kalmuks and Kirghiz, who have even been able to prepare asphalt from the naphtha. By means of the river, naphtha from these wells could easily be sent to Hodjent, if not to Tashkent, in quantities far surpassing any present demand. The merchant Feodorof obtained a concession for working these wells from the Khan of Khohand on payment of ten per cent. as duty, but as far as I can learn work has not yet been begun there.[1]

On leaving Hodjent we were obliged to cross the Syr Darya in a large boat. A wooden bridge was at that time being constructed by a Mr. Flavitsky, a retired artillery officer, and is now finished and opened to traffic. This gentleman succeeded in making a contract with the authorities, by which the ferry tolls during the construction of the bridge, and the bridge tolls, for thirty years, were made over to him.

In the steppes and gravelly plains of this part of the Syr Darya there are enormous lizards (*Stellio Lehmanni*), two of which I saw in captivity at Hodjent. They were about four feet long, of a dark greyish brown colour, and greatly resembling a small crocodile, except that the jaws were much shorter. They seemed to be quite harmless, and their owner was unable to ascertain on what they lived. He had had several of them, and after keeping them two or three weeks, they always disappeared; whether they died, or ran away, he was unable to tell. After making three stations through a hilly country and an elevated steppe, we descended into the lowlands, watered by the Angren (or Agengeran) and Tchirtchik, with their numerous branches and irrigating canals. The fields,

---

[1] After what I have stated above, it is perhaps hardly necessary for me to say that the account of the mineral wealth Central Asia in the 'Geographical Magazine' for January, 1875, based on the exaggerated reports of Mr. Feodorof, a mining speculator, must be taken with some allowances.

which were chiefly planted with rice, were everywhere covered with water, and besides that, there were great overflows from the rivers. At this time of year, the end of May, the roads were detestable, and we had at times great difficulty in getting through the marshy land. Once we were detained an hour in crossing a small canal not more than fifteen feet wide, where a bridge had been carried away. The post-horses were unruly, and we had at last to send to a neighbouring village on the other side for the aksakal, who furnished us with horses and men to get the carriage across. A few miles further, and we came to the town of Piskent (also Biskent and Pskent), situatd on a high steep river bank. Many of the houses and balconies projected over the bank, supported by beams; and I can imagine that the palace of Baber's father at Akhsi was built in this way over the Syr Darya, when he was precipitated into the river with his pigeon-house and all his pigeons. Piskent is a thriving little town, chiefly noted for the immorality of its inhabitants, and for being the birth-place of Yakub Khan, the Amir of Kashgar, one of whose wives and many of whose relatives still reside there. We went on through a small fertile country, seeing peasants everywhere ploughing and harrowing their fields, until we arrived at the main river Tchirtchik, which we had great difficulty in crossing. It here divides into seven or eight branches, some of which are four or five feet deep, and the current is always very rapid. Guards of Kirghiz are stationed here with carts to assist travellers over the streams. It has long been the aim of the Russians to facilitate communication by building a bridge over this river, but the difficulties have been very great.

The history of this bridge is a singular one. The rich and influential natives petitioned the governor to allow them to construct a bridge at this point. Permission was at first given, but subsequently one of the Russian engineers handed in a proposition to construct the bridge at the expense of the treasury. He estimated the cost at 42,000 rubles. The permission was then withdrawn from the natives, on the ground that they had not the necessary technical knowledge, and the matter was given to a specialist, who seemed to have even less. What he constructed in one summer was carried away by the floods of the next spring, and he demanded 9,000 rubles more. This was insufficient, and still more was paid, when the bridge was again carried away. Up to the autumn of 1874, 65,000 rubles had been spent on the bridge, and it is even yet incomplete.[1]

On the other side of the Tchirtchik is Kuiluk, a small village but the residence of the Prefect of the district of Kurama. He has here a fine house, almost a palace, with large gardens and well-kept grounds, which he makes no pretence of keeping up on his salary of 2,400 rubles. All this and much more is provided for him out of the district funds, although by virtue of what law it would be difficult to ascertain. The funds for this and for similar purposes are supposed to be freely voted by the representatives of the inhabitants; but they, while nominally elected, are in reality appointed by the prefect, or by his creatures, and they are given from time to time documents and resolutions written in Russian, to which they are ordered to put their seals or signatures. These papers are seldom if ever translated to them, although an explanation of some sort may be given. To avoid any possible difficulty in the future, however, the official interpreter, when he has time, writes a translation in Turki on the opposite page of the record book.

This region is the district of Kurama, and it is the richest and most populous after that of the Zarafshan. Besides pure Uzbeks and Kirghiz, a great part of the population is of a mixed breed of uncertain origin, called Kurama. The natives say that this country was settled by fragments and deserters of all the tribes which formerly inhabited Central Asia.

The quantity of land irrigated by the Angren and the Tchirtchik is at best but limited, and a large portion of the inhabitants therefore devote themselves to stock raising. It is not customary here to stable the cattle for the winter, or to provide them with hay. For the winter pasture a place must therefore be chosen where the wind is not too violent, so that the cattle may not suffer from the cold, and where the snow does not lie too deep to prevent them from finding the stubble and the young grass underneath. The horses are sent out first of all, because with their hard hoofs they remove the snow so much better. They are followed by the horned cattle,

---

[1] See 'Golos,' September 24 (October 6), 1874.

by the sheep, and then by the camels. The best wintering places are along the banks of the Syr Darya, or in the north-eastern part of the district in the upper regions of the river Keles, which are excellent pasture grounds in summer. It is estimated that in the district of Kurama there are 33,000 camels, 60,000 horses, 53,000 cattle, and about 700,000 sheep; but these figures are probably very much less than the real ones, for although in 1870, on account of the extreme heat in the summer, and the sudden cold in the winter, there was great mortality among the cattle,—more than 250,000 head perished,—it did not seem to produce any appreciable effect upon the well-being of the inhabitants. At the average prices of 3 rubles for a sheep, 15 rubles for a horned beast, 30 rubles for a horse, and 50 rubles for a camel, the value of the live stock, according to these figures in the district of Kurama, would be 6,300,000 rubles (863,000*l.*)

The sheep are either with *kurdiuks* and without tails, or with tails and without *kurdiuks*. In Bukhara there is another breed of sheep, somewhat smaller, with grey wool, called *Arabi* (Arabian). The *kurdiuk* is a protuberance of pure fat growing out of the rump, and is sometimes very large; but the stories about sheep having such fat tails as to be obliged to carry them on wheels, is an exaggeration of some story-teller, coming down, like all Joe Millers, from most ancient times. One day I made the Kushbegi of Bukhara laugh heartily at this story, which had been gravely related by one of my predecessors.

Until 1873 no regular system of meteorological observations had been undertaken in Central Asia, and it is therefore difficult to obtain accurate information with regard to the climate. Private observers, however, have kept registers of the temperature in various places, and from these it is possible to obtain some general ideas of it. In general the climate, especially in the northern zone, is to a marked extent what is called 'continental,' that is, having extreme heat in summer, and extreme cold in winter. Roughly speaking, the territory of the district of Turkistan may be divided into four climatic zones.

The *northern zone*, extending south about 45 degrees north latitude, includes the lower course of the Syr Darya to Fort No. 2, and the lower course of the Ili. The climate here is in general cold, and apricots and vines do not grow. At the western extremity of Kazala, the average temperature is 43·2 degrees Fahr.; while at the eastern extremity, Kopal, the mean temperature of the year is 45·5 degrees. Snow remains on the ground for about three months, although on the lower Syr Darya it is constantly drifted by a violent wind from the north and west. The summer at Kazala lasts about five months without rain, and is exceedingly hot. At that place, taking an average of 19 years, the Syr Darya has been covered with ice for 123 days in the year, or from December 3 to April 5. At Kopal the summer heat is moderated by the snow-covered mountains in the immediate vicinity, and the western wind blowing from Lake Balkash.

The *apricot zone* lies next to the south, and includes Perovsky, Turkistan, Aulié-ata and Vierny. At Vierny the mean temperature for the year 1861, the only one of which there is any record, was 44·6 degrees. Grapes ripen in Vierny, but they are of an inferior quality to those farther south. The winter is here shorter than in the northern zone, but the winds blow with as much violence. At Perovsky and Julek the prevailing wind is north-west, from the Aral Sea. At Aulié-ata a north-easterly wind prevails, and all along the northern side of the Alexandrofsky range the wind is very violent. At Vierny there is generally a north-westerly wind from Lake Balkash. At Perovsky an experience of seven years has shown that the river is covered with ice on an average 97 days, from December 19 to March 26. The winter may be compared to that of Central Germany, although the cold sometimes reaches 30 degrees below zero Fahr., and in summer the thermometer has marked in the shade over 99 degrees Fahr.

The *peach and almond zone* includes Mankent, Tchimkeut, Tashkent, Tokmak, the district of Kuldja, Ura-tepé, Jizakh, and the district of the Zarafshan. From Tashkent southwards, grape-vines do not have to be covered in winter. The district of Kuldja, although lying far to the north, is protected on every side by high mountains, which accounts for its comparatively high temperature, the yearly average of which is 48·5 degrees Fahr. It is possible therefore to raise apricots, peaches, grapes, pomegranates, and other tender fruit. The yearly average of the temperature at Tashkent, as observed at the Chemical

Laboratory in 1872-73-74, was respectively 56·3°, 56·1°, and 55·9°, with the barometer at 722·24°, 722.4°, and 723·1°. The temperature at Tashkent in February is similar to that at Sevastopol, and in July to that of Derbend. The winter is short; snow falls for about a month, but quickly melts. The winter of 1871-2 was considered very remarkable, because the snow remained on the ground for a month and a half. The cold in winter sometimes reaches 6 degrees below zero Fahr., and the heat in summer 110 degrees in the shade. The winter, however, is accompanied with a great deal of rain, which begins to fall in October, and lasts till March. There are seldom any violent winds.

The *fourth zone* comprises the valley of Hodjent and all the small mountain valleys south of 42 degrees of latitude. Here, even pistachio trees can grow. The winter is milder than at Tashkent, and the Syr Darya rarely freezes. The summer is much longer, and fruits ripen two weeks earlier than in Tashkent, or in Jizakh and Ura-tepé. Pistachio trees will grow as far as 3,500 feet above the level of the sea; wild peaches reach 4,000 feet, wild almonds 4,500, apricots 5,000, and wild apples 6,500 feet.[1]

Since the Khivan Expedition, a meteorological observatory has been established at Nukus, on the Amu Darya, but only observations from July to November in 1874 have been published. The temperature during these months was about the same as at Tashkent, the highest point reached by the mercury being 107·4 degrees. It would be interesting to investigate the old writers to see what changes the climate of Central Asia has undergone. Baber, in the winter of 1502, speaks of the intense cold, and of crossing the Syr Darya on the ice near Hodjent, and in another place says that his father led his army across the river Arys on the ice, and defeated the Uzbeks.

Earthquakes are very common throughout Central Asia, especially in the mountainous districts, and it has been remarked that they most frequently occur in March, or about the time of the vernal equinox. As this is the time of the beginning of the new year, it has become a belief among many that the new year cannot really begin until an earthquake has been

---

[1] See an article on the subject in the 'Turkistan Gazette' for 1873, No. 12.

felt, and it is said that some Sarts even stick a knife slightly into the ground, and do not celebrate the new year's feast until the knife has been shaken down. One of the most violent earthquakes of recent times was on April 4, 1868, at 2.20. A.M. It lasted two minutes, and at Tashkent overthrew many houses, killing 20 persons. In 1869, at 5.20. A.M. on March 25 there was also a very noticeable earthquake, and in 1870 there was another on March 10. At Tashkent there are on an average five earthquakes a year, but many of them are so slight that they are scarcely noticed.

Where so many races have met as in Central Asia, there is naturally a conflict in the modes of computing time. Three calendars are in habitual use—the ordinary Mussulman religious calendar, with its lunar year; an agricultural solar year; and the Kirghiz calendar; and to these has now been added a fourth, the Julian in the Russian form with a new series of festivals.

The Mohammedan lunar year, *Kamariya*, is well known; but the solar year, *Shamsiya*, of 365 days, beginning at the vernal equinox, with twelve months named from the signs of the Zodiac, has never, as far as I can learn, been thoroughly investigated. This year is habitually used by all agriculturists, it being the only computation of time by which they can know when to till their ground and sow their crops.

The names of the months in common use are the Arabic names for the signs of the Zodiac, as follows: (I give the pronunciation there heard) *Hamal*, Aries; *Saur*, Taurus; *Jauza*, Gemini; *Saratan*, Cancer; *Asad*, Leo; *Sumbula* (*Sambla*) Virgo; *Mizan*, Libra; *Akhrab*, Scorpio; *Kaus*, Sagittarius; *Jadi*, Capricornus; *Dalu*, Aquarius; and *Hut*, Pisces. As these names are not all entirely intelligible to the people, one or two of them are otherwise explained.

For instance, *Jauza* is connected with the word *jauz*, a nut; *Saratan* is called an insect resembling a death-watch, as crabs are there unknown; *Sumbula* is explained as a beard of rye; and *Dalv*, aquarius, is simply a water-pail. With the natural desire of simple people to find reasons for words in common use, explanations are given to each of these names.

Thus, the first month, it is said, is called *Hamal*, because the sheep then get their fill of green meat; the second month, *Saur*, because cattle can find sufficient pasture; *Jauza* is so-called because it is then warm enough for children to play in the street with nuts and pebbles; in *Saratan* the death-watch appears in the houses and does harm; in *Asad* lions do not go out of their dens; *Sumbula*, the beard of rye, is the month of harvest; in *Mizan*, the balances, the days and nights are equal: in *Akhrab*, the scorpions hide themselves: in *Kaus*, it is no harm to kill game; *Jadi* is an excellent month for goats; in *Dalu* water freezes, and it is impossible to use it without employing a pail; while the last month, *Hut*, is the best of all for eating fish.

At Tashkent these months are given 30 and 31 days alternately; the last, *Hut*, having only 29 days in ordinary years: but in Samarkand and Bukhara, another mode of calculation is adopted, which is kept in mind by means of a distich:

La u la, lab, la u la, la, shash mahast,
Lal kat u kat lal, shuhúri kutast.

In the Arabic alphabet l stands for 30, a for 1, b for 2, k for 20, and t for 9, and giving the combinations of letters their numerical meanings (the vowels in the last line being unwritten and therefore without force) these lines would read, 'Thirty-one and thirty-one, thirty-two, thirty-one and thirty-one thirty-one, six months; two thirties twenty-nine and twenty-nine two thirties, short months. The same distich for remembering the number of days in a month is common in Persia, where this solar calendar is also in use by the agricultural classes and is employed by the government for the collection of taxes. It will be seen that the number of days given to the Zodiacal months differ somewhat from the number of days during which the sun actually remains in each sign of the Zodiac; these being, beginning with Aries, 31, 31, 31, 31, 32, 31, 30, 30, 29, 30, 30, and 29 respectively. An intercalary day is inserted once in four years at the end of the last month *Hut*. The first day of the year, as in Persia, is called *Nauruz*, new year, and is always a popular festival.

In searching for previous mention of these Zodiacal months, I find them frequently used for dates in 'The History of the Moguls' of Abul Ghazi, Khan of Khiva, who wrote in 1663.

There can be no doubt here that the names *Saratan, Hut,* &c., are used as true month-appellations, although commentators seem to have overlooked the fact, probably ascribing the use of the Zodiacal signs to a mere freak of the author. El Maqrizi, who wrote in the beginning of the fifteenth century, in a passage about Egypt, speaks of this solar year, and calls it *Haradjia,* or the *Haradj* year, referring probably to its use there as now in Persia, for collecting the taxes. Going much farther back, we find in the Almagest of Ptolemy seven observations of Mercury, Mars and Jupiter, between 272 and 241 B.C., which are referred to a special era called that of Dionusos and to the months Tauron, Didumon, Leonton, Parthenon, Scorpion, Aigon, and Hudron, which are evidently named from the signs of the Zodiac, showing that such a calendar was then in use. The Arabic names for the signs of the Zodiac were translated from the Greek. There has been much discussion as to the origin of the Greek names; but it has now been conclusively proved by Assyriologists that they were derived either directly, or through Egypt, from the names given by the Chaldean and Babylonian astronomers. We find from the labours of these scholars that the Chaldeans and Babylonians had with regard to the twelve months of the year myths coming down from very early times, which were localised by them in the different epochs of the year when they already inhabited the plains of the Euphrates and the Tigris, in accordance not with agricultural occupations, but with the great periodical phenomena of the atmosphere and the phases of the annual circuit of the sun as it appeared in that region. The months received names corresponding to these myths, such as the month of the favourable bull; the month of the construction of bricks; the month of the seizer of the harvest; the month of the burning fire; the month of the messenger of the goddess Istar, which were usually shortened into expressions such as the month of the bull, of the bricks, of the seizer, of fire, of the messenger; and in accordance with these legends were designed the symbolic figures given to the solar 'mansions' in the Zodiac. In the cuneiform inscriptions we find the signs of the Zodiac exactly the same as those now in use, except that Virgo is replaced by the archeress, that is the Goddess Istar; Libra by the Scorpion's claws; Sagittarius by the arrow; and Aquarius by the pail: the last two being the same now in use in Central Asia.[1] It would thus seem that the solar calendar, or the *Shamsiya* year, now under consideration, has a very high origin; in all probability it has remained in these regions of Central Asia since the times of their earliest colonisation, or rather the introduction of the civilisation of the Assyrians, or of their Iranian successors.

It is to be regretted that such a sensible calendar will probably be replaced by that of the Russians, which is already twelve days out of its reckoning, and the correction of which will for some time be prevented by a superstitious reverence for church festivals, it being thought that the peasants would be unwilling to lose twelve saints' days and consequent holidays out of one year. It is still more to be regretted that Europe, from a traditional reverence for the beginning of the Christian religious year, should have changed the beginning of the civil year from March, its natural beginning near the time of the vernal equinox, to January.[2]

The ordinary word used by the Sarts for the week is *hafta*, the Persian for seven; while the Kirghiz and nomads usually call it *atna*. The usual names for the days are principally of Persian origin. *Jumma*, the day of prayer, is Friday; *Shambé*, evidently a corruption of Shabat, or Sabbath, is Saturday;[3] then come *Yakshambé*, Sunday; *Dushambé*, *Sishambé*, *Tcharshambé* and *Peshambé*; that is, the first day after *Shambé*

---

[1] 'Les Premières Civilisations,' par François Le Normant, ii. 67. Paris, 1874.

[2] It is curious that the reformed calendar made under the Sultan Jelal-Eddin Malik Shah in 1079, and which is still the official calendar in Persia, was more exact than the Gregorian reform. The mean year has 365·2422 days, the intercalation of Aloyse Lilio gives an error of 3 days in 10,000 years, while this error would be only 2 days with the Persian intervalation. We are bound to say that the astronomers of Malik Shah were much nearer the truth. Instead of adopting uniformly 8 bissextiles in 33 years, they established the period $\frac{7}{29} + \frac{4\cdot 8}{4\cdot 33} = \frac{39}{161}$ that is, that they counted 39 bissextiles in 161 years. This period gives for the mean year 365·2422 days, precisely the same as that of our modern tables. 'Prolégomènes des Tables Astronomiques d'Oloug-Beg, Notes et éclaircissements,' p. 235. Paris, 1847.

[3] It is curious that not only the institution of the sabbath as a day of rest, but the word sabbath itself is probably of Assyrian origin. See a letter of Professor A. H. Sayce in 'The Academy' for November 27, 1875.

or the Sabbath, the second day after *Shambé*, and so on.[1] Among the Kirghiz it is very common instead of *Yakshambé* to say *Bazaar*, as most of the bazaars are open on that day.

The Kirghiz have no era by which to date their years, but use the twelve-year period which they call *Mutchal*, or *Müshel*, originally introduced from China by the Mongols. Each of the years in this period is named after an animal, and they are ranged in the following order: Mouse, Ox, Leopard, Hare, Fish, Serpent, Horse, Sheep, Ape, Fowl, Dog, Hog. The same cycle is also used among the Sarts and Persians, by whom it is placed in all official documents and proclamations. I have before me a Persian official almanac for the year 1874–5, which is marked for the year of the Dog, and bears on each cover a representation of that animal. The present year is that of the Hog. If a Kirghiz should be asked how old he is, he would seldom tell the number of years, but for example would simply say, 'My year is that of the Horse,' leaving you to guess how many twelve-year cycles back he was born; or if he wished to be more precise he would add, 'and I am in the third *Mutchal*,' which, supposing the question to be asked in 1875, would make him out to be thirty years of age. No attention is paid to the day of the birth, and therefore everybody who is born in the same year is considered to be of the same age. The Kirghiz word for year, *jil*, means not only a whole year, but also half a year; so that sometimes a Kirghiz, seeing your difficulty in calculating the *Mutchal*, will tell you that he has so many *jils*, and thus apparently make himself out twice as old as he really is, be taking the *jil* as half a year and you as a year. The Kirghiz have a legend that when the animals came up in procession to have the years named after them, the camel, as the noblest of all, came first, but that a mouse crept up on his head and succeeded in getting the first year named after himself, so that thus the camel was entirely omitted.

Besides the twelve years' cycle, or *Mutchal*, there is another called *Karn*, which was explained to me as being thirty-six

---

[1] The Russian names for the days show something similar. *Ponedyelnik*, Monday, means the day coming immediately after *Nedyela* (literally, without work), the old name for Sunday, but now used as a general term for the week, the word *Voskresenye*, resurrection, being substituted for Sunday.

years, or three *mutchals*; but more probably this word, which is of Arabic origin, meaning a member or a horn, is used as we would use age or generation. The Kirghiz year, like that of the settled inhabitants, begins with the feast of *Nauruz* at the vernal equinox, and is divided into twelve solar months, which are usually known by the zodiacal names I have just mentioned. A solar month is called *Yulduz*, or constellation, while a lunar month is called *Ai*, or moon; and this is divided into two parts, the *Yang-ai*, new moon, and *Isk-ai*, old moon. The winter months are frequently called after a complicated system, which it would seem very difficult to apply. The first month of winter is that when on the eleventh day of the month the moon is equal with the Pleiades, *Ur-kar*, and is therefore called *On-bir-tugush*, that is, the eleventh conjunction. The second month of winter, when the moon and the Pleiades are together on the ninth day, is called *Tokuz-tugush* (ninth conjunction); in the third month, *Yedi-tugush*, they are together on the seventh day; in the fourth month, *Bish-tugush*, they are together on the fifth day; in the fifth month, *Utch-tugush*, on the third day; and in the sixth month, *Bir-tugush*, on the first day. Besides these the simple folk, instead of months, give names to certain times of the year, chiefly according to various events of steppe life, as the lambing season; the mare-milking season; May, the rainy time, which lasts for about a fortnight about the end of May and the beginning of June; *Tchillé*, the subsequent forty days (of heat); the sheep-shearing season; and the slaughtering season. It would be interesting to make a careful comparison of the Kirghiz names of the months with those of the Altai, Shor, and Kommandin Tartars, part of which are given by Radloff in his 'Journey through the Altai,'[1] where we find such denominations as white month, wind month, summer month, the great heat, old woman's month, great month, and small month. The Tunguses, as well as the Altai Tartars, have a year of thirteen lunar months named in this way after the phases of nature and the occupations of a regular life, and even in more highly cultivated societies, as in America and England, country people refer events to the natural calendar

---

[1] Erman's 'Archiv für Wissenschaftliche Kunde von Russland, vol. xxiii p. 261.

in which sowing-time, haying time, and harvest are strongly marked seasons.

The day, from sunrise until sunset, is divided into four parts, called sunrise, eating time, mid-day, and sunset In general the Kirghiz know well the stars, for these assist them not only in calculating time, but also in finding their way over the steppes. The Polar star is called *Temir Kazyk*, the iron pole; the Great Bear, *Jitti Karaktchi*, the seven robbers; and the Milky Way, *Saman yul*, the straw road, or *Kük gaz yul*, the path of the wild geese.

APPENDICES.

APPENDIX I.

A SKETCH OF THE HISTORY OF KHOKAND IN RECENT TIMES.

KHOKAND, or the Valley of Fergana, was included among the provinces given by Tchinghiz Khan to his son Jagatai, and shared the general fate of the countries of Mavcrannahr. We know its condition as an appanage to the throne of Samarkand during the time of Baber; and after that it was sometimes rebellious, sometimes conquered, sometimes in the possession of this or that prince, and does not emerge as a separate and independent country until toward the beginning of the present century. No written historical account of the country by a native author has yet seen the light, and what we know of its modern history is derived chiefly from traditions and oral accounts, strengthened here and there by numismatic and documentary evidence.

Both popular tradition and the Chinese accounts agree that in the middle of the last century Khokand was not under one rule, but was divided into separate cities, provinces and clans, each with its own Bek or Hodja. According to the account of Mahsum Hodja, quoted by Ritter,[1] some time in the last century Shahrukh Bek, with some of his country people, went from the Volga region

---

[1] My chief authorities have been:—

1. An article, 'Description of the Khanate of Khokand in its present condition,' published in the 'Memoirs of the Imperial Russian Geographical Society,' Book III. 1849.

2. An article by V. Veliaminof-Zernof, 'Historical Information about the Khanate of Khokand from Mohammed Ali to Khudayar Khan,' published in the 'Labours of the Oriental Section of the Imperial Archæological Society.' Vol. ii. 1856.

3. 'Contemporary coins of Khokand,' by V. Grigorief; *ibid.*

4. 'List of known coins of Khokand,' by A. Savelief; *ibid.*

5. An article by the Kirghiz Sultan, Nurekin, 'Sketches of the History of

to Fergána, and married the daughter of Ediger Hodja, the ruler of the town of Khurram-Sarai, and then settled with his Uzbeks in Kukan, twelve miles west of the present Khokand. He then murdered his father-in-law, and made himself ruler of the district, and, profiting by the dissensions and weakness of his neighbours, soon extended his sway. He was succeeded by his eldest son Rahim Bek, and he by his brother Abdul Kerim Bek, who built the present city of Khokand, to which he transferred his residence. He was succeeded by his nephew Irdana, or Erdeni, son of Rahim, (according to some a son of Abdul Kerim). The Chinese geographer[1] says that the Beks of all the other towns in Fergana were under the rule of Erdeni Bek, and obeyed his orders. In 1759, the Chinese General Tchao-hoei was in pursuit of Khodzidjan, and detached some officers to put down the Buruts. Erdeni entertained these officers in Khokand, and when they departed, sent one of his officials to tender his submission to the Emperor Khian-lung. The other Beks, among them Tokto Mohammed of Andijan, and Ilas Ping-li (Kuli?) of Marghilan, followed his example, and, in 1760, sent embassies and tribute to Pekin, Tokto Mohammed going thither in person. Among the gifts sent to the Chinese Emperor, were ' horses that sweat blood (*argumaks*[2]), great eagles and falcons for hunting, *and plates of the fountain of the dragon.*' Tashkent had submitted to China in 1758. In 1762, Erdeni invaded the country of Oshi (Ush), which belonged to Adzi Bii, but was ordered by the Chinese Governor-General to withdraw his troops. In 1763, there was another invasion of the country of the Buruts, which was blamed by an imperial decree. Erdeni died in 1770, and was replaced by

Khokand from 1841 to 1864,' published in the 'Turkistan Gazette,' No. 35, 1872.

6. The report of Mahsum Hojda, as given in Ritter's 'Erdkunde von Asien,' Vol. v. p. 772.

7. The 'Memoirs of Mirza Shems,' Kazan, 1861.

8. 'Eastern Turkistan,' by V. Grigorief; St. Petersburg, 1873.

9. 'The Uzbek State of Kokan' by W. H. Wathen, in the 'Journal of the Asiatic Society of Bengal,' August, 1834.

10. Notices in the accounts of various travellers, such as Nazarof, Kliutcharef, Pospielof and Burnashof, and Mir Izzet Ullah.

11. Personal observation; the Russian newspapers; official reports; private letters from Tashkent and Khokand; and accounts taken down from the lips of Tashkentians and Khokandians, some of whom were actors in the events described. Some of these last have also been used by Mr. N. Petrofsky in his 'Sketches of the Khanate of Khokand,' in the 'Messenger of Europe' for October, 1875.

[1] *Thai thsing y thoung tchi*, or Great Geography of Chinese Empire, edition of 1790, sect. 420, translated by Klaproth in 'Magasin Asiatique,' vol. i. 82.

[2] 'Horses sweating blood' in the early times always formed part of the tribute to the Chinese Emperors from the countries of Central Asia.

his nephew, Narubutu (Narbuta), who sent an embassy and tribute to Pekin.

Here contradiction begins, for Mahsum Hodja says that Erdeni was succeeded, after twenty years' rule, by Suleiman Bii, and then by Shahrukh Bek, who only reigned three months. It is a question, too, who Narbuta Bii was. Mahsum Hodja says that he was a grandson of Abdul Kerim, and apparently Abdul Kerim and Rahim are in some way confused. But according to local tradition, Narbuta Bii was the son of a certain Abdurrahman Batyr, an Uzbek of the tribe of Ming, and ruler of the town and district of Isfara, once much more important than now, and was descended from a certain Tchumatch Bii, a great local hero.[1] Abdurrahman Batyr married the sister of Erdeni Bek, and was treacherously killed by the latter, who wished to get possession of Isfara. Narbuta, then a child, was spared on account of his tender age, and when on Erdeni's death his heirs were killed or dispersed, was chosen by the Khokandians to succeed him.

Narbuta passed his whole reign in wars with his neighbours, and added to his dominions Andijan, Namangan and Ush, besides other smaller towns, which had been thitherto independent. His last years were occupied in a contest for the possession of Hodjent, with Fazil-Bii and his son Khudayar Bek, the ruler of Ura-tepé. Hodjent was sometimes in the possession of one party, and sometimes of the other, but was never permanently annexed to Khokand until after Narbuta's death. Abul Gaffar Bek,[2] the grandson of Khudayar Bek, says, that during the reign of Fazil, Narbuta Bii in alliance with Rahim Bii of Bukhara, attempted to take Ura-tepé, but were beaten back, when Khudayar sallied out, completely routed them, killed 20,000 men, and made a pyramid of their heads in Ura-tepé. In 1799, Narbuta undertook an expedition against Tashkent, but was beaten and captured together with many of his followers by Yunus Hodja, the ruler of all that place, and in 1800 was beheaded there.[3] Narbuta left three sons, Alim, Omar, and Shahrukh, of whom the eldest, Alim, succeeded him.

[1] Khanikof says that the father of Narbuta was Iamtchi Bii (probably the same as Tchumatch), a descendant of the Sultan Baber. *Frachn*, Nova Supplementa, p. 336.

[2] See pp. 88 and 310.

[3] See 'Travels of Pospielof and Burnashof to Tashkent,' in 1800. 'Messenger of the Imperial Russian Geographical Society,' 1851, vol. i, p. 23. Narbuta Bii is here called Khan Hodja, which accords with the Chinese account that the cities of Khokand were governed by Hodjas; they were probably connected in some way with the Hodjas formerly reigning in Kashgar. In one of his notes to this journey Mr. Khanikof gives some information with regard to the history of Tashkent,

After the defeat given to Narbuta Bii, Yunus Hodja raised an army, including the Kirghiz tribes subject to him, and marched against Khokand, making a treaty with Bek Murad Bek, the son of Khudayar Bek, then ruling in Hodjent, for mutual action against the Khokandians. The armies of Khokand and Tashkent met on opposite sides of the Syr Darya; but although the fire was kept up for some time, it was without effect, and both armies retreated. Yunus Hodja, however, again took the field, with the intention of placing on the throne of Khokand one of the sons of Narbuta Bii, whom he held prisoner. In connection with Bek Murad Bek, he besieged Ura-tepé, but could not take it, and was obliged to retreat. Baba Bek of Ura-tepé, brother of Khudayar, therefore allied himself with Omar Khan, the second son of Narbuta Bii (who was apparently even then on bad terms with his brother), and succeeded in driving Bek Murad Bek from Hodjent. Baba was subse-

which may be an interesting addition to what I have said on pages 111-12. 'Even in the beginning of the seventh century Tashkent, or Tchash, was considered as in vassalage to the Chinese. In 713, the ruler of Tashkent, who had thitherto been called Khan, was raised by the Chinese Emperor to the rank of King. In 714, he complained to the Emperor of the invasion of the Arabs and asked for help, but the Chinese instead of complying with this request only confirmed the high-sounding titles which he assumed. Soon after that a Chinese official was sent there to arrange the disturbances among the petty princes. The ruler of Tashkent submitted unconditionally, but his nephews were put to death, and he in consequence turned for help to the Arabs; thus their dominion became established in that region. In the tenth century, according to Ibn Haukal, Tashkent, under the name of Khas, was one of the strongest barriers of Turkistan. In the beginning of the thirteenth century it belonged to the possessions of Ala-Eddin, the ruler of Kharezm, under the name of Bin_ket. Lying on the frontier, Tashkent was one of the first regions of Central Asia which felt the attack of the Mongols, and was speedily subdued. In 1390, Tashkent again appeared as an important military point, being the rendezvous for the army of Tamerlane on his second campaign against Toktamish. At the end of the fifteenth, and during the first years of the sixteenth centuries, Tashkent was under the rule of Omar Sheikh Mirza, and of his son Baber, the ruler of Khokand. In the middle of the fifteenth century the Uzbeks, taking advantage of the dissensions between Abul Soid and Abdullatif, princes of Maverannahr, penetrated under command of the latter into the district of Tashkent as well as across the Syr Darya, and although in 1456 Abdullatif was obliged to submit to Abul Seid yet the Uzbeks made use of this road under the command of Sheibani Khan for the complete expulsion of the Timurides from Maverannahr, among whom was Baber, the ruler of Fergana as well as of Tashkent, who was forced to flee to Kabul, where he laid the basis for the empire of the Great Mogul in India.'

From the reports of Kushelef and Müller, who were in Tashkent in 1789, we learn that at that time the city was ruled by Yulhars Khan, and that the city of Turkistan under Seid Sultan, was in a certain measure subject to it. This Yulbars, who appears not to have been a Tashkontian, but a Kirghiz Sultan, was killed by the Sarts on April 17th, 1740, three days after Müller had left the city.

quently murdered by his nephew Bek Murad, in return for which Bek Murad was himself killed by the children of Baba Bek in Samarkand, whither he had been invited by the Bukharan Amir Haidar. Yunus Hodja, however, was finally unsuccessful, and was obliged to retreat to Tashkent, which city was captured by Alim Khan either in 1803 or in 1805. He then turned his attention southwards, and took Ura-tepé, but having been unfortunate in a campaign against Jizakh, Ura-tepé was retaken by Mahmud Khan, a nephew on his mother's side of Khudayar Bek. Alim Khan took up his residence for some time in Tashkent, in order to look after the administration of that province and put down rebellions, and was constantly engaged in forays against the Kirghiz. The people of Khokand got disgusted with the continual wars, and more than all others the courtiers and officials of Alim, who wished to profit by the wealth they had acquired. They therefore conspired to kill him, and to put on the throne his brother Omar. Having succeeded in getting Omar to their side, they withdrew to Khokand, when some of the faithful followers of Alim, getting wind of the conspiracy, reported it to their master, and urged him at once to advance to Khokand and put it down. Alim, however, was unwilling to believe it, and for a long time refused to take any decided measures, in consequence of which the band of conspirators daily increased. Instead of following the advice of his friends, and taking a round-about way, Alim insisted upon going the shortest way through the defiles of Kendyr-tau, where he was attacked in the little village of Shaitan, and was killed by a shot from a certain Maidan Yuldash, an adherent of Omar, who wished to find favour with his master. Happily he did not get the expected reward for his treachery, for on telling Omar of his exploit, he was himself immediately executed.

The death of Alim Khan probably occurred in 1812. How long the sovereigns of Khokand continued to pay tribute to the Chinese, is unknown, but Mahsum Hodja and others say that Alim Khan was the first who gave himself the title of Khan, who ordered his name to be recited in the *Khutbe,* or daily prayers, and who coined money. Mahsum Hodja says that these coins, which were of bronze silvered over, were struck from old cannon, left by Nadir Shah at the time of his conquest.

Omar Khan,[1] in spite of the reasons for his elevation, found it difficult to keep the peace with his neighbours, captured Mahmud

---

[1] Called also Homar and Gomar. By Mir Izzet-Ullah, probably by some mistranscription, he is called *Amir Khan*, and by Nazarof *Amir Valliami*, i.e. Omar-Veli-n-niem.

Khan of Ura-tepé, sent him prisoner to Khokand, and appointed one of his own adherents Governor of that place. In three months the new Bek was turned out, and the struggle began again. After many changes of fortune, Jizakh fell to Bukhara, and Ura-tepé to Khokand, and Tiura-Bek-Yiura, the son of Mahmud Khan, went to Khokand, and occupied an honorary position at the court of the Khan. About the same time Turkistan and several smaller towns to the north were conquered by the generals of Omar. The last descendant of the Kirghiz Khans, Tozai Khan, notwithstanding a brave defence, was forced to seek refuge in Bukhara, where he was killed in the troubles accompanying the accession of Mozaffar-Eddin.

In 1822, Omar Khan, who was greatly loved by his people, died, or, as it is said, was poisoned by his elder son Mohammed Ali, who then became Khan, and is the first of whom we have some detailed accounts. His name, according to a frequent custom, has been abbreviated to Madali Khan. His accession was accompanied by no revolutions, but he found it necessary to exile many of his relatives. His younger brother, Sultan Mahmud, escaped to Shahrisabs, where he lived for many years, having married a daughter of its ruler. He was also in favour with the Amir Nasrullah, and was appointed by him for a short time Bek of Urmitan, and after its capture of Hodjent.

The disagreement with Bukhara, which broke out soon after the accession of Madali, ended peaceably in 1825, and in the following year he joined Jihangyr Hodja, one of the Appak family, in his efforts to recover Kashgar, from the throne of which his ancestors had been driven by the Chinese, in 1756. Some slight, but bloody, skirmishes with the Chinese seemed to Madali sufficient to warrant the title of 'Ghazi,' or 'Conqueror of the Infidels;' and after a twelve days campaign he returned home, leaving a part of his troops to help Jihangyr Hodja, who succeeded in taking Kashgar, and making himself temporary master of the country. But soon a Chinese army of 70,000 men arrived and turned the tables. The Khokandians withdrew in time with their booty, but Jihangyr was captured, it is said, by the treacherous consent of Madali, and was sent to Pekin, where he was executed. This was in 1827.

In 1828-29 there was another attempt made on Kashgar by Yusuf Hodja, the elder brother of Jihangyr. Madali Khan again lent the services of his army and of his best generals. Again Kashgar, Yangy-Hissar and Yarkand were taken, and again the Khokandians withdrew with their booty on the approach of a Chinese army. Yusuf Hodja escaped to Khokand, where he died five years afterwards. Many thousands of Kashgarians were massacred by the Chinese, and 70,000 took refuge in Khokand, where they were colonised in the city of Shahri-Khana, built by Omar Khan, and on the Syr Darya below Hodjent.

On account of the depopulation of Kashgaria, and the dangers of constant hostile relations with Khokand, the Chinese resolved to resort to their former practice of buying peace and quiet, for they had at one time paid a large yearly sum to Khokand for that purpose. A treaty was therefore readily concluded at Pekin, in 1831, with Alim Patcha, Madali's envoy, by which the Khan of Khokand was to receive the duties on all foreign goods imported into Aksu, Ush-Turfan, Kashgar, Yangy-Hissar, Yarkand, and Khotan, and was allowed to maintain *aksakals* in all those towns to collect the duties and to protect the Mohammedans, and by which he bound himself to prevent the Hodjas from leaving his dominions, and to punish them if they did so. In this way Khokand acquired a great influence over its neighbour Kashgar.[1]

After this Madali Khan conquered Karategin, and forced Kulab, Darvaz, and Shugnan, to recognise his authority. In this way, up to 1840, Madali Khan had the reputation of a brave and active sovereign, and was exceedingly popular. At that time a sudden change came over him. He threw aside his occupations, ceased to think of military expeditions, and gave himself up to complete licentiousness. This change is supposed to have been due to the remorse which he felt at having murdered the Ming Bashi Hakk Kul, by whose intelligent counsels he had been previously guided.

At this time Madali received a letter from the Amir of Bukhara, accusing him of breaches of Mussulman law in marrying two sisters, and even his step-mother—one of the wives of Omar Khan —and upbraiding him for his licentious life. Madali was in such a rage that he imprisoned the envoys, had half of their heads and beards shaved, and gave orders for an immediate campaign. At the first meeting of the hostile troops Madali was cut off from his army, and only saved himself from capture by running away. His army dispersed without fighting, and the war thus ignominiously ended.

Soon the whole realm fell into disorder, there was general discontent, and a conspiracy was raised against Madali Khan with the aim of placing on the throne Murad Bii, the son of Alim Khan, or Shir Ali, the son of Hadji Bii, the brother of Narbuta. Not feeling themselves, however, strong enough to overturn their ruler,

[1] See 'Memoirs of Mirza Shems' and Grigorief's 'Eastern Turkistan,' part ii. 443-460.

the conspirators fled for assistance to Nasrullah, the Amir of Bukhara. Though he was most ambitious to obtain possession of Khokand, yet from distrust he refused to have anything to do with the conspirators. Not deterred by this, they tried again, and at last he consented to lead an attack against Khokand, and set out from Bukhara in the middle of April, 1842, with an army of 18,000 men, and in a fortnight encamped a few miles from the city of Khokand.

This sudden invasion terrified Madali Khan, and he could think of no means to save himself but by peace, and sent out his eldest son, Mohammed Amir (Madamin), with other ambassadors, to propose to admit himself the vassal of the Amir of Bukhara, and to allow the Amir's name to be used in the public prayers, and to be stamped on the coins. The Amir received the embassy kindly, and sent back the prince, but after a conversation with the Kush Begi Leshker, and on ascertaining that the inhabitants of Khokand were not disposed to defend their sovereign, but were ready to open the gates to him, he demanded that Madali Khan should himself come to him for personal explanations.

Madali Khan, however, thought it better to save himself by flight, and quickly collecting his valuables, sent them off in a hundred carts to Namangan, whither he himself soon followed, with a suite of a thousand men.

The Amir of Bukhara was immediately received into the city, and thinking that he could better lay the inhabitants under subjection by terror, gave the city up for half a day to pillage by the soldiery, and immediately sent to capture Madali Khan and his family. The unfortunate Khan, after leaving Khokand, had thought it might be best to return there, and to go personally to the Amir and make what peace he could with him, and had come to Khokand for that purpose when he was discovered by the persons who had promised to capture him, and was brought to the Amir, who resolved to execute him.

This intention was opposed in council by the magnates of Khokand, as well as by Irdane, the Kush Begi of Bukhara, who said how much better it would be for the Amir to rule the country by love than by fear. This council displeased the Amir, and the Kazi Kalian of Bukhara, who was present, knowing his master's wishes, immediately accused Madali Khan of the crime of having married his step-mother, and insisted on his death. Madali Khan, his mother, and his eldest son Madamin Bek, were immediately brought before the council, and executed in their presence.

A second son, Mozaffar, was also killed by the Amir's orders, and a third son by another wife, Ashula, was killed near Tchusta in 1866-7, by the orders of Khudayar Khan. It was really true that Madali Khan had married his step-mother, the widow of his father Omar Khan. She was apparently an attractive person, for after Madali Khan's death, the Amir Nasrullah married her himself, although he put her to death in the same year after his second expedition against Khokand. The other wives of Madali Khan were sent in forty carts to Bukhara. Two hundred and fifty of the chief Khokandians were also taken to Bukhara as hostages.

The Amir appointed as Governor of the Khanate Ibrahim Datkha, formerly Governor of Samarkand, and left with him 600 soldiers, and after arranging affairs there to suit him, made a triumphant entry into Bukhara, the whole campaign having lasted only fifty-four days.

Hardly three months had elapsed, however, since this easily gained triumph, when the whole of Khokand was in an insurrection, and the Bukharan power there was destroyed. It seems that Ibrahim Datkha greatly oppressed the people, and made them pay not only all the taxes which existed in Bukhara, but others introduced at his own pleasure. The people, indignant at these exactions, resolved to rid themselves of the Bukharan yoke, and sent to the Kiptchaks where Shir Ali, the son of Hadji Bii was living, and asked them to come and deliver them. Shir Ali was himself extremely feeble, and unfit for governing, but the leading Kiptchaks thought it would be a good opportunity for their own personal aggrandisement, and for restoring the supremacy of the Kiptchaks and Uzbek tribes in the Khanate. In former times they had had possession of all the important offices, and had ruled the country, but had afterwards been turned out by the town people, or Sarts, who surrounded Madali Khan, and were his favourites.

Shir Ali had taken refuge among the Kiptchaks on account of the designs of Madali Khan against his life, and had there married daughters of two of the prominent chiefs.

The Kiptchaks then were moving in a mass on the capital, when the inhabitants threw themselves on the Bukharans and killed nearly all of them. Ibrahim Datkha and his brother with difficulty saved themselves by flight. Shir Ali immediately entered the city, occupied the citadel, and was at once proclaimed Khan.

The news of this successful rebellion threw the Amir into a great rage, and he immediately ordered the punishment of Ibrahim Datkha and his brother, confiscated their property, and finally decided to send another army to Khokand, thinking that the Kiptchaks, hearing of its approach, would at once run away, and in the autumn set out with an army of 20,000 men, taking with him the 250 Khokandian officials, whom he had previously taken to Bukhara as hostages. He feared to leave them in Bukhara, lest they might enter into some plot with Allah Kul, the Khan of Khiva, who had long been in disagreeable relations with him, and was particularly jealous of his extension of dominions.

The Amir laid siege to Khokand, but the garrison refused to surrender.

One of the hostages, a Kiptchak, who had formerly been a Yuz Bashi, or centurion, in Khokand—a person of remarkable intelligence and capacity—called Mussulman Kul, and popularly known as Tchulak (cripple) on account of his lameness, resolved to save his country. He adroitly flattered the Amir, and offered to obtain for him the possession of the city, and was therefore allowed to enter Khokand. Once arrived there, however, he energetically preached 'no surrender,' and urged the inhabitants to fight till the last drop of blood. As he had previously been much respected, his words inspired them with confidence, and consequently sorties were made, in some of which the Bukharan army met with heavy losses. At the same time he had recourse to cunning. He addressed a letter to some of the Bukharan notabilities, urging them to fulfil their promise of rising against the Amir during the present campaign, and contrived that these letters should fall into the hands of the Amir. At the same time, by a most lucky coincidence intelligence arrived from Bukhara that the Khan of Khiva, by intrigues with Khokand, had invaded the country, and had carried off a large amount of spoil.

Nasrullah, terrified by this news, at once raised the siege, freed the 250 hostages, and returned to Bukhara. The whole siege lasted forty days.

After the departure of the Amir, Shir Ali was maintained in peaceful possession of the throne. He was simple and good-natured, and was a kind and mild ruler, so weak as to get the nickname of *pustiak* (mat or rag), and distinguished the beginning of his reign by causing the body of Madali Khan to be dug up and re-buried with great funeral ceremonies conducted by all the clergy.[1]

The reign of Shir Ali was chiefly marked by a struggle for supremacy between the nomads and the settled inhabitants. The

---

[1] A distich composed by Shir Ali, quoted by Petrofsky, s' ows his character. It is addressed to himself:

Adat buldyr Khanlar tchiksa yagmur yagar;
San na Khan san? tulga Xchiksang khalk kusindan kanlar yagar.

What sort of a Khan art thou? when thou goest out, blood flows from the eyes of the people.'

The tradition is that when Khans go out of doors, rain falls (i.e. blessings come)

Uzbek party had put Shir Ali on the throne, and it was therefore only natural that, knowing the Khan's weakness and inability to rule, their leader should insist upon governing the country. Their chief, the Kiptchak Yusuf, was made Ming Bashi, and began to remove all the Sarts from influential positions, and to fill up their places with his own favourites and adherents. But the head of the Sart party, Shadi, was more loved by the people; and, therefore, with the consent of Shir Ali, he poisoned Yusuf, and ordered many of his adherents to be executed. Desiring to get rid of Mussulmen Kul, the hero of the revolution, who was his greatest enemy, he ordered him to come to Khokand. Mussulman Kul replied politely that he was on his way, and that he was rejoiced to hear of the death of Yusuf, who had been ill-disposed to him, but in reality be collected an army, and took into his service all the fugitive adherents of Yusuf. When Shadi heard of this, he sent hired assassins to Andijan, but they were caught and hung by order of Mussulman Kul. An open war now began between the two parties, and their armies met at Tuz, where the Uzbeks defeated the Sarts; Shadi was killed, and the Khan Khudayar, who had accompanied him, was taken prisoner. Owing to difficulties in finding a successor, he was retained on the throne, and Mussulman Kul occupied the place of Shadi Ming-bashi. But Mussulman Kul found it impossible thoroughly to propitiate the Sarts, adherents of Shadi, for he could not give them all the offices they desired; and the more he endeavoured to make friends with them, the more he displeased the Kiptchaks, who were jealous of his prominence in the government, and there was consequently a strong opposition to him, and every means were used to overthrow him. Finally the dissatisfied party, in 1845, sent deputies to Shahrisabs, and invited Murad Bek, son of Alim Khan, who was living there, to come to Khokand and take possession of the throne.

On the accession of Madali Khan, Murad Bek had gone to Khiva, where he had married his daughter to the Khan Allah Kul, but after her death had quarrelled with his son-in-law, and had sought refuge in Bukhara. Murad Bek easily persuaded the Amir Nasrullah to assist him, and with a small body of soldiery made his way to Khokand, and, profiting by the absence of Mussulman Kul, who had gone to the mountains in the east to collect tribute, seized the capital by a *coup-de-main*, put to death Shir Ali, and proclaimed himself Khan, but at the same time vassal and lieutenant of the Amir of Bukhara. Had it not been for this, he might perhaps have been successful, but the people so hated the Bukharans, that word was at once sent to Mussulman Kul, who advanced with his forces, stopping at Marghilan on the way, and taking with him

Khudayar, one of the younger sons of Shir Ali, and Bek of that place, who was at the same time his son-in-law.

As soon as Murad heard of the approach of Mussulman Kul, his courage deserted him, and he fled from the city and returned to Shahrisabs. According to other accounts he was killed. The Bukharan troops for the most part escaped.[1]

Shir Ali had left five sons: by his first wife Jarkin, the daughter of the Kiptchak Tokhta Nazar, Sarymsak, then twenty-two, Bek of Tashkent, Khudayar, sixteen, Bek of Marghilan, and Sultan Murad; and by his second wife Suna Aim (also a Kiptchak), Malla, seventeen years old, Bek of Andijan, and Sufi.

Mussulman Kul was in unpleasant relations with Sarymsak, the eldest son, and preferred one of the younger boys as Khan, because in that way he could really govern the country himself. He therefore sent a letter with the seal of Khudayar to Sarymsak, who was then at Tashkent, asking him to come to Khokand and become Khan. Sarymsak believed this and started, but was murdered on the way. It is generally believed that this execution took place without the knowledge of his brother. On the next day his death was announced, and Khudayar was proclaimed Khan.

After the accession of Khudayar, there ensued a painful epoch for Khokand. The Khan himself was too young to engage in business, and was kept by Mussulman Kul in most strict seclusion. He was, for instance, rarely allowed any money, for fear he should buy himself friends, and only obtained a little through the good offices of the Aftobatcha Abdurrahman, the son of Mussulman Kul, then his best friend.

Mussulman Kul himself was a kind and naturally a just man; but he now removed from the government all of the Sarts who had been hostile to him, and the persons who surrounded him oppressed the people with their extortions. Mussulman Kul himself was not a man who could be contradicted, and insisted on the fulfilment of

---

[1] Atalyk, the second son of Alim Khan, had been sent to Karategin with his brother Murad on the usurpation of Omar. He was subsequently invited to Bukhara, where he married, going afterwards to Balkh. In 1844 he headed a trifling insurrection in Khokand, but was defeated by Shir Ali at Kara Yasi and was killed. Six years after his death his widow went to live at Samarkand, accompanied by her son Pulad, then a boy of seven, and by a daughter, who afterwards married Mohammed Rahim Subankul, the Mutevali of the Medressé Hodja Akhrar. In 1872 Pulad went to Khokand where he was arrested by Khudayar, and was only set at liberty on the intercession of his sister. In the insurrection of 1875 Pulad took no part, and the person bearing that name, who was subsequently executed by the Russians at Marghilan, was an impostor, a Kirghiz from near Andijan, named Mullah Islak, who was a tobacco-seller at Piskent, and was put forward by the leaders of the Kiptchak party.

his will, whether it was according to law or not. He had raised up for himself enemies even among his own Kiptchaks, and the rulers of Ura-tepé, Hodjent, and Marghilan, and Nur Mohammed, the Bek of Tashkent, became especially hostile to him. In 1850, too, the Khan Khudayar reached his majority, and was less disposed to submit himself to the arbitrary will of his regent.

Open rebellion did not, however, begin until 1851, when Nur Mohammed led armed forces towards the capital, with the view of meeting with Utenbai, the Governor of Marghilan, and overthrowing Mussulman Kul. The latter, however, got wind of this, and cut off their intercourse, and forced Nur Mohammed to retreat to Tashkent, while Utenbai came to Mussulman Kul and declared that he had come to his assistance, and not to that of Nur Mohammed. He was, however, removed from office.

In consequence of various disputes arising out of the collection of the tribute due from Tashkent, in the next year another rebellion broke out, and in March 1852, Mussulman Kul marched with an army of 40,000 men, and laid siege to Tashkent, taking the Khan with him, as he dared not leave him in Khokand. The siege, owing in part to the treachery of the Bek of Marghilan, and to the violent rains, was unsuccessful, and after a fortnight, the Khokandian army was obliged to retire.[1]

This disaster was followed with very important consequences for Mussulman Kul. The intrigues against him grew stronger, and were secretly supported by the Khan. He tried to disarm and propitiate his enemies with favours and promises; but at last, in July, he was obliged to besiege Tashkent again with 30,000 men. As, however, preparations for defence had been made, he found it impossible to take the place by storm, and contented himself with besieging the small fort of Niazbek, and with cutting off the water supply of the city; and then, turning to the north, took Tchimkent. In his absence, however, he found that a sortie had been made from Tashkent, the force blockading Niazbek defeated, and the water supply restored to the city. Hurriedly returning to Tchimkent with his army, he met the Tashkendians on the Tchirtchik. When just on the eve of battle, it was found that the Khan Khudayar and numerous of his followers had abandoned him, and gone over to the enemy. The Khokandian army, losing heart, ran away, and Mussulman Kul himself was obliged to take refuge among the Kiptchaks.[2]

[1] The Russian merchant Kliutcharef, then living in Tashkent, kept a very interesting diary of all these proceedings from February $\frac{5}{17}$ to $\frac{6}{17}$ June 1852, which is published as an appendix to Mr. Velyaminof-Zernof's article.

[2] Nurekin relates this differently. According to him Mussulman Kul won in the battle and captured the Khan, and the fall of Mussulman Kul was owing to the explosion of a subsequent intrigue.

Khudayar Khan had, however, not freed himself from the despotism of Mussulman Kul to fall into the hands of new regents, and a party among the Sarts of Khokand being formed, adverse to the Kiptchaks, he readily joined with them. Nur Mohammed was executed, and his friends were overthrown. Malla Bek, the brother of the Khan, was sent to govern Tashkent. General orders were now given for the massacre of all the Kiptchaks in the Khanate from Ak Masjid (Fort Perovsky) to the mountains separating Khokand from Kashgar, and they were killed everywhere, in the bazaars, in the streets, and on the steppe, wherever they were found. Khokand was thus turned into a vast place of execution, and in all the three months during which this massacre lasted, 20,000 men, it is supposed, were killed. Khudayar was himself by his mother's side a Kiptchak, and this act of carnage was never forgiven nor forgotten.

In the beginning of 1853, while these murders were still continuing, Mussulman Kul was caught, and publicly punished. He was made to sit loaded with fetters, with a tall cap on his head, on a wooden platform, while 600 Kiptchaks were killed before his eyes, and at last he himself was hung. To please the people, who were delighted with the fall of their former oppressors, new and most unheard-of kinds of torture, were applied. It is said that when Mussulman Kul witnessed the horrible spectacle of the punishment of his partisans, he at first sat pale and silent, with difficulty sustaining his emotion; but that when he saw the heads fall of persons entirely innocent, he could no longer contain himself, and cried out, 'For God's sake kill me first.'

After the reign of the Kiptchaks came that of the Sarts. Malla Bek soon quarrelled with his brother and declared war against him, and being defeated fled to Bukhara. Subsequently, at the request of his mother, he was pardoned and recalled to Khokand, but received no new position.

Mirza Akhmet, one of the Sart leaders, and a great opponent of Mussulman Kul, was appointed Bek of Tashkent in his place.[1]

Mirza Akhmet by his severity excited great discontent among the Kirghiz who lived in the district surrounding Tchimkent and Aulié-ata; and finding it impossible to put them down, was obliged to make a compromise with them and satisfy their demands.

This was in 1857. At the same time the Kara Kirghiz and what was left of the Kiptchaks entered into negotiations with Malla Bek and gained to their side many influential Uzbeks, especially Alim Kul, a person who afterwards rose to great promi-

---

[1] Mirza Akhmet is now one of the chief advisers of Yakub Khan, the Amir of Kashgar.

nence. They at once proclaimed Malla Bek their Khan and marched against Khokand.

The Khan with his army went out to meet them, but suffered a decisive defeat at Samantchi. His most trusted adherents immediately turned against him, and he was obliged to give up his throne and fly to Bukhara, while Malla Khan was received as the lawful ruler.

Another reason of dislike to Khudayar Khan had been the advance of the Russians, who in 1853, after the fall of Mussulman Kul, had captured Ak Masjid, and founded Fort Perovsky, and had made considerable progress in the north, having captured Pishpek, Tokmak, and other forts near Vierny.

Khudayar Khan was very well received at the Court of Bukhara, for Nasrullah thought that this might prove another opportunity for him to obtain possession of Khokand, a country the loss of which he had never ceased to regret, and Khudayar was given a sort of honorary position at Court, and subsequently went to live at Samarkand. When he had lived there for some time, for some reason or other the Amir suddenly changed his disposition to him, and sent him to live at Jizakh, at the same time giving strict orders to the Bek of that place to assist him in no possible way, and to prevent all people from holding any communication with him. Khudayar Khan saw himself, therefore, on the point of starvation. He lived with two personal adherents in a little hut made of mud outside of the walls. Afraid to appear in public himself, his attendants gathered reeds and roots which could be used as fuel, and disguising themselves sold them in the town, and with the money thus obtained purchased provisions. Then the mother of Khudayar Khan managed to send him from time to time small sums, and with this money, under an assumed name, he procured two or three camels, which he hired out to carry freight, and when events recalled him to Khokand he had laid the foundation of a fortune, and was standing the chance of becoming a rich merchant.

Malla Khan reigned for two years, during which time he succeeded in making himself much loved by the people. Alim Kul became his chief adviser, but, contrary to the hopes of the other Biis who had taken part in the insurrection, he gave them no share in the Government, and allowed no one to approach the Khan. Their discontent increased to such a degree that some of their leaders, including Shadiman Hodja, resolved to murder the Khan, and taking advantage of the absence of Alim Kul, who had been appointed Bek in Andijan, and having gained over the attendant who always watched over his master, they murdered him during his sleep and proclaimed as Khan Shah Murad, a boy of about fifteen years old, the son of Sarymsak, and therefore nephew of Khudayar Khan.[1]

Malla Khan had left a son, a boy of about thirteen years, Seid Sultan, whom it was the intention of the conspirators also to kill, but Alim Kul, who had quick intelligence of what was taking place, sent to Khokand, and managed secretly to get him out of the palace and bring him to Andijan. The conspirators were very much frightened, thinking Alim Kul had intended immediately to proclaim Seid Sultan the Khan, but were soon quieted by receiving a message from him that he merely wished to save him from death, and that he was devoted heart and soul to the new government. He probably temporised in this way on account of the danger of being disunited in view of the position taken by Tashkent, for this city, with its usual rebellions spirit, under the influence of Shadiman Hodja, one of the murderers of Malla Khan, and of Khanayat Shah, Bek of Turkistan, had just recalled Khudayar Khan from Jizakh, and he had occupied it with his adherents. The army of Khokand, under the command of Shah Murad, with most of the conspirators, immediately moved on Tashkent and besieged Khudayar Khan; but as Tashkent held out strongly, after thirty-one days' siege, they retired. On the homeward march, while the army was resting, Alim Kul, who had just arrived from Andijan, put to death in the Khan's presence four of the leading murderers of Malla Khan, who had just plotted to go over to Khudayar, and on the same day another, Alim Bii, was also killed by his orders. Contrary to expectation Shah Murad, who was with the army, remained Khan, the only change being that Alim Kul was made regent, as he had been in the time of Malla Khan.

Khudayar Khan and his army at once followed and attacked Hodjent. Alim Kul at first began to defend Khokand, but finding general treachery he retired to Marghilan, and then to the mountains.

The young Khan, Shah Murad, somehow disappeared, and it was ascertained afterwards that Khudayar had succeeded in capturing and murdering him. He was also desirous of getting hold of Seid Sultan, but was unsuccessful.

Khokand received its old tyrant, Khudayar Khan, with great delight, and there were now two strong parties in the country—that of Khudayar, who was once again the lawful ruler, and that of Alim Kul, the Regent; and a violent contest lasted between them for three years, all the Uzbeks, with the exception of the Kara Kalpaks, supporting Alim Kul, and the Sarts and townspeople being on the side of Khudayar. Not only the two armies fought, but the indi-

[1] I have given the detailed account of this murder on p. 92.

viduals of the two classes of populations murdered each other whenever they had an opportunity.

The Uzbek party was somewhat divided in consequence of three new pretenders to the throne, descendants of the former Khans— Shahrukh, who had been proclaimed by Mirza Akhmet, Sadyk Bek, and Hadji Bek—and it was said that Alim Kul, to rid himself of opposition, enticed these young men to himself and had them all murdered in Ush, where they are buried on the side of the hill called 'Solomon's Throne.'

After this Alim Kul proclaimed Seid Sultan Khan, and began decisive operations against Khudayar, and soon took Marghilan and Andijan, and twice defeated the Khan's army. Khudayar Khan then sent Sultan Murad Bek to the Amir of Bukhara, asking for assistance, and the Amir—now Mozaffar-Eddin, the son of Nasrullah—came in person with a large army. Alim Kul retreated and shut himself up in the defiles of Kara-Kuldja, where he was for a long time besieged.

At last the Amir became disgusted at his want of success, got angry with Khudayar, sent to Alim Kul as presents a golden staff, a cap, a belt, and a fine Koran, and retired to Bukhara. Upon this Alim Kul advanced from the mountains, took Khokand without difficulty, and Khudayar for a second time sought refuge in Bukhara.

Alim Kul was now supreme ruler of Khokand, for Seid Sultan bore but the nominal title of Khan. Fully understanding the difficulties which internal disputes were causing the country, while lenient to ordinary offenders, he punished with unexampled severity all those accused of political offences, and is said to have executed over 4,000 men.

At first by these means he restored quiet to the Khanate, but soon reaction took place, and he was greeted with general discontent. Prayers from every city went out to Khudayar to return and assume the throne. Khudayar in the meantime was living in Jizakh, where he had renewed his former mercantile operations, but this time on a larger scale. On making representations to the Amir he succeeded in persuading him again to attempt an expedition, and preparations were being made when news arrived of the death of Alim Kul in Tashkent. He had been wounded in the first attack the Russians had made on the city in 1865, under General Tchernaief. The partizans of Alim Kul, fearing the vengeance of Khudayar Khan, immediately fled, most of them going to Kashgar, where Yakub Bek was now making for himself a throne under the pretext of being the general of Buzruk Khan.

About the same time that the Russians took Tashkent, the Bukharan Amir took Hodjent, and one of the first propositions of the Russians in their efforts to make a peace was that the Amir of Bukhara should place on the throne of Khokand the rightful Khan Khudayar, even offering him the support of the Russian troops for that purpose. This, however, he did not accept, feeling confident of his own strength, and advanced to Khokand and reinstated Khudayar. He insisted on retaining Hodjent as the price for his services, and that town therefore remained a Bukharan possession until it was taken by the Russians in 1866. Seid Sultan Khan escaped for the time, but was brought to Khokand and executed in Isfara in 1871.

The Khanate of Khokand, by both Russian and Bukharan conquests, had now been reduced to but a small portion of its former dimensions, but the Khan succeeded in escaping complete conquest by following the shrewd advice of Ata Bek in sending to congratulate the Russians upon the capture of Hodjent. While in his heart hating the Russians, Khudayar became apparently submissive, and for the remaining ten years of his reign was unmolested by them. Fear of the Russians in a great measure restrained his subjects from rebellion, although they were no more contented with his rule than they had previously been; in fact, his reign had become much more severe. He did not give himself up so much to open licentiousness as he had previously done, but he began to make money as fast as possible out of his dominions, both by seizing the bazaars and taking the profits arising from them, and by imposing taxes of every kind upon the country. The Kirghiz and Kiptchaks, although they have not been the greatest sufferers by these taxes, have been the most indignant at them, and in all of their projects they have had the full support of the settled population—a thing which has never before occurred. It was with difficulty that anything could be attempted, as there was great fear that the Russians would march in and reduce the population to submission to the Khan, it being thought that the new conquerors looked upon him as their instrument.

In 1871 an open revolt broke out, but was speedily terminated.

During 1873 a much more serious movement began. The Khan desired to impose additional taxes upon the Kara-Kirghiz in the mountains to the south of Ush and Andijan, and asked as much as three sheep instead of one from a family. There were also some new taxes upon the cultivated land in the mountains. These taxes the Kirghiz refused to pay, and stripped and beat the officers who were sent to collect them; and when troops were sent, conflicts ensued, and the Kirghiz in a mass retired to the inaccessible defiles of the mountains.

At this time the Aftobatcha Abdurrahman Hadji, the son of Mussulman Kul, and brother-in-law to the Khan, who had just returned from a pilgrimage to Mecca,[1]—to the great surprise of all, who had supposed he had been secretly murdered by order of the Khan,—and who enjoyed a great influence among the Kiptchaks, was put in command of the troops, and was sent to bring the Kirghiz to obedience.

The Aftobatcha persuaded the Kirghiz to send to the Khan a deputation of forty men to represent their grievances, and to try to come to some understanding. At the same time he urged the Khan to retain them as hostages, but on no account to harm them, and to treat them well, as order could only be restored by pacific means. The Khan stupidly had all of them executed, and the Aftobatcha was obliged at once to return to Khokand, as the Kirghiz were thoroughly aroused at this act of perfidy, and the Kiptchaks were threatening to join them. All this occurred while I was in Khokand.

Open hostilities commenced at once, and the Kirghiz immediately took Uzgent and Suk, a small fortified place in the mountains, where was part of the private treasury of the Khan. In the low country the rebels met with little success, as they were too badly armed and disciplined to cope with even the poor soldiers of the Khan. A large number of them were taken prisoners, and 500 of them were executed in the bazaar at Khokand; and the pretender to the throne, who called himself Mozaffar Khan, son of Madali Khan, was impaled alive. At the same time the Khan sent two or three special envoys one after the other to Tashkent asking for assistance, and making complaints to the Russians that the Kirghiz subject to the Emperor had invaded Khokand, and were devastating it. On investigation the facts proved to be that several thousand Kirghiz from Khokand, on the breaking out of the disturbance, had emigrated from Khokand into the Russian territory; but when the rebels began to get the upper hand, with the exception of a few Kiptchaks, they all returned. The Russians refused to interfere on the side of the Khan, and the commander of the forces even telegraphed to St. Petersburg for permission to occupy Khokand if the insurrection continued, as

[1] Although the pilgrimage was the avowed object of the Aftobatcha's journey, he had been in reality sent by the Khan to the Sultan at Constantinople to ask his aid against the Russians. *Aftobatcha* is an honorary title meaning ewer-holder.

such a state of affairs was very injurious to Russian interests. This permission was, however, refused.

The position of the Khan was very unpleasant; he felt he could not even rely on those persons who ought to be the most devoted to him. Mirza Hakim, the Khokandian envoy at Tashkent, told me that he himself was strongly in favour of the insurgents, and that he, as well as many others, would abandon the Khan as soon as they saw that the rebellion had any prospect of success. He said that the Khan had promised him in case his mission were successful to make him Bek, but if it were unsuccessful, he was to have his head cut off. It was known that conspiracies were on foot in Andijan and Khokand, and the Khan had great fear of his son the Khan-Zada Nasr'eddin, Bek of Andijan, and desired to bring him to Khokand. The Khan-Zada, however, feared for his life, as some time before the Khan had openly told him that as long as *he* lived he could feel no safety. He therefore refused to go. At the same time three high military commanders in Andijan laid a plot to seize upon the person of Khan-Zada, carry him to the mountains, and proclaim him Khan, hoping that this would add confidence to the insurgent's cause. The Khan-Zada refused to be a party to this plot, and personally wounded two of the conspirators, and had them all arrested and sent to Khokand, where they were executed. It was not, however, until the good offices of his aunt,—a sister of Malla Khan, and much respected at Khokand,—had been brought into play, that he consented to go to his father at Khokand, resigning at the same time the Bekship, and taking his family and treasure with him, saying that he no longer wished to hold any public position.

Ush and Andijan were immediately after taken by the rebels, and various smaller places, such as Suzak, Utch-Kurgan, and Balyktchi. This last city greatly suffered from the insurgents. Its Bek was put to death by being pinned to the ground by a stake driven through his mouth.

The Khan now took command of the troops in person, together with Ata-Bek and the Aftobatcha, although the two former soon retired, leaving the Aftobatcha in sole command. He had several small engagements with the rebels; but a large number of the Khan's soldiers,—it is said several thousand,—passed over to the enemy, and the Aftobatcha shut himself up in the small fort of Tiura-Kurgan, near Namangan, and refused to take any further action.

Messages from Khokand and other cities were sent to the Kirghiz, asking them to advance more quickly, as they would at once rise against the Khan; and the aid of the Kiptchaks, who had hitherto taken no active part in the rebellion, was promised, and it was hoped that the Aftobatcha even might be on their side.

It was now, however, autumn; and with the approach of cold weather the insurrection died out, and the Khan retook his cities with but little opposition, and the country during the winter returned to its usual quiet state. In 1874 the insurrection began again with a plot to put on the throne Mohammed Amin, or Madamin Bek, the second son of Khudayar, who, it is said, himself let out the conspiracy by his great talkativeness. The plan had been prepared by his uncle Batyr Khan Tiura, and it was proposed to seize the Khan about April 1, in one of his towns outside of the capital. Batyr Khan and sixteen of the conspirators were called to the palace, and never returned; it is supposed that they were drowned in a pond within its precincts. Madamin himself was placed under strict surveillance. The Mekhter, Mullah Mir Kamil, was also one of the victims, and was poisoned by order of the Khan, for not having given him previous information. Before that, the Mekhter had been suspected of embezzling the custom-house funds, and had been subjected to a severe ordeal. He was bound on a thin lattice work, which was thrown over a deep ravine, and a horse was made to gallop several times over this frail bridge, threatening at every moment to break through. As the Mekhter came out alive, he was considered innocent—at least, of that offence. The Kirghiz and Kiptchaks now united, and sought for another claimant to the throne, entering into negotiations with Abdul Kerim Bek, a boy of sixteen, and a grandson of Fazyl Bek, the Khan's uncle, who was living at Hodjent. As an infant of a year old, his mother had taken him from Khokand to Hodjent, where she soon after died, and, it is said, that he did not even know of his extraction. At a request of Khudayar, the Russians compelled Abdul Kerim to remove to Tashkent, where he would be under the strictest surveillance, and sent his chief adviser, Abdul Kaum, to Tchimkent.

The failure of these two plots did not restore to the Khan that tranquillity and quiet which he had previously enjoyed. He became sombre and distrustful. His body-guard, composed of 400 picked men, educated to that trust from their infancy, ceased to inspire him with the same confidence as before. He felt himself menaced everywhere and at all times, and he even saw dangers where there were none. For a long time he did not even leave his palace. The entry of his room was usually guarded day and night by a black slave, Nasim Toga, who was blindly attached to him, and who was ordered to let no one—not even his wives or children— enter without consulting him. His distrust and fear were so great, that he was only lulled asleep by the noise of the voices of three of his most faithful servants, who were ordered to remain in the adjoining room, and to make themselves constantly heard, as a palpable proof that watch was being kept.'[1] His eldest son Nasreddin was placed under strict surveillance, and the system of espionage throughout the Khanate was carried to its utmost limits. His best spy was a certain Mir Alim, a rich merchant of Khokand, who had agents in the Russian possessions, as well as everywhere within the dominions of the Khan, and who naturally played upon the affairs of the Khan in order to gain for himself a good fortune.

One of the most popular chiefs of the insurrection of 1873, was a certain Mamyn Batcha, from Andijan, who had taken refuge first on Russian territory, and then in Kashgar, where he had tried to find support. Not succeeding in this, he returned with some adherents to Khokand, but was defeated, and took refuge in Russia, where he was arrested and sent to Siberia. A Kiptchak, too, Mussulman Kul, a relative of the former Regent, Alim Kul, in June, 1874, collected a band of partisans in the mountains north of Namangan, and finally succeeded in taking the town of Kasan, from which the Bek had fled. The Khan sent against them 7,000 men, under the command of the Aftobatcha, and of Issa-aulié, the Bek of Shahrikhana, and defeated the insurgents at Tiura Kurgan. Mussulman Kul died in the fight, and Said Pulad Khan, a new pretender, together with a certain Mumyn, a Kirghiz chief, fled to Russian territory, where they were caught. Another slight insurrection of the Kirghiz to the north of Namangan, was also easily put down.

In 1875, General Kaufmann, in order to make a bargain with the Khan, resolved to give up Abdul Kerim, and sent him to Khokand. While the Russian embassy was still there, the rebellion broke out again; and the Aftobatcha, who had been waiting his own time to avenge the murder of his father, Mussulman Kul, appeared as its leader. Everything must have been well prepared, for the army deserted in a mass, and Khudayar's brother and sons immediately went over to the rebels. Khudayar was forced to fly for the third time, and escaped with all his treasure to Tashkent, where he was well received by the Russians. He was subsequently sent to live at Orenburg. His eldest son, Nasreddin, was proclaimed Khan, but did not long keep the title, for he allowed himself to be drawn into a war against the Russians, the details of which I have given elsewhere—and eventually lost his throne, after which Khokand was annexed to Russia under the historic name of Ferghana.

---

[1] 'Journal de St. Pétersbourg,' No. 24. January 26 (February 7), 1875.

HISTORY OF KHOKAND. 359

GENEALOGICAL TABLE OF THE SOVEREIGNS OF KHOKAND.

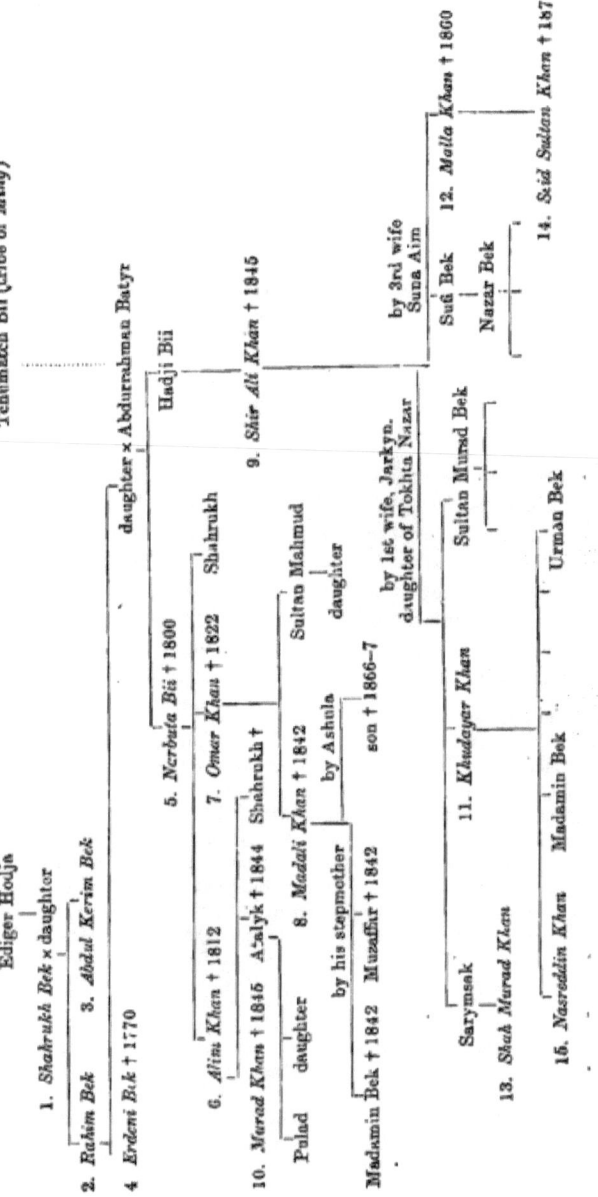

APPENDIX II.

REVIEW OF VÁMBÉRY'S 'HISTORY OF BUKHARA,'
BY PROFESSOR GRIGORIEF.[1]

History of Bukhara from the Earliest Period down to the Present, composed for the first time after Oriental known and unknown historical manuscripts, by Arminius Vámbéry, London, 1873, xxxv. 419 pp. 8vo.

IN the very title of this work the author represents that it is the *first* which has appeared in Europe on this subject, and that it has been based in a great measure on Oriental historical manuscripts *unknown* in Europe. In the preface he expatiates still more on his services. 'It seems, however, to be the lot ordained for me to traverse regions where I have had scarcely any, or absolutely no, predecessors;[2] and having now to explore with the pen an entirely new field,' he says (p. viii.), and further on (p. xvi.): 'The second

---

[1] As this review was published in a journal, but little circulated in Russia, and hardly known abroad—the 'Journal of the Ministry of Public Instruction' for November 1873—I have thought that a translation of it would be interesting and valuable to students of the East. I have in some cases slightly condensed it without changing the ideas of the author.

[2] As is evident from this and other passages, Mr. Vámbéry seems to think that he was almost the first traveller in Central Asia in recent times.

Without speaking of the numerous Russian merchants and agents who went to Khiva and Bukhara during the seventeenth century, I subjoin an imperfect list of European travellers in Central Asia from the beginning of the eighteenth century up to the date of Mr. Vámbéry's journey, the most of whom have left published accounts of their travels.

- 1690. *Dubrovin*, Khiva.
- 1725. *Florio Beneveni*, Khiva and Bukhara.
- 1727–30. *Basilio Batazzi*, Turkistan and Persia.
- 1732. *Colonel Garber*.
- 1741. *George Thompson* and *Reynold Hogg*, Khiva and Bukhara
- 1740–1. *Muravin* and *Gladishef*, Khiva.
- 1743. *Müller*, Tashkent.
- 1752. *Nikolai Grigorief*, Bukhara.
- 1774. *Philip Yefremof*, Bukhara and Samarkand.

part of my work (i.e. the 'History of Bukhara, from its Conquest by the Uzbeks') deals almost entirely with data hitherto little known, or entirely unknown even to the world of scholars, for they bring before us *a series of princes and even whole dynasties regarding whom scarcely anything has, as yet, been written in Asia, and not a single word in Europe.*' In conclusion the author says that 'it must always be a difficult task to write the *first* history of any country,' and that the present is 'the fruits of many years' toil.'

Statements of such a kind from a professor of Oriental languages, who has personally visited the country, the history of which he writes, and who has already succeeded in giving himself a reputation as a writer, would naturally cause every Orientalist, interested in the history of Central Asia, to read this 'History of Bukhara' with the expectation of finding in it, if not an artistic historical work, at least a whole mine of new information, of new facts, and of new conclusions penetrated with the spirit of European criticism, and enlivened by the author's acquaintance with the nature of the country investigated by him, and with the character of its inhabi-

1793-4. *Blankennagel*, Khiva.
1793-5. *Metropolitan Chrysanth*, Balkh, Bukhara and Khiva.
1794. *Timothei Burnashof* and *A. S. Bernosikof*, Bukhara.
1800. *Pospielof* and *Burnashof*, Tashkent.
1813-4. *Nazarof*, Tashkent and Khokand.
1819. *Muravief*, Khiva.
1820. *Negri* and *Baron Meyendorf*, Bukhara.
1821-2. *Fraser*, Khorasan.
1830. *Potanin*, Khokand.
1831-3. *Burnes*, Bukhara.
1834. *Honiberger*, Bukhara.
1834. *Demaison*, Bukhara.
1836. *Vitkevitch*, Bukhara.
1840. *Abbott*, Khiva.
1840. *Thomson*, Khiva.
1840. *Shakespeare*, Khiva, Merv.
1841. *Nikiforof*, Khiva.
1841. *Connolly*, Khiva, Khokand, and Bukhara.
1841. *Stoddart*, Bukhara.
1841-2. *Khanikof, Lehmann, Butinief*, Bukhara and Samarkand.
1842-3. *Danilefsky* and *Basiner*.
1842-3. *Eversmann*, Khiva.
1843. *Dr. Wolff*, Bukhara.
1851. *Kliutcharef*, Tashkent.
1858. *Admiral Butakoff*, the Oxus to Kungrad.
1858. *General Ignatieff, Lerch*, and *Kühlewein*, Khiva and Bukhara.

An interesting map by Mr. Jacob Khanikof, giving the routes of many of these travellers, is appended to Book X. of the Memoirs (Zapiski) of the Imp. Russ. Geogr. Soc., 1855. [E. S.]

tants. Unfortunately, every page of Mr. Vámbéry's book only disappoints such expectations, and the general result of reading it shows that the very small particle of what is really new in his book is lost in the mass of what is old and well-known, which in most cases, too, he has misunderstood and has erroneously studied. It appears that instead of communicating new sources of information he has not even made use of very important books accessible to all, and has not even known of their existence. It seems, in short, that Mr. Vámbéry, in beginning his work, had not the slightest acquaintance with the history of Central Asia; and in the simplicity of his soul regarded his own gradual emancipation from complete ignorance on this subject as discoveries which would astonish and delight the learned world.

In consequence of this relation of Mr. Vámbéry to his subject, we have not in his book a conscientious and learned work, the result of many years' study, but a very light and superficial compilation, put together somehow or other in a few months, and with very frequent errors and omissions of the most unpardonable character—a compilation which would not be worth speaking about had it not been received both in the West and in Russia by unlearned persons with full credence in the boast of the author, as a monumental work, and in this quality been lauded to the skies.

To show the foundation of our own unfavourable opinion of the last work of the noted traveller who has shown himself such a poor historian, we shall look more or less minutely at the contents of all the nineteen chapters of his book, together with the preface and the introduction.

In his preface, Mr. Vámbéry, after naming eleven works in eastern languages, which were his chief materials for the first part of his book – the 'History of Bukhara to the Uzbek invasion'—adds that besides these he has made use of all that he 'could find relating to the past history of Transoxiana in Oriental works, both printed and in manuscript, or in European histories, biographies, or books of travel' (p. xii.). 'As extensive a knowledge as can possibly be obtained of all literature bearing on this subject,' he adds directly afterwards, 'is now-a-days the first requisite for an author attempting any work.' This is of course true, and yet there can be no doubt that the author of the 'History of Bukhara' did not refer in preparing it to such European writers on the history of Central Asia as Deguignes, Abel Remusat, Klaproth, and Ritter, to say nothing of those less known. This circumstance alone shows what kind of a writer Mr. Vámbéry is, as well as what kind of a professor. Further on he enumerates five sources of information for the history of Bukhara which he supposes to be *new* and *un-*

known to anyone but himself; and what are they? The most important of these, and that which has furnished him with the whole 'series of princes and even dynasties,' about which, as he boasts, 'not a word has been written in Europe,' is the 'Tarikhi Mukim-Khani,' the text of which, with a partial French translation, was published fifty years ago in St. Petersburg by the late Professor Senkofsky.[1] The second in importance, the 'History of Bukhara,' by Narshaki, has been known to the learned world for more than thirty years, thanks to the extracts made from it by our Orientalist Khanikof. There are five manuscripts of this work in the libraries of St. Petersburg alone. The third source, 'Tarikhi Seid Rakim,' was obtained by Mr. Lerch during his visit to Bukhara in 1859, and is well known by extracts made from it in various works by Mr. Lerch and by the Academician Veliaminof Zernof.[2] Thus only two out of the five sources mentioned appear to be really new and unknown to anyone but Mr. Vámbéry—the poem in the Jagatai language, 'Sheibani Nameh,' and a collection of poems, 'Dakhme-i-Shahan,' both of which, as is evident from the citations of Mr. Vámbéry himself, contain almost nothing historical.[3] There was no reason on account of this to raise a cry throughout all Europe and boast of the abundance of the new information communicated to the world.

In calling his book the 'History of Bukhara,' its author was obliged to explain what he meant by the name of Bukhara, for the boundaries of the country, the capital of which is the city of Bukhara, have greatly differed in different times. Part of the introduction is dedicated to this explanation, from which it is evident that by Bukhara the author means the Khanate of Bukhara within the limits which it had before the Russian movement beyond the Syr Darya, and in addition the countries on the left of the Amu Darya, north of the Hindukush and of the Paropamisus, beginning from the sources of that river to the Murghab on the west—countries very often in historical times independent of Bukhara. Let it be so, although this extension of the term Bukhara is not entirely correct; but why does the author then identify Bukhara with Maverannahr, or Transoxiana, and try to prove that the Arabs meant by Maverannahr not only the country to the north of the Oxus, or Amu Darya, but also the left bank of that river from its

---

[1] The title is 'Supplément à l'histoire générale des Huns, des Turks, et des Mogols,' par M. Joseph Senkowski:—St. Pétersbourg, 1824. [E. S.]

[2] Among others in 'Archæological Journey in the Region of Turkistan in 1867,' by P. Lerch. St. Petersburg, 1870. [E. S.]

[3] A copy of the 'Sheibani Nameh,' has long been in the Imperial Library of St. Petersburg. [E. S.]

source to the Murghab, we can in no way understand, especially as all that is nonsense, and is not even proved by the only Arab geographer whom Mr. Vámbéry read and whom he cites. We find, however, that this geographer says entirely the contrary to that stated by Vámbéry (see 'Viæ Regnorum, auctore al-Istakhri' in edit. M. I. de Goeje, Lugd. Batav., 1870, pp. 286, 287). Indeed, it could not be otherwise, for the very name Maverannahr means 'what is beyond the river,' and by the river is there meant the Jaihun, the Oxus of the ancients, and the Amu of our times. Quite mistakenly, too, does Mr. Vámbéry call this geographer (El Belkhi) the oldest Arabian geographer; and finding there the name of a country 'Udjan,' explains that this would be more correctly written 'Vadjan,' when this is the well-known 'Vakhan'; and in the same place in enumerating the districts on the left bank of the Amu he omits Badakshan, and informs us that the Amu means among the natives 'river,' while it is well known that the Amu Darya was so called from the city Amuye, or Amulye, on its left bank. He there repeats his absurd idea that it is necessary to pronounce Khahrezm and not Kharezm.[1] In the same place, speaking of the thirty-fifth degree of latitude he calls it longitude, and the seventy-first degree of longitude he calls latitude, and in addition does not think it necessary to say from what meridian he calculates, probably supposing that on all maps the degrees are counted from the same meridian. All this is on one page of the introduction (p. xxii.), not counting the statement on the same page that according to his 'historical researches' the left bank of the Amu was an integral portion of Bukhara, or Maverannahr, from the time of the Samanides; whereas there is nothing in the book to show any ground for this wrong assertion. No less ignorance of the history and geography of Maverannahr under Arab rule is evident on the two following pages (xxiii, xxiv). The chief town in the district of Osrushna he positively calls Bu Mekhet, although in the manuscripts the name of this city is written without diacritical points in so many different ways that it is by no means known how it should be read.[1] In the neighbouring district of Tchatch (Tashkent) there appear, according to him, the cities Otrar, Siganak, and Sirem (i.e. Sairam), of which Balkhi (that is, Istakhri) makes no mention whatever, and which only became known in very late times. Mr. Vámbéry is even surprised that during his journey in Bukhara he

---

[1] Mr. Lerch in his 'Khiva oder Khârezm' ('Russian Review,' vol ii. pp. 445, 447), has conclusively shown Mr. Vámbéry's error, and takes Khârezm to mean *Lowland*. [E. S.]

[2] In the same passage 'Sabad or Savat' should be identified not with Sarvad, but with Savat between Zamin and Ura-tepé. [E. S.]

heard no mention of the 'great wall, which Belkhi describes as having been built by Abdullah bin Hamid between the mountains and the Yaxartes.' No wonder, because there is not a word about any such wall neither in Belkhi nor, as far as we know, in any other Arabian geographer or historian. Turning then to the history of Tchatch, Mr. Vámbéry informs us that 'in the pre-Islamite period these northern shores of the Yaxartes formed an independent state governed by Turks, which, however, was annexed to Bukhara during the Arabic rule there in the time of the Samanides.' But in the pre-Islamite period all Maverannahr consisted of independent districts, for the most part having Turkish rulers; and the district of Tchatch was subdued by Mussulman arms long before the appearance of the Samanides. 'It asserted its independence again under the Seldjukides,' continues our historian, 'and the Turkish prince Kadr Khan rose to considerable power.' The fact is that the district of Tchatch, which fell under the power of the Samanides, together with the other dominions of the Abbasides in Maverannahr, never again obtained its independence, but with the enfeebling of the Samanides became subject to the Turkish sovereign ruling in Kashgar. This happened at the end of the tenth century, when the Seldjukides had not yet become important. And the power of the sovereigns of Kashgar did not begin with Kadr, or Kadyr Khan, who died in 1032, but at least with Bogra Khan, who took from the Samanides both Samarkand and Bukhara. 'From the date of the Mongolian invasion,' we read further in Vámbéry, 'Tchatch became a bone of contention between Khâhrezmians in the west and Uigurs in the east; and after the death of Djenghiz Kadr and his successors, waged a long fratricidal war with the Jagataides about this very territory.' Here there is hardly a word that is not erroneous. After the Mongol invasion of Maverannahr there were neither Khârezm-Shahs who could fight with the Uigurs, nor Uigurs who could fight with the Khârezm-Shahs; and even before the Mongol invasion the Khârezm-Shahs contended, not for Tchatch, but for Bukhara, and not with the Uigurs but with the Karakhatai or Karakidans, of the very existence of whom, as is evident further on, Mr. Vámbéry is ignorant. But what is best of all is the 'fratricidal' war, which, after the death of Tchingiz, Kadr Khan and his successors had with the Jagataides. Kadr Khan, as we have seen, died in 1032, and Mr. Vámbéry makes him outlive Tchingiz Khan, who died in 1227. The result is that Kadr Khan lived two centuries and a half, to say nothing of the fact that the power of his successors was destroyed by the Karakidans in 1120; so that the Jagataides, even if they had wished, could not have fought with the descendants of Kadr

Khan, who did not then exist, and who besides had not the slightest relation to them.

To show all the mistakes of Mr. Vámbéry we should be obliged to write a book three times larger than his 'History of Bukhara.' Therefore, in his introduction we shall note only two more capital errors. On page xxviii. Mr. Vámbéry says that Samarkand 'never became a centre of inland commerce,' for 'it lay a little on one side of the great high-road to India' (whence ?). This shows that Vámbéry has no idea of the great and active traffic which was formerly carried on through Samarkand between China and Eastern Turkistan on the one hand, and Western Asia and Europe on the other, to say nothing of the fact that even part of the goods coming from India arrived at Bukhara only through Kashgar and Samarkand. On page xxxii we read that Bukhara has 'grain, fruit, silk, cotton, and dyes, all unrivalled of their kind,' and that 'the same may be said of its cattle, for besides their horses, which are celebrated throughout Asia, their camels surpass all the other kinds of this most useful domestic animal in the south and west of Asia, and their mutton, finally, is equal to any in the world.' This is not history. Mr. Vámbéry was himself in Bukhara, and therefore allows himself such inadmissible hyperboles. In what part of Asia are Bukharan horses celebrated, and why does he think that Bukharan cotton is unrivalled? With regard to camels and sheep, it is well known that Bukhara obtains animals of this kind chiefly from the Kirghiz steppes.

The first chapter of his work Mr. Vámbéry devotes to the history of the country before the introduction of Islam. It is natural to expect that the reader should find here the information about this period given by the Greek writers,—for the Greeks reigned over Transoxiana a long time after the conquest of the country by Alexander the Great,—as well as from the Chinese writers; for in the second century, B.C., this country was visited by Tchjan-Tsiang, and the beginning of the seventh century, A.D., by Hioneu Thsang; and both of these travellers communicate very important details with regard to it, irrespective of the information contained in the Chinese official histories of the Han dynasty, of the elder and younger dynasty of Bei, of the 'Northern Courts,' and of the dynasties of Su and Thang. Instead of this, Mr. Vámbéry has apparently never heard of the Greek and Chinese authorities on the past of the country, the history of which he undertook to write. There is not even one word in his history to show that the Greeks ever ruled there, or that there was a time when the sovereigns of Maverannahr considered themselves vassals of the Emperor of China. The ancient history of Bukhara, according to Vámbéry, begins with the legeudary tales of Narshaki about the origin of the city of Bukhara, and the people who reigned there not long before the invasion of the Arabs, and about the early times of their conquest; and these tales are besides set forth without any criticism, with the name of a town *Eskedjiket* (Sekedjiket) taken as the name of its ruler. After that, he tells us, as one of his own discoveries, that Maverannahr was anciently inhabited by a race of Persian origin distinguished by high culture, and ascribes to the Roman historian Justin (p. 6) a phrase about Bactria which belongs to the Greek writer Apollodorus of Artamis, and refers, not to Bactria, but to India; and further on he makes the erroneous statement that 'the Persian dialect of modern Central Asia contains both in its words and forms more traces of the old Persian language, before it was disfigured by Semitic and Turanian elements, than all the other dialects of the language put together;' and that in the Tadjik dialect, 'the pronoun and verb appear to be less influenced by the Turkish language, than is the Persian or modern Iran.' Those who wish to assure themselves of the contrary, may read the grammatical notes on the Tadjik dialect appended to the edition of the 'Memoirs of Mirza Shems,' in that dialect.[1] On the west of Bukhara the old Transoxanian civilisation could not extend itself, we read further in Mr. Vámbéry's work (p. 8), because there, on the west of Bukhara, began sandy steppes, while on the previous page he cites from Rawlinson a quotation of Al Biruni, with regard to the high state of the civilisation of Khârezm, the present Khanate of Khiva, on the west of Bukhara.

In the same way, when beginning to talk about the Turanian neighbours of Transoxiana, Mr. Vámbéry at the first step displays his complete ignorance of the subject. He does not know where is the fatherland of the Guzz, because Balkhi (the only Arabian geographer read by the celebrated traveller), places them on the north of Tchatch, while Persian authorities many centuries later apply the same term to the Persian nomads in the neighbourhood of the modern Andkhoi. When a man is not able to put together such simple things, he should not write history, but confine himself to sketches of travel. Immediately after this, Vámbéry ascribes to the Turks what Rawlinson says of the Scythians, and then expresses a doubt whether the first migration of the Turks over the Oxus could have taken place 700 years before Christ. This doubt is very well put, since the Turks appear in history only in the sixth century after Christ; and with such information, and

---

[1] See Note, p. 109. [F. S.]

such an historical method, people set themselves to write history, and wish even to teach and to astonish. . . . The learning of the author is also well recommended by his derivation of the name *Balkh*, from the Turkish *balyk* (p. 11); his book abounds in similar derivations, of which he is evidently proud, thinking that they are discoveries. According to him, *Bukhara* is also a Mongol word (p. 14), for *Bukhar* is even now the word for a Buddhistic 'temple' or 'monastery.' This Sanscrit *vihara*, borrowed by the Mongols, he takes for a Mongol word. As to when and how the nomad population of the steppes of the north of the Syr Darya came into Maverannahr, the celebrated traveller has not the slightest idea, and therefore with childish *naïveté* asks the question whether the Turks at their earliest appearance in Transoxiana played the parts of rulers, or served as auxiliary troops of native princes; and with still greater *naïveté*, says this is difficult to decide. But he has no difficulty in deciding that the Sogdian ruler *Maniakh* mentioned by Zemarkhus was a Turanian. Why? Because *Maniakh* is a Turkish word, meaning 'prince, noble, distinguished,' and must have this meaning, because the chiefs of the Diko-kamenny Kirghiz are called *Manaps*, as if *Maniakh* and *Manap* were the same word. He also has no difficulty in deciding that Buddhism penetrated into Maverannahr before the beginning of history (p. 14), for he evidently does not know that the teaching of Buddha began in India only five centuries, B.C., as he is also ignorant that Hiouen Thsang travelled in this country not in the fifth (p. 15) but in the seventh century, A.D.

The second and third chapters, treating of the conquest of Bukhara by the Arabs, and of the rule of the Khalifs there, to the time of the Samanides, are perhaps the best of the book, *i.e.*, least filled with mistakes of every kind. Unfortunately here, as in the remaining parts of his book, the author does not cite the sources whence he borrows his facts, which turns his history into a child's book. In applying himself to his work, the author, it appears, did not suspect that an historian who is not contemporary with the events which he describes, *i.e.*, who is not himself an authority, is bound to show whence he derives his information, because, among other things, the probability of the event is to some degree determined by the character of the person who recounts it. Writers like Mr. Vámbéry always avoid this duty, because if they should give the sources of their information, they would show their want of acquaintance with the literature of their subject, and their inability to become oriented in it. Concerning the facts relative to this period of Bukharan history, the 'Geschichte der Chalifen' of Weil, gives them much better than the special work of Vámbéry,

who cares for nothing more than the tales of Narshaki. With
regard to the choice of these facts, their grouping and their
meaning, Mr. Vámbéry's work is beneath criticism. The struggle
of Maverannahr with the Arabs for independence, and its struggle
a thousand years before with Alexander the Great for the same
independence (of which there is not a word in Vámbéry's book),
are events almost unparalleled in the history of all Asia; and
Mr. Vámbéry, in telling of this struggle, overlooked such characteristic moments as the last efforts of Ezdedjerd to oppose
the attack of the Arabs with forces which he chiefly drew from
his vassal possessions on the north of the Amu. For Mr. Vámbéry
this struggle begins only in the forty-sixth year of Hejra (666 A.D.).
In this connection,—the relation of the victories of the celebrated
Kuteibi-ibn-Muslim,—our historian communicates facts which are
neither in Tabari nor in Narshaki;—whence did he get them?
—and makes Kuteibi take Vardan (that is Vardan-Khudat, according to Narshaki), in the ninety-ninth year, A.H. (717-718 A.D.),
although Kuteibi had died long before. The year 89 A.H. (corresponding to 707-8 A.D.), he makes 698 (p. 26) and a little further
on, 94, A.H. (712-713 A.D.), he makes 742; while 95, A.H. (713-714
A.D.), he makes 711 of our era. In general, Vámbéry considers
chronological accuracy as superfluous, and to put one year instead
of another is apparently of no importance to him. The best of all
is his account of the invasion of Kashgar by Kuteibi in the
beginning of the eighth century of our era. Vámbéry finds there
Uigur (?) princes whom he makes call in Kalmuk auxiliaries from
north Jungaria (p. 31), while the name of Kalmuk, as is well
known, appears in history for the first time in the fifteenth
century. The following phrase too is good: 'we are told that the
Arabs extended their incursions into the province of Kansu' (in
Western China). There are no references for this, and judging
from the character of the information, we should suppose that
during his wanderings in Bukhara Mr. Vámbéry heard about this
from his Dervish companion. From the same source he probably
also obtained the information that Turfan in Eastern Turkistan
embraced Islam on the very first appearance of the Arabs (p. 32).

In the third chapter, the most amusing thing is the part which
Mr. Vámbéry makes the well-known Abu-Muslim (whom he calls
'founder of a dynasty') play among the present Turkomans and
Uzbeks, and his reflections on that favourite as well as on the
false prophet *El-Mokanna*; nowhere in other parts of the book
does his historical tact shine so brilliantly. No, we are mistaken;
further on he is still more amusing about Tamerlane.

The fourth page is devoted to praise of the flourishing period of the rule of the Samanides, which he describes under the guidance partly of Narshaki, and partly of Mirkhond, a compiler of the fifteenth century, and of *Zinet-et-Tavarikh*, a compilation made in the beginning of the present century. Neither here nor further on is there any mention of Ibn-el-Athir, or of his copyist Ibn Khaldun. We are mistaken; Vámbéry knows of the existence of Ibn-el-Athir, but only by a quotation of this chief Mussulman chronicler in Defrémery. This would be the same as writing the history of the ancient east, and ignoring Herodotus. Mr. Vámbéry also displays a total absence of any knowledge of the whole literature of the coins of the Samanides which have been found in Northern Europe, and which show how great was the trade of Maverannahr under their rule. There is not one word on this subject of the highest importance and interest. Instead of this, in his efforts to show the political power of Samanide Ismail, he erroneously ascribes him dominion over Shiraz (p. 67), which was never in his power.

The fifth chapter relates to the fall of the Samanide power, and the transition of Maverannahr to the 'rule of the Turks;' but what Turks they were, he certainly does not know. Without hesitation he calls them *Uigurs*, while if he had carefully read the only Arabic geographer known to him, Balkhi (*i.e.* Istakhri), to say nothing of Ibn Khordadbah, Ibn Khaukal, Masudi or Edrisi, he would have seen at once that these were not Uigurs, but Kharlukhs. Mr. Vámbéry, as an Uigur specialist, ought to have understood this long ago; but even in his 'Uigurische Sprachmonumente' he displayed an astonishing historical ignorance on this subject. This fifth chapter also exposes Mr. Vámbéry's knowledge of the Persian language to great doubt. *Amiri Reshid*, he translates, 'the *brave* prince,' instead of 'the just;' and *Amiri Shedid*, 'the *just* prince,' instead of 'the austere' (pp. 78–9.) But the Uigurs, or Kharlukhs, had Turkish rulers, who took Maverannahr from the Samanides, and the history of these rulers Mr. Vámbéry knows very unsatisfactorily. It is given by him chiefly in the sixth chapter, which is especially devoted to a detailed history of the Seldjukides,—very much out of place in a history of Bukhara,— a country which fell under their sway only temporarily. With regard to the struggle of Ilek Khan with the famous conqueror of India, the Sebuktekinide Mahmud, in the very beginning of the eleventh century, about which Utbi, Ibn-el-Athir, and others speak, there is not a word in Vámbéry. He knows only of the last intervention of Mahmud in the dispute of the successors of Ilek, and the Khans Arslan and Kadyr. He makes Ilek Khan live till

e time of this dispute, and take part in it, although in reality he
d died some years previously; and not knowing that Ilek and
s successors were vassals of Mahmud, presents the events related
them in a false light (p. 91). However the history of the
harlukh sovereigns, who, besides Maverannahr, ruled over
estern Jungaria and Eastern Turkistan, has never been well
udied, and presents much that is dark and perplexing; the confusion
Mr. Vámbéry is, therefore, perhaps excusable. But what is inex-
sable is to take, as he does in his whole book, *Karakidans* for
igurs, and to suppose that *Kara Khatai* means the modern Chinese
rovinces of Shansi and Hansu (p. 101). This is the height of
istorical distortion, the like of which is not even found in the
orks of Mr. Vámbéry's famous countryman the late Viennese
ientalist Hammer.[1] Before these two colossi of historical,
hnographical, and geographical ignorance, comparatively little
nportance should be given to all the other errors of the famous
aveller; such as his admission, that he is unable to discover any
ention of Jend in the geographers (p. 89), his statements that the
untry between the Oxus and Yaxartes, that is, all Maverannahr,
as the inheritance from their fathers of the grandsons of Seldjuk
p. 91-2); that the authority of the Seldjukites was felt even in
frica itself; that the Gurkhan (Mr. Vámbéry does not know that
is is the title of a man called Yeliu-Tashi, but takes this title for
is proper name) extended his authority over a portion of the 'so-
alled' Khatai (p. 103), to say nothing of other charming passages
the sixth chapter.

The struggle for the supremacy over Bukhara and Samarkand
etween the sovereigns of Kara Khatai on one side, and the
hárezm-Shahs on the other, constitutes the subject of the eighth
hapter. Even there Mr. Vámbéry continues to call the Kara
hatayans Uigurs, and besides, does not understand the events of
his struggle, which, for the Khárezm-Shahs, had a religious cha-
acter. He does not understand, too, that it was constantly
xcited by the rulers of Bukhara and Samarkand with the aim of
aking themselves independent, both of the Khárezm-Shahs, and
f their Kara Khatai suzerains. He does not know that these
ulers were descendants of these Kharlukh Karakhanides, who
ook Maverannahr from the Samanides, and as such had certain
easons for their political claims. The sway of the Khárezm-Shahs
xtended on the north, according to Vámbéry, to the very Volga

[1] The orientalists of St. Petersburg say that Hammer can never be quoted or
elieved without the verification of his citations, which are very frequently
rroneous. [E. S.]

(p. 109), but in conclusion, the Kara Kidan ruler who fought against the Khârezm-Shah, Kutb Eddin Mohammed, Vámbéry considers as the same Gurkhan (Yeliu Tashi) who founded the sovereignty of Kara Kitans, and seriously remarks that the Gurkhan was now 90 years old (p. 113). This campaign took place in 1213, and Yeliu Tashi (the Gurkhan) died in 1136, and had he lived till 1213, would have been not 90, but more than 130 years old. This great mistake Mr. Vámbéry made, notwithstanding that the historian Juveini, whom he quotes, calls the Gurkhan who fought with Kutb Eddin by his name *Tchiluka*.

To relate the conquest of Maverannahr by Tchinghiz Khan, following Juveini only as Vámbéry does in his ninth chapter, is no great service when this conquest was recounted by D'Ohsson forty years ago from all the other sources. Vámbéry apparently cannot know of the existence of the first volume of such a work as D'Obsson's 'L'Histoire des Mongols.' If he knew of it he would not derive the name of the Kerait Van Khan (Ong Khan) from the Uigur *un*, 'right' (p. 120), because Van is a Chinese title; and if he had known even a little Mongolian he would not have derived the name of the Kerait from the Turkish words *kir-it*, 'grey dog' (*ibid.*), for *t* in the name Kerait is evidently the Mongolian sign of the plural. This tribe, which still exists, is called Kirei or Kerai. Had Mr. Vámbéry been acquainted with the work of D'Ohsson he would not have said that Tchinghiz Khan fixed his residence in the fortress of Karakorum (p. 121), since Karakorum was constructed only by his successor, Ugedei, and was never a fortress; and he he would not have said that Tchinghiz gave his son Tuli Khorasan Persia and India, when the appanage of Tuli was Mongolia itself; and if he had read the traveller no less famous than himself, Marco Polo, he would not have made the Emperor Khubilai send Marco Polo on a mission to Kerman (p. 139)! When we know what kind of an historian Mr. Vámbéry is, we of course do not blame him for blindly following the Mussulman stories of the complete depopulation of Maverannahr by Tchinghiz Khan; but we should have considered it the duty of anybody else to turn his attention to what is said on this subject in the travels of the Taoist monk, Tch'ang Tch'ung.

The rule of the Tchinghizides over Maverannahr is considered in the ninth chapter. But we were wrong in saying *considered*; he does not consider it there, but copies extracts from Mussulman historians, chiefly after the incorrect Hammer, about the ruin and devastation that were brought on this country by the quarrels of the different members of the family of Tchinghiz. About the genealogy of the Jagataides, who inherited Maverannahr, Mr.

Vámbéry has very confused ideas. For instance, he considers Kabul-Shah to be the last of this race (p. 157), and while thus ignorant has the boldness to accuse the Persian historian Mirkhond of error in saying that the Jagataides long after appear as rulers in the Djete Ulus and in Mongolia, when that fact does not admit of the slightest doubt. Nevertheless, taking into account the absence of detailed authorities for the history of the Jagataides, we must say of the ninth chapter that it is one of the most satisfactory in Vámbéry's book. He very truly remarks that it was in the period of the Jagataides that various religious teachers obtained in Maverannahr an immense importance, which the Mussulman clergy have kept up to this time; for under the Mongolian sway it was only with the religious class that the population could find support, defence, and protection (p. 160).

There now comes on the historical scene a personage about whom writers like Vámbéry love to speak in grand and sounding phrases—the terrible Tamerlane; and our historian of Bukhara of course does not let pass an opportunity of showing himself the panegyrist of such a hero, and devotes to him fifty pages of his book—the tenth and eleventh chapters. Unfortunately, in these fifty pages we find nothing new, except mistakes of various kinds, and a complete misunderstanding of the causes and character and influence of the events of the history of Central Asia. The explanation of the psychological contradictions united in the character of Tamerlane would be a very new and interesting problem—incomparably more interesting than an account of all the well-known campaigns of this conqueror beyond the boundaries of Maverannahr, an account with which Mr. Vámbéry feasts the learned world, forgetting that the biographies of Tamerlane by Sheref-eddin and Arabshah have existed in European translations for more than a hundred years. Mr. Vámbéry begins his biography of Tamerlane by the discovery that the title of *Kurkan*, the only one borne by this 'scourge of the world,' is the name of that branch of the family *Berlas*, from which he was descended (p. 163). Without going into an explanation of what this title means, we may remark that Tamerlane himself ought to know the source of this title, at least as well as Vámbéry, and Tamerlane in his autobiography, speaking of his ancestor Karajar Noyan, says that among other favours from Jagatai, the son of Tchinghiz Khan, his ancestor received the title of *Kurkan* (the 'Mulfuzat-i-Timury,' translated by Stewart, p. 28), and therefore this was not the family name of Tamerlane. The remark of Vámbéry that Karajar Noyan is a mythical personage was made before him by Defrémery.

Our Hungarian historian in general prefers silence with regard to those learned men whose ideas he borrows. It is also strange that in many places he textually cites the 'Autobiography of Tamerlane,' when from his quotation on page 164 we must believe that he knows it only through the 'Indian Surveys' of Markham, an excellent book in its way, but not an authority on the history of Jagatai literature.

On page 179 Vámbéry does a thing very unusual for him—he names his authorities. He enumerates the biographies of Tamerlane which are accessible to European readers, that is, which have been translated into European languages, but he forgets to mention such authorities as Arab Shah, the 'Autobiography' and 'Decrees' ('Tuzukat') of Tamerlane himself, long ago translated by Mangère, Davy, and Stewart. On the same page he explains that *Tokhtamish* is a modern Jagatai name, although it is one of the oldest peculiarly Turanian names known to us, and means not 'immortal' or 'immoveable,' as Vámbéry states, but 'magician.' The meaning of 'immortal,' our historical linguist ascribes to it for the reason that a certain Khokandian in the presence of Mr. Vámbéry, changed the name of his son, *Tokhta*, to *Baki*, which in Arabic means immortal —a very good reason! That in recounting the campaign of Tamerlane against Tokhtamish Vámbéry did not make use of the special work on this campaign, written by Professor Charmoy in French, can be easily explained. How should he know of such specialties, when he has not even read Deguines? But what are all his remaining mistakes in comparison with his apology for Tamerlane on pages 195-197, where he tries to justify his cruelty and his lust for conquest? He there shows the depth of his historical sense. The six pages following are extracted from the account of Ruy Gonzalez de Clavigo, who was sent as ambassador to Tamerlane by Henry III. of Castile; of the existence of Schiltberger's account Vámbéry says nothing. The well-known motto on Tamerlane's seal he reads *Rusti rasti*, and translates 'Justice is Strength,' when he should read *Rasti resti*, which means, 'If Thou be Right, Thou shalt be saved,' or ' Safety is in Right.' On page 210 the well-known Mussulman *savant*, Taftazani, receives the unintelligible surname of *Ulama*, and on the following page, to Jezeri, a contemporary with Tamerlane, is attributed the composition of an Arabic dictionary, the author of which was not *Jezeri* but *Jougeri*, who lived four centuries before Tamerlane.

In the history of the Timurides, which constitutes the subject of the twelfth chapter, Mr. Vámbéry ascribes to Khudaidad, an official of Khalil (p. 216), the insults heaped on Khalil's wife, the famous Shadi Mulk (with whom her husband was passionately in love), when, according to all historians, these insults were heaped upon her by Khalil's uncle Shahrukh; and Mr. Vámbéry does this, not from ignorance, but because he is a great psychologist. 'Shahrukh,' he says, page 216, 'had a romantic passion for his wife, Gowher Shadi, and it seems difficult to imagine him capable of thus further torturing his love-sick nephew.' In consequence of this acquaintance with the human heart the historian considers it just and logical to place the crimes of one man on another who was perfectly innocent of them. It appears that his psychology is worthy of his logic and *vice versâ*. It also appears from his note on Khudaidad that he confuses this official of Khalil with the Khudaidad, the son of Puladji, the famous chief of the Ulusses in the possessions of the Djete Jagataides. We see this confusion also in the fact that Vámbéry makes his Khudaidad (called Hussein), give over to Khalil, after defeating him, the government of Kashgar (p. 215), whereas Kashgar was in the hands of Khudaidad, son of Puladji. On the bottom of page 217, where there is printed *Khalil* we should read *Shahrukh*. This is perhaps only a slip of the pen, but we cannot explain so easily the statement that Sheikh Nur-Eddin, after rebelling against Shahrukh, was beaten by his commander Shahmulk, when, on the contrary, Shahmulk was twice beaten by Nur-Eddin, who was obliged to retreat (not to Tashkent as Vámbéry says), only in consequence of a defeat inflicted on him by Shahrukh himself. On page 218 our historian makes Ulug Bek, the son of Shahrukh, fight with the Mongolians (he does not know that from the time of Timur the name *Mongol* or *Mogol* was given by the Mussulman historians not to the Mongols but to the Turkish subjects of the Jagataides who ruled in Jungaria and the western parts of what are now the Kirghiz steppes), and penetrate to Ak-su in Eastern Turkistan, when his authority, Abd-er-Rezzak, speaks not of Ak-su but of Akhsi, the old capital of Ferghana. In addition to this Mr. Vámbéry gets his knowledge of the astronomical tables of Ulug Bek from the same source from which he drew that about Tamerlane's autobiography, that is, from Markham.

Not having at hand the Mussulman writer who is the authority for our historian in the accounts of the Timurides (that is, Abd-er-Rezzak, who can only be used in the translation of Quatremère, which stopped at the year 1420), and being unable to verify how correctly he cites him, we shall not go into any further investigation of the twelfth chapter; but the examples quoted are enough to convince any one how carelessly the author of the 'History of Bukhara' refers to his authorities, how badly he understands them, and consequently how he confuses and misstates events. Mr. Vámbéry, however, does not found his reputation as an historian on the part of his work of which we have spoken, but rather on that which still remains to be considered—his account of the fate of Bukhara from the time of the Uzbek conquest. Let us see if this part be any better than the preceding.

'One of the most pleasing traits in the character of the Turkish people' (Mr. Vámbéry ought to say *race*, and not *people*, for there is not one Turkish 'people' in the world, and there are many peoples of Turkish race) 'has always been the custom of adopting the names of those princes whose glorious reigns, or whose exertions for the public weal, had given them special claims on the gratitude of posterity, as surnames.'

Thus Mr. Vámbéry begins his thirteenth chapter about the commencement of the Uzbek rule in Bukhara, and it must be said begins very unfortunately. Whence did he get the idea that such a custom exists among the Turkish peoples, when we do not find a single example of it in their history? He apparently took this, although, of course, he did not mention his authority, from Bentinck's notes to the French translation of Abul Ghazi, on page 458. In making this plagiarism, Mr. Vámbéry did not notice that what is pardonable in a *savant* in the beginning of the eighteenth century, is not allowable to a writer in the second half of the nineteenth. In our times it is not possible seriously to say that the Mongols received their name from a certain Mongol Khan, or the Tartars from Tartar Khan. To the examples of Bentinck Vámbéry adds one of his own; that is, that the present Osmanlis (Turks of Constantinople) called themselves so in remembrance of their leader Osman. In reality, the present Osmanlis are called after Osman, the son of Ertogrul, but not in remembrance of him. The companions of Osman—the band of which he was the chief—received and accepted the name of Osmanlis, just as in our time the companions of Garibaldi got the name of Garibaldians, and as the robbers of the band of Lisofsky, that plundered Russia in the beginning of the seventeenth century, were known under the name of Lisoftchiki. Subsequently the name of Osmanlis was extended over a mixture of various races which came under the banners of the successors of Osman. But there never existed, and does not now exist, any people that can be called Osmanli. What relation, however, does this have to the Uzbeks? This; that even this popular name Mr. Vámbéry considers adopted by Turkish tribes in remembrance of a Khan of the Golden Horde,—one Uzbek, as the Khivan historian Abul Ghazi affirms. But if one comes to that, Abul Ghazi believes also that the Turks are so called from Turk, the son of Japhet, and repeats on this head no end of nonsense. If we allow that the Uzbeks received this name in remembrance of an Uzbek Khan, then we can also allow the existence of some benevolent Khan called Kazak, from whom the present Kazak people must have derived its name (by us wrongly called Kirghiz Kaisak, or simply Kirghiz). The fact is, that it was no more known to Abul Ghazi than to us, when, or in consequence of what circumstances, the name of Uzbek arose in the steppes north of the Syr Darya and the Aral Sea,—a name under which the population of these steppes began to be called by the Mussulman historians of the last half of the fifteenth century. As an Asiatic, without any idea of historical criticism, Abul Ghazi might easily refer the origin of this name to Uzbek Khan; but we in the nineteenth century must be more careful than Tartars of the seventeenth, and if we do not exactly know, we ought to say we do not know, and not repeat stupid fables. Stupid, we say, because in the Golden Horde, where Uzbek Khan lived, there were never any Uzbeks; but the Uzbeks appear in the Blue Horde, over which the power of Uzbek Khan never spread, and they only came on the scene a hundred years after his death. According to Vámbéry, a whole century must have passed before the population of the Blue Horde had sufficiently digested the services of Uzbek Khan, and had thought of adopting his name. This is about as probable as that in the beginning of the present century, the Poles, from a deep sense of the services of Peter the Great, should have suddenly called themselves Petroftsi. Vámbéry, however, says that the name of the Uzbeks is mentioned by a contemporary with Uzbek Khan, the celebrated Arabic traveller Ibn Batuta, but how he discovered the passage where Ibn Batuta speaks of this, is a mystery. He does not cite it, and we can find no such mention in Ibn Batuta, and do not believe that he can do so.

Explaining in this brilliant way the origin of the Uzbeks, Mr. Vámbéry passes immediately to the well-known Uzbek ruler Abul Khair Khan, saying that his name was found in the list of chiefs and vassals who renounced their allegiance to the ruler of Sarai during the reign of Ivan III. Vasilievitch, and exercised the right of sovereignty as grey beards or independent Khans. We should be glad to see this list in which 'aksakals' are put on an equality with Khans, and where Abul Khair is represented as the vassal of the ruler of Sarai, if such a detailed list exist. But, alas! it only exists in the imagination of Mr. Vámbéry, as does also the fact that Abul Khair ' retired (whence?—apparently from the banks of the Volga, from the encampments of the Golden Horde), with the tents and herds of his nomads, before the storm which was gathering in the north of Christendom against the Mussulman power, and sought refuge in the eastern steppes.' According to all known authorities, Abul Khair was the descendant of Sheibani, the brother of Baty, who had his own special *ulus*, and was never considered a vassal of the rulers of the Golden Horde, who were descended from Baty Khan, never separated himself from them, and always reigned within the domains of the Blue Horde as an independent ruler by virtue of hereditary right. Is it allowable to destroy facts and their relations in this unceremonious way? According to Vámbéry, Kitchik-Mohammed was the Khan of the Blue Horde, instead of the Golden Horde, and the last one too, notwithstanding the fact that after him reigned Seid Akhmed, who brought such terror upon Russia. Vámbéry calls Akhmed Yasavi, the 'national saint' of the Uzbeks, and says that these Uzbeks invaded Maverannahr 'wrapped in horse skins!' The further fate of Abul Khair and of his descendants, he gives, according to Abul Ghazi, a writer whom Europe has known for a century and a half in a French translation, according to Baber, whose 'Memoirs' were translated into English more than forty years ago, and according to other well-known works, with the addition of some unimportant details from one new source, the poem *Sheibani Nameh*, but with mistakes, such as that he represents the Jagataide Mahmud Khan, son of Yunus Khan, and Yunus Khan himself, as rebels against the Timurides, and the Uzbek Khan Sheibani (p. 263). This is in a certain way even more radical than the idea of the Russian common people, who, when we had a war with the Turks, always insisted that the Turkish Sultan had again *rebelled* against our Tsar. The conqueror of Maver an nahr, and the introducer of Uzbek rule there, Mohammed Sheibani, of course appears to Vámbéry as a hero, for the reason that whoever succeeds must be a hero. In conclusion, we learn that there existed in the world the historically celebrated 'State of Transoxiana' (p. 270) about which, however, no one has ever yet heard, excepting Mr. Vámbéry.

The history of the successors of Sheibani in Maverannahr is the subject of the fourteenth chapter. It is well-known that the beginning of this history is very confused, both in the Mussulman writers who constitute the sources of our information, and in the works of Europeans who have written on this subject. We should expect therefore that a new historian of Bukhara would investigate these contradictions, and would explain the character of the Uzbek monarchy, which was undoubtedly divided up into appanages for a very long time; but we do not find here a word about the contradictions in the authorities, or even of this peculiar character of the Uzbek kingdom. He states events as if there were nothing at all doubtful or dark, and, besides this, does not tell us whence he gets the material for such statements. On the death of Mohammed Sheibani, who fell in battle with Ismail Sefevi, the

Uzbek sultans were deprived of a leader; but we read that immediately after this, a treaty was concluded with Ismail, according to which the boundary between the dominions of the Uzbeks and Sefevides should be the Amu Darya (p. 273). With what Uzbek rulers this treaty was concluded, or which of them had the right to conclude it without asking the rest, Mr. Vámbéry avoids telling us. Sheibani was killed unexpectedly, but we read that at his death he gave as appanages to his eldest son and presumptive heir, Mohammed Timur Sultan, Samarkand, Kesh, Miankal, and even Bukhara and Karakul, which before that had been the appanage of his brother Sultan Mahmud (p. 64). How could Sheibani make this disposition at his death, when he fell in battle very unexpectedly? According to Vámbéry, this Mahmud inherited Bukhara from his father, but only reigned a few days, and died apparently a violent death (p. 274); while, according to other authorities, Mahmud did not reign in Bukhara, but in Samarkand, and even had command of the army, which, in 1512, three years after Sheibani's death, defeated Baber, who had taken from the Uzbeks Bukhara and Samarkand. According to Vámbéry, Kutchkunji Sultan was chosen as Sheibani's successor before the proposed invasion of Maverannahr; whereas it is stated by trustworthy authority that this happened only after the battle of Hidjuvan. Such and similar contradictions should not be passed over in silence. Further, according to Vámbéry, Ubeidullah, the nephew of Sheibani, appears in relation to Kutchkunji, up to his very death, as his generalissimo, but was really only an appanaged prince of the district of Bukhara. Of the other appanages we find no mention made. On this subject we find only the following phrase :—' The Government of Transoxiana had hitherto (*i.e.* to the death of Ubeidullah) been more or less divided between the children of Kutchkunji and Sheibani, and the result was general confusion amongst the Uzbeks after the death of Ubeidullah (p. 281).'

As regards the division of which he speaks, Vámbéry had a very confused idea, as is evident from his remark that the division was between the children of Kutchkunji and Sheibani, when he ought to have said between the descendants of Abul Khair, for the son of this latter Siundj-Hodja had the appanage of Tashkent, and the grandson of Abul Khair, Jani Bek, had Miankal, Sogd, and Nur. Maverannahr was therefore not the general inheritance of the descendants of Sheibani Khan, but of those of Abul Khair, and consequently the dynasty, which is called by Vámbéry (as well as by his predecessors, of whom he makes no mention) the Sheibanides, it would be more correct to call the Abul-Khairides.

Such misunderstanding of the tribal relations between the Uzbek sultans, makes Vámbéry consider the election to the Khanate on the death of Ubeidullah, Abdullah, and then Abdullatif the sons of Kutchkunji, as the work of a party (p. 281), when this was perfectly legal—that is, in conformity with Uzbek custom —and makes him represent Abdul Aziz, son of Ubeidullah, as the supreme Khan, whereas Abdullatif was such until his death in 1551, and Abdul Aziz from 1541 to 1551 was only the prince of the appanage of Bukhara. Further, the successor of Abdul Aziz in the Khanate is called by Vámbéry Mohammed Yar, and his successor Burhan, whereas both were princes of the appanage of Bukhara, and on the death of Abullatif, the dignity of Khan fell to Nouruz Akhmed, son of Siundj Hodja, and on the death of Nouruz Akhmed in 1556 to Pir Mohammed, the son of Jani Bek, who reigned till 1561. The names of these Khans are not even mentioned by Vámbéry. No; Nouruz Akhmed *is* mentioned, but how ?—not as a lawful Uzbek Khan, but as a Jagataide, son of Mahmud Khan, a cruel tyrant, who pillaged and devastated Maverannahr from Otrar to Bukhara. That would be the same as if an historian said that Ivan III. Vasilicvitch, was a Khan of the Golden Horde, who devastated Russia from Saratof to Moscow. In this accurate way has the historian of Bukhara stated the events of that period, about which he thinks that his every word is a discovery for Europe. Representing, as is quite just, Abdullah, the son of Iskender, as the most remarkable of the Sheibanide sovereigns, Mr. Vámbéry knows so little of this celebrity, that he makes him first appear on the historical scene not earlier than 962 A.H., when this Abdullah had long before, by his ambition, spread disorder throughout the whole of Maverannahr. And all these errors are to be found on page 282 alone. On the following page he confuses Nouruz Akhmed (whom he constantly calls Borak) with Burhan Sultan, the appanaged prince of Bukhara, and makes Abdullah kill Burhan, whereas this latter died by the hands of quite a different personage. We then read, 'Having thus driven out the invaders' (there were no invaders; Vámbéry has, as we have said, taken for an invader the lawful Khan Nouruz Akhmed, and no invaders were driven out;—driving out here means the seizure by Abdullah of Bukhara which belonged to his relative Burhan Sultan), 'he firmly re-established once more the authority of the Sheibanides in Transoxiana' (which had never been menaced by any danger from without, and, besides, Abdullah was not a Sheibanide) 'in imitation of Sheibani and Ubeidullah, who, although practically sovereigns of the country, had left the actual seat of the Khanate to others, the more freely to pursue their military career. Abdullah placed his father Iskender on the throne of Samarkand, and put himself at the head of the army to reconquer the original frontier of the Uzbek empire' (p. 284). Here there is not a word which does not show a complete misunderstanding of events, and a falsification of facts. Sheibani never gave up the throne to anybody. Ubeidullah, we have seen, could not give it up, because he was in 939 A.H. by right, and in reality, only prince of the appanage of Bukhara; and Abdullah, when he defeated Burhan and seized Bukhara, made himself only the appanaged prince of Bukhara, and could not dispose of the throne of the Khanate. The Khan at this time, 964 A.H., was his uncle Pir Mohammed, who reigned from 963, *i.e.* from the very death of Nouruz Akhmed, until 968; and only in this last year, on the dethronement of Pir Mohammed, was Iskender, the father of Abdullah, chosen Khan

With such complete misunderstanding of the juridical relations of the descendants of Abul Khair, that ruled in Bukhara, and with mistakes of a similar kind does Mr. Vámbéry narrate also the remaining period of the rule of this race to the end of the sixteenth century. Although boasting of the abundance of new authorities unknown to previous orientalists, he did not use, nor even know of the existence of such works as the 'Lubb-ul-tevarikh' of Kazvini, and the 'Abdullah-Nameh' of Hafiz Tanysh, or even of the extracts from them, published by the academician Veliaminof-Zernof, to whom belongs the honour of explaining, as many as fifteen years ago, the greater part of the misunderstandings with regard to the descendants of Abul Khair in Bukhara, which have completely confused our new historian, who has worked over, in his own words, 'a field untouched' before him. He was led astray in part by his chief authority, the 'Tarikhi Mukhim-Khani.' In reading it, he did not notice that it is not the history of all Maverannahr under Uzbek rule, but only of the appanage of Bukhara, and it is probably for that reason that Mr. Vámbéry constantly gives to the appanaged sultans of Bukhara the rank of the supreme Khan, or Khakan, and is either ignorant of the existence of these latter, or considers them intriguers, and even invading foreigners. The appanage period of Russian history would not have come out very well if some one had related it as Vámbéry relates the Bukharan history of the sixteenth century.

The history of the so-called Ashtarkanides or Astrakhan dynasty —we prefer to call it with Frachn the *Janide*—we find in the fifteenth and sixteenth chapters of Vámbéry, related for the seventeenth century after the 'Tarikhi Mukim-Khani,' with additions from Abul Ghazi and other well-known authorities. There is very little new there, and there are not such mistakes as in other parts of his book. In the beginning of the eighteenth century the oriental sources for the history of Bukhara are, so to speak, dried up. The facts must be obtained chiefly from the accounts of Europeans who have visited the country in one way or another, or from the few described coins of the later Astrakhanides; but of numismatics as an aid to history Mr. Vámbéry has no idea. In his whole book he does not once refer to this source of information, and the works of orientalists on this subject are utterly ignored by him.

The Europeans who penetrated into Bukhara during the eighteenth century were almost exclusively our countrymen, who have left accounts in Russian of which Mr. Vámbéry has apparently not known, or which, at least, he has not used.[1] But Mr. Vámbéry does not even know of the information collected somewhat later by

---

[1] These authorities are not abundant in historical information, but still as they were contemporaries and eye-witnesses a skilful hand can get profit from them. Such are—1. The report and letters of *Florio Beneveni*, the secretary of the 'Oriental Expedition of the Ambassadorial *Prikaz*,' who was sent by Peter the Great to Bukham, and remained there from the autumn of 1721 to the Spring of 1725, published by A. N. Popof, in vol. ix. of the Memoirs of the Imperial Russian Geographical Society. 2. The report of the Greek *Nikolai Grigorief*, who traded in Bukhara for more than ten years. It was taken down from his words in Orenburg, in 1752, and was printed by Vellaminof-Zernof in his 'Historical Information about the Kirghiz-Kaisaks,' Ufa, 1853. 3. The recollections of *Philip Yefremof*, who, about 1774, was made a slave in Bukhara, and put into the military service, where he served several years taking part in various expeditions, and at last escaped to Russia through India. These recollections were published by Yefremof himself at St. Petersburg in 1786 under the title 'Ten Years' Wanderings and Imprisonment in Bukhara, Khiva, Persia, and India, of the Russian Non-commissioned officer Yefremof, now a College Assessor.' 4. The Memoirs of the Mining Official *Timothei Burnashof*, who went to Bukhara in 1794 and returned in 1795. Extracts of these Memoirs were printed by G. J. Spaski in the 'Siberian Messenger' 1818. Besides this, information about the events in Bukhara in the eighteenth century is contained in the works of Russian travellers, who visited this country in the nineteenth, such as Meyendorf, Eversmann, and others. Mr. Vámbéry did not even use these sources, although Meyendorf wrote in French and Eversmann in German.

In the archives of the Ministry of Foreign Affairs preserved at Moscow there are still other materials for the history of Bukhara and Khiva. Such are the papers relating to the missions of *Boris* and *Semen Pazukhin* to Bukhara, 1669–1672; of Vassily *Daudof* to Bukhara and Khiva, 1677–8; of Ivan *Khokhlof* to Bukhara and Samarkand, 1620–23; of Anisim *Gribof* to Bukhara and Khiva, 1642; to the affair of the Boyar's son Ivan *Sorokin*, who in 1643 was ordered to be whipped for going to Bukhara without leave; to the mission of Ivan *Fedotof* to Khiva in 1670–73; and to the numerous embassies from Khiva and Bukhara to the court of the Tsars at Moscow, of which full accounts are preserved, from 1616 to 1739, with lists of presents, and details of ceremonies at the receptions. As regards the Russian embassies, not only are all the instructions preserved, but in most cases the

Izzet-ullah, and long ago translated into English and French. It is easy to imagine how short, therefore, is his account of the history of Bukhara during the greater part of the eighteenth century. The campaign of Nadir Shah against Mavérannahr during the reign of Abul-Feiz Khan is told, of course, after Nadir's historian, Mirzá Megdi; but Vámbéry ascribes to Abul-Feiz a reign of forty years, and in another place of almost fifty years, although in his own words this Khan came to the throne in 1717 and died in 1737. At the same time coins of Abul-Feiz are known which were struck in 1154 A.H., and which therefore show that in 1741-2 A.D. this Khan was still living; and other authorities lead us to believe that he died in 1747, or ten years later than when Mr. Vámbéry kills him off. Even Vámbéry in another place (p. 342) speaks of the meeting of Nadir Shah with Abul-Feiz in 1740. What he says on p. 341 of the treachery of Rahim Bii was first invented by Burnes, and Vámbéry without studying the matter repeats Burnes, although he does not mention him. Nothing is said of the service of Rahim Bii under Nadir Shah in Persia, although it was due to this circumstance especially that Rahim Bii was afterwards able to get into his hands the power over Bukhara, to depose Abul-Feiz Khan, and to put him to death. Mentioning this latter circumstance our historian continues—' A similar fate befell his son, who had married a daughter of Rahim Bii, and although a third prince, said to be an Astrakhanide, was raised to an illusory sovereignty, in point of fact Abul-Feiz closed the line of rulers of that dynasty' (p. 343).

Why should such a conclusion be drawn with regard to Abul-Feiz, who, in the hands of Rahim Bii, was just as much of a puppet as were his successors, whose names are evidently unknown to Vámbéry? The first of these successors was named—if Mr. Vámbéry cares for the information—Abdul Mumin, and had the title of Khan apparently from 1747 to 1751. In any case there are coins of his marked 1160 and 1163 A.H. (1747 and 1750 A.D.). The successor of Abdul-Mumin was called Ubeidullah, and hardly belonged to the Astrakhan dynasty. On the other hand there is evidence that the Astrakhan dynasty did not cease with Abdul-Mumin, because Abul Ghazi, who after him had the title of Khan, was the son of a cousin-

detailed journals (*stateiny spisok*) of the mission. Some short extracts from a few of these papers were printed by Mr. Khanikof in his 'Explanatory Memoir to the map of the Aral Sea and the Khanate of Khiva'—(Memoirs of the Imperial Russian Geographical Society, Book V. p. 268; 1851). They contain so much that is interesting and curious that they should either be published in full, or a careful abstract should be made of them. In 1869, Mr. P. N. Petrof read before the Imperial Russian Geographical Society, a paper on the reports of the mission of Dubrovin and the expedition of Colonel Garber in 1732, but nothing has yet been printed on the subject. [E. S.]

german of Abul-Feiz, and Mr. Vámbéry himself calls this Abul Ghazi, with what reason is not plain, the grandson of Abul-Feiz. Therefore this grandson or nephew of Abul-Feiz, and not Abul-Feiz himself, must be considered the last Astrakhanide on the throne of Bukhara. But it could scarcely have been in 1199 A.H. that Abul Ghazi was deprived of the throne, as Vámbéry says on page 350, for we have a coin of this Khan with the date of 1200 A.H., of which apparently the historian of Bukhara knows nothing, although it has been described more than seventy years.

The last and the now ruling dynasty in Bukhara is called *Manghit*, from that Uzbek family to which its founders belonged. The account of these founders is also given in the sixteenth chapter, but in such a way that it is evident that the author did not know even a fact of such importance as that Mohammed Rahim, whom he speaks of as *Atalyk*, was the first of the Manghit Biis who took the title of Khan. This is indubitable, because we have his coins with this title. Mohammed Rahim, Vámbéry rightly calls Rahim Bii, but his successor, Danial Bii, he calls Danial *Bai*, and explains that *bai* means 'superior grey-beard' (p. 347), which shows that he does not know the present meaning of the word *bii* among the Uzbeks, those very Uzbeks whose language and life, according to him, no one in Europe knows so well as himself.[1] Of the date of the death of Rahim Bii and of the date of the coronation of Abul-Ghazi, Vámbéry does not speak. He does not know that Danial Bii was the own nephew of Rahim Bii, but instead of that tells us without authority that he was related on his mother's side to the Astrakhanides. The accusation which he makes against Danial Bii of 'the most disgraceful excesses, of covetousness and tyranny,' is doubtful, for he does not mention his authority, and in all the authorities known to us nothing like this is ascribed to Danial. Shah-Murad, too, was not the immediate successor of Danial in the rule of the Khanate, as appears according to Vámbéry, for on Danial's death the management of affairs passed to the Kush Begi Doulet, of whom Vámbéry makes no mention. We will state also that there is in Persian a whole history of Rahim Bii and Danial Bii, unknown to Mr. Vámbéry, a copy of which, obtained in Bukhara by Mr. P. I. Lerch, is now kept in the library of the Asiatic Museum at St. Petersburg.

Shah-Murad, son of Danial Bii, was one of the most remarkable political personages in the modern history of Asia, and the sketch of him by Vámbéry is lively, and full of relief; but this is not a merit of Vámbéry, but of the English historian of Persia, Malcolm,

---

[1] *Bii* has the sense of judge or ruler, *Bai* that of rich. [E. S.]

from whom Vámbéry took bodily all that he says of Shah-Murad, and without the slightest use of quotation marks. Those who wish to be assured of this, may compare pp. 348 to 355, and 361 of Vámbéry's history, with pp. 243 to 261 of the second volume of Malcolm's 'History of Persia' (London, 1815). Not in vain did Mr. Vámbéry play for a long time the part of a shameless Dervish: in writing a book in English, he has dared to rob a well-known and respected English writer, and to think that no one would notice it. To cover it up, he adds to what he has taken from Malcolm a few mistakes, which we do not find in the English writer. Among such errors is the statement that Shah-Murad, when he removed Abul Ghazi in 1784, mounted the throne of Bukhara (p. 350). We have already remarked that coins of Abul Ghazi are known with the date of 1200 A.H., =1785-1786, A.D. If, therefore, Shah-Murad mounted the throne, it could not have been in 1784, but later, and there are strong reasons for supposing that he never took the title of Khan, was never raised on the felt (a ceremony equivalent to the European coronation), and until the death of Abul Ghazi, which did not take place earlier than 1796, considered himself nothing more than the regent of the Khanate, with the title of *Naib* (viceroy), and the honourable appellation *Veli-n-niem*. At least, he coined no money in his own name, and there is evidence that his name was not mentioned in the *Khutbe*; and the right to coin money and to be named in the *Khutbe*, are characteristics of supreme power in the Mussulman East. Shah-Murad, too, did not die in 1802, as Vámbéry states (p. 360), for we have coins of his successor Mir Haidar, dated 1215, A.H. (1801 A.D.), and therefore cannot say, as does Vámbéry, p. 362, that Mir Haidar mounted the throne in 1803. For the history of the reign of Mir Haidar, Mr. Vámbéry evidently had no materials at all, and did not use either Izzet-Ullah, or even Meyendorf, and therefore says that Mir Haidar 'enjoyed for twenty-three years the peaceful possession of his dominions,' p. 363. If this historian and professor had known of the 'Memoirs of Mirza Shems,'[1] he would have seen that the years of Mir Haidar's reign did not pass in such quiet. On one side he was constantly fighting with the Khans of Khiva, and on the other his own subjects were rebelling against him. And whence did Vámbéry get an idea that Mir Haidar reigned under the name of Amir Said? Various titles he certainly gave himself, as we see from his coins, but no such title is stamped on them, unless by *Said* Mr. Vámbéry means *Seyid* (Seid). *Seyid*, descendant of Mohammed, Mir Haidar really called

---

[1] See note on page 109, vol. i. [E. S.]

himself at times, on the ground that his mother was the daughter of Abul-Feiz Khan, and that this latter was descended from Din-Mohammed (the first Bukharan Khan of the Astrakhan dynasty), who was married to the daughter of Mirza Abul-Talib, really a direct descendant of the Khalif Ali. But besides this title, Mir Haidar bore others,—the Persian *Padshah*, and that of the Khalifs, *Amir-el-Muminim*.

The eighteenth chapter of the book is devoted exclusively to the reign of the Amir Nasrullah, who ruled from 1826 to 1860. The history of his reign up to 1842 is told according to the excellent book on Bukhara, written by our countryman N. V. Khanikof, which was translated into English; but although Vámbéry is guided by it, he has not a single reference to it, perhaps considering Khanikof a personal enemy because he was in Bukhara before him; for he tries to convince himself and the world that up to his time nobody had been there, nobody had seen anything, or had written anything about the country. Mr. Vámbéry spoils Khanikof with his additions in the same way as he spoils Malcolm. In entering upon the account of the conquest of Khokand by Nasrullah, he communicates some historical information about this Khanate, which is enough to make the hair stand up on the head of any one who is at all acquainted with the history of Central Asia. It is enough to say that he makes Mohammed Ali Khan of Khokand, genealogically related to Kaidu Khan of the thirteenth century, and says not a word either about Erdeni Bek, or Narbuta Bii and his successors, and assures us that there are no historical accounts of Khokand during recent times, and therefore follows what was told him by a Khokandian whom he met in his travels in Central Asia. Such an addition to the account of Mr. Khanikof is also the statement that, in 1841, when in war with Nasrullah, Mohammed Ali did not dare to risk a battle, because he had to detach a considerable portion of his forces to watch the Russians on the lower Yaxartes, p 374. But in 1841, not only had we not moved to the lower Syr Darya, but we had not even established our power in the Kirghiz steppes further than Orsk, which had been built a century before. The account of Khanikof ends with the war of Nasrullah in Khokand in the spring of 1842, and Vámbéry says nothing more of an intelligible character about the further acts of Nasrullah in regard to Khokand, or about the events in that country. We may mention that he seriously says that the well-known Mussulman Kul was a pretender to the throne of Khokand, put forward by Nasrullah (p. 376)! The events in the neighbouring Khanate of Khiva are no better known to him. He makes Rahim Kuli Klan reign from 1841 to 1843 (p. 377), whereas this Khan occupied the throne from 1842 to 1845. As concerns Russia, of the relations of which country with Bukhara Vámbéry speaks on page 379, the mistakes are endless. The first Russian mission in Bukhara, he thinks, was the one of Negri in 1820, although even in 1620 Bukhara had seen a Russian mission within her walls. In 1834, Russia, according to Vámbéry, sent as an envoy to Bukhara, Demaisons, and in 1835, Vitkevitch, as a political agent, both to procure the liberation of Russian slaves (p. 380); whereas both of these persons went there secretly, *incognito*, the first under the guise of a Tartar Mullah, the last as a Kirghiz, which, we may say, demanded of both no less boldness, no less adroitness, and no less acquaintance with the languages and customs of the East, than the travels of Vámbéry himself disguised as a Dervish. Russian cannon had never at that time sounded on the Syr Darya, as Vámbéry says (p. 380), &c. &c.

The English relations with Bukhara, beginning with the mission of Stoddart in 1838, are much better set forth.

Let us pass to the last chapter of this book, which tells of the events from 1860 up to the present time. Here, Mr. Vámbéry, who constantly, as a publicist, had incited England against Russia, and had proclaimed to all the world our duplicity and lust for conquest, very unexpectedly appears as the apologist of Russian policy in Central Asia, and is even enthusiastic over our victories. We might therefore risk being considered prejudiced, if we should say that the end of his book is incomparably better than the middle or the beginning. In the first plan in this conclusion appear the Russian actions against the Khokandians, and those against the Bukharans. In recounting them, Mr. Vámbéry had no recourse to Russian authorities, and knows of these matters apparently only by the compilations of the Messrs. Michell ('The Russians in Central Asia.' London, 1865), and the German Hellwald's ('Die Russen in Central Asien,' Wien, 1869). But as these compilations are very good, we do not meet with many mistakes in the way in which he has retailed them. Some, however, we will point out. Mussulman Kul is again put forward as a usurper of the throne of Khokand (p. 393); and it is said that he was assassinated by Bukharan intriguers, and that the throne then reverted to Khudayar Khan, while the fact is that Khudayar Khan was placed on the throne by Mussulman Kul, and that Mussulman Kul was publicly executed on the scaffold by Khudayar, in consequence of a general uprising of the Sarts against the supremacy of the Kiptchaks, at whose head he was. Further, Khudayar Khan is not the grandson of Mohammed Ali, as Vámbéry states (p. 393), because the father of Khudayar Khan, Shir Ali, was not the son of Mohammed Ali, as Vámbéry says (p. 373), but his cousin. Moreover Khudayar Khan never personally led his armies against the Russians, never was in Bukhara previous to his dethronement by Malla Bek, and never found the gates of his capital shut in his face on returning from a campaign against the Russians, as Vámbéry recounts (p. 394). He ran away to Bukhara only after he had been defeated by Malla Bek between Tashkent and Khokand, and took refuge, not with Mozaffar Eddin, who had not then ascended the Bukharan throne, but with Nasrullah; and neither Mozaffar nor Nasrullah commanded the Bukharan army sent afterwards against the Khokandians to restore Khudayar to the throne. These are all inventions of Mr. Vámbéry, and all on the 394th page. But this unlucky page has still other and more improbable facts, viz., that Malla Bek was killed by the partisans of the Amir of Bukhara, and that Shah Murad was the younger brother of Khudayar, and that he did not succeed in getting on the throne after Malla Bek's murder, because he was forestalled by Mozaffar Eddin, who reinstated Khudayar, and then returned to Bukhara. This was not at all so. Malla Bek perished, assassinated by the leaders of the Kiptchak party, who were discontented with him, and who had nothing in common with the Amir of Bukhara. Shah Murad, the son of Khudayar's elder brother Sarymsak, was the nephew of Khudayar; and on the murder of Malla Bek, he was proclaimed Khan, and reigned until Khudayar was recalled from Bukhara by the inhabitants of Tashkent, and with their aid got possession of Khokand, when Shah Murad was dethroned. With all this, neither Nasrullah nor his son Mozaffar had anything to do. In the seventh line from the bottom of the same page, *Samarkand* is an error for *Khokand*.

The further account by Vámbéry of the events in Khokand, we do not at all understand; it is so confused, and has so utterly distorted what we know to have taken place there.

We remark further: 1. *Kutebar* means in Kirghiz not the lucky one, as Vámbéry translates it on p. 399, but 'podicem habens' in the sense of 'magna podice praeditus;' and that the robber known as Iset Kutebarof not only did not undermine the Russian supremacy in the Middle Horde, nor even in the Lesser Horde, but enticed into temporary disobedience in all only two or three tribes; and Mr. Vámbéry has no idea of what he is talking of, when he speaks of the gold medal given to Kutebarof. 2. Mir Said was not the son of Sarymsak, but of Malla Khan. 3. General Tchernaief was not the successor of General Perovsky, and in 1865 there was no Russian army on the banks of the Syr, but only an insignificant detachment. The historian of Bukhara does not know the position of our affairs in the region of Tashkent in 1866 sufficiently well to make a proper estimate of the acts and capacities of Generals Tchernaief and Romanofsky, as he does on p. 403. 4. The fort of Ura-tepé was not captured by Count Vorontsof-Dashkof alone (p. 408), as he commanded only one of the storming columns. 5. Yany Kurgan was occupied without any opposition on the part of the Bukharans, who had abandoned it, by Lieutenant Colonel Abramof, and not personally by General Kaufmann. 6. The affair of June 2 between the Russians, under the command of General Kaufmann and the Bukharans, took place not at Serpul, but on the heights of Zera-Bulak.

We have concluded, and we hope that we have confirmed our opinion of the character of Mr. Vámbéry's 'History of Bukhara' by a sufficient number of proofs. We have pointed out many errors, but it must not be thought that we have exhausted the supply of them. Persons who wish to assure themselves of this, may look in the review of Mr. Vámbéry's book published in the *Literarisches Centralblatt* of Leipzig, No. 19, 1873, written by Professor A. von Gutschmidt. Mr. Gutschmidt does not find words enough to brand the manner in which the author set about the work, for which he was not at all fitted by his education, the want of conscientiousness which he has displayed in his labour, and the vain-gloriousness with which he has proclaimed the unusual qualities of his history; but there is no evil in the world without some particle of good, and so there is one good side to Mr. Vámbéry's work, that is, his endeavour to correct the orthography of peculiarly Turkish names, which has been corrupted by the ignorance of the Turkish dialects both by the various Arab and Persian historians who wrote of the Turks, and perhaps even more by European orientalists who have used these historians, and who have not been able to read aright the names as given by them. However, in sometimes happily correcting the false orthography of peculiarly Turkish names, Mr. Vámbéry himself acts very illogically with regard to the Arabic names of Central Asiatics, writing them most frequently, not as they are pronounced by the natives, but as they are pronounced in Constantinople only.

APPENDIX III.

MEDIÆVAL TRAVELLERS IN CENTRAL ASIA.

ALTHOUGH much has already been written on the routes of the early travellers from Europe through Northern Central Asia, it may not be profitless briefly to review some of them again in connection with the Chinese records of similar journeys.

1. ZEMARCHUS.

In the fragments of Menander Protector, we find an account of an embassy of Turks, accompanied by Maniach, the chief of Sogdia, which arrived at Byzantium in 568. The next year the Emperor Justinian sent Zemarchus on a mission to Dizabulus, the ruler of these Turks. Dizabulus appears to be Dalobian Khan, the younger son of Kigin, or Muyui Khan, who established the power of the Turks (Tu-hiu) from the Western Sea to the Gulf of Corea, and from the Northern Sea to the steppes of Shamo, and who ruled from 553 to 572. Dalobian Khan, after his father's death, rebelled and founded the Western House of the Tu-hiu. He must have exercised a viceregal sway during his father's lifetime. He lived on the northern slope of the Tian Shan, which was then called the White Mountains, by the Chinese Bo-shan or Pe-shan, and by the Turks Ak-tag.

According to Menander, Zemarchus went to the mountains *Ek-tag*, which he translates Golden Mountain, where he found the camp of Dizabulus in a hollow, very probably the same 'Thousand Springs' mentioned by Hiouen Thsang. As Altai means golden, the residence of this Turkish Khan has been placed by some in the Altai Mountains, and Ritter on the strength of this even names a portion of the Altai range the Ek-tag Altai, an appellation unknown on the spot, and against which Captain Sosnofsky protests. ('Mem. Imp. Russ. Geog. Soc.'; vol. v. Geography, p. 566; St. Petersburg, 1875).

After Zemarchus had been fitly entertained, the most of his suite was sent back to the land of the *Choliatae* or *Chliatae* (probably the *Kangli*), while he himself accompanied Dizabulus on an expedition against the Persians. On the way they stopped at *Talas* (near Aulié-ata), where they were met by a Persian ambassador). Here, being dismissed, and being allowed to take with him a deputation from the Choliatae, he crossed the river *Oech*—which it would be difficult to identify—and after a long journey, came to a huge wide lagoon, perhaps the northern shore of the Aral Sea, or the Mertvii Kultuk Bay of the Caspian. Travelling for twelve days across the sandy shores of this lagoon, and having to cross some very difficult places, he came to the stream of the river *Ich* (the Emba?), then to the *Daich* (the Yaik or Ural), and then by other swampy tracts to the Attila (the Ethil or Volga), and then again to the land of the *Ugors*. Then passing down the west shore of the Caspian, he crossed the Caucasus, and got to Trebizond, whence he posted to Byzantium. (See Yule's 'Cathay and the Way Thither,' clx–clxvi). The Vech is by some (see Review of Marco Polo in 'Edinburgh Review' for January, 1872) identified with the Wakh, a name once given to the Upper Oxus. According to this supposition Zemarchus must have crossed the Syr Darya without mentioning it, and the Oxus a little below its mouth.

2. Hiouen Thsang.

Sixty years after Zemarchus, in 629, Hiouen Thsang, a Buddhist pilgrim and student, started on his long journey through Central Asia. Leaving China by Liang-tchow and Kua-tchow, at the western extremity of the Great Wall, he went to Khamil (Hami), Kharashar and Kutche, and then leaving the high road to Kashgar, by which he returned fifteen years later, and passing through the borders of Pa-lu-kia (Ak-su), north-east, he crossed a stony desert, and arrived at an icy mountain (Ling-tchan, the Muzart Pass, close to the peak Khan Tengri), where 'snow had been heaped up from the beginning of the world, which never melts either in spring or in summer. Smooth fields of hard and glittering ice stretch out unendingly, and join with the clouds. The way is often between icy peaks overhanging on each side, and over high masses of ice. These places are passed with great trouble and danger, with constant blasts of piercing wind and gusts of snow; so that even with warm boots and a fur coat, the cold penetrates to the bones. There is no dry place in which to lie down or to eat. You must cook your food and sleep on the ice.' 'One is often a prey to the ferocity of dragons, which attack travellers. Those who follow this route should not wear red clothing, or carry calabashes, or cry aloud. Should these precautions be forgotten, the greatest misfortunes would come. A violent wind would suddenly arise, whirl about the sand, and engulf the traveller with a shower of stones. It is very difficult to escape death.' Such were then the terrors of the Muzart Pass. Seven days' journey through these mountains brought Hionen Thsang to a great lake, called *Thsing-tchi*, about 1,000 *li* in circumference. 'It is lengthened from east to west, and narrowed from south to north; on all sides it is surrounded by mountains. A number of rivers throw themselves into it, and are lost there. The colour of the water is a greenish black, and its taste is at once salt and bitter. Sometimes its vast waves extend in immense sheets, sometimes they swell up and roll impetuously. Dragons and fish inhabit it, and from time to time extraordinary monsters are seen to rise out of it. For this reason the travellers who go and come pray for good luck. Although the guests of the lake are very numerous, no one dares to fish there.' In this description it is impossible not to recognise Lake Issyk Kul. After travelling 500 *li* north-west from this lake, he arrived at the city on the river *Su-ye*. 'The city is from 6 to 7 *li* in circumference, and is the meeting-place of merchants from different kingdoms.' There can be no question that this river is the Tchu, and judging from the distance travelled, the city would be near Tokmak, where an ancient town existed. We are further told that, 'from this city to the kingdom of *Kie-choang-na* (Kesh), the country is called *Su-li*, and the inhabitants have the same name. This name is also applied to their writing and to their language. The radical forms of the graphic signs are very few, and are reduced to thirty-two letters, which, by being combined together, have gradually given rise to a great number of words. The inhabitants possess but few historical memoirs. They read from top to bottom.' An interesting description of the inhabitants follows. *Su-le*, which nearly resembles *Su-li*, was the Chinese name for Kashgar.

'West of *Su-ye*, there are many isolated towns. In each city chiefs are established, who are independent of each other, but who are all submitted to the *Tu-kue* (Turks).'

After travelling about 400 *li* west of the river *Su-ye*, he arrived at the 'Thousand Springs.' 'The country of the Thousand Springs is about 200 *li* square. On the south it is bounded by snowy mountains, and on the three other sides by level plains. The land is abundantly watered, and the forest trees offer beautiful vegetation. In the last month of spring the most varied flowers beautify the earth like a rich embroidery. There are a thousand basins of living water, whence have come the name of the Thousand Springs. The Khan of the *Tu-kue* (Turks) comes to this place every year to avoid the warmth of summer. Here are a multitude of stags ornamented with little bells and rings. They are familiar with men, and do not flee their sight. The Khan likes to see them. He has published a decree, in which he says that any one who dared to touch one of them, would be punished with death without pardon. This is why all these stags can tranquilly end their days.'

The Khan of the Turks at this time, as we find from the annals of the T'hang dynasty, was Sy shekhu Khan, who had just dethroned Sybi Khan, and the 'Thousand Sources,' *Ming-bulak*, or *Thsian Thsionen*, where he passed his summers, was probably the same place as that at which Zemarchus had found his predecessor sixty years before. Mr. Severtzof places Ming-bulak in the valley of the Ters, a little west of Aulié-ata, where there is now a locality of the same name, noted for its fine pastures, but this does not seem to answer the requirements of the narrative, and at the same time Ming-bulak is not an uncommon name in any part of Central Asia. A glance at the map, which shows numerous streams descending the Alexandrofsky range and watering the triangle formed by the Tchu and its chief branch, the Kurgati, can leave little doubt as to the probable situation of the 'Thousand Springs,' which, according to Hiouen Thsang was a locality about fifty miles square. According to the distances given it would be between Merke and Aulié-ata.

After travelling 140 or 150 *li* west of the Thousand Springs, he 'arrived at the city of *Tu-lo-sse* (Talas, at or near Aulié-ata), eight or nine *li* in circumference. Merchants from different countries live in it indiscriminately. As regards the products of the soil and the climate, this country resembles that of *Su-ye*.' About ten *li* south of this he found an isolated city, inhabited by 330 families of Chinese origin, who, although they had adopted the dress and tastes of the Turks (*Tu-kue*), had yet preserved the language and usages of their country. 'Leaving this kingdom and travelling 200 *li* to south-west, he arrived at the city *Pi-shui*, or White Water (in Persian *Isfidjab*, the modern Tchimkent). This city is six or seven *li* in circumference. With regard to the products of the soil and the nature of the climate this country is much better than that of *Ta-lo-sse*.'

'Travelling about 200 *li* to the south-west, he arrived at the city of *Kong-yu* (Yangy ?), which was five or six *li* in circumference. The plains were rich and fertile, and the gardens and forests offered magnificent vegetation.' Thence he went 40 or 50 *li* south to the kingdom of *Nu-tch'i-kien* (the old Nejkat or Nujkent), and thence 200 *li* west to the kingdom of *Tche-shi* (Tchatch, Shash, or Tashkent).

Hiouen Thsang then went to Ferghana, Usrushna (Ura-tepé), Samarkand, and Kesh, and through the Iron Gates, to the Oxus.

The full account of the travels of Hiouen Thsang is to be found in the 'Voyages des Pèlerins Bouddhistes,' par M. Stanislas Julien.

3. YE-LÜ TCH'U-TSAI.

The celebrated Chinese statesman, Ye-lü Tch'u-tsai, accompanied Tchinghiz Khan in his conquest of the West, and wrote a book about his travels, which he named 'Si-yu-lu,' or an 'Account of a Journey to the West,' an abstract of which was made and published long afterwards by Ju-tze. I quote some passages from the translation given in Dr. Bretschneider's 'Notes on Chinese Mediæval Travellers to the West':—

'In the next year (1219) a vast army was raised and set in motion towards the west. The way lay through the *Kin-shan* (Chinese Altai). Even in the middle of the summer, masses of ice and snow accumulate in these mountains. The army passing that road was obliged to cut its way through the ice. The pines and larch trees are so high that they seem to reach heaven; the valleys (in the Altai) all abound in grass and flowers. The rivers west of the *Kin-shan* all run to the west, and finally discharge into a lake (Nor Zaisan). South of the Kin-shan is *Bie-shi-ba* (*Bishbalik*, Urumtsi), a city of the *Hui-hu* (Mohammedans, Uigurs). There is a tablet of the time of the T'ang dynasty, on which it is said that here at that time was the station of the army of the northern desert. The desert is several hundred *li* distant from the city (of Bishbalik). There is a lake with an island in it, on which a great number of birds used to mew. West of the city (of Bishbalik), 200 *li* distant, is the city *Lun-t'ai-hien*, where also a tablet of the time of T'ang is found. South of the city (of Bishbalik) 500 *li* (beyond the Tian-Shan) is *Huo-tchou*, the same place which at the time of T'ang was called *Kao-tch'ang*, and also *Yi-tchou*. West of *Kao-tch'ang*, 3,000 or 4,000 *li* distant, is the city of *Wu-duan*, which is the same as the realm of *Yi-t'ien* (Khotan), of the T'ang dynasty. There is a river there, in which is found white and black jade.

'At a distance of more than 1,000 *li*, after having crossed the desert, one arrives at the city of *Bu-la*. South of this city is the *Yin-shan* mountain, which extends from east to west 1000 *li*, and from north to south 200 *li*. On the top of the mountain is a lake (Sairam Nor), which is 70 or 80 *li* in circumference. The land south of the lake is overgrown with apple trees, which form such dense forests that the sunbeams cannot penetrate. After leaving the *Yin-shan* one arrives at the city of *A-li-ma* (Almalyk). The western people call an apple *u-li-ma* (*alma*), and as all the orchards around the city abound in apple trees, the city received this name. Eight or nine other cities and towns are subject to *A-li-ma*. In that country grapes and pears abound. The people cultivate the five kinds of grain as we do in China. West of *A-li-ma* there is a large river, which is called *I-lie* (Ili). Further on, west of this river, is the city of *Hu-sze-wo-lu-do*, the capital of the *Si-liao* (Karakhitai), several tens of cities are subject to it. To the west of *Hu-sze-wo-lu-do*, several hundred *li*, is the city of *T'a-la-sze* (Talas). From this place, 400 *li* and more to the south-west, are the cities *K'udjan* (Hodjent), *Ba-p'u*, *K'o-san* (Kassau) and *Ba-lan* (Badam, Kanabadam).'

After this follow notices of Hodjent, Badam, Otrar, Samarkand, and Bukhara, from which I have previously given some quotations.

Two places in this account deserve mention, *Bu-la* and *Hu-sze-wo-lu-do*. *Bu-la* is probably the same place as that marked on ancient Chinese maps *P'u-la*, the *Bolo* of Tchang-Te, the *Phulad* of Hethum, and the *Pulad* of the historians of the Mongols. It was a little to the north or north-east of Lake Sairam Nor, and may perhaps derive its name from the river Boro-tala, *r* and *l* being interchangeable, as in Talas and Taraz, and is perhaps *Ulan-buru*; or it may come from *Bulak*, a spring, which enters into several names in this region. May this not be the city which Rubruquis calls *Bolok*, to which the German prisoners were sent from Talas, and which he passed at a distance of three days' journey?

Hu-sze-wo-lu-do was the capital of the *Si-liao* or Karakhitai, and should, therefore, be Bala Sagun, though whether it is meant for that is hard to tell. *Wo-lu-do* is simply *ordo*, or camp.

4. TCH'ANG TCH'UN.

Tch'ang Tch'un, the Taouist monk, also passed through this region in 1221 and 1224, on his way to and from the court of Tchinghiz Khan.

After leaving *Bie-sze-ma* (Bishbalik, the modern Urumtsi), and going along the northern slope of the Tian Shan, and passing several towns, he came after seven days' journey to *Tch'ang-ba-la* (Tchangbalik, a town on old Chinese maps, but not otherwise known). After travelling westward several days, during which he crossed a sandy desert, and then, turning southward on a long slope, he came to a lake, which he calls the *Lake of Heaven* (the modern Sairam Nor), the description of which, as well as of the Talki defile, which I have elsewhere quoted, is still very exact.

What a slope this was which he ascended may be seen from the fact that Sairam Nor is 7,200 feet above the level of the sea, while Ebi Nor, at a distance of less than 80 miles, is but 700 feet. After passing through this defile he came to the city *A-li-ma*. This was the old Almalyk, situated near the modern Kuldja, and its name he rightly derives from the Turkish *alma*, apple. Having been entertained by the ruler of the *P'u-su-man* (Mussulmans), he journeyed 'further to the west, and arrived in four days at the *Ta-la-sumo-lien*. The river, which is deep and broad, comes from the east, and cutting across the Yin-shan mountains, runs in a north-western direction. To the south of the river, again, are snow-covered mountains. On the first of the tenth month (end of October) we crossed the river in a boat, and proceeding southward arrived at a great mountain, on the northern side of which was a small town. Thence we travelled five days to the west. . . . Travelling again westward during seven days, we crossed a mountain, and met a Chinese envoy who was returning to China. . . Next day there was a great snow-fall, and we reached a small town of the Hui-ho (Mohammedans). The snow was one foot deep, but it was quickly melted by the sun.

'On the 16th of the tenth month, we went in a south-western direction, crossed the river on a bridge of planks, and in the evening reached the foot of the southern mountains. Here were (formerly) the dominions of *Ta-shi Lin-ya*. . . . Here the climate is quite different from that of the regions north of the Yin-shan (Tian Shan). The country has many plains, and the people are employed in agriculture and breeding of silkworms. They make wine from grapes. The fruits are about the same as in China; but it does not rain there during the whole summer and autumn, hence the fields are irrigated artificially by canals led off from the rivers, and the corn is brought to maturity. To the north-east are mountains, to the south-west valleys, which stretch out for ten thousand *li*.

'This kingdom (of Tashi-Linya), existed about a hundred years. As the power of the *Naiman* was broken, they (*i.e*, Gutchluk and the Naimans), fled to the Ta-shi, and after becoming powerful, overthrew that nation. Subsequently the *Suan-tuan* (Sultan of Kharezm), conquered the western part of their dominions, then Tchingiz arrived, the Naiman were totally destroyed, and the *Suan-tuan* was also overthrown.

'We were told that the way still before us presented many difficulties. One of our carts was broken, and we were obliged to leave it behind.

'The 18th of the tenth month, we travelled westward along

the hills, and after seven or eight days' journey, the mountains suddenly turned to the south. We saw a city built of red stones; and there were the traces of an ancient military encampment. To the west we saw great grave mounds, which resembled the Great Bear. Passing over a stone bridge, and travelling five days along the south-western mountains, we arrived at the city of *Sai-lan* (Sairam).'

The chief, and, indeed, only difficulty in fixing the localities mentioned on this route, lies in the river called *Ta-la-su mo-lien*. *Mulien* is the same as *Muren*, the Mongol word for river, and there is no question but that literally it must mean the river Talas. But Tch'ang Tch'un could not possibly have travelled the distance from Kuldja (Alima) to the Talas, about 600 miles, in four days, and have taken twenty-five days to go from the Talas to the city of Sairam, only about 100 miles.

On the return journey, the account is more easily understood. Tch'ang Tch'un left Sairam on the 16th of the third month. On the 23rd of the month he was joined by the Imperial envoy, A-gou, who had been ordered to accompany him along the southern bank of the *Tch'uimu-lien* (the Tchu). Ten days later, he was at a distance of more than one hundred *li* to the west of Alima, and crossed a large river. On the 5th of the fourth month, he arrived at a garden east of the city of Alima, and in the evening reached the foot of the Talki defile.

Dr. Bretschneider, in his 'Chinese Mediæval Travellers,' pp. 34-36, in order to explain these difficulties, supposes there must be some confusion in dates, or that parts of the diary have been transposed. Mr. Lerch thinks that by the *Ta'-la-su mo-lien*, Tch'ang Tch'nn does not mean the modern Talas, but the Tchu. It seems to me, however, very much more simple to suppose a slip of the pen on the part of the diarist. If we look attentively at the account, we shall see that he must have meant the Ili, although he called it the Talas. He had probably entered in his note-book the names of all the rivers he crossed, and of the places to which he came, and by an easily intelligible error placed here the wrong name. In no other way is it possible to understand the route. This must be the same river which was last crossed on the return journey before reaching Alima, but which is not named there.

After crossing the Ili in a boat, for it is too deep to be fordable, and probably was never bridged, and proceeding southward, he arrived at a great mountain, on the northern side of which was a town, probably somewhat to the east of the modern Vierny. Following these mountains, the Alatau, to the west, he crossed them probably at the Kastek Pass, on the route of the old post road, and then came to the river Tchu, which he crossed on a bridge, and

reached the foot of the Alexandrofsky range, where he came into
the country of the Karakhitai, the history of which people he briefly
relates. Then travelling westward along the foot of this range,
he came to the ruins of Akhyr-tash, of which I have spoken on
p. 121, vol. ii, and crossing the Talas on a stone bridge, arrived at
Sairam, near Tchimkent. This supposition, that the river of which
Tch'ang Tch'un speaks is the Ili, will make his dates properly agree.

For a note on the translation of the account of Tch'ang
Tch'un's journey, see vol. i. p. 238. I have chiefly followed Dr.
Bretschneider.

5. TCH'ANG TE.

In 1259, Tch'ang Te was sent by the Mongol Emperor Mangu
Khan to his brother Hulagu, who had just defeated the Khalif of
Bagdad. On his return an account of his journey was written by
Liu Yu, who gave it the name of 'Si-shi-ki.' I quote a portion of
it from Dr. Bretschneider's translation, which is much fuller and
better than those of Rémusat and Pauthier.

'On the 20th day of the first month of 1259, Tch'ang Te set out
as a courier despatched to the west (to the prince *Hü-lie-wu* or
Hulagu.) After leaving *Ho-lin* (Karakorum), he travelled through
the country of *Wu-sun* in a north-western direction, more than
two hundred *li*, the ground rising gradually. After a halt, the
traveller then crossed the desert. The country was very high and
cold, and notwithstanding the great heat in summer, the snow
never melts there. The rocky mountains were covered all over
with fine pine trees. After seven days' travelling in a south-
western direction, Tch'ang Te had crossed the desert, and descending gradually for three hundred *li*, arrived at a river several
li broad. It was called *Hunmu-lien* (the modern Dsabgan), and
in summer often overflows the country. He crossed in a boat
and a few days later passed the river *Lung-gu* (Ulungur).

'Thence Tch'ang Te proceeded again in a north-western
direction; the distance by road southward to *Bie-shi-ba-li* (Bishbalik), at the nearest point being five hundred *li* (through a
country inhabited by a great number of Chinese). They cultivate
wheat, barley, millet, and *setaria*.

'The river (Ulungur) flows to the west, stagnates, and forms
a lake, which is more than a thousand *li* in circumference. The
name of this lake is *Ki-tse-li-ba-sze* (Kyzyl bash). It abounds in
good fish. There are mills (on the river), which are put in motion
by the running water. Proceeding gradually westward, Tch'ang
Te arrived at a city called *Ye-man*. Further to the south-west a
city, *Bo-lo*, was reached. In this country wheat and rice are

cultivated. On the mountains many cypresses are found, but they do not thrive vigorously, and grow tortuously between the stones. The dwelling-houses and bazaars stand interspersed among the gardens. The houses are built of clay, and the windows furnished with glass.

'To the north of this place (Bo-lo), is the *Haie t'ie shan* (the iron hill of the lake). A furious wind comes out from the mountains, and blows people passing there into the lake.

'Proceeding south-west twenty *li*, Tch'ang Te reached a defile, which is called *Tie-mu-r-ts'an-ch'a* (the Talki Pass). It was guarded by Chinese. The way leading through the defile was very rugged, with overhanging rocks. After quitting this defile, Tch'ang Te arrived at *A-li-ma-li* (Almalyk). There the reservoirs in the market-places were connected by running water. As regards fruits, there were melons, grapes, and pomegranates of excellent quality. The *Hui-ho* (Mohammedans) in Alimali lived mixed up with the Chinese, and gradually their customs had got changed into the customs of the middle kingdom.

'South (of Alimali) there was a city called *Tch'i-mu-r*. Amongst the inhabitants were a great many Chinese from *Ping* and *Fen*.

'Going from the city of Bo-lo westward, the coins in use are made of gold, silver, and copper, and bear inscriptions; but they have no square holes.

'Tch'ang Te now entered the country called *Ma-a* (Maverannahr, *i.e.*, Turkistan). In this country the people (in winter) put horses to sledges, and carry heavy burdens in this manner from station to station, going very quickly. It is reported that the *Ki-li-ki-sze* (Kirghiz), instead of horses, use dogs (for drawing sledges).

'On the 24th of the second month (in the first half of April), Tch'ang Te passed *Yi-tu*, situated between two mountains. The ground there was level, and the population numerous. The country was intersected in all directions by canals, which irrigated the fields. Numerous ancient walls and other ruins were seen. The people said that in former times the *K'i-tau* (Karakhitai) dwelt there. Tch'ang Te calculated that this country was fifteen thousand *li* distant from *Ho-lin* (Karakorum). In the neighbourhood there is a river called *Yi-yün* (probably the Kurgaty). It runs bubbling to the east. The natives say that this is the source of the Yellow River (the Tchu).

'On the 28th of the second month, Tch'ang Te passed *T'a-la-sze* (Talas), and on the 1st of the third month, arrived at *Sai-lan* (Sairam). There is a tower in which the *Hui-ho* (Mohammedans) worship.'

Yeman is perhaps *Imil* or *Emil*, a town supposed to be situated on the river of that name, running into Lake Ala Kul, and frequently mentioned by the historians of the Mongols. It was the appanage at one time of Kuyuk Khan. It was probably somewhere near the present Tchugutchak. *Yi-tu* is apparently the country near Pishpek and Tokmak, between the Ala-Tau and the Alexandrofsky range.

6. Plano Carpini.

In 1245 John de Plano Carpini, a Franciscan monk, was sent as a missionary by Pope Innocent IV., to Mongolia. With Friar Benedict, the Pole, he reached the encampment of Batu on the Volga in February 1246, in Comania, and crossing the Yaik, or Ural, entered the land of the Kangli (Kangittae), an arid and desert region. Thence they went into the land of the Bisermans, or Bussurmans (a Russian corruption of the word Mussulman, used in all the old chronicles, and even now by the common people) who spoke the language of the Comanians, but observed the law of the Saracens. Here they found many ruined cities and forts, and saw on a great river a certain town called *Janckint* (the old Yany, or Jany-kent, on the lower Syr Darya), as well as others, among which were *Barchin* and *Ornas*. The ruler of this land was called *Alti soldanus*, which Mr. Lerch thinks is probably a corruption of the name of the Khârezm Shah ruling at that time, Ala Eddin Mohammed Sultan. Thence they went into the land of the Black Kitayans (Kara Khitai), in which they saw the city *Omyl*, which had just been rebuilt, and after that came upon 'a certaine small sea, upon the shore whereof stands a little mountaine, in which mountaine is reported to be a hole, from which in winter time such vehement tempestes of wind doe issue, that travellers can scarcely, and with great danger, passe by the same way. In summer time the noise indeede of the winde is heard there, but it proceedeth gently out of the hole. Along the shores of the foresaid sea we travailed for the space of many dayes, which, although it bee not very great, yet hath it many islands, and wee passed by, leaving it on our left hande.'

The friars then passed by the lands of the *Naimans*, and arrived at *Karakorum* on July 22, remained there until November 13, and reached Kief again on June 8, 1247.

English translations of the relation of Plano de Carpini were published in 'Hakluyt's Voyages,' and in 'Purchas, His Pilgrims,' but the best text of the original with all the variations of reading in different manuscripts, is to be found in the fourth volume of the 'Recueil de Voyages et de Mémoires publié par la Société de

Géographie,' Paris, 1839, accompanied by learned and interesting notes on ancient travellers, by M. D'Avezac.

After crossing the Yaik, Plano Carpini went through the southern portion of the steppe now belonging to the Lesser Horde of Kirghiz, and passing, as Friar Benedict says, many salt marshes, pools, and streams, and then a vast sandy waste (the Great and Little Barsuk, and the Kara-Kum), until he arrived at the Syr Darya, which is evidently the large river of which he speaks. At that time the lower regions of the Syr Darya were inhabited and cultivated, and contained many cities, which, up to the Mongol invasion, had been under the Khârezm Shahs. The people which Carpini calls Bisermins or Mussulmans, were apparently of Turkish race, and of the Mohammedan religion. Of the cities there mentioned, Janckint is evidently Yanikent, the ruins of which were investigated by Mr. Lerch in 1867, and were described by him in his 'Archæological Journey in Turkistan.' Barchin is probably the same as Partchin, mentioned in the journey of King Hethum, and appears also to be mentioned by Shchab-Eddin, in his enumeration of the cities of Turkistan. The name is apparently also found, although without diacritical points, in a coin of Jutchi, described by Fræhn (see Lerch, *ibid.* p. 10). As to Ornas, Karamzin, D'Avezac, Kunik, and others identify it with the city of Tana or Azof, at the mouth of the Don, while Fræhn and others think it to be Urgentch, the modern Khiva. It seems probable that Carpini has confused in the two passages where he speaks of this place, cities with similar names. A full discussion of the various identifications proposed for Ornas is to be found in Professor Philip Braun's notes to his Russian translation of Schiltberger in the 'Memoirs of the Imperial University of New Russia' (Odessa, 1867), vol i. pp. 30–34. *Lemfinc* (Lemfinc, or Lemfint), mentioned in the last chapter, is otherwise unknown.

From the Syr Darya Carpini probably went by the usual road, through Talas, &c., but there is no means of settling his route until we come to the lake with islands and a violent wind, which is commonly believed to be Lake Ala Kul, or *Alak-tugul-nor*, as the Mongols call it, and which is mentioned by Tch'ang Te, as well as by Rubruquis. Ala Kul means the spotted lake, either on account of the islands in it, or because, as the Kirghiz think, it lies among the mountains Ala-tau. The Mongol name means the 'lake of the spotted bull.' It is the only lake on this route with large islands, and was explored first by Schrenk, and then by Golubef, whose account is printed in the 'Memoirs of the Imp. Russ. Geog. Soc.:' Geography, vol i. p. 349.

The difficulty here is that if *Omyl* be Iymil or Emil (or Yeman in Tchang-Te), which is some distance beyond Lake Ala Kul, the lake must be the Kyzyl-bash, which has no islands, though it is frequently disturbed by violent winds. Ala Kul is the only lake in this part of Asia, except Balkash, which has any islands.

The place of the violent wind is the defile in the mountains on the road from the Ala Kul to Sairam Nor, of which I quote the account of a recent traveller, Mr. Zakharof, on p. 191 of vol. ii.

7. Rubruquis.

In 1253, William de Rubruk, or Rubruquis, a Flemish Franciscan friar, was sent by St. Louis of France on a mission to the Tartars. He set out from the Volga on September 16, 1253, and went to the Court of Mangu Khan, at Karakorum, and got back to Antioch about the end of June 1255.

Twelve days from the Volga, the missionaries came to the *Jayag* (Yaik, Ural), and travelled through the land of the Kangli eastward till October 31; the inhabitants of the country having all migrated southward, they went straight south through certain Alps eight days, when they saw high mountains south of them (the Alexandrofsky range), and on November 8, they came to the city of *Kenchat* (Kentchak, near Merke). 'Here there descended a great riuer downe from the mountaines, which watered the whole region, according as the inhabitants would give it passage by making diuers chanels and sluices; neither did this riuer exonerate it selfe into any sea, but was swallowed up by an hideous gulfe into the bowels of the earth (lit. was absorbed by the soil); and it caused many fennes or lakes' (probably the Tchu).

Hence they travelled eastward, and in a few days after ' entered upon those Alpes where the *Cara Catayans* (Karakhitai) were woont to inhabite (Ala Tau). And there wee found a mightie riuer: insomuch that wee were constrained to imbarke our selues, and to saile ouer it (the Ili). Afterward we came into a certaine valley, where I saw a castle destroyed, the walles wheroof were onely of mudde: and in that place the ground was tilled also. And there wee founde a certaine village, named *Equius*, wherein were Saracens, speaking the Persian language; howbeit they dwelt an huge distance from Persia. The day following, hauing passed ouer the aforesaid Alpes (spurs of the Ala Tau), which descended from the great mountaine southward we entred into a most beautiful plaine, hauing high mountaines on our right hande, and on the left hande of us a certaine sea or lake, which containeth fifteene dayes journey in circuite (Lake Balkash). All the foresayde plaine is most commodiously watered with certaine freshets distilling from the said mountaines, all which do fall into the lake. In summer time wee returned by the north shore of the saide lake, and there were great mountaines on that side also. Upon the forenamed plaine there were wont to bee great store of villages; but for the most part they were all wasted, in regarde of the fertile pastures, that the Tartars might feede their cattel there. Wee found one great citie there named *Cailac*, wherein was a mart, and a great store of Merchants frequenting it. In this citie wee remained fifteene dayes, staying for a certaine Scribe or Secretarie of Baatu, who ought to have accompanied our guide for the despatching of certaine businesse in the court of Mangu. All this countrey was wont to be called *Organum*: and the people thereof had their proper language, and their peculiar kinde of writing. But it was altogether inhabited of the people called Contomanni. The Nestorians likewise in those parts used the very same kinde of language and writing. They are called Organa, because they were wont to be most skilfull in playing upon the Organes or citherne, as it was reported unto me. Here first did I see worshippers of idoles, concerning whom, bee it known unto your maiestie, that there be many sects of them in the East countries.'

After leaving Kayalik on November 30, Rubruquis came to a 'small city of Nestorians, and then, after three days, arrived at the chief place of that province, at the extremity of the aforesaid sea, which seemed to us to be as tempestuous as the ocean. We saw in it a great island. My companion approached its shore, and dipped his linen cloth into it to taste the water, which was a little salt, but drinkable. Then there came a certain valley between the great mountains in the region between the south and east, and there among the mountains there was another great lake, and a river came through that valley from that lake into the other, and so great a wind continually comes through that valley, that men pass it with great danger of being carried into the lake. We then crossed this valley, going northward to great mountains covered with the deep snow which was then lying on the ground.' Here, the population being small, they hastened their journey, and on the second Sunday of Advent, passed between very horrible rocks, so that they were requested to say some good words to put to flight the demons which were accustomed there to fall on man. After that they entered into a plain, where was the Court of Kenkhan (Kencan or Kencan), formerly the land of the Naimans (the valley of the Black Irtysh). The place mentioned was not seen at that time, but only on the return journey. Then again they crossed mountains, always going northward, and at length on

November 26, came into a great plain like a sea where no hills appeared, and on the next day arrived at the Court of Mangu Khan.

The best text of Rubruquis is that given by D'Avezac, but I have quoted in part from the quaint, though imperfect translation, given in Hakluyt. There are certain things in the account of Rubruquis which it is very difficult to explain until we come to Kentchak. What the Alps were which he crossed, it is impossible to say, unless they are the high lands south of Akmolinsk, but the high mountains which he saw to the south of him, and which he evidently did not cross, are the Alexandrofsky range, as is evident from the position of Kentchak.

Quatremère ('Notices et extraits,' vol. xiii. p. 226), cites various passages from Mussulman historians, mentioning Kentchak, and nearly always in connection with Talas. For instance, Rashid Eddin speaks of the prairies of Talas and Kentchak, and Haider Razi says 'the meadows of Talas and Kentchak which are commonly called *Meski* and *Taraz*.' *Meski* is so similar to Merke or Mirky, that it seems to me plain that Kentchak was situated in the neighbourhood of the present Merke. I had come to this conclusion even before reading the passage in Quatremère, from what Rubruquis says of Talas, for in the village close to the mountains, which he reached the day after leaving Kentchak, he made inquiries about the situation of Talas, and was told that it was six day's journey behind him (*VI dietas post nos*). The VI may here be a misprint for IV, or even for II, or it may be that his question was not accurately answered. As at that time there was ice there, and as since Michaelmas they had had frost, it is probable that Rubruquis crossed the Tchu without noticing it, and the river which irrigated the country must therefore be either the Kurgaty, or one of the branches of the Tchu, or possibly the Tchu itself, which he approached from the other side. A few days afterwards he entered the Alps where the Karakhitai lived, and found there a large river, which he was obliged to cross in a boat, *i.e.*, he crossed over the spurs of the Ala-Tau going toward Vierny, where the hills were not particularly high, and came to the Ili, which is the only stream in this region deep enough to need a boat to cross it. After crossing this, he comes to the town of Equius. Colonel Yule ('Cathay,' p. cc.), leans to the opinion that Equius is a translation of *asparah*, the *asp* of which is the Persian for horse. This, however, seems to me somewhat strained, as Rubruquis is always very careful to give the native names for places, and not a translated name of this kind without the original. Mr. Howorth would make Equius *It-kitchu*, the 'dog's ford,' on the right bank of the Kurgaty, ten miles above its junction with the T'chu. Its name is indeed somewhat similar, but it is impossible in any way to reconcile this identification with the topography of Rubruquis. The next day after leaving Equius, certain other Alps were crossed, which branch off from the mountains from the south, which must be the high lands through which the post road now runs, going from the station of Ili towards Kopal. He then had the high mountains of the Ala-Tau on his right hand, and Balkash on his left, and soon came to the town of Kayalik, which Colonel Yule is probably right in placing near Kopal (*ibid.* p. ccxiii). This land, he says, was called Organum. This name, as Colonel Yule says (*ibid.* p. 522), is probably derived from that of the Princess Regent Organa (Organab), widow of Kara Hulagu, grandson and successor of Jagatai, then reigning in Almalyk, and was probably given to the country through some misapprehension of Rubruquis. His derivation of the name is, of course, utter nonsense. The description of Lake Ala Kul, which Rubruquis apparently and very easily mistook for a part of Lake Balkash, seems to be very excellent and accurate. From here he went northward towards the present Tchugutchak, across the mountains north-eastward toward the Black Irtysh—the country of the Naiman, and where they even now live—turned in the direction of Lake Kyzyl Bash, and came out on the plain to the south of that lake, and probably ascended the river Ulungu or Urungur.

8. KING HETHUM.

'Hethum, King of Armenia, very faithful and a friend of Christ, reigning at Sis, in the regions of Cilicia, had previously sent his brother, the General Sembat (Sempad), with presents and offerings to Giug (Kuyuk) Khan, who received him honourably, and sent him home with confirmatory letters.

'When Mangu Khan became sovereign, the great Generalissime Batu, bearing the title of 'Royally Descended,' residing in the north with his innumerable legions, on the banks of the great and deep river Etel (Volga), which falls into the Caspian Sea, requested for himself and Mangu Khan a visit from King Hethum. This prince, who feared Batu, left secretly in disguise, for fear of being recognised by his neighbours, the Turks, and their Sultan, Ala-Eddin of Roum, who mortally hated him for his friendly relations with the Tartars. Having quickly traversed the Turkish dominions, in twelve days he arrived at Kars, where he saw Batchu-Nuin, commander of the Tartar army in the East, as well as other lords, who treated him honourably. He stopped at the village of Vardenis, in the district of Aragatzofu, and opposite Mount Arai, in the house of Prince Kurd, of Armenian race, and in religion a Christian. Here he remained until he received from home the things intended for presents and offerings. These things were sent to him by his father Prince Constantine, already an old man. . . . Accompanied by them the King went through Agovanie (Albania), and by the Gates of Derbent, *i.e.*, the fortress of Tchor, to Batu, and his son Sartakh, a Christian. They welcomed him with honour and affection, and fitted him out for his long journey to Mangu Khan, beyond the Caspian Sea.

'Having set out on the 6th of the month of *Mareri*, or May 13, the King and his suite crossed the great river *Aiekh* (the Yaik or Ural), and arrived at *Or* (the river Or, or a town on it), midway between the camp of Batu and Mangu Khan.

'After crossing the river *Ertitch* (Irtysh), they arrived in the country of the Naiman, thence among the *Karakhitai*, and reached *Tataristan* on the 4th of the month *Hori*, September 13, and on the festival of the elevation of the Holy Cross, were presented to Mangu Khan, who was sitting in all the greatness of his fame.

'King Hethum offered him his presents, and was treated with due respect, and remained in the Horde fifty days. Mangu Khan gave him a special rescript, forbidding any one to disturb him or his states, as well as an order granting liberty to all churches.

'Starting thence on the fiftieth day, the 23rd of *Sahmi* (November 1), in thirty days he reached *Gumagur*, then went to *Berbalikh* and to *Beshbalikh* (Bishbalik), and to the sandy countries where live savage men who are quite naked with the exception of the hair on their heads; the breasts of their women are long and enormous. They are quite dumb. Here there are also wild horses with yellow and black skins, and white or black mules, much larger than horses or asses, as well as camels with two humps.

'Thence they went to *Arlekh* (or Lekh), to *Kulluk*, *Enkakh*, *Janhalekh* (Tchangbalik, see in Tch'ang Tch'un), *Khutapai*, and *Ankibalekh* (Yangybalik). Thence they entered into Turkistan, and came to *Ekopruk*, *Tingabalekh*, and *Pulad*.

'Crossing the *Sut-Kul* or Milky Lake (Sairam Nor), they came to *Alualekh* (Almalik) and *Ilan-balekh* (serpent town). Passing over the river *Ilan-su* (the Ili), and crossing an arm of Mount Taurus, arrived at *Talas*, and came to Hulavu (Hulagu), the brother of Mangu Khan, who had taken for his share the countries of the East.

'After that, turning to the north-west, they came to *Kutuktchin*, *Berkent*, *Sukulkhan*, *Urusokan*, *Kaikand*, *Khuzakh* (Suzak ?), *Kamotz*, *Khendakhuir*, and *Segnakh* (Saganak), or the Mountains of *Khartchukh* (a river near Turkistan), whence come the Seldjukides, and which begin at the Taurus, and reach to *Partchin* (Barchin), where they end.

'Thence they came to Sartakh, son of Batu, who was going to Mangu Khan. Then they went to *Sengakh* (var. *Sengan, Ongan*), *Savran* (Sauran), which is extremely large, *Kharatchukh, Ason* (Yassy, Turkistan), *Sori* (or *Savri*, Sauran), *Otrar, Zurnukh* (on the left bank of the Syr Darya), *Dizakh* (Jizakh), and thence in thirty days to *Samarkand*, *Saripul, Krman* (Kermineh), and *Bukhara*.

'After crossing the great river *Jaihun* (Oxus), they went to *Mrmn, Saraskh, Tus*, situated opposite to *Khorasan*, or *Rokastan*. Then they entered into *Mazanderan*, and then came to *Bestan*, then to the country of *Erak* (Irak), on the frontiers of the *Mulhids* (the assassins), to *Damgan*, the large town of Rei, to *Kazuin, Avher, Zongian, Miana*, and in twelve days to *Tauriz*.

'Twenty-six days after they traversed the *Eraskh* (Araxes), and went to *Sisian*, to Batchu-Nuin, chief of the Tartar army, who sent them on to Hodja-Nuin, to whom he had entrusted the command of his army, while he himself with the other chiefs went to meet Hulavu (Hulaga), brother of Mangu Khan, who was going to the East (*i.e.* Persia and Armenia). . . .

'The King related to us with regard to barbarous peoples, marvellous and unknown things which he had seen, or of which he had heard. There is, he said, beyond the Khatai, a country where the women have the shape of human beings, and are gifted with speech, while the men have that of dogs, and are dumb, large, and hairy. These dogs allow no one to penetrate into the country, and hunt beasts, with which they feed themselves as well as the women. When the dogs lie with the women, the males are born in the shape of dogs, and the females like women.

'There is also a sandy island, where there grows like a tree a kind of precious bone, called the "fish's tooth," and when it is cut, it sprouts again like a stag's horns.

'In another country there are numbers of idolators, worshipping very large idols of clay, called *Shakmunia* (Shakya-Munya, or Buddha), which they say has been a god 3,040 years, and is yet to live 37 *tumans* of years, of 10,000 each. At the end of this time his divinity will be taken away by another god, called *Madrin* (*Maidari*, the future successor of Buddha), in honour of whom they have erected clay statues of an immense size, and have placed them in five temples. These people, including their women and children, are all priests; they are called *Toins*. They shave off their hair and their beards, wear yellow *filons* like christians, not on the back, but round the neck. They are temperate in eating, and with regard to marriage. Taking a woman of twenty, they lie with her until she be thirty years old, three times a week; until forty, three times a month; until fifty, three times a year; after the fiftieth year they touch them no more.

'The wise King related about barbarians many other things, which I omit, that I may not be taxed with exaggeration. He entered Armenia eight months after leaving Mangu Khan. This was in the year 704 of the Armenian Era (1255-1256).'

The King Hethum, whose journey to Mongolia I have just given, was Hethum or Hayton, the Armenian form of the name which is in Arabic *Hatem*, who reigned over Cilicia, or, as it was called in the Middle Ages, Little Armenia, from 1226 to 1270. This journey constitutes the fifty-ninth chapter of the 'History of Armenia,' by Kirakoz of Gantzak, the whole of which is translated by Brosset in his 'Deux Historiens Arméniens.' This chapter also previously appeared in a Russian translation in the 'Siberian Messenger,' vol. xix., St. Petersburg, 1822, and subsequently in a French translation from that edited by Klaproth, in the 'Journal Asiatique' for October 1833. It has also been translated into French by N. Emin as an appendix to his translation of the 'History of Vardan the Great,' Moscow, 1861, and by K. P. Patkanof, in the 'History of the Mongols from Armenian sources,' St. Petersburg, 1874. I have chiefly followed Patkanof, who has given much care to the correct orthography of the proper names.

Hethum had been obliged to deliver up to the Mongols the mother, wife, and daughter of the Turkish Sultan of Iconium, who had sought refuge in his dominions, and had in this way gained the favour of the Mongols, but had become hated by the Turks, and, as an ally of the Mongols, was also distressed by attacks from the Sultans of Egypt, which finally put an end to this little Christian kingdom. He had previously, as stated in the text, sent to Knyuk Khan his brother Sembat, the constable of Armenia, but the Khan commanded that Hethum should himself come. It was in consequence of his terror of the Turks, that he disguised himself and went *incognito* through the Turkish country in the suite of his own ambassador. Two years after his return, he told the historian Abul Faradj that he was not recognised until he came to Arzengan; but that there a man who had lived some time in Cilicia, exclaimed, 'If these be my eyes, this is the King of Sis.' On hearing this, the ambassador, whom he was accompanying, struck him, and said, 'Thou most abject little man, art thou like a king?' 'But I,' he says, 'patiently bore the blow to turn from me his correct suspicion.'

Rubruquis, on his way back from Karakorum, passed Hethum, and on arriving at the Horde of Batu, learned that Hethum, during his stay there, had rendered assistance to the men whom he had left there, who had been badly off. Hethum gives few details of his outward journey, and appears to have gone directly east until he crossed the Irtysh. The Or, which he describes as being half way, is probably so in point of time, and not of distance; so that it is probably, not as Klaproth suggested in Jungaria, but the river Or, from which both Orenburg and Orsk derive their names. On returning, he arrived in a month at Gumagur, Gumsgur, or Kumakur, which Patkanof suggests may be a corrupted form of Karakum, then at Berbalik, which Klaproth thinks is the modern Barkul, then at Urumtsi, then keeping along the rocky highway skirting the northern slope of the Tian Shan, and south of Lake Ebi Nor to Lake Sairam Nor and Kuldja, and then through Semiretch to Aulié-ata. From this point Hethum turned southwards to Samarkand, and returned home by the way of Khorassan and Persia.

Among the wondrous tales told by King Hethum of the strange people that he had seen is one about the race of dogs and women. Plano Carpini speaks of the same story. According to Klaproth there is also a story of the 'Keou koue,' or Kingdom of Dogs, in the Chinese books of that epoch. The Chinese Encyclopædia, 'San-thsai thou hoeï' ('Affairs of Man'), in book xii., folio 27, says that 'In the Kingdom of dogs the men have the bodies of dogs. Their heads are covered with long hair, they are not dressed, and their language resembles the barking of dogs. Their women are of the human race, and understand the Chinese language. Their clothes are made of sables' skins. These people live in caverns. The men eat raw food, but the women cook it. They contract marriages with these dogs. Formerly a Chinaman lived in this country, and the women, who desired to run away, gave him little sticks, and asked him when he returned to his country to drop one of these sticks every ten li. The dogs, then seeing that their dwellings were deserted, set out in pursuit of this man, but could not catch him. To go from Nankin to this country requires two years and two months.'

In reading these stories one is struck with their resemblance to the legend of the origin of the Kara-Kirghiz from forty maidens and a red dog, and it seems probable that both Hethum and Carpini during their travels heard of these and similar legends, which they converted into actual present facts.

The moral of all this is very simple. In all countries where there are inhabitants there are roads or tracks, or lines of communication; and travellers in general journey by those roads, and do not go across the open country. Where the country is shut in by a mountain range with a limited number of passes, it is comparatively easy to ascertain where those roads must run.

Now we know that in ancient times there were from Pekin three roads to India, full descriptions of which are given in writers of the Thang dynasty, as well as in others. One, the southern road, went through China itself to the coast; the second, the middle road, went through Central China to Kashgar and Thibet; the northern road, with which we have concern, after leaving China at the extreme north-western corner of the empire, skirted the great mountain ranges, and near the present Ak-su divided into two branches, one of which went on to Kashgar, and the other going through the Muzart Pass along the shore of Lake Issyk Kul, came into the valley of the Tchu, then went along the northern side of the Alexandrofsky range to Talas, and then southward to Tashkent, Samarkand, Balkh, and Kabul; in fact, was almost exactly the present post and caravan road. This was the route taken by Hiouen Thsang, and the description of it given by the writers of the Thang dynasty in some respects supplements his account, and in others is almost exactly coincident with it. Tchinghiz Khan, after defeating the Naimaus, who lived in the Upper Irtysh, descended into Central Asia from the neighbourhood of Lake Nor Zaisan; but immediately after his conquest a new road was built, or perhaps an old one was improved, which left the old northern road at Bishbalik or Urumtsi, went close to the mountains to Lake Sairam Nor, then through them by the Talki Pass, where many bridges had been constructed to Almalyk in the valley of the Ili, then down that valley towards the modern Vierny and Tokmak. That road was from the time of the Mongols until the late Dungan insurrection maintained as one of the great Imperial Chinese post-roads, and even now in the Talki Pass but slight repairs would be required to make it perfectly available. At the same time another road was in frequent use, which has been maintained until recent times; and which, deflecting northwards before reaching Urumtsi, followed the River Urungur to Lake Kyzyl Bash, and then went by the Irtysh to Lake Nor Zaisan. South of Lake Nor Zaisan, near Lake Ala Kul there was a province, the capital of which, Imil, was situated near the present Tchugutchak, and there was a road going south connecting this with Almalyk. What seems strange is that anyone going to Central Asia should choose this northern road in preference to the more direct one from Urumtsi to Sairam Nor, and then turn south from Imil to Almalyk, instead of going directly on and joining the main road further west, as Tchang Te seems to have done. Still this may have been caused by reasons of state which have been omitted in the short form in which the account has come down to us.

For travellers going to Central Asia from the West the case is somewhat different. Here there are no mountain passes to concentrate the roads in particular places, and nothing but fresh water and pastures to tempt travellers in one direction more than another out of the direct road. Apparently, we may judge not only from travellers but from accounts of campaigns, that the road from the Volga was much what it would be now had Orenburg not been built, that is, by the old caravan road from the neighbourhood of Astrakhan to the northern shore of the Sea of Aral, and then up the Syr-Darya as far as Tchimkent, where the road turned, as at present, southward for Central Asia proper, and north east by the way of Aulié-ata for China and Mongolia. Different seasons of the year naturally made differences in the routes pursued, and for that reason we find Rubruqnis, who started late in the year, took a much more northerly route than others, for there probably he found much better forage, and afterwards, there being snow on the ground, the want of water did not trouble him.

END OF THE FIRST VOLUME.

www.ingramcontent.com/pod-product-compliance
Lightning Source LLC
Chambersburg PA
CBHW022145300426
44115CB00006B/354